The Southeast Maya Periphery

The Southeast Maya Periphery

EDITED BY PATRICIA A. URBAN AND
EDWARD M. SCHORTMAN

University of Texas Press   Austin

Requests for permission to reproduce material from this work should
be sent to Permissions, University of Texas Press, Box 7819, Austin,
Texas 78713-7819.

Library of Congress Cataloging-in-Publication Data
Main entry under title:
The Southeast Maya Periphery.
  Bibliography: p.
  Includes index.
  1. Indians of Central America—Antiquities.
2. Mayas—Antiquities.   3. Central America—Antiquities.
I. Urban, Patricia A. (Patricia Ann), 1950–
II. Schortman, Edward M.
F1434.S68   1986   972.8'01   85-22678

ISBN: 978-0-292-74195-9

First paperback printing, 2012

For reasons of economy and speed this volume has been printed from
computer-generated disks furnished by the editors, who assume full
responsibility for its content.

Contents

PART II. THE GREATER SOUTHEAST

The Southeast Maya Periphery

**EDWARD M. SCHORTMAN AND
PATRICIA A. URBAN**

1

Introduction

Background

The southeastern periphery of Mesoamerica, which forms the focus of this volume, has traditionally been defined by the distribution of certain material traits which, in their aggregate, are considered to be the hallmarks of Maya "culture" in the Classic period (ca. A.D. 200–900; see Schortman, Table 1, this volume, for a list of these material markers). The distribution limit of these traits is generally taken to mark the southern boundary of Maya culture and, hence, the southernmost extent of well-defined Mesoamerican culture patterns. The territory thus demarcated includes the Southeast Lowland Maya zone, that is, the area immediately surrounding, between, and including the southernmost known Classic Maya centers of Quirigua and Copan, sites which clearly possess the hallmarks of Classic Maya civilization. Surrounding and enveloping this region is the Greater Southeast zone, distinguished by the presence of complex, ranked societies not as socially or materially elaborate as the Maya in the Classic era. These "non-Maya" polities show evidence of differential participation in Maya culture patterns as expressed, once more, by the distribution of Maya material items. In sum, the Southeast Periphery, including both the Greater Southeast and Lowland Maya zones, represents the southernmost extent of Classic Maya culture and the area most greatly influenced by that culture.

Clearly the focus of this definition is on but one time period in the long prehistory of the area. There are several reasons the Classic era was selected for the purpose of definition. First and foremost, this is the best-known time period both in the Maya area and along its southern fringes: it has attracted the greatest amount of archaeological interest over the years and, as a result, the greatest number of known sites date to this period. Second, it is the period when the lines demarcating the different cultures in the area appear to have been the clearest, i.e., there seems to have been a clear Maya material culture pattern intruded into a markedly different cultural milieu of simpler societies. This condition makes the job of distinguishing "Maya" from "non-Maya" sites relatively easy and the simple dichotomy has thus remained with us to this day.

The Preclassic and Postclassic cultural situations in the southeast are much less clear both because less work has been devoted to the elucidation of these time periods and because, on present evidence, the material distinctiveness of the cultures involved seems to have been less marked (see Sharer 1974, however, for an innovative attempt to consider the Southeast Periphery in all prehistoric time periods). As a result, the tendency has been simply to assume that the entire southeastern periphery zone, as defined by the distribution of Classic Maya material traits, was also peripheral to broader Mesoamerican cultural developments in earlier and later periods as well—that it has always been on the fringes of, and influenced by, cultures to the north. While this Classic Maya-based definition of the region certainly has its difficulties, as noted by various authors in this volume (e.g., Demarest and Sharer, Kennedy, Schortman; and the later parts of this essay), it has, nonetheless, been adopted as the framework of this volume.

The area covered here, then, encompasses the central and western portions of the modern nation of Honduras, eastern Guatemala, and the state of El Salvador. The region is marked by a variety of topographic and environmental zones ranging from the high, cool mountains of El Salvador, central Honduras and eastern Guatemala, to the lower, more rolling hills of western Honduras and the hot, wet, low-lying tropical plains along the Caribbean and Pacific coasts of Guatemala, Honduras and El Salvador. This environmentally diverse zone, for so long little-known archaeologically, is now recognized to have had a rich diversity of cultural patterns during the course of its long prehistory. Before considering the contributions that the papers in this volume have made to the elucidation of this culture history, a brief synopsis of earlier research is necessary to indicate the intellectual context of this more recent work.

The definition of the Maya's (or Mesoamerica's) southeastern boundary has long been of concern to archaeologists (Longyear 1947; Lothrop 1939; Thompson 1970), and discussions of the problem have utilized linguistic, ethnohistoric, and archaeological data. The sporadic field investigations carried out in the Greater Southeast, however, showed little initial concern with understanding the local culture history of the southeast in its own right. Rather, the primary focus was ties between the area and the Maya, with secondary emphasis on other areas of Mesoamerica further to the north. As a result, most of the early work in the periphery concentrated on the major Maya centers in the Southeast Lowland Maya zone, specifically on Copan in western Honduras and Quirigua in eastern Guatemala. Also significant is that, following the custom of the times, research centered firmly on the study of site cores themselves; there was relatively little interest in the broader, regional settlement that surrounded, and was presumably integrated with, these major centers (e.g., Hewett 1916; Longyear 1952; Morley 1920; Stromsvik 1941). Recording of the elaborate inscriptions and sculpture for which Copan and Quirigua are justly famous was extensive and there was also some excavation of the monumental constructions which dominate these centers. All of this work provided data which was comparable to that being collected in the better-known major sites of the lowland Maya core in Guatemala and southern Mexico, and, hence, led to a better understanding of the variation and consistency of Maya material patterns, at least those associated with major monumental sites.

Moving beyond the clearly Maya centers, research in the Greater Southeast zone was minimal and dispersed. Gordon (1898b) initiated data collection and reporting in this area and he was followed by a restricted but distinguished company of scholars which included Boggs (1944, 1945a, 1950a), Canby (1949, 1951), Longyear (1944), Popenoe (1934), Stone (1941, 1957), Strong, Kidder, and Paul (1938), and Yde (1938). This widely scattered work provided tantalizing clues about prehistoric developments in the southeast, but the lack of sustained investigation resulted in a dearth of systematic information. As noted earlier, much of this work was devoted to determining the relationship of this nebulous area to more completely understood developments to the north and west.

It has only been during the past 20 years, principally since the inception of the Los Naranjos project (Lake Yojoa, Honduras) in the late 1960s (Baudez and Becquelin 1973) and the Chalchuapa Project (eastern El Salvador) in the same general time period (Sharer, ed., 1978) that the Southeast Periphery outside of Copan and Quirigua has been the focus of large-scale work designed to reconstruct the culture history of specific regions within it. Similarly, it is only with the initiation of the Harvard Copan Project in the mid 1970s, under the direction of Gordon Willey (succeeded by subsequent phases of research under, first, Claude Baudez and, most recently, William Sanders), and the University of Pennsylvania Quirigua Project under William Coe and Robert Sharer, that systematic research has been devoted to reconstructing the full culture histories of these two sites and relating them to their surrounding hinterlands (e.g., Ashmore 1981a; Willey, Leventhal, and Fash 1978; and the authors in the first portion of this volume). The result of this tardiness in research has been that while information on Maya culture history in the core area has become increasingly complete and specific, comparable basic knowledge of the southeast has severely lagged.

We do not want to give the impression that all research prior to 1965 in the southeast was misguided and incomplete; far from it. Given the historical fact that research was first initiated in the lowland Maya heartland and that this became, early on, a focus of Mesoamerican studies, it was totally logical that the first efforts in the southeast should have been devoted to defining the southern borders of the Mayan culture area. Without such an areal definition there would have been no clear limit to the region over which generalizations about Maya culture were supposed to apply. Further, concentrating on the area's largest Maya centers was sensible if data were to be provided for comparison to that obtained at monumental sites in the Maya core zone. Moreover, the Maya phenomenon is clearly associated with monumental centers (see Schortman, this volume) and its definition would require, at least as a start, intensive investigations at the largest of these southern sites. The use of the trait list approach by many scholars was also probably inevitable as a beginning way to define the Maya culture area; it certainly had ample precedent in the anthropological theory of the day (e.g., Kroeber 1939; Wissler 1917). As a result, the fact that the Southeast Periphery was seen primarily in terms of developments elsewhere was an appropriate response in the initial stages of research. This, of course, does not mean that such approaches are still warranted or very fruitful today. As the papers in this volume indicate, the limits of this view of the southeast have been reached. As more information is gained about boundary areas in the periphery the old core culture-boundary culture distinction is increasingly recognized as an oversimplification.

In response, a series of questions has arisen in southeastern research reflecting the growing dissatisfaction with earlier frameworks. The most basic of these is defining the so-called "marginal" cultures of the area and their individual histories of development. Further, without such information, more theoretical questions about the prehistory of the region remain unanswerable. The old concern with how southeastern societies interacted with the "core" cultures to the northwest remains but is now more sophisticated. Specifically, interest has developed in precisely identifying the flow of influences between and among specific Maya and non-Maya societies and in addressing the question of the effects these influences had on local developments on both sides of the interactions. A further question being considered in southeast research is how the cultures involved in these various interactions changed through time and how the changes affected the process of interaction. Needless to say, these lines of inquiry are not limited to the Classic period and there has been an increasing amount of effort devoted to reconstructing the full culture history of various areas of the southeast, as attested by the papers presented here. Increasingly, the question asked is whether or not the non-Maya cultures in the southeast were "marginal" in prehistory and if so, when. To discuss this question adequately it is necessary to develop a theoretical framework and related terminology to aid study in this complex area. We will return to this last question at the conclusion of this essay.

As the above synopsis indicates, systematic and intensive research in the southeast is far too young to fully answer all of the basic, let alone the interesting, questions. Large gaps in our knowledge of the area remain and many zones do not have even the most rudimentary foundations for understanding their culture histories. For example, our continued amazement at the discovery of large, complex sites in previously unstudied portions of the periphery where none were expected (e.g., the Cajon region of central Honduras, as reported in Hirth *et al.* 1980, 1981) attests to how little we still know of this important region. The papers presented here, however, reflect both the processes of questioning and constructing adequate data bases from which new questions can be answered. The results advanced in the current volume are not always equally well-established at present; given the various stages of completeness of the different projects represented such a situation is inevitable. All of the contributions do reflect, however, the current state of our knowledge of this important and complex area and, more importantly, they reveal the questions and concerns that are guiding current investigations.

Organization of the Volume

Most of the papers which appear here are revised and updated versions of contributions presented at the 1980 Society for American Archaeology meetings in Philadelphia during two related symposia: The Southeast Mesoamerican Periphery: Copan and Quirigua; and

The Southeast Mesoamerican Periphery: Western Honduras and El Salvador. Several papers from these sessions have not been included here, but three additional works, by Bruhns, Demarest and Sharer, and Sheets, have been newly contributed.

The goal of this book is to provide a one volume, up-to-date cross-section of archaeological research in the Southeast Periphery involving projects begun and/or completed in the 1970s and early 1980s. The papers encompass both reports of newly-collected data and re-evaluations of earlier material. Disagreements among the authors are as obvious as points of agreement, and almost as numerous. This is simply a reflection of the state of current southeastern research, which has great vitality and some uncertainty as new data are acquired and the record is interpreted from different perspectives.

The contributions are divided between two general sections which roughly correspond with the original 1980 symposium boundaries. The first part concerns the two major sites of Copan and Quirigua within the Southeast Lowland Maya zone. These papers are based on research recently completed at the latter center and still in progress at the former. The basic questions addressed here are several: The early histories and origins of these centers are considered in the papers by Jones and Sharer, Baudez, and Ashmore, while their developmental sequences of construction and their relationships to wider political and social events are discussed in the contributions by Cheek, and Jones and Sharer. These matters have long been discussed by Maya archaeologists and the data provided here should go a long way towards resolving earlier arguments. The relationships of these two major centers to each other, the changes in these relationships through time, and how these changes affected local developments in each area are dealt with in contributions by Jones and Sharer, Cheek, Riese, Bishop *et al.*, Vlcek and Fash, and Leventhal. Traditionally, such questions have been considered largely in terms of epigraphy and, to some extent, sculptural similarities between the two sites (e.g., Hatch 1975; Kelley 1962; Proskouriakoff 1973), but the authors here have brought to bear on these important questions information from a number of different data categories including architecture and constructional sequences (Cheek), ceramics (Leventhal; Bishop *et al.*), and settlement (Vlcek and Fash), as well as new material from epigraphy and sculpture (Riese; Jones and Sharer). The result is the introduction of novel insights into the complex problem of relations among the Maya on the southern periphery.

The relationships of Copan and Quirigua with other areas both within and outside the Southeast Lowland Maya zone are addressed in papers by Ashmore, Jones and Sharer, Schortman, Cheek, Baudez,

Vlcek and Fash, Leventhal, and Bishop *et al.* As the number of these papers indicates, the question of relationships between the Maya and the non-Maya is far from dead though it has now been raised to a more sophisticated plane than the simple attempt to draw fixed boundaries. Once more, data on settlement (Schortman; Vlcek and Fash), architecture and site planning (Ashmore; Jones and Sharer; Cheek; Schortman), sculpture and epigraphy (Baudez) and ceramics (Leventhal; Bishop *et al.*) are brought to bear on this question. The nature of the settlement in the area surrounding Copan is addressed by Fash while settlement in the larger region around and between Copan and Quirigua is described in papers by Vlcek and Fash, and Schortman.

The Copan and Quirigua papers are the most definitive in their results largely because of the significant amount of effort invested over the years in understanding these two sites and their surrounding hinterlands. As the papers presented here indicate, Maya research in the southeast has gradually shifted away from the exclusive study of the largest centers and the assessment of their similarities with sites in the Peten heartland towards placing these massive sites in both their immediate and larger regional contexts.

Turning to the papers on the Greater Southeast zone, the second portion of the volume, we find that the results reported are somewhat more tentative. The area these papers cover is broader than that encompassed by the Copan-Quirigua contributions and the previous work here was less systematic than that at the Maya sites. As a result, researchers in this zone are still in the process of developing a coherent data base.

The contributions in this second section of the volume are based on different forms of data, and many present information not previously published elsewhere. The papers by Urban, Robinson, and Agurcia are founded, largely, on the results of settlement survey work, while those by Demarest and Sharer, Kennedy, and Bruhns derive from the analysis of various material culture classes, especially ceramics. Wonderley's paper reports on the intensive investigation of a particular site (Naco), as do Bruhns (Cihuatan) and Kennedy (Playa de los Muertos). The papers cover all of the major time periods in the area: Kennedy, and Demarest and Sharer deal with the Preclassic; Robinson, Agurcia, and Sheets discuss events in the Classic; Bruhns and Wonderley consider the Postclassic; and Urban presents a sequence of occupation and settlement change spanning the Late Preclassic through the Early Postclassic in one region, the Naco valley. On the theoretical level, the authors address a number of different issues. The primary concern of most is reconstructing the nature and development of southeastern societies in specific areas, and this is clearly seen in the papers by Urban, Demarest and Sharer, Sheets, Robinson, and Wonderley. The nature of the interactions among southeastern societies and representatives of Maya, or more generally, Mesoamerican societies is dealt with by all of the authors in this section, revealing once more the continued attraction of this question. The effects of outside influences on local developments are dealt with by Bruhns and Wonderley, while Sheets considers the effects of a natural disaster, specifically a volcanic eruption, on such developments. The definition of prehistoric ethnic units, a point considered earlier by Schortman, is dealt with in detail in the contribution by Demarest and Sharer, as well as by Kennedy.

Each of the major sections is followed by a synthesis of the papers in that portion of the volume. Gordon Willey pulls together the strands of the Copan-Quirigua arguments while Robert Sharer and Claude Baudez do the same for the Greater Southeast papers.

The Outlook for the Southeast

Different areas of the world are variably suited to addressing certain basic archaeological questions. The Southeast Periphery, for example, is uniquely situated to address questions of the nature and effects of intercultural interaction. Located on the fringes of two major cultural zones, Mesoamerica and Lower Central America, between which contact was maintained prehistorically, local sociocultural developments were probably always influenced to a great extent by outside contacts and cannot be understood apart from those contacts. This is not to say, however, that southeastern cultural developments were totally the result of these interactions. Each local group occupying its own territory would have reacted to outside stimuli in its own creative way, fashioning its development from both intrinsic and extrinsic forces. That the reactions of particular southeastern societies to these contacts have been far from uniform is just now being documented and is amply seen in the contributions to this volume. Quirigua's culture history, for example, represents the process of outright colonization of a southeastern site by a group or groups from the Maya core; in contrast, the Naco valley some 90 km to the northeast in Honduras has a long sequence of occupation documenting nothing so much as a strong regional tradition in some contact with outside societies but resistant to their influences through most of prehistory. If two such markedly different examples of interaction and its consequences can exist so close together in this region, what great variation in the nature and effects on local development of culture contact can be expected in the wider area of the southeast?

There is a long history of anthropological concern with intercultural intercourse and the culture change that results from that exchange (frequently called acculturation studies). Archaeologists have often been urged to put their extensive time spans of observed culture contact and change at the service of these studies (Willey 1953; Willey *et al.*1956). More recently, Central Americanists have called for such studies within this broad area—Panama to eastern Guatemala—encompassing the Southeast Periphery (Helms 1976; Lange 1976, 1979). Nonetheless, while there has been some very exciting work carried out with foci on intercultural contact and its results (Fox 1981; Hodder 1977, 1979; Hodder, ed., 1978; Wells 1980), this aspect of archaeology is relatively under-exploited. One of this volume's major strengths is that the various authors are each struggling with such questions, ones which, in fact, constitute the book's underlying general theme.

Southeastern scholars are becoming increasingly aware of how important complexly structured interactions are in understanding local developments. Concomitantly, we are less satisfied with using simple plots of trait distributions as guides to defining the supposed boundaries of the "high cultures" which border the area. We want, more and more, to know what sorts of societies, with their various interactions, produced the trait distributions that we see. What do these distributions mean behaviorally? What do they say about the nature of the societies in contact and their interactions? What were the results on local developments of these exchanges of goods and ideas? Such basic questions structure considerations of Classic period Maya-non-Maya interactions but also can be extended to interactions among Maya peoples or non-Maya groups during any time period. Further, as the papers in this volume reveal, there is an increasing realization among southeastern scholars that we are not dealing with contact between two monolithic entities, even at any given archaeological "moment" in time such as the Late Classic. There was not one homogeneous Maya culture interacting in every region, and in the same manner, with an equally homogeneous non-Maya culture. The differences among the Maya are clearly seen at Copan and Quirigua and, as the evidence indicates, relations were far from consistently friendly. Among southeastern societies of this era the differences were apparently even greater and the papers here point to variations in social complexity, material elaboration, extent of contact with Maya and Mesoamerican societies in general, and the degree to which that contact influenced local developments. Out of this complexity a new picture of the southeast is emerging in which various groups of Maya elites were in contact with differently organized southeastern societies. As a result there is a remarkably complex distribution in the Late Classic southeast of material traits, Maya and non-Maya, presumably reflecting the equally complex diffusion of concepts and innovations associated with these material items.

It should, therefore, be no surprise that among southeastern scholars dissatisfaction has occurred with such terms as "boundary" and "frontier" when applied to the southeast. The first implies stasis and rigid lines of demarcation, while the latter indicates the existence of at least one more-or-less homogeneous culture, with well-defined limits at any point in time, that is expanding into an area of presumably less "developed" culture(s). Such situations may have existed at certain times in prehistory, but neither term is particularly appropriate for describing the southeast through time. Further, both imply a conceptual framework for research more concerned with defining cultural limits than identifying the processes which underly those ephemeral limits, although the frontier concept does embrace the dynamic of expansion.

For these reasons, we southeastern researchers must develop a conceptual framework with its own terminology which will allow us to take full advantage of the research potential of this complex area, acknowledging its immense variation yet not becoming swamped by it. The scheme proposed below was derived by the authors both from their own work in the area and from the suggestions embodied in the contributions to this volume. The focus of this outline is interaction between regions and results of interaction as seen in the distribution of distinctive material items and the development of local cultures. This orientation was chosen because, as noted, the area seems to be a fruitful one for such a consideration, and by using interaction as a research focus it is possible to integrate the diverse Southeast Periphery research interests into one coherent program. As indicated below, in order to study prehistoric interaction, culture history investigations must be carried out together with technical analyses of materials, the definition of ethnic units, and stylistic studies reflecting the spread of ideas. We note at the outset, however, that not all of the contributors would necessarily agree with the appropriateness of this scheme; it is simply our contribution to the ongoing debate as to how best to treat the Southeast Periphery.

The first, most obvious, step in southeastern research has already been taken: the recognition that there existed a number of different cultures at any one time, and that these interacted in any period with an array of other distinct cultures, under different circumstances, with different purposes in mind. Our first goal, therefore, must be to define the cultures involved in different time periods. This basic goal of culture history has already been achieved in some areas though major spatial and temporal gaps still remain. Clearly, without this basic data for large portions of the southeast, questions of interaction cannot be fully resolved. For example, the flow of goods and ideas cannot be established until we have well-dated cultural sequences from a variety of areas, allowing us to establish the precedence of one area over another in the development of a particular idea or good. Beyond this, since the nature of a culture provides the matrix into which any introduced innovations must fit, a culture's organization provides an effective screen determining which innovations/goods are rejected, which accepted, and how the latter have to be adapted to fit within the existing culture system.

Once these cultures are defined, their interactions in different time periods must be specified. This can be done by verifying through technical analyses the actual movements of goods (see Bishop *et al.*, and Demarest and Sharer, this volume) or using stylistic studies of different media to examine the movement of ideas. In this volume the last approach has been employed by Demarest and Sharer, and Kennedy, for ceramics, both Ashmore and Schortman, for site planning, and Riese, Baudez, and Jones and Sharer, for sculpture, all with good results. Glyphic texts, where available, provide further insights into intergroup interactions (Riese, and Jones and Sharer, this volume), though their limited extent in the southeast restricts their utility to the study of groups in the Southeast Lowland Maya zone.

The material items used to establish contacts between cultures must be understood in terms of the behavioral contexts in which they functioned in the donor and recipient cultures. Only in this way can the behavioral significance of the distribution of particular material traits be understood. This may be done, as Schortman indicates in this volume, by defining the different behavioral realms within a culture in which the items were presumed to function and then seeing the spread of these items as reflecting the spread of innovations associated with those realms. Along this line it should also be asked how the item and, presumably, the ideas and behaviors with which it was originally associated have been adapted to fit within the new cultural system and how has adoption affected that system? Awareness must exist that any internal changes in the cultures involved will, most probably, affect the course of their interactions. As a result, a positive feedback system is at least potentially present, with contacts producing cultural changes which, in turn, result in changes in the form of the interaction.

Attempts must also be made to specify the conditions of intergroup interactions, for these play a role in determining the results of the relations. Some of the more important conditions controlling ethnographically known interactions which can be expected to have played important prehistoric roles are these: the goals of the interacting groups; the nature of the social segments actually in contact (i.e., the subcultures interacting directly with each other as distinct from the wider societies of which they are a part and which may experience the results of the interactions only indirectly); the effects of the environment on the interaction; the relative power relations of the groups involved; and the presence or absence of competition among the parties to the interaction.

Finally, we must recognize that no interaction situation is static. Change in any one of its variables, whether it be the cultures involved or the conditions of the contact, will produce change in that interaction, and, hence, change in the material distributions which are the manifestations of interaction. Ultimately, therefore, we must understand the cultures involved in an interaction, the conditions of their contact, and the changes in that contact if we are to fully comprehend the significance of observed trait distributions and make full use of the available data in the southeast.

As all of the foregoing implies, attention cannot be focused solely on the Classic period, nor exclusively on Maya-non-Maya interactions. Interest should be expanded to include interactions *internal* to both Maya and non-Maya populations, as well as *between* Maya and non-Maya groups. Additionally, all time periods must be subject to analyses. This approach requires that we adopt a supra-regional scale of reference, to be concerned not simply with what was going on in one particular region at one point in time, but with how this region was articulated with other neighboring regions and what the results of those interactions were in the developments of all the groups involved. We are, in fact, arguing for an expanded perspective which looks beyond individual cultures and even culture areas to stress the importance of extra-regional ties in understanding the prehistory of any one population. In recent years archaeologists have become increasingly aware of the need to place the phenomena they study within broader contexts in order to understand their significance. Projects within Mesoamerica focused on the investigation of individual sites have been largely replaced by broader regional studies which seek to reconstruct the settlement systems within which specific sites originally functioned (e.g., Flannery, ed., 1976; Parsons

1971, 1974; Sanders 1965, 1970). The setting of these regions within the context of the larger interaction networks in which they participated seems to us to be only the next, logical step in this process of broadening our understanding of the past. Ultimately, the southeast is well suited to produce data for such a massive comparative study of intercultural interactions and their effects on cultural developments through time in one diverse area. As the papers in this volume indicate, we are now on the threshold of being able to accomplish this goal.

This brings us back to the question of terminology, for our choice of a term to designate the area will very much condition our perception of the study zone and, hence, the questions we will ask in our research there. What term can be used for the southeast that will reflect our concerns with cultural diversity and interaction and that will serve to set the Mesoamerican southeast apart as a valid area for study with its own research problems related to, but distinct from, those of adjacent zones? We advocate the use of the term "periphery" for the following reasons. First, it is established in the literature and its use would not involve the introduction of a new word which most people will probably not use (see Sharer 1974). Second, it implies the presence of a permeable barrier and not a fixed and necessarily clearly defined one. This seems to be more in line with our present understanding of interactions in the area, with ideas and their material manifestations traveling differentially across the barriers between interacting cultures—and in some areas and time periods barriers were more impermeable than in others (see Urban, this volume). Further, the term periphery does not pre-judge the nature of the contacts involved and allows for a variety of different interactions, with different results, in different time periods, thereby suggesting the dynamic nature of these interactions. Finally the area is a "double periphery"—for both Mesoamerica to the north, and Lower Central America to the south—and the term can be useful for either perspective.

Unfortunately, this term also has certain disadvantages, foremost of which is its implication of marginal status for non-Maya southeastern societies: it suggests that cultures in the southeast were neither as complex socially nor as elaborate materially as Mesoamerican cultures to the north. As Baudez indicates below, this imputation of marginality may have been true in the Classic period, but the Postclassic situation is less clear, and in the Preclassic attributions of marginality to the southeast appear to be totally unwarranted (Demarest and Sharer, and Kennedy, this volume; Healey 1974). The term periphery also implies a one-sided perspective in which the societies in the Greater Southeast zone are still seen in relation to developments to the north and west and not in their own right.

Despite these drawbacks, we feel that periphery is the most appropriate available term to be applied to the area and best expresses the concerns embedded in the conceptual scheme outlined above. We fully recognize that some southeastern scholars would disagree with this view, including several of the authors appearing here.

In sum, there is much to be done in southeastern research and much refinement of conceptual schema must be carried out before we can fully extract the maximum amount of information from this potentially productive area. Further debates and exchanges can be eagerly anticipated, but in the meantime the current volume will serve as an initiating step in this process. We look forward to future advances in our knowledge of this important area and the contributions that the southeast will make to Mesoamerican archaeology and general anthropological theory.

Acknowledgments

We first wish to thank both the participants in the symposia which gave rise to this volume and the many colleagues who attended the sessions: their enthusiasm for recent work in the Southeast Periphery was so contagious that we were motivated to produce this volume in hopes of reaching an even wider audience. In preparing the book, we were ably assisted by Sharon Duchesne and Alison Trofatter, who typed and retyped manuscripts with accuracy and good cheer. We are also grateful to Gordon Willey, Robert Sharer, and Wendy Ashmore, who read earlier versions of this introduction. Their comments were taken to heart, although they might not recognize this from the finished work, for which we bear full responsibility.

PART I

Copan and Quirigua

CLAUDE F. BAUDEZ

2

Iconography and History at Copan

Introduction

The monumental stone sculptures from Copan offer an excellent opportunity for the study of stylistic and iconographic changes through time. Most of the monuments carved before 9.9.0.0.0 have been found in pieces and in secondary reuse contexts, therefore providing little information. On the contrary, freestanding monuments of the Late Classic period and sculptures associated with architecture are not only numerous, but also generally well-preserved and securely dated.

Spinden (1913) was the first to present a stylistic sequence for the Copan stelae and in 1950 Proskouriakoff made few deviations from his analyses in her monumental work. Both studies deliberately focused on style and made no attempt to study iconographic changes. As Proskouriakoff's goal was to build up a seriation "to place monuments in time," she quickly realized that "the significant change was in the artist, not in the subjects of his art" (1950: 2–3). This statement remains true assuming one encompasses the whole repertoire of Classic Maya productions. Most motifs indeed seem to be already extant at the very beginning of the Classic epoch and are found scattered over great distances and many centuries. When one considers the amount of artistic diversity found from one site to the other in the Maya area (even those which are geographically close like Copan and Quirigua), one may expect to face deep differences in meanings and symbolism as well. An alternative is the intrasite study in which the variables of time and space are controlled, making more reliable the discovered regularities, continuities, and changes. Furthermore, comparisons of different forms manifested in the same contexts lead to the discovery of equivalences and oppositions, which in turn may be used for the construction of a lexicon of images, whose value is provisionally restricted to the site under study.

Monuments before 9.9.0.0.0

The earliest sculptures ever found at Copan are the two decapitated potbellied statues which were used as foundations for Stelae 4 and 5. Dating most likely from the Late Preclassic, they are probably derived from comparable forms produced in Pacific Guatemala and El Salvador. In 1978, a large stela fragment picturing practically identical standing figures on the front and back was found reused in the construction of Str. 10L4-1st. Carved of local tuff, this monument shares some traits with the late Cycle 8–early Cycle 9 productions of the central Peten (for example Tikal, Uolantun, Yaxha) but it is with the Leyden Plate that our Stela 35 shares a closer resemblance (fig. 1). This implies that we have evidence of an early colonization of the Copan valley by a Maya group coming from the Peten. No glyphs are evident on Stela 35 but it may have included an inscription on the missing upper portion. Stylistic considerations date Stela 35 to approximately A.D. 400 assuming that it is Peten-derived. Be that as it may, the next monument with a secure date is Stela 24 which bears an inscription (9.2.10.0.0 or A.D. 485) but no iconography. All the following stelae are text-bearing until 9.9.0.0.0 (Stela 7), when iconic monuments resume[1].

The Late Classic Period

Proskouriakoff's Formative Phase

During this phase (dated at Copan to A.D. 613–706) the stelae form a rather homogeneous group of eight monuments, but for two exceptions which will be discussed later. As Spinden (1913) noticed, relief is rather low, the typical monument is more trapezoidal than rectangular, the figure holds a flaccid serpent against his chest with his vertical or oblique forearms, the feet are completely turned out forming a 180 degree angle, the head is small relative to the body, and so on. The regalia characteristic of this phase which will not be in use later are the mask under the chin, the skirt, and the loincloth composed of one or two broad trapezoidal flaps. The only entities which accompany the main figure are closely interrelated: the Jaguar, the Sun God, and Death figures. Most of the conventional symbols which are used on the costume can be demonstrated as having death or sacrifice implications. In short, all recognizable motifs and themes are related to a war-sacrifice-death complex. It can be postulated that if the ruler surrounds himself with this imagery it is because he wants to appear as the warrior "par excellence" and that his major role is as a war captain.

Figure 1

Figure 2

Figure 1. Copan, Stela 35; height: 130 cm. (drawing by B. Fash, Proyecto Arqueologico Copan).

Figure 2. Copan, Stela P; height: 320 cm. (photo by J. P. Courau, Proyecto Arqueologico Copan).

Intrusion: Stelae 1 and 6

The eleventh katun is celebrated with unusual pomp as six stelae (most of them carved only with texts) are erected on the same day at distant locations, as though marking the limits of the city of Copan. Stela 1, with a date of 9.11.15.14.0 appears as a break with the established tradition and is erected 15 years later (fig. 3). Stela 6, erected another 15 years later at 9.12.10.0.0, pictures the same individual in an even more exotic accoutrement (fig. 4). Proskouriakoff (1950: 116) wrote that Stela 1

> marked a radical departure from the conventional mode of carving stelae at Copan. . .an increased emphasis on the conception of the design as an arrangement of masses or three-dimensional forms, expressed in the composition of receding and projecting surfaces. Oblique masses, however, are not yet introduced, and the figure can still be adequately envisaged on perpendicular planes, in spite of its rounded contours.

The two stelae are shorter than the other monuments of the same kind either preceding or following them, and present the following exotic traits: more elaborated ankle-guards (Stela 6); no anklets (6); superimposed decorated bands from which hang triangles, as garters (6); one single loincloth flap without a superimposed tassel-like apron (6 and 1); no tinklers hanging from the belt (6 and 1); no belt medallions (6 and 1); "Tlaloc" jaguars (6); no chin mask (6 and 1); unique bracelet forms—ribbon wrapped three times around the wrist (1); band and two shells (6); turban (6 and 1); circular earplugs (6 and 1); more realism in the way the clothes are worn and fixed (6 and 1), and so forth.

As these new traits have no precedents at Copan, a foreign origin has to be postulated. Proskouriakoff (1950: 116) suggests "inspiration from the outside." I think it can be put more strongly and that we can interpret Stelae 1 and 6 as statues of a foreigner who seized power at Copan. From where did this intrusion come? The Pacific slope of Guatemala is suggested by similarities with sculptures of the Cotzumalhuapa culture: high relief, Tlaloc-like images, long tradition of the turban, etc., but this hypothesis still rests on shaky grounds.

The turban, which appears for the first time on Stela E, becomes frequent on the Copan late monuments of the reign of Madrugada and is characteristic of Copan rulers on monuments of political character (Altar Q, Temple 11, and so forth). One may interpret the small turbanned figures on the stelae as representations of ancestors, as their faces are irrefutably human with none of the grotesque elements reserved for the gods. The ruler on Stela 1 wears not only a large turban on his head but also has a turbanned head at both ends of the flaccid serpent, which later will become the ceremonial bar. He is presenting himself, therefore, as a "man-with-the-turban" and placing himself under the patronage of ancestors or predecessors "with-the-turban." Either the turban is already a Copan emblem and

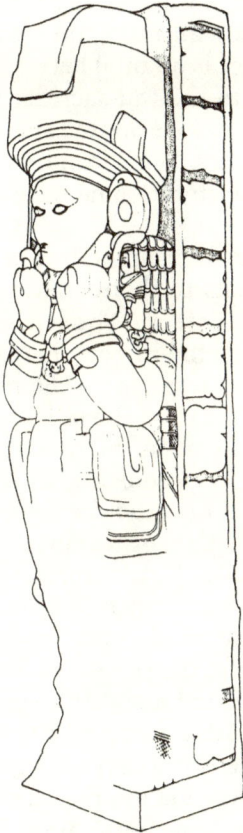

Figure 3   Figure 4

Figure 3. Copan, Stela 1; height: 290 cm. (drawing by A. Dowd, Proyecto Arqueologico Copan).

Figure 4. Copan, Stela 6; height: 212 cm. (drawing by B. Fash, Proyecto Arqueologico Copan).

the ruler claims Copan citizenship, or it is the emblem of the invader's group, which has previously infiltrated Copan iconography on Stela E. One will also note that if the motifs on Stelae 1 and 6 are distinct from those on the other monuments, they have, in fact, the same meaning and value. The change affects the form not the content; there is no departure from the role or function embraced by the ruler. For instance, the so-called "Tlaloc" images on Stela 6 are blends of the Jaguar Tlaloc and Crocodile Tlaloc from Teotihuacan (Pasztory 1974). It is essentially a Jaguar exhibiting similarities to the Jaguar patron of the month Pax and that of war and sacrifice, both well defined at Copan on Stela I by the following traits: no lower jaw and a long protruding tongue (which in fact is a knife) between two fangs in scroll forms. Other images refer to the war-sacrifice-death complex: the belt made of several lengths of rope around the waist, the shells (death sign) fixed to the bracelets, and a band wrapped three times around the wrist (apparently with the same meaning as the "bow-ties").

If the figure on Stelae 1 and 6 is viewed as an usurper, it is because Stelae I and 5 which follow are throwbacks to the technique, the style, and the iconography of the preceding stelae. The reaction to the innovations proposed by the "man-with-the-turban" may be interpreted on the political level as the return to power of the ruler of the dynasty temporarily put aside. Stelae are larger, the relief lowers, and the path which would have led to the true in-the-round sculpture is provisionally abandoned. Stela I is trapezoidal, just like the earlier monuments. The main figure has on his head the traditional jaguar helmet with chin mask, he wears square or rectangular earplugs and bracelets, and from the two heads of the serpent that he holds against his chest emanate jaguar heads with the axe-and-smoke element. Apparent on his belt are the masks of the two main aspects of the Jaguar: the patron of Pop and the patron of Pax. Although the Tlaloc-like form of the Jaguar is not visible on Stela I, it surfaces once more in the iconography of Stela 5 (apron of the west figure), but will not reappear in later stelae. Curiously enough, this motif will continue to be used in later times and in other contexts: the Hieroglyphic Stairway, palaces of the Cementerio area, and so forth.

The foreign intrusion lasted a minimum of 15 years and a maximum of 25; it was put aside and at first glance did not leave a deep impression. However, it raises questions about some epigraphic interpretations.

A glyph (T 122:1030) called "Smoke-Jaguar" by Riese and frequently followed by the Imix Monster (T 1031) would designate a ruler just preceding 18 Rabbit's reign. This name can be read on Stelae E, 2, 1, 6, J and on the altar of Stela I. According to this interpretation, the man-with-the-turban of Stelae 1 and 6 would be the same individual who is depicted on Stelae E and I. I would argue against the possibility that one ruler rebelled against the established sculptural tradition by commanding that his portrait be carved in smaller scale, in higher relief, and surrounded by new symbols, only to later revert to the original patterns.

Proskouriakoff's Ornate Phase

This epoch is dated at Copan to A.D. 721 to 810. Only 16 years elapsed between Stelae 5 and F, but what a contrast between the two monuments! With the introduction of Stela F (fig. 5), the relief is highly accentuated and, as Spinden (1913) observed, the feet are less open, the forearms holding the ceremonial bar—no longer a flaccid serpent—are now horizontal and no longer oblique, and the figure's anatomical proportions have shifted. Iconographic changes are also very obvious. From the collection of ceremonial regalia the skirt and chin mask disappear and the trapezoidal loincloth is replaced by a Sun God mask and narrow apron. The motifs on the anklets, the garters, and the bracelets change but generally retain the same meaning. The Jaguar loses its importance, vanishing almost completely from its position on headdresses and belts, having been replaced by an anthropomorphized Sun God. New creatures are seen emanating from serpent jaws or distributed along the sides of the monument where they grasp the serpents' bodies which frame the stela. Many belong to the war-sacrifice-death complex: the Pax Jaguar with its tongue-knife gives way to an ophidian creature with a lancet as a tongue; one also encounters deified flint or obsidian eccentrics and other patrons of sacrifice with knotted hair. The Sun God, now rarely represented in its guise as a jaguar, clearly continues to be associated with sacrifice and blood-letting, but the serpent also assumes aggressive roles. There are stelae (e.g., F) which, like those of the first phase only, illustrate themes of the war-sacrifice-death complex. But others—and this is the major departure from the former period—exhibit new icons belonging to an earth-water-fertility complex: i.e., the Maize God, the Cauac Monster, the Crocodile, God K, etc. On Stela H, for instance, the dead sun and the Moan bird stand in opposition to the Maize Gods; on Stela B, the Sun Macaw and the Cauac Monster are together. If these new themes were not previously noted at Copan, this does not mean that they were nonexistent in Copan culture before A.D. 720; they were merely excluded from the official art of the monuments erected to the ruler's glory. If he surrounds himself with new images, it is because he envisions himself as having a broader field of action with more responsibilities (terrestrial and cosmic) and a more expansive role in the universe. The iconography of the first phase placed the ruler under the patronage of the Jaguar and/or Sun God, and surrounded him with symbols of death, war, and sacrifice. From A.D. 721 on, the ruler is placed amidst opposite yet complementary forces, life and death, blood and rain, sun and earth. He is no longer pictured solely as the war captain who offers the gods his own blood as well as blood from his captured enemies; he is also the protector of the crops and the guarantor of fertility on earth.

Figure 5. Copan, Stela F; height: 340 cm. (drawing by A. Dowd, Proyecto Arqueologico Copan).

The mask of the Cauac Monster appears for the first time on a stela dated 9.13.10.0.0 (Stela J, A.D. 702). It will emerge 30 years later on the back of Stela B. Stela J has another peculiarity, as it is the first to be associated with a non-geometric altar. Previously, all altars were round or rectangular and, when carved, bore an inscription and knotted bands. These altars were sacrificial, as the knots imply (see, as an example, in the Diccionario de San Francisco, the word *Kax* which means 1; *penitencia, pena que se impone* or 2; *atar*). The altar of Stela J represents a jaguar head with a crown of feathers, and on the back is the crossed-bands motif which belongs to the war-sacrifice-death complex. With Stela F, we have another zoomorphic altar: it is the double head of the Pax Jaguar with a whole jaguar on the sides, presented upside down (negative sign). The altar of Stela H is so much destroyed that it cannot be described with confidence—it seems that there are two "god" heads on the north and south corners, and two large monster heads on the sides of the monument. The altar of Stela A is geometric; Stela B does not have an associated altar. In front of Stela 4 there is a spherical sculpture encircled by a knotted rope, which has a small basin on top drained by two canals curving in opposite directions. So with the possible exception of the altar of Stela H, all other altars up to and including that of Stela 4 are sacrificial (autosacrifice and/or sacrifice of victims, human and/or animal). The picture shifts with the appearance of Stela D's altar; it is a cubic sculpture which represents the two-headed dragon. So the evolution of the altars parallels the evolution of the stelae: during the first phase sacrifice is the only theme, but from the fifteenth katun we find figurations related to universal dualism, with special emphasis on earth and rain powers.

Most of these important innovations borrowed from other regions in the Maya area coincide with the accession of 18 Rabbit. Was he a second foreigner, bringing from abroad many new beliefs, symbols, and images? The changes are so sudden that one is inclined to come to this conclusion. It is true that at the end of the eighth century— corresponding to the beginning of Proskouriakoff's Ornate Phase— most of the Maya cities were experiencing major changes; if these appear more sudden at Copan it is probably due to its peripheral location. In any event, there is no doubt that Copan breaks out of its former isolation and claims access to the major trends of the period. Not content to simply receive and assimilate ideas, original forms were created and successfully worked out in Copan's characteristically high relief.

The carving of small zoomorphic altars is an innovation which coincides at Copan and Quirigua and suggests one site borrowed from the other. Quirigua alone will elaborate and transform the zoomorphs to an unprecedented degree. In spite of their vicinity and political relationships they entertained, the two centers guarded their independence in the realm of artistic productions.

During the last part of the phase corresponding to the reign of Madrugada, the altars gather growing importance. They bear texts and/or complex scenes, and are no longer subordinate to the stelae, which seem to vanish. The last sculptural accomplishments put emphasis on warfare (Structure 18) and give evidence for outside contacts, primarily with the Usumacinta drainage and the northern Lowlands.

There is nothing else to announce the imminent cessation of all elite activities, which we refer to as the Maya collapse.

Note

1. The readings are by Riese (personal communication 1979). All the monuments referred to in this paper bear an unequivocal date, with the exception of E (between A.D. 647 and 665), 2 (probably 9.11.0.0.0), H (probably 9.14.19.5.0) and C (between 9.15.0.0.0 and 9.17.12.0.0). The chronological order of the iconic stelae is as follows: 7, P, E, 2, 3, 1, 6, I, 5, F, H, A, B, 4, D, C (?), M, N, 11.

CHRISTOPHER JONES AND ROBERT J. SHARER

3

Archaeological Investigations in the Site Core of Quirigua, Guatemala

In this paper we summarize and update our preliminary reconstruction of Quirigua's dynastic and constructional history. Since we last considered these topics (Jones 1977a; Sharer 1978a) several new findings at Quirigua have provided information that considerably amplifies the time span of the site's history. Thus, our purpose here is to integrate these new findings into our former reconstruction of Quirigua's development.[1]

Our knowledge of the origins and early development of Quirigua was significantly increased in late 1978 by the discovery of Monument 26, and by the 1979 excavations conducted as a consequence of this discovery. Details of the monument's recovery and the subsequent excavations of the associated Str. 3C-14 have been summarized by Ashmore, Schortman, and Sharer (1983).

Monument 26 was discovered accidently by a drag-line excavating new drainage canals for the Del Monte banana plantation just north of the site core, reportedly from a depth of ca. 1.6m beneath the alluvium. Ashmore's excavations at this location indicate that Monument 26 probably rested on a low paved platform that was bisected by the drag-line. This platform also supported a small plain circular "altar" (left in situ by the drag-line) and a small rectangular structure. The excavations located an elaborate cache in the structure, containing six Early Classic vessels filled with burned jadeite artifacts, pyrite mirrors, and cinnabar reduced to metallic mercury.

Here we wish to comment upon the epigraphic and stylistic evidence provided by Monument 26 that relates to Quirigua's origins and early development. A fuller treatment of Monument 26 may be found in Jones (1983).

The initial series date of Monument 26 is not only incomplete but actually displays incongruous information, and therefore cannot be read with certainty. Out of various possibilities we prefer the more straight-forward reading of 9.2.18.0.0 at 19 Ahau 8 Pax, even though the two dots of the katun coefficient are oddly connected by a bar, and the patron of the month sign would be better read as Cumku or Yax. Our opinion is based first on comparison to the previously-discovered Monument 21 (Stela U; Morley 1937–8, IV: 89–92; V; Pl. 169b). In Morley's photographs and our own, Monument 21 clearly carries a Katun 2 initial series date. The two monuments are of a similar bluish schist stone, are of a similar size and shape, and feature a front-facing figure with a horizontally-held bar. More specifically, on both monuments the frontal design extends onto the stela sides. Also, an animal glyph with band headdress appearing on Monument 26 is carved in large size on Monument 21 as if it represented a ruler's name.

Certain features of style also support our Early Classic dating. The tun and uinal glyphs on Monument 26 carry distinctive tied head-dresses with frontal tassels found only on early monuments (Tikal Stelae 29 and 6, the Leyden Plate, Copan Stela 24, and Yaxchilan Lintel 48, all from 8.12.14.8.15 to 9.4.11.8.16). Other specific elements of style, such as the blunt-ended scroll work, the peculiar split ends of the serpent head fangs, the lack of panelling on the belt, and the flared tassels on the collar ornament, are all early traits (Proskouriakoff 1950: 29–70). The wrap-around design as well as the costuming resemble most strongly those of Tikal Stela 2, style dated to 9.3.10.0.0±2 katuns (Proskouriakoff 1950: 195). William Coe (personal communication, 1980) has pointed out to us that a similar full-front figure is found on Uaxactun Stela 20, probably dated to 9.3.0.0.0 (Morley 1937–8; I: 188–91; V: Pl. 61).

Altar de Sacrificios and Copan possessed carved monuments before 9.2.0.0.0, but Quirigua's Monuments 26 and 21 are the earliest known dated figural stelae outside of the core area. Although they retain the bas-relief carving tradition of the Peten, Monuments 26 and 21 were the first to pull together the wrap-around idea and the full-frontal pose which later became the hallmark of Quirigua and Copan stelae. This break from, or re-combination of, Peten modes established a new regional style of incipient three-dimensionality, which progressed at Copan into the almost free-standing "statue" stelae.

A very interesting set of glyphs on the back of Monument 26 shows a coefficient three with a hel-and-spiral glyph, followed by three undeciphered glyph-blocks and then a coefficient four with an identical hel-and-spiral compound. According to Riese (1979a), similar hel-with-coefficient notations are associated with rulers' names in a count of succession at Copan and other sites. By this interpretation Quirigua's great ruler, Cauac Sky (also called "Two-Legged Sky"), inaugurated at 9.14.13.4.7, labeled himself the fourteenth ruler. Thus, these hel notations support the early date for the monument. However, it must be remembered that none of the above epigraphic and stylistic arguments constitutes proof of a specific Katun 2 date and we must continue to allow for later possibilities, at least until Katun 7.

Peter Matthews (personal communication, 1979) has pointed out to us the relevance of the text on the west side of Quirigua Monument 3 (Stela C; dated at 9.17.5.0.0, A.D. 775; see Morley 1937–8 IV: 156–162). Following an Initial Series date of 9.1.0.0.0 (A.D. 455) this text includes a clause consisting of a possible name distinguished by a mah-kin-a title and the Quirigua Emblem Glyph. This text may be seen as an historical reference to an Early Classic Quirigua ruler, perhaps the local dynastic founder, made at or near the end of the reign of Quirigua's dominant Late Classic ruler, Cauac Sky (see below). The Initial Series date associated with this reference (9.1.0.0.0), some 37.5 years earlier than the presumed third or fourth ruler associated with Monument 26, is chronologically consistent with the suggestion that the person named on Monument 3 was Quirigua's founder.

After this apparent founding period in the Early Classic, the historical record at Quirigua is mute for some 200 years, or until the dedication of Monument 13 (Altar M) at 9.15.0.0.0 (A.D. 731) and Monument 19 (Stela S) at 9.15.15.0.0 (A.D. 746). The only exceptions are Monument 20 (Stela T) which Morley (1937–8 IV: 86–89) preferred at 9.13.0.0.0, and Monument 12 (Altar L) that Satterthwaite (1979) placed at ca. 9.12.0.0.0 (A.D. 672). The archaeological record indicates that it may have been during this intermediate period at Quirigua (ca. A.D. 550–720) that construction began in what was to become the Late Classic site core, with the earliest buildings in the Acropolis (Construction Stage 4; cf. Jones 1977a) dated to this era by associated ceramics and a single radiocarbon determination (A.D. 590±50 MASCA corrected). The origins of the Acropolis as an elite residential complex are reflected in the recovery of a single dedicatory burial in a stone-lined crypt under the eastern "shrine" structure. This is consistent with the pattern of residential settlement and associated dedicatory burials encountered at Tikal, and designated as "Plaza Plan 2" at that site (Becker 1972).

During this era Quirigua seems to have consisted of little more than a small elite residential compound with the platform of Monument 26 to the north, all constructed of masonry in contrast to the scattering of surrounding, less-substantial dwellings. The eastern "shrine" in the Acropolis began as an earthen mound over the burial and was then capped with cobble fill and roughly-hewn masonry steps and terrace facings. The south structure was raised only three steps above plaza level. Its building floors were mostly mud, mixed with a little lime. Its walls, composed primarily of large cobble-stones, were too thin to have supported a masonry roof. Opposite the shrine on the west was another low building built on an earthen core. This structure has a relatively elaborate interior platform bench embellished with a red-painted cornice and trapezoidal legs in relief. What we have seen of the Acropolis at this early stage is not grand in its design. The cobble masonry rather resembles that found in other lower Motagua valley sites (Schortman 1980a) and in the Chamelecon drainage of Honduras (Urban 1980).

At this point, we cannot determine whether Construction Stage 4 began as early as Katun 2, or signaled Quirigua's later resurgence. Likewise, we cannot be sure when Construction Stage 3 began. We have suggested (Jones 1977a; Jones, Ashmore, and Sharer 1978a) that the major constructions of this period, Str. 1B-2 and the buried ballcourt, Str. 1B-Sub 4, built as they are of well-cut rhyolite blocks, might correlate in time to the rhyolite monuments such as Monument 13 (Altar M, at 9.15.0.0.0?) and Monument 14 (Altar N) and therefore to the early part of Cauac Sky's rule, before 9.15.6.14.6. We also suggested that Quirigua's three small round flat monuments, Monuments 12, 17 and 18 (Altars L, Q, and R), might have been markers for the buried ballcourt. If so, of course, then Construction Stage 3 would have begun earlier than the 9.14.13.4.17 inaugural date of Cauac Sky. We can detect some time-depth for Construction Stage 3, however, with Str. 1B-2 looking later in masonry style than the ballcourt itself.

The cache vessels associated with the ballcourt are of a later type than those from the Monument 26 platform. The correlation between Construction Stage 3 rhyolite masonry and the rhyolite monuments is in itself a tenuous one, but it gains credence from the fact that a clearer correlation can be made between the architecture and masonry of the succeeding Acropolis construction (Construction Stage 2) and the series of Cauac Sky's monuments from Monument 19 (Stela S at 9.15.15.0.0) to Monument 7 (Zoomorph G at 9.17.15.0.0). The prevailing material of both is sandstone, the craftsmanship is superb, the design is grandiose. Furthermore the mosaic masonry figure on Str. 1B-Sub 1, the great western wall of the Construction Stage 2 Acropolis, matches the figures on the monuments in scroll-work and in costume details.

In any case, Quirigua was fully transformed architecturally during Construction Stage 2 (ca. A.D. 740–810), when some 70 years of seemingly continuous building activity replaced the former small residential compound with the monumental architectural and sculptural remains recognizable as a Late Classic Maya center. The Acropolis was considerably enlarged and its structures rebuilt burying all the previous constructions except Str. 1B-2. The Great Plaza was expanded to the north, ultimately, by the construction of a huge cobble-filled platform (100 by 85 m) to support the latest and largest of Cauac Sky's monuments. The Ball Court Plaza and its surrounding "reviewing stand," along with Str. 1A-11, were built adjacent to the Acropolis. All this rapid growth follows a single historical event, possibly the capture of Copan's ruler, 18 Rabbit, by Cauac Sky in 9.15.6.14.6 as identified from multiple references in the Quirigua inscriptions (Marcus 1976: 135; Proskouriakoff 1973: 165–178; Riese, this volume). As we have suggested elsewhere (Jones 1977a; Sharer 1978a: 66–68), the archaeologically detected transformation of Quirigua after this event reflects a new status as an independent political and mercantile power, commanding the Motagua valley jade and obsidian routes.

In a paper for the conference from which this volume derives, kindly submitted in advance, Riese has pointed out that Copan did not undergo a hiatus after the capture of 18 Rabbit at 9.15.6.14.6, but built and carved the great hieroglyphic stairway. However, there is little in Quirigua's Construction Stage 2 that can be considered of Copan derivation or inspiration. The exquisite sandstone mosaic masonry and decoration has its forerunner in Construction Stage 3, specifically in Str. 1B-2, and as we have mentioned, models for the stelae of this time can be found in Monuments 26 and 21 at Quirigua itself. The other possibly imitative features mentioned by Riese, such as the bench-panel inscriptions of Str. 1B-1 and the frieze inscription of the same structure, belong to Construction Stage 1, probably beginning around 9.18.0.0.0. It is at this late stage that the Quirigua Acropolis takes on a Copan appearance, because of the building of the great stairways leading up to it from the new Ball Court Plaza. For all we know, Copan's mosaic masonry might have been inspired by Quirigua Str. 1B-2. Even the mat design inscription on Quirigua Monument 8 (Stela H) seems more closely related to Cancuen Stela 3 (Tourtellot, Sabloff, and Sharick 1978: 229–230), since both share an apparent simple unwoven diagonal text, unlike the interwoven pattern of Copan's Stela J (Miller 1980).

In sum, we still see Quirigua's great period (Katuns 16 and 17) as one of cultural independence from Copan. Its architecture and its monument style are both taken from local models. The size of Quirigua's monuments and its plaza are at a scale not found at Copan. In contrast, the ballcourt markers of the earlier Construction Stage 3 and the buildings of the later Construction Stage 1 might indeed have been designed with an eye on Copan. The data suggest that for a while, Quirigua was able, perhaps through the well-touted capture event, to gain sufficient political and economic independence to exploit its position between Copan and the Peten and perhaps attain fuller control over the jade and obsidian sources and the rich bottom lands of the Motagua valley.

Quirigua's role as a commercial power is supported by several lines of archaeological evidence. Geomorphological investigations in 1978 and 1979 have revealed that the ancient course of the Motagua shifted continuously in the vicinity of Quirigua. It is likely that the course of the Motagua was much closer to the site core during its occupation, probably flowing adjacent to the western side of the Great Plaza (Ashmore 1980c). Excavation immediately west of Str. 1A-11 in 1979 discovered that the northwest edge of the Ball Court Plaza consists of a precipitous embankment faced with cobbles. This embankment was the edge of a large anciently water-filled basin. The extent of this basin is unknown, but its proximity to the apparent eighth century course of the Motagua suggests that it served as an embayment to provide shelter and docking facilities for river canoes.

Quirigua's prosperity and building activity continued through the reigns of Cauac Sky's successors. The two largest structures of the Acropolis, Str. 1B-1 with an associated Initial Series date of 9.19.0.0.0 (Morley 1937–38, IV: 229–237), and Str. 1B-5 shortly thereafter, were apparently built during the reign of the last historically identified ruler, Jade Sky (Jones 1977a; Sharer 1978a).

It might be interesting to point out that Quirigua's two periods of monument carving activity, and its long hiatus, at least as now known, fall within those of Tikal. Copan, in contrast, although it has an early stela of Southern Maya style, and some Early Classic all-glyphic monuments, begins its great period of stela erection around Katun 9, halfway through Tikal's long hiatus. This is roughly at the time when Piedras Negras, Naranjo, Coba, and Palenque, the new centers of the Maya periphery, begin their spectacular and creative careers. Likewise, Quirigua and Tikal continue their monumental activity longer than these other sites. To us, the timing suggests that

Quirigua's economic fortunes were more closely connected to Tikal's than to Copan's. In our view, Quirigua and Copan were rivals. Quirigua's connections were with the Peten, either by way of the coast and the Motagua and Belize Rivers, or more directly by way of overland trails through the lower Verapaz and the southern Peten. As Miller (1980) has pointed out, Copan's sculptural styles owe much to a non-Peten influence and are more free and creative than the stiff Tikal-like forms of Quirigua. We should point out that this conclusion was reached independently from, but is in agreement with, findings based upon ceramic studies presented in the volume's symposium (i.e., the 1980 SAA Symposium, The Southeast Meso-american Periphery: Copan and Quirigua, Willey *et al.* 1980; also see Sharer, in press).

Although the end of Quirigua's dynastic and occupational history remains unknown, results of our archaeological excavations indicate that while the site continued to be occupied into the Postclassic period, it may have come under the control of outsiders. For the first time, occupation debris from the latest levels of areas such as the Ball Court Plaza contain sizeable proportions of "foreign" pottery. The closest affinities for these ceramics are from the East Coast of Yucatan. Other new elements appear at this time, including chipped-stone projectile points. This suggests contacts with areas to the north, probably via the newly emerging seacoast long-distance trade networks (Sabloff and Rathje 1975a). The Central Mexican flavor of such Postclassic contacts may explain the earlier reports of "non-Maya" artifacts found at Quirigua, including a "chacmool" sculpture (Richardson 1940) and a carved metate of apparent Coastal Veracruz style (see Thompson 1970: 131).

Despite these indications of lingering occupation, Quirigua was surely abandoned before the end of the Postclassic era. When Cortes (1908) and his party marched through the Maya lowlands to Honduras (1524–1526) they visited the prosperous commercial center of Nito on the Rio Dulce 80 km to the northeast of Quirigua. This location was significant, for Nito undoubtedly served as Quirigua's replacement as a trade center serving the commerce between the Maya highlands and the Caribbean.

To summarize, then, although there certainly is a clear regional southeastern Maya artistic and architectural style shared by Quirigua and Copan, the great period of Cauac Sky cannot, in our view, be characterized simply as imitative of Copan. We think, rather, that it derives from earlier local models and ultimately, perhaps, from the central Peten. Quirigua's Postclassic occupation, with its suggested

Yucatecan connections and the subsequent transfer of commercial power to Nito on the coast, can be viewed as a continuation of this association with the north that began in the Early Classic.

Note

1. The Quirigua Project was formed in 1973 under a contract between the University Museum, University of Pennsylvania, and the Government of Guatemala, under the auspices of the Instituto de Antropologia e Historia (IDAEH). The Project conducted archaeological research at Quirigua and within the surrounding lower Motagua valley region for six seasons (1974–1979). IDAEH is currently continuing their program of architectural consolidation within the site core. Funding for the Quirigua Project was provided by the University Museum (Francis Boyer Fund), the National Science Foundation (Grants BNS 7602185, 7603283, and 7624189), the National Geographic Society, the Ford Foundation, the Tikal Association of Guatemala, the Ministry of Defense of Guatemala, and several private benefactors. The consolidation program at Quirigua is funded by the Ministry of Education, Government of Guatemala, and is directed by Arq. Marcelino Gonzales C. of IDAEH. Our appreciation is extended to all these institutions and individuals for their generous support.

WENDY ASHMORE

4

Peten Cosmology in the Maya Southeast: An Analysis of Architecture and Settlement Patterns at Classic Quirigua

Introduction

Settlement pattern research at the Classic site of Quirigua[1] has identified a series of distinctive group plans for monumental architecture. Combination of groups into clusters likewise appears to follow
recognizable norms. Comparison of these architectural assemblages
with equivalent units elsewhere, in the lower Motagua valley and
beyond, suggests the use at Quirigua of site planning principles derived from both local and distant sources. Furthermore, source distinctions seem to correlate with functional identity of the complex:
while domestic and administrative groups in the area resemble architectural groups elsewhere in the lower Motagua valley and immediately adjacent areas, architectural groups with primarily public or
ceremonial function follow arrangement canons that are here argued
to have been derived from Tikal and other sites in the Classic Maya
heartland, over 200 km to the north. These canons can be linked to a
cosmological system with roots in this lowland core area, and trace-
able there to Preclassic times. This suggests that those in power were
using public-oriented architecture, just as they used publicly displayed sculpture and inscriptions detailing dynastic genealogy with
links to Peten, to express participation in the elite tradition of their
more prestigious neighbors and probable allies to the north.

Background: Site Planning and Quirigua

Site planning refers to adherence to preconceived norms for the arrangement of structures and spaces and is most easily recognized through repetitious patterns. Although small, unprepossessing residential groups may evince principles of planning (e.g., Ashmore 1981b; cf. Glassie 1975; Pollock 1965: 389), the primary focus in this paper is on norms executed in monumental architectural groups,[2] and therefore presumably associated with the aristocracy of local society. In part, such a narrowing of focus reflects an interest in examining intercommunity elite interactions, but it also derives from the nature of the Quirigua data, to which we now turn.

The site periphery program of the Quirigua Project conducted reconnaissance, survey, and excavation in an irregular 95 km² area surrounding the Quirigua site core (see fig. 1). Because of discovery problems related to alluvial burial of Precolumbian remains, the program was divided between intensive investigations in a 10.4 km² area of the floodplain periphery, ringing the site core, and a more superficial examination of remains in the rest of the area, or wider periphery. Details of method and results of this research are presented elsewhere (Ashmore 1980a, 1981a, in press). What is important here is that despite some excavation in both parts of the program, the research still constitutes primarily a survey project. As with most archaeological survey research, data on architectural group plans are fuller for monumental units. This is due, at Quirigua, both to the greater visibility and presumably enhanced survival rate of the more imposing remains, and to the fact that, on the northern floodplain, only relatively imposing Late Classic construction was visible at all at ground level. Smaller and/or earlier construction in this zone was generally undetectable except as exposed in cross-section in modern drainage ditches. Thus while hundreds of features of various kinds were recorded in site periphery investigations most data on structure and group plans pertain to monumental architecture. This does not mean that data on small or early groups is totally absent, only that it is less common and, when available, comes usually from the wider periphery.

Also like most other Maya archaeological settlement samples, the majority of the data, at any scale, describe terminal occupation, in this case, Terminal Classic/Early Postclassic remains. Materials recorded in the deep ditch exposures and in periphery test excavations have, however, allowed delineation of a gross sequence of occupation spanning half a millennium, from the mid-fifth to at least the mid-ninth centuries A.D., with tantalizing evidence suggesting local population in the area for several centuries prior to the fifth century florescence. Internal divisions of this sequence, called Periphery Time Spans (PTS), are necessarily linked to ceramic complexes; the reasons for this, as well as details of the occupation sequence, are described elsewhere (Ashmore 1981a, 1984). Relevant aspects of the sequence will be noted below as needed.

The combination of the periphery data set and that from the site core (Jones and Sharer, this volume) has allowed tentative identification of seven plaza plans at and within five kilometers of Quirigua. Their distribution within the occupation sequence is shown in Table 1. There is not space here for a detailed consideration of all seven

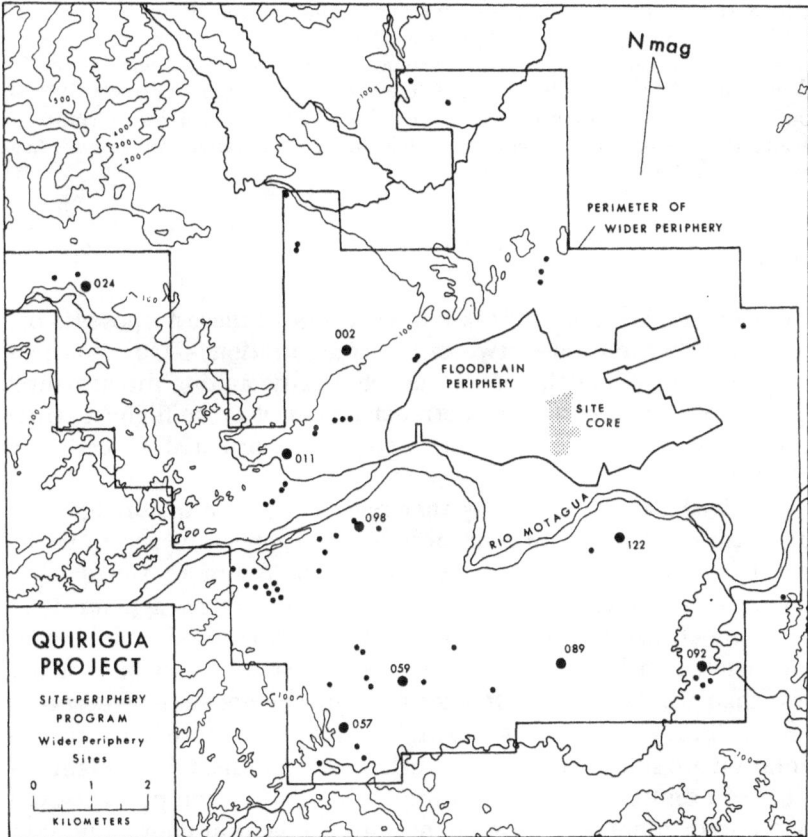

Figure 1. Limits of the Wider Periphery Research Universe around the site of Quirigua.

Table 1. Distribution of Quirigua Patterns in the Site Core
and Site Periphery, According to Periphery Time Spans

		QP 1	QP 2	QP 3	QP 4	QP 5	QP 6	QP 7
A.D. 900+	PTS 1			ABANDONMENT				
A.D. 810	PTS 2	x	x?	x	x	x	x?	x
			|	|	|	|	|	
A.D. 700	PTS 3	x	x?	x	x	x	x?	
			|		|		|	
A.D. 600	PTS 4		x		x		x	
					|		|	
A.D. 400	PTS 5	x?			x		x	
	PTS 6							

Note: An "x" indicates presence of the particular pattern during the specified time period; vertical lines indicate sure or probable continuity in use of groups established in the earliest time period. Not all patterns are discussed in this paper, since the focus of the essay is on identifying site planning principles associated with either the southeast or the Central Maya lowlands. QP 3 seems an indigenous pattern; QP 2, 4, and perhaps 5 derive from northeast Peten. QP 1 simply designates ballcourts, of widespread Mesoamerican occurrence. QP 6 and 7 have uncertain sources. See Ashmore (1981a) for further discussion.

patterns (see Ashmore 1981a). What matters for these purposes is the form and distribution of two of the configurations—Quirigua Patterns 3 and 4—and the occurrence generally, among monumental groups, of a preferential northern placement of 1) the highest structure in a group and/or 2) the more public-oriented spaces in a cluster[3].

Quirigua Pattern (QP) 3 is that referred to as a quadrangle[4]—a patio group with central court at least 15 m across and access to the court blocked at two or more corners (cf. Ashmore 1981a: 239; Sharer et al. 1979: 55–56), although the latter trait is apparently at least sometimes a secondary feature, due to growth and/or deliberate alteration. Substructures are generally at least 20 m long but usually less than 3 m high, even after excavation. The northern structure is often, although not always, the highest. Superstructure form and orientation are seldom clear from surface indications. Of the eight excavated examples (Strs. 1B-1 through 1B-6, 3C-5 and 089-2), seven had one or more doorways facing into the central court; one (Str. 3C-5) faced away from it.

Quadrangles were identified at Loci 059, 089 (fig. 2; southern patio group) and 092 in the wider periphery, and Groups 1B-1 (Acropolis) and 3C-2 in Quirigua proper. Other potential examples of QP 3 are Groups 1A-3, 1A-5, 1B-2, 1B-4, 1B-5, and 13B-1, with full confirmation of the form prevented by alluvial masking. All are identified with PTS 3 and 2.

The architecture of quadrangles seems to stress privacy or restricted entry (cf. Andrews 1975: 63–64), as well as externally visible grandeur, and artifacts recovered in quadrangle excavations suggest domestic activities took place there. Furthermore, the groups are either located immediately adjacent to the architectural epicenter of the ancient community or arranged in systematic subdivision of the fertile plain to the south. It is difficult to avoid the inference that these groups were residences and/or administrative centers of at least some of the local aristocracy. Even more suggestive in this regard is the distribution of somewhat larger quadrangles as the core groups of sites spaced regularly along the south side of the Motagua valley northeast of Quirigua, apparently dividing the valley

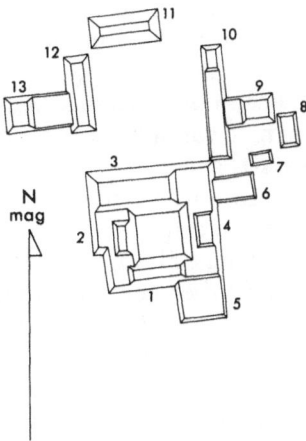

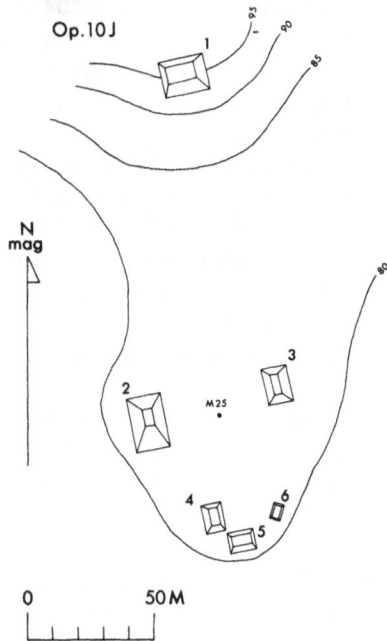

Figure 2. Locus 089, Jubuco Site.

Figure 3. Locus 011, Morley's Group C.

into politico-administrative units (Schortman 1980, 1984, this volume). Quadrangles are therefore interpreted, overall, as the residences and administrative offices of Quirigua's ruler (i.e., in the Acropolis), and other ranking nobles (cf. Sharer 1978a; Jones and Sharer, this volume; Ashmore 1981a).

Another patterned assemblage, QP 4, is similar to Andrews' (1975: 56–59) "temple group," and is referred to here as a triad group. Its defining characteristics at Quirigua are an elongated plaza, bounded on the west, north, and east, but with no obvious restriction on access. The northern structure, at one end of the long axis of the court or plaza, has the highest summit elevation of the group. Examples of this pattern include Loci 011 (Morley's Group C; fig. 3), 057, and 089 (fig. 2; northern patio group), and probably floodplain periphery Group 7A-1 (Morley's Group B). In one case (Loc. 057), the south end of the court remains open, but in the other three it is bounded by a likely residential structure or group, in one instance (Loc. 089) a quadrangle. At least Loc. 011 seems to have been founded in PTS 5; all cited examples were apparently in use in PTS 3/2.[5] The seemingly earliest triad groups (Loci 011, 057) are located at river control points, adjacent to Motagua tributaries either where these emerge from the foothills or at their Motagua confluence. Later instances are likewise located on the rivers and/or in association with administrative centers (e.g., Loc. 089)—in other words, in prominently public positions.

Functionally, triad groups seem to have been public arenas, with easy access to an open plaza that could have held variably large numbers of people. Morley's Groups B (Group 7A-1) and C (Loc. 011) incorporate stone monuments within the plaza, but in both cases, placement of the monuments may postdate the original establishment of the groups. Indeed, Group 1A-1, the Great Plaza of the site core, with its multiple monuments, may be a further example of QP 4, although there is now no known evidence of construction along its west side. Whether this identification *per se* is correct, the Great Plaza, nonetheless, does represent a large public space, with its tallest immediately flanking structure to the north and a residential group (the Acropolis quadrangle) to the south.

Together, examples of triad groups and quadrangles constitute the principal public-ritual and elite-residential-administrative groups at Quirigua. And it is in these two patterns that the greatest emphasis on the importance and elevation of the northern position is found, at both the group and cluster scale.[6]

The layout of groups of non-monumental structures is less well documented at Quirigua, largely because of the cited alluvial masking in the floodplain periphery. Where small-structure groups have been encountered, however, in wider periphery sites such as Loc. 024, they constitute patio groups and informal groups with no more strikingly consistent principles of arrangement.

Site Planning Principles as Cultural Diagnostics

The interpretive implications of these observations can be seen when the patterns are fitted into a larger temporal and cultural context. That is, first, the quadrangle pattern, as described, seems to be a lower Motagua valley trait; its origins and development remain obscure, but during PTS 3/2 it became the exclusive plan found in the focal groups of the major sites along the south side of the valley[7] (Schortman 1980, 1984, this volume). It has no real known precedents in other areas, but is reminiscent of structure groups in the Copan valley.[8] Triad groups and the northward focus of monumental assemblages, however, are lacking as systematic organizing norms in the settlement remains from southern valley sites beyond Quirigua's periphery. These norms do have precedents and analogs in Classic sites of the central Maya lowlands, especially at Tikal. Furthermore, both seem—given the present data base—to have been introduced at Quirigua during periods marked by an influx of other central-lowland-elite material traits.

Coggins (1967), Jones (Jones, Ashmore, and Sharer 1983) and Hammond (1981) have contended that the fundamental elements of Classic lowland Maya centers can be reduced to a mutually complementary, paired combination of ritual-ceremonial and elite-residential-administrative facilities. The first author, however, has noted a further regularity, in placement of the principal ritual areas to the north of the main elite residential complex (Coggins 1967), an arrangement observed at 13 Classic centers of various sizes, all within 100 km of Uaxactun—that is, in the core of the Classic heartland.

In a different context, Coggins (1980: 728–31, 737) argues that directionality of elements in some public-oriented Classic Maya architectural groups depicted a 90 degree rotation of the sun's path: east and west represent the rising and setting points, respectively, but north represents the zenith or "up" while south is the locus of the underworld (cf. Bricker 1983). For Coggins (personal communication, 1982), the east-west dimension in Classic architectural assemblages is initially prominent, but north is nonetheless the most revered position, associated with the celestial and the divine.

From his analyses of Preclassic cosmology as expressed in architecture, Freidel (1981b) likewise stresses the north-south axis as dominant. He has described in intricate detail the Late Preclassic monumental sculptural portrayal of the sun's daily cycle at Cerros Str. 5C-2nd and elsewhere, and has further suggested the association of stations in the sun's yearly transit with elements of some three-sided architectural groupings, such as atop Str. 29B at Cerros or in coeval structures[9] at Lamanai (Pendergast 1981) and El Mirador (Morley, Brainerd, and Sharer 1983: 296–97). However, it is 5C-2nd, now visibly marking the northern extreme of the community, that served both to establish the original north-south centerline of the elite center and simultaneously to begin the local tradition of such elaborate solar-related pyramid decoration (Freidel, personal communication, 1982). It would seem that whether dealing with Pre-classic or Classic orientations, with Freidel's or Coggins' analyses, north represents the heavens.[10] That is, the north-as-eminence and north-ritual vs. south-residential associations found in Classic architecture of the Peten heartland seem to express a cosmological ordering incorporated into publicly imposing architecture since Pre-classic times (cf. Freidel 1981b).

Certainly by the Late Classic, Tikal had developed several examples employing this and related principles. Coggins (1980) describes both the twin-pyramid groups (Jones 1969) and the North Acropolis-Great Plaza-Central Acropolis as instances of architectural directionality expressing cosmological structure (cf. Guillemin 1968). Indeed, I would suggest Tikal's northernmost twin-pyramid Group 3D-2, together with Temples IV and VI, may mark an even grander version of the same triadic arrangement, with the Great Plaza complex near the center of the huge triad. Group 3D-2, and Temples IV and VI were all built during the reign of Ruler B (Jones 1977b), and all are termini of the great causeways built or refurbished at the same time. The layout may have been first attempted by Ruler A, whose twin-pyramid Groups 3D-1 and 5C-1 were subsequently dwarfed and partly obliterated by the causeways leading to Ruler B's Group 3D-2 and Temple IV. It has been suggested that Ruler B seems to have had a penchant for grandeur (Jones 1977b; Ashmore and Sharer 1975), and these architectural monuments of his surround and dwarf his father's and other predecessors' constructions, restating the basic cosmological scheme on an unprecedented and truly impressive scale.

Beyond Tikal, Coggins says there are few known examples of Classic triad groups, the only one cited being the Cross Group at Palenque (Coggins 1980; see Cohodas 1976 for a different cosmological interpretation of this group). Like Ruler B's putative grand construct at Tikal, however, the Palenque Cross Group seems to lack a southern element. In complexes where the southern position is occupied, it represents either the underworld (e.g., the nine-doorwayed structures within twin-pyramid groups) or the mundane aspect of a sacred-north vs. secular-south distinction (e.g., the Tikal Central Acropolis, beyond the nine-doorwayed Str. 5D-120 fronting the Great Plaza; cf. Coggins 1967). It may be that the southern position could be left unfilled, its use suppressed and its meaning implicit, just as the underworld lies below and beyond view (cf. Freidel n.d.). More speculatively, the placement of palace groups in this southern position (cf. Coggins 1967) may then reflect less a part of the cosmological structure than simply occupation of the one remaining cardinal position.

What is suggested here is that the principles underlying north-oriented triad groups along with the north-eminence and north-south functional dualism were indeed developed by Classic times in the monumental architecture of the central Maya lowlands, derived from a cosmological system whose development and use in public architectural display went back to Late Preclassic times in the same core area. It is further asserted that these principles were exported to more distant centers as part of an elite Maya "culture," and that their appearance in Classic times at places such as Quirigua serves as a sign of identification of those who commissioned the architecture— that is, the local rulers—with the cosmological system of the source area. While simple emulation of more powerful nobles by less powerful ones is possible, a more usual interpretation of the appearance of locally intrusive, elite-related architectural forms is that they reflect a closer political identity between the two areas, such as colonization or confederation. Examples include Teotihuacan-style architecture at Kaminaljuyu in the Early Classic (Brown 1977; Kidder, Jennings, and Shook 1946; Santley 1980); "Toltec" Chichen Itza-style buildings in northern Belize (Chase and Chase 1982); Mayapan-style dwellings on Cozumel Island and elsewhere in the Late Postclassic (Freidel 1976, 1981a); and Quiche/Cakchiquel architecture in the eastern frontier area of Mesoamerica also during the Late Postclassic (Fox 1981).

Evidence for such interpretation of the Quirigua data comes from the apparent earliest occurrence of the cited principles there in Early Classic PTS 5, at Loc. 011 and probably Loc. 057. More certainly attributable to this same (admittedly long) span are: 1) the earliest Quirigua ruler, cited in glyphic inscriptions of the eighth century but referring back to his existence in A.D. 455 (cited on Monument

Table 2. Detailed Quirigua Chronology, Nonsettlement Sources

Gregorian Dates	Pottery Complexes[a]	ACS[b]	Monument Dedicatory Dates[c]	Ruler[d]	
	?	?		Jade Sky	
	Morley	1	Str. 18-1 Frieze	(Ruler 16)	Regent?
A.D. 800			Mon. 11		("Imix Dog")
			Mon. 9		Sky Xul
			Mons. 16, 24		
		2	Mons. 15, 23		
			Mon. 7	Cauac Sky	
750	Hewett		Mon. 2	(Ruler 14)	
			Mons. 1, 3		
		3	Mon. 5		
			Mon. 4		
			Mon. 6		
700		4	Mon. 10		
			Mon. 8		
			Mon. 19		
650	Maudslay (late facet)		Mon. 13		
			Mon. 20		
600					
550					
	Maudslay (early facet)				
500			Mon. 26	Ruler 3 or 4?	
			Mon. 21		
A.D. 450				Ruler 1?	

[a] Pottery complexes are given in Table 1, except that Catherwood is omitted here; arrow at end of Table 2 indicates continuation of Maudslay Complex beyond limit of table. Sources are Bullard and Sharer (n.d.) and Willey et al. (1980).

[b] Acropolis Construction (ACS) sequence was outlined by Jones (1977a; Jones, Ashmore, and Sharer 1983).

[c] Includes date from Str. 1B-1. Sources are Sharer (1978a) and Morley (1937–8).

[d] Rulers given when known; data from Jones and Sharer (1980: Fig. 7).

3; Jones and Sharer, this volume); 2) the earliest known Quirigua stelae, Monuments 21 (A.D. 478) and 26 (A.D. 493), with references on Monument 26 to local rulers 3 and 4 and sculpted in Peten style (*Ibid.*; Jones 1983); and 3) locally manufactured Peten-style painted pottery.

On the latter three grounds, Jones and Sharer (*op. cit.*) have suggested that Quirigua's Early Classic florescence was directly attributable to intervention (colonization) from Tikal. Other evidence suggests further coeval local ties with centers such as Copan and Kaminaljuyu (Ashmore 1980b; Ashmore, Schortman, and Sharer 1983), but even granted the sampling problems in the early Quirigua data, the dominant political affiliation seems to be with the central lowland core area.

Note again that all the indices cited are associated with more elite-oriented aspects of culture, and the sculpture, inscriptions, and architecture are all items on public display. The settlement pattern and site planning data, then, can tentatively be seen to comprise further corroboration of a political link, using public architecture to express allegiance. The principles were assuredly well established at Quirigua by the Late Classic, and are clearly and abundantly present in PTS 3/2 monumental architecture, as outlined above.[11] They are less clear, if truly present at all, at Copan,[12] and, as stated earlier, are essentially absent at other Motagua valley sites.

Such political expressions at Quirigua were probably intended less for local people than for dignitaries and emissaries from other power centers. That is, the latter category of visitor, whether from the Peten, Copan, or elsewhere, would most likely have been conversant with the ideas of the aristocracies of the lowlands, and would have recognized the cited sculptural, epigraphic, and architectural manifestations as symbols of allegiance. The spatial contexts of the symbols support this interpretation, for they occur in the most publicly prominent and accessible locations—the Great Plaza core of Quirigua, its Late Classic administrative satellites (e.g., Loc. 089), and the Early/Late Classic sites dominating local tributary access to the Motagua (e.g., Loci 011, 057). Moreover, at least with respect to Late Classic architecture, one may note the functional distinction between public-ritual assemblages which follow the northeast Peten system, while it is precisely the suppressable southern element of that system that follows putatively local canons (that is, the quadrangles), and does so within the bounds of Peten norms (i.e., placement of residential groups to the south).[13] The less regularized arrangement of the known small-structure groups only underscores the distinction and further supports the interpretation.

Conclusion

Analyses of architectural layouts in the Quirigua area have highlighted several apparent principles employed in local site planning. Those associated with public and ritual precincts are argued to reflect adoption of ideas from elite culture in centers far to the north, in the Classic lowland Maya core area. Conversely, groups associated with residential functions seem to have been arranged according to local southeastern norms, yet fit within the overall context of the foreign-derived system. The particular nature of this juxtaposition of norms is further interpreted as reinforcing the interpretation of the corpus of Quirigua architecture as a symbolic expression of the center's Classic period alliance with a polity based in the northeast Peten.

Although architecture and settlement patterns are molded by natural environmental, economic, and social organizational constraints, they are also media for communication of values and other ideas of a given culture (e.g., Andrews 1975; Glassie 1975; Leone 1977; cf. Agrest and Gandelsonas 1977; Rapoport 1982). The ancient Maya embedded their complex and intriguing ideas in a variety of media. Surely we are just beginning to read the messages preserved in the form and distribution of their buildings.

Notes

1. The Quirigua Project, of which the Site Periphery Program was a part, was formed by the Instituto de Antropologia e Historia, Ministerio de Educacion, Guatemala, and the University Museum, University of Pennsylvania. Financial support was provided by the University Museum (Francis Boyer Fund), the National Geographic Society, the National Science Foundation (BNS 7602185, 7603283, 7624189), the Ford Foundation, the Tikal Association, the Guatemalan Ministry of Defense, the Museum Applied Science Center for Archaeology (University Museum), the Department of Anthropology of the University of Pennsylvania, Messrs. Landon T. Clay and Alfred G. Zantzinger, and Dr. John M. Keshishian. Among the people who have contributed to the development of ideas contained in this paper, I would especially like to thank R. J. Sharer, E. M. Schortman, P. A. Urban, M. C. Coggins, D. A. Freidel, M. C. Arnauld, J. B. Carlson, Y. A. Cohen, J. W. Fox, D. Grove, N. Hammond, and P. D. Sheets.

2. At Quirigua, that which is referred to as monumental architecture encompasses construction having 1) substructures greater than

one meter in height, and/or 2) incorporation of masonry. While substructure height could be attributable to longevity of occupation and repetitive rebuilding, excavation reveals little such rebuilding at Quirigua beyond the Acropolis (Jones and Sharer, this volume; Ashmore 1981a).

3. Groups and clusters are defined here in line with previous definitions of Bullard (1960) and Ashmore (1981b).

4. Andrews' quadrangles seem to differ conceptually and probably functionally from those of the Motagua valley (cf. Andrews 1975; Ashmore 1981a).

5. The basis for dating Loc. 011 to PTS 5 is the age of ceramics associated with basal construction at Str. 011-2. It must be noted that the presently measurable main north-south axes of the putative PTS 5 triad groups (Loci 011, 057) are closer in alignment to well-dated PTS 3 groups in the site core and Loc. 089 (i.e., ca. 5−11 degrees west of magnetic north, 1975) than to firmly dated PTS 5 elite Groups 3C-7 and 3C-8 (that is, 5−6 degrees east of magnetic north, 1975). If the contrast has chronological significance, it may counter attribution of Early Classic antiquity for the triad group pattern at Quirigua, but affects neither the importance of the pattern in PTS 3 nor the broader arguments offered here.

6. Another pattern of PTS 3/2, QP 5, is conceivably an incomplete version of either QP 3 (quadrangle groups) or QP 4 (triad groups) and is characterized by a large structure (again, most commonly on the north) and a smaller flanking structure oriented at a right angle to the first. Although details of development of these three Quirigua patterns are still unknown, they did co-exist in PTS 3/2, supporting the mutual distinctiveness of the three. At least the smaller structures of QP 5 were residential, but whether the overall functional emphasis of these groups was residential, administrative, ritual, or otherwise cannot be decided on present evidence. A dramatic complementarity of QP 3 and QP 5 distributions, both within and beyond the floodplain center, suggests functional and/or social (e.g., moietal) complementarity for these two group types, but interpreting the meaning of the complementarity must remain at the level of hypotheses to be tested in the future (Ashmore 1981a: 422−24; 1984).

7. Sites on the northern side of the valley, east of the Quirigua site periphery, are not yet as well known; they may incorporate parallels to QP 5 (see note 6). Analyses of the relative roles of QP 5 and QP 3 and of the northern and southern sites in the valley at large are still continuing (see Ashmore 1981a: Chapter 6; Schortman 1984).

8. Schortman (this volume) suggests the quadrangle form diffused

from Quirigua to other lower Motagua valley centers. I continue to believe that the quadrangle, as exemplified in its final PTS 3/2 form has significant, if perhaps not sole, roots in the southeast.

9. One derivation of Cerros' west-facing Str. 29B might be the Early Classic E-Group solstice-equinox tracking complex at Uaxactun. Surely it is worth noting in this regard that the immediate Preclassic predecessor of the western structure of this group was the famous Str. E-VII-Sub., whose elaborate masks Freidel describes as exemplifying the same Late Preclassic sun-cycle symbolism as its Cerros contemporary, Str. 5C-2nd.

10. See, for example, Fritz's (1978) provocative parallel argument concerning cosmological structuring in architectural forms and settlement patterns in Chaco Canyon, New Mexico, or the comment by V. Garth Norman (1981: 37) on north as "up" among many Mesoamerican peoples.

11. In fact, another Tikal-derived group plan appears in the earliest version of the Acropolis, which was founded in the seventh century during a parallel resurgence of prosperity at both Quirigua and Tikal. The pattern (QP 2) is the equivalent of Tikal's Plaza Plan 2, a patio group where the eastern structure serves as a shrine housing the burials of the senior males resident in the group (Becker 1971). Becker (1972) had suggested that the Quirigua Acropolis was an instance of this plan, and excavation in 1977 verified the presence of a burial of an adult male underlying the earliest eastern structure (Str. 1B-6-2nd; Jones, Ashmore, and Sharer 1983). The further distribution of this plan at Quirigua is poorly understood, but it is not known from Copan or the lower Motagua Valley sites east of Quirigua. It does apparently derive from Tikal (Ashmore 1981a; cf. Johnson 1975), and its occurrence in the residence of the paramount family is fully in line with the contentions of this paper, particularly during the cited renaissance of the seventh century.

12. There is, of course, the Great Plaza-Acropolis combination (Ashmore 1980a; Leventhal 1979; Pollock 1965), but little else at Copan strikes one as following these principles. A competing prominence of easternness may have been operative (e.g., Schele 1981). This observation indirectly underscores Webster's (1980) and Thompson's (1939) calls to deal with smaller centers—such as Quirigua—as presenting less "cluttered" views of ancient Maya culture than do mammoth centers such as Tikal and Copan.

13. The distinction at Quirigua between Peten-influenced serving vessels and locally derived storage vessels in the Early Classic may further reflect the likelihood that visiting dignitaries would be the

intended audience of the symbol manipulation: such visitors would be presented with food, but were rather less likely to be taken back into the kitchen. Hence the ceramics of Quirigua's Maudslay complex offer further possibilities of political symbols, in Peten Tzakol-like bowls and plates but southeastern-style jars (Willey *et al.* 1980; Ashmore 1981a).

5

Construction Activity as a Measurement of Change at Copan, Honduras

Introduction

Construction data is an underexploited source of information on cultural processes (Sidrys 1978: 9). Since public structures reflect the amount of surplus energy available to the societies that build them (Price 1979), they should be able to be used on an intra- or inter-site scale to measure the degree of social organization and control over resources exhibited by the unit under study.

The sequence of development in the construction at a site may also provide information on social processes. The scale of the work and its rhythm or periodicity are important variables that reflect the larger social processes which control the organization of the work and the distribution of resources at a site. The best place to identify such variables is in the main group of a settlement since it is the center of political power, organization of work, and control over the distribution of resources.

The studies of both settlement pattern and of the function of structures are an important part of Maya archaeology today, but although Mayanists use architectural information in such studies, they seldom use construction data *per se*. The energetic information contained in the size of structures in their excavations is infrequently exploited. Only a few recent studies have taken advantage of the information inherent in construction data on the relative access to scarce resources (labor and materials) and the societal and political implications of this differential access.

One reason this is so is the problems associated with trying to utilize such data. A primary impediment was the Maya habit of incorporating earlier structures into the fill of later ones at times partially destroying them. Measurement of the volumes of final construction stages masks the developmental processes leading to that final stage. A structure, or a site for that matter, could have reached its final stage by gradual accretion representing no major change in the degree of organizational complexity or construction all at once, or by a combination of the two processes. Given the normal constraints of time and money few research projects have the resources to dissect large architectural masses like acropolises and/or palace groups. And when they do they are faced with the problem of missing data due to prehistoric demolition.

The only report that I am aware of that copes with the problem of sequential additions is that of Bebrich in a Late Preclassic structure at Kaminaljuyu, Guatemala (1969; also reported in Sanders 1974). The studies by Adams and his collaborators (Adams 1981; Adams and Jones 1981; Turner, Turner, and Adams 1981) and by the Harvard Copan Project (Willey and Levanthal 1979) have both used courtyard counts and volumetric-type measurements to place sites and groups within sites in a relative hierarchy of wealth and resource control, during the last phase of their occupation. Michels (1979b: 206) also uses volumetric data to "mirror hierarchical variation" for the Middle Classic at Kaminaljuyu. Sidrys (1976b) has compared the ratio of the volumes of ceremonial groups and extended family residential compounds in northern Belize. For northern Yucatan, Rathje (1975) demonstrated that Postclassic rooms were more comfortable, larger and cheaper to build than Late Classic rooms. Using labor figures modified from Erasmus (1965), Arnold and Ford (1980) have produced the only study that has calculated labor demands for construction of housemounds at Tikal.

One important variable which must be considered when analyzing the significance of both the relative and absolute size of construction activity is their relationship to population growth. The two factors, population growth and construction activity, are intricately interrelated and to understand the latter the former must be controlled. This fact has been recognized (Rathje 1973: 439–40; 442), but no published study has yet applied this idea.

Looking at construction data from another perspective, few studies have been done using the sequence in the site center to examine internal cultural processes and none at all which have quantified the increase and decrease in energy devoted to construction. Some studies have employed the construction data from a major center to address broad developmental problems; these have resulted in a coarse-grained analysis of major trends. To take one recent example (Culbert 1973), at Tikal a combination of data including construction, and ceramic change resulted in a clearer view of the relationship among the changes in these variables. Unfortunately, there is no quantification of the amount of construction in the different phases. Thus we know little more than that Tikal underwent a surge of Late Classic construction, a phenomenon found in other sites throughout the Maya zone. The dates and therefore the timing of these changes are defined, however, which enable comparisons with other areas. In another example, Cheek (1977a) used a closely-dated construction sequence from Kaminaljuyu to reconstruct the progress of a cultural process. No quantification was employed here either.

The analysis undertaken in this paper is an attempt to combine a quantitative approach to the problem of resource allocation and work expenditure with a detailed study of the development sequence at the Main Group at Copan. The problems mentioned above were avoided for the most part through the application of specific techniques described below and through very few restrictions on time and money variables. The methods of excavation and their results are discussed first. The means of quantification are defined and then the data are examined for the contribution they make to three specific problems.

Methods

Excavation

The data to be examined were derived from the construction sequence defined for the Main Plaza at Copan, Honduras. An electrical resistivity map was made of the entire plaza (2.6 ha) by Albert Hess of the French National Center for Scientific Research (CNRS). Areas which showed marked changes in resistivity were tested to determine if the changes were caused by buried constructions. When cultural features were found, excavations were extended to determine their nature and extent. About 20% of the surface area of the plaza was tested in this fashion. The resistivity tests revealed that the technique was primarily picking up fill changes which may or may not have been separated by structural features. Eight buried structures, five platforms, and two earthen plaza surfaces were discovered.

This technique aided our excavation strategy tremendously by saving a great deal of time and effort. It also gave us confidence that all major building events of which any evidence remained were discovered.

Besides the excavations under the plaza surface, two above ground structures, Strs. 10L-2 and 10L-4, were completely excavated and their relationship to the surrounding plaza established. Data from the Carnegie Institution of Washington's tunnels into Strs. 10L-26 and 10L-11, which front on the plaza, and data from the excavations of M. Becker and G. Guillemin on the north edge of the Acropolis provided information on the relation of these areas to the Main Plaza.

A sequence of over 100 construction events—major and minor— was identified (fig. 1), which could be grouped into phases and stages. The sequence was first divided into a series of phases which include a major construction event or a number of related events that occurred at approximately the same time. A major alteration of the Main Plaza plan was called a "stage" and included one or more phases.

The temporal parameters of the phases cannot currently be identified with much precision. The temporal boundaries of the stages are firmer although more absolute dates would be beneficial.

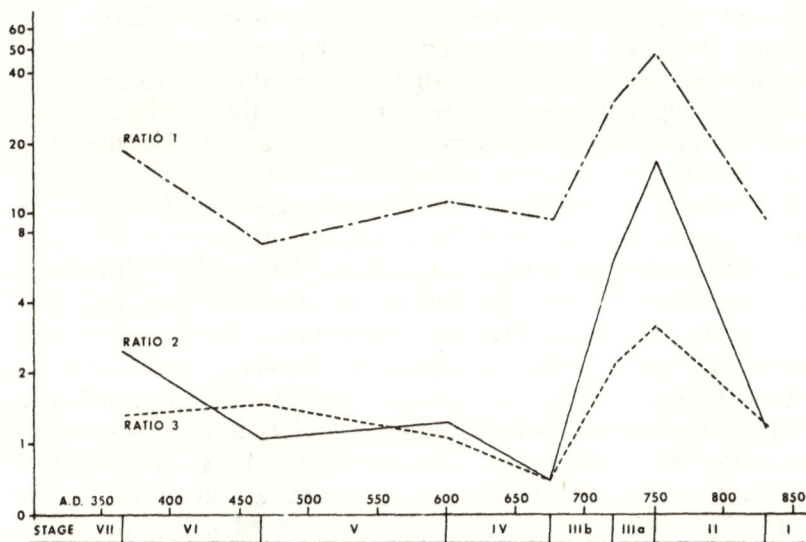

Figure 1. Graphic representations of construction activity within the Copan Main Plaza; ratios employed are defined in the text.

Summary of the Sequence

No structural remains were found in the earliest two cultural stages, IX and VIII. These stages correspond to the Middle Preclassic Uir and the Late Preclassic Chabij ceramic phases. In fact, ceramics were not found from the latter era; although some Chabij materials were found south of the Acropolis, Chabij deposits have not yet been identified in the Main Group. Only a small scattering of Uir sherds was found in the Main Plaza on what may have been the ground surface at that time.

The next stage, VII, sees the first identified construction in the Main Plaza. Two foci of construction appear to have existed at the time—one in the south and one in the north sectors of the Plaza. To the north, a large area was leveled and filled with as much as 1.5 m of soil, apparently producing a plaza area (F. 139). No evidence of stucco was found and this plaza was almost certainly unpaved. The north plaza was contemporary with the structures in the south sector of the Main Plaza.

In the south sector of the Main Plaza, there is an extensive fill of living debris from early in this stage. The debris might have come from either a nearby habitation zone or from a leveling operation. This postulated Early Classic zone would have been located either to the south under the present Acropolis or west just outside the Main Group. The area with the living debris, whatever its origin, was leveled for a series of buildings in what is today called the Courtyard of the Hieroglyphic Staircase, referred to here as the Southern Courtyard. In this courtyard a stucco floor (F. 17) was laid. The floor was surrounded by at least three (Strs. sub. 6-3, sub. 2, and 26-6) and possibly five stuccoed buildings. Only one of these is well-preserved— Str. sub. 2, a long, narrow (80 by 18 m), low structure on the north side of the courtyard. To this complex was later added Ball Court I, east of, and connected to, Str. sub. 2. Two structures (26-5 and 11-7) with identical facades—the lowest terrace exhibiting a tablero supported by a vertical wall—were added on the south and east sides of the courtyard. To the north of this courtyard complex and at a slightly later date was built Str. sub. 1, which faced north away from the complex just discussed. This structure had a stuccoed frontal platform on the north and a main structure, now destroyed, to the south. The main structure apparently continued with some modifications into Stage III. One should also note that the South Courtyard complex is very similar to the Late Classic plan, indicating considerable continuity of plan in this area.

The sherds associated with the construction of the various buildings of this stage, including those from two trash pits and two caches, are Bijac in date.

To the southwest under the Acropolis, a floor similar to that in the Southern Courtyard was found. The sherds located under it are the same as those under the South Courtyard floor. Thus the construction in the Main Plaza is not an isolated event and indicates the early importance of the Main Group, contrary to Morley's observation (1920).

The next stage, VI, marks the first major transformation of the Main Plaza plan: the individual structures were integrated into a group. The South courtyard remained essentially unchanged except for Str. sub. 2, which was shortened and covered by a low platform, designated a plaza platform (Pl. 1-5). This connected directly to Ball Court I and Str. sub. 1. This platform is the first of three in this stage that gradually expanded the stuccoed plaza platform to the east and north becoming, in essence, the plaza surface.

The second expansion of the platform (Pl. 1-4) was primarily to the east, and included the construction of two buildings (Strs. sub. 3-5, sub 3-4) on the platform, between Str. sub. 1 and Ball Court I. Following this, the platform was expanded primarily to the north (Pl. 1-3). The unstuccoed north plaza surface was raised to the level of the platform surface and stuccoed. Although the north edge of the new surface has not been firmly identified yet, it is possible that Str. 4-4th may have been built on this edge in this stage. While the eastern extension of the platform was not as extensive, another structure (sub. 5) was added to the east edge. A new structure (sub. 6-2) was built on the west side of the South Courtyard at the beginning of the stage: this structure was destroyed and rebuilt (sub. 6-1) at the end of the stage.

By the end of the stage the north sector of the plaza was stuccoed. The south sector had not changed very drastically but the courtyard and the playing alley of the ballcourt were now sunken below the level of the platform and structures around it. Although most of the ceramics associated with the constructions of this stage can be assigned to the Acbi ceramic phase, at least one of the structures, Pl. 1-5, was probably built at the end of Bijac.

The beginning of the next stage, V, is signaled by the construction of Ball Court IIa and the raising of the South Courtyard (F. 18) to the level of the plaza platform. The stage is primarily characterized by a series of alterations of the structures around the South Courtyard. The building under Str. 11 was rebuilt four times and the one under Str. 26 at least once. The structure on the west side of the South Courtyard was razed and covered by a stuccoed floor (F. 56) that extended over much of the southwest and west sector the Main Plaza, expanding the South Courtyard westward to the size it was to have in the Late Classic.

In the north sector Str. 2-3rd was probably built at this time, at the north end of the Main Plaza. If the stuccoed plaza surface had not extended this far north before, it was extended to Str. 2 at this time.

All constructions of this stage are associated with ceramics assigned to the Acbi phase. Unlike the earlier stages, two dates are available for the end of this stage, one each from the north and south edge of the Main Plaza. The one on the north is an archaeomagnetic date on a burnt posthole. The one on the south side is a style date assigned to a hieroglyphic step. Both suggest the stage ends between A.D. 575 and 600.

The next stage, IV, actually saw very little construction activity. The plaza platform (Pl. 1-2) was expanded east; a structure on the platform (sub. 3-2) was remodeled and Str. 4-3rd was built in the north sector. The platform extension covers a fill of Late Acbi sherds which also appear in Str. 4-3rd.

For the Acropolis, we have not been able to tie the sequence to that of the Main Plaza until the Late Classic in Stage III. However, we do know that construction activity was intensive during Acbi times. At one locus on the Corte, just before the massive remodeling of Stage III, Becker (personal communication, 1979) has noted that the structures became smaller and possibly not as well made. This phenomenon could correspond to the slowdown in construction in the Plaza during Stage IV times. Until firmer dates are determined, this will remain only a possibility.

Stage III can be divided into two parts both of which contain a great deal of building activity. In Stage IIIb there was a massive expansion of the plaza platform (Pl. 1-1) to the east, and a concommitant expansion of the Acropolis platform (Pl. 2-2) to the north. These two activities were undertaken at the same time. Slightly later, a series of structures was built on the north Acropolis platform, and Ball Court IIb was constructed. The ceramics associated with this stage, in the fill of the Main Plaza extension, did not include any Copador, but did include some sherds of utility wares from the Copador phase (called Coner). The structures on top of the Acropolis platform did include Copador in their fills. This indicates that this stage started at the very beginning of the Copador phase, or perhaps, at the very end of the Acbi phase.

Stage IIIa structures all contain Copador sherds and are therefore Coner phase. The various constructions are also associated with dated stelae. The Late Classic Main Plaza was given its form in this stage. The *graderias* around the north sector of the Plaza were built in this phase, as were Str. 3 and its platform in the northeast corner of the Main Group. The west side of the Main Plaza was also probably built at this time. Structures 2-1st and 4-2nd were erected in the north sector as were the majority of the stelae. Slightly later than these events, Str. sub. 1 and the early ballcourt were destroyed and Ball Court III with its attendant structures was built in their place. Structure 26 was built at the same time as the ballcourt, and a floor was added in the east and south sectors of the plaza at the base of Str. 26.

The last construction stage, II, was primarily restricted to the Acropolis area. The only major work in the Main Plaza was a floor in the east sector and a possible sacbe connecting Str. 3 with the north Acropolis platform. Structures 2 and 4 were modified and Strs. 5 and 24 were built. This is also the Coner phase.

The last stage, I, refers to the Postclassic. No structures and no new information on this stage were identified by the Copan Archaeological Project in the Main Plaza.

Quantification

As mentioned above, a problem that any quantitative assessment of construction events must overcome is missing data. Construction events may be missed completely because of insufficient excavation, because complete structures may have been removed by the prehistoric builders, or because structures were partially razed during new construction.

The first problem has been avoided within the restricted area excavated (the Main Plaza and the surrounding structures). The electrical resistivity technique provided a map of the earlier constructions and, based on our experience with the map, we can affirm that it is extremely unlikely that any major construction event was unidentified. The only exception would be if structures were removed without leaving any trace. This situation cannot be controlled but is unlikely to have happened at Copan given the typical construction patterns. However, one must note that there are three large architectural masses, Platforms 10L-3 and 10L-4 and the Acropolis, which were not explored and construction may have occurred on them at a different tempo than in the Main Plaza.

Partially razed structures present partial data. Horizontal and vertical dimensions may be missing preventing the measurement of structure volume. These data can still be treated in a quantitative fashion if one simply counts construction events or constructs a weighted counter based on known and projected volumes. Both approaches have been taken here.

The simple count considers each construction event equal to any other no matter the size.[1] In the weighted count, weights were assigned on a scale of 1 to 10. The highest number was assigned to a base volume (12,500 m³) which is the largest known volume of a completely new construction. This includes both Plaza Platform 10L-1-1st and the original north sector plaza. The volumes of the other construction events were ranked proportionately. Known volumes were calculated first; these events were assigned scores in proportion to the base volume. Other events with some unknown dimension were compared to those of known volume and assigned the score of the event to which they seemed most similar. Such weighted counts can be considered as measuring the relative amount of effort that went into a particular construction event.

Certain very large structures, such as 10L-11 and -26, had final volumes twice as much as the base volume, but were also scored as 10 to compensate for the fact that they were built on earlier structures of unknown size. In general, major alterations of a structure were given a score half as much as the original score, and minor events half of that. The ranking of the floors varied considerably depending on the amount of fill under them.

Stages were used as the unit of analysis rather than phases for two reasons: first, there is better chronological control over the limits of the stage divisions; second, the assignment of construction events to the broader stages is more certain. The sequences in the various sectors of the Main Plaza are clear but the connections between the sectors is sometimes tenuous. Thus the larger time period (the stage) is the better unit of analysis.

Various indices were developed which produced further information. When the weighted score is divided by the simple count (Ratio 1) the result is the average weight of each construction event per stage. This provides information on the average amount of effort expended in each construction event. Both the score and the count were divided by the number of years in each stage to get, respectively, the average score per year (Ratio 2), the average yearly effort, and the average number of events per year (Ratio 3), for a particular stage. It was also found useful to divide the number of years per stage by the number of construction events in that stage. The result (Ratio 4) is the number of years between construction starts. These indices are presented in Table 1 and in chart form in fig. 1.

Table 1. Quantitative Measures of Construction Activity in the Main Plaza, Copan

Stage	Weight W	Construction Event Count C	Years Y	Ratio 1 W/C	Ratio 2 W/Y	Ratio 3 C/Y	Ratio 4 Y/C
II	9.625	10	80	0.963	0.1203	0.125	8.0
IIIa	48.000	10	30	4.800	1.6000	0.330	3.0
IIIb	29.125	10	45	2.900	0.6470	0.220	5.6
IV	3.625	4	75	0.910	0.0483	0.050	25.0
V	18.700	16	140	1.170	0.1336	0.114	8.8
VI	10.125	14	90	0.720	0.1125	0.156	6.4
VII	18.500	10	70	1.850	0.2640	0.143	7.0
Totals	137.700	74	530	1.86	0.259	0.139	7.2

Results

Assuming that the weight is a relative measure of the amount of energy expended in construction, several trends are quite clear on the graph of fig.1. All indices show three trends: 1) a decline in construction activity from the initial stage of construction to a low point in Stage IV; 2) a sharp increase in Stages IIIb and IIIa; and 3) a sharp decline to Stage II with no construction at all in Stage I.

The steep increase in the Late Classic Stages IIIb and IIIa primarily is due to increases in the amount of effort for each construction event and not so much to an increase in the number of construction events. The latter are two to three times as frequent as in the Early Classic Stage VII (the one with the larger amount of prior construction); but the amount of construction effort is up to eight times as much. The change (decreased energy expenditure) at the end of the Late Classic is also due to a change (this time decline) in size or amount of effort rather than a change in numbers.

The low point in Stage IV is due to both a fall-off in the number of events per year and the amount of effort per year. Ratio 4 reveals that there was only one construction event for every 25 years as compared to the other stages which varied from one every three to every nine years. During Stage IV construction was done at half the rate and about one-third of the effort per year of the next lowest stage.

The reader should be reminded that the data from the Acropolis are not incorporated here because they are so poorly known. However, we do know that during Stage II considerable construction was occurring on the Acropolis which would dramatically increase the amount of actual construction effort recorded for this stage if included in the calculations. The same could be true of other stages as well. However, until the time arrives that those data will be available, we have to work with the material from the Main Plaza alone, and can consider, for the moment at least, the Main Plaza as an adequate microcosm of elite construction activity.

Problems

It is generally recognized that there were four major transition points in the development of Classic Maya society: the origin, the Classic hiatus, the Late Classic development, and the collapse. All these have been recognized as significant because of major changes in the expenditure of energy by the societies involved. No new data on the origin were discovered at Copan and existing data on the collapse are obscured by our current inability to subdivide the ceramics dating the end of the Late Classic. Much data, however, from both the period of the hiatus and the start of the Late Classic are available. These two topics will be examined to see how these processes are manifested at Copan and what their relationships to other variables such as population growth and stela production are. A third question examined is the effect Quirigua may have had on Copan during the Late Classic.

The Classic Hiatus

One question of general interest is the existence of the Classic hiatus at Copan: Does it exist and if so what shape does it take? The hiatus was originally defined by Proskouriakoff (1950: 111). She noted a decline in stela dedication between 9.5.0.0.0 (A.D. 534) and 9.8.0.0.0 (A.D. 593) and a major stylistic change in the way the subject of the stela was presented. Changes in both ceramic and architecture were noted for the same period by Smith (1950) at Uaxactun. Stelae were particularly rare in the central Maya zone but a few were found in sites on the peripheries. Extensive excavations at Tikal and increased survey in other Maya regions have done little to change this picture (Willey 1974, 1977). It can be noted that some sites, such as Tikal (Coe 1970), also experienced a slowdown in major construction projects or even a decline in population (e.g., in the Pasion-Usumacinta region).

The events of the hiatus are particularly pronounced at Tikal and last considerably longer there than at other sites. There is only one stela dedicated between 9.5.0.0.0 and 9.13.0.0.0 and it dates within the traditional limits of the hiatus (St. 17, 9.7.0.0.0; Jones, personal communication, 1980). Thus there is a 6 katun or 120 year gap between known dedication dates, twice as long as the traditional length of the hiatus. Construction in the North Acropolis also slowed and even stopped during this period. The resumption of construction occurred at 9.11–9.12.0.0.0 or between A.D. 650 and 670 (Jones, personal communication, 1980), before the resumption of stela dedication.

The causes of the hiatus are perhaps even more nebulous than the causes of the Classic collapse. Willey (1974) has suggested that Tikal was intimately involved in the Teotihuacan trade network and may have actually been administrating it. The close ties between Tikal and Teotihuacan demonstrated by Coggins (1975) support this idea. When Teotihuacan withdrew from participation in this network, Tikal and the other northeast Peten sites which seemed to be benefiting the most from the trade suffered a decline. Presumably the mechanism for this decline was the loss of the major market for various lowland products and a general loss of income. Disruption of the trade routes would cut off the flow of goods to the elite, and reduce their access to wealth and redistributable items by which they maintained their position and level of elite activity.

The predicted relationship of Copan to such disruption of trade networks depends on the position Copan is thought to have held in the trade network at that time. Although Copan is considered a major Classic Maya center, it is not by any means in the core of the Maya zone, nor is it even in what Rathje (1973) has called the buffer zone. Copan's location places it within easy reach of a series of highland products: obsidian from Ixtepeque, jade from the Motagua, and hard stone for metates from within the Copan pocket itself (M. Spink, personal communication). It could be considered a highland resource zone site in Rathje's Core/Buffer Zone scheme, and thus could be expected to respond to economic and political processes in different ways than sites in the other zones.

Another factor to consider is that Copan has major cultural ties with the highlands. There are many ceramic similarities between the Middle Classic Acbi ceramics from Copan and the assemblages from the same time period in the Guatemalan Highlands (R. Viel, personal communication). Other links are suggested by an elite interment from the Main Group which is buried in the Middle Classic Kaminaljuyu style (Cheek 1977a) and includes a Teotihuacan Thin Orange bowl and various highland-derived goods. These facts suggest that Copan may have been participating in a somewhat different network of trade than the sites in the Peten, one which tied it more closely to events in the highlands.

If Copan were involved in a highland commercial sphere, it may still have been affected by a disruption of trade, since Teotihuacan seems to have been deeply involved in highland affairs (Brown 1977, Cheek 1977a, Sanders 1977), as witnessed by the information for the valley of Guatemala. However, this would only occur if Teotihuacan ceased participation in trade in both areas simultaneously. This may not have been the case. Teotihuacan influences continued at Kaminaljuyu well beyond their purported withdrawal from the Peten. Teotihuacan did not withdraw from the highlands until between A.D. 550 to 650. The latter half of this period, between A.D. 600 and 650, probably saw some decline, with major architectural changes away from Teotihuacan patterns around A.D 650 (Cheek 1977b).

This possibility creates two alternative hypotheses. If Copan were participating primarily in a trade system coming out of the Peten, a hiatus at Copan should have occurred more or less synchronously with that in the Peten around A.D 530. On the other hand, if it were integrated into a trade network centered in the highlands, little or no change should be evidenced during the lowland hiatus, but some change should have occurred between A.D. 600 and 650, which reflects the breakdown of the highland networks. To examine these hypotheses, construction activity and frequency of stela erections will be examined.

The use of construction as an indication of economic well-being is easily understood, but the use of the frequency of stela dedication for the same purpose is somewhat uncertain. We do not really know what factors contributed to the erection and dedication of one of these monuments. Economic well-being is certainly not the only factor. The erection of Stela 11 at Tikal at the very end of the Classic Period (10.2.0.0.0) after the Peten had suffered what had to be an economically disastrous population collapse demonstrates this point. Political and perhaps ideological factors also played a role. It is now generally accepted that many of these monuments functioned as status validation documents. If no person existed who had an undisputed claim to rulership, or who had sufficient force to support such a claim, then monuments may not have been erected during the time when such conditions existed. If Coggins (1975: 347) is correct, such a situation may have existed during the hiatus at Tikal.

A gap in stela dedication may also have been artificially produced by a regular or periodic destruction of stelae. For example, at Copan virtually all stelae dated before 9.9.0.0.0 appear as broken fragments, reused as fill or as building stones (Riese 1979b). But since stelae were originally used to define the hiatus, they will be considered here as well.

The graph of construction activity at Copan during the Classic (fig.1) suggests that a construction slowdown did occur during the transition from the Middle to the Late Classic. Construction events per year (Ratio 3) drop from an Early Classic high in Stage VI to a low in Stage IV. A look at Ratio 4, the spacing between events, makes this clearer. Whereas in all other phases a construction is started every three to nine years, in Stage IV it is every 25 years. Ratio 2, effort per year, is also lowest in Stage IV. However the intensity of effort per construction event (Ratio 1) changes very little from Stage VI to Stage IV, and is even a little higher in Stage IV then in Stage VI.

Thus, while the amount of effort put into each event remains relatively constant over about 300 years (Stages VI to IV), the rate of construction starts drops after a peak in Stage VI. From State VI to V the rate is halved and from Stage V to IV it is halved again. Thus the data suggest that Stage IV can be looked upon as a major construction slowdown which may have started in the preceding stage.

When the stelae are examined a different pattern emerges. In order to attempt to control for broken and missing monuments, I have included in the analysis a number of fragments which Riese (1979b) has tentatively dated on stylistic grounds. For the period of the Classic hiatus, only one dated stela and eight fragments exist. The fragments are stylistically dated from 9.5.0.0.0 to 9.9.0.0.0, which is one katun longer than the hiatus. Some of these pieces could have been dedicated between 9.8–9.9.0.0.0 and therefore be outside the hiatus, but it is unlikely that all of them were. Only one or two of the fragments could possibly have come from the same stela. This number is by far the most recorded at any Maya site for this period, but then fragments have generally not been available for study unless a site has been excavated.

The number is even more than in the preceding period. Only one dated monument and four fragments have been placed before 9.5.0.0.0. Thus around nine stelae were erected during the hiatus compared to, possibly, five before it, an increase rather than a decrease during the hiatus. We might note that without excavation, we would not know of any stelae from Copan before 9.9.0.0.0.

For comparison, we can note that during the four katuns after 9.9.0.0.0 to 9.13.0.0.0 which correspond to the continuation of the hiatus at Tikal, eleven stelae were erected, approximately the same number as during the hiatus. Eight of these were erected around 9.11.0.0.0 and two date to the ninth katun. Thus the rate of stelae construction seems to increase during the Classic hiatus and continues at that level with a very slight increase during the duration of the Tikal hiatus. The long nature of the Tikal hiatus, of course, may be an artifact of a systematic program of destruction of monuments from that period whose fragments have not yet been discovered or identified.

It was hypothesized that if Copan were going to reflect a breakdown in trade networks, it would experience a decline in elite activity at either A.D. 530 or A.D. 600. The data best fit the latter date. At Copan the period of the Classic lowland hiatus is included in the last part of Stage V. The frequency of construction does decline slightly but probably not significantly. Stela erection continues during this time at a rate higher than that evinced in the earlier periods. The data therefore reflect little or no reaction to the events of the Classic hiatus.

However, the succeeding stage, Stage IV, starting at A.D. 600 exhibits the low point in construction activity in the plaza, while stela erection continues. If construction is taken as a better indicator of economic problems than stela production, as I have argued, it can be concluded that Copan underwent a hiatus of its own, unconnected to the one in the central lowlands, but seemingly reflecting events in the Guatemalan Highlands.

As I have suggested elsewhere (Cheek 1983), Stage IV may be divisible into two sub-stages, around A.D. 650, with both the few construction events and mass of stelae erections, eight out of eleven, in the post-A.D. 650 part. A number of these stelae were erected around the periphery of the Copan valley and may have signaled the reassertion of the political authority of the central government after a period of decline in centralized authority. This interpretation will remain speculative until finer control of the dating can be exercised or more, and more informative, texts from this period are discovered.

One remaining problem with the identification of a localized hiatus is the possibility that significant construction could be occurring on the Acropolis analogous to the events in Stage II. Only further extensive excavations can answer this question.

The Late Classic

As mentioned earlier, public structures reflect the surplus energy supply available in societies (Price 1979). Thus, if there is an increase in the amount of labor energy invested in public/elite construction, one should expect to find a comparable increase in the energy supply (human labor and the food to support it) in the society concerned. However, the interesting question is how this increase is achieved. Two possibilities exist, each of which has implications for the development of the society. These are an increase in population and an increase in the labor tax. Population growth can result from the colonization of new lands or from an intensification of the agricultural system possibly through the development of a more productive agricultural technology. An increase in the labor tax can be applied to a stable, increasing, or even decreasing population base. These options are examined below.

All the known major Late Classic sites underwent substantial growth at the beginning of, and during, the Late Classic period, as evidenced by major construction projects at these sites. It has been suggested that this growth was fueled by increasing demands on the peasant populations (Thompson 1966) in the form of increased labor and food taxes. The quantified data at Copan can be used to explore this question.

In examining the growth of investment in monumental public architecture at Copan, it is most informative to focus on effort expended as measured by Ratio 2, the weight divided by the number of years. In terms of this annualized measure of effort, the increase from Stage IV to Stage IIIa (the first of the two major growth stages in the Late Classic) was approximately thirteen-fold. However, it does not seem reasonable to use the score for Stage IV as the bench mark. It is likely that the low point in construction that is observed in Stage IV was due to a period in which centralization at Copan had deteriorated rather than that the population had declined. Thus the level of effort recorded for the preceding stage, Stage V, is employed as the base from which to assess the magnitude of the changes in the construction program. Ratio 2 increased over five times from Stage V to Stage IIIb and increased another 2.5 times from IIIb to IIIa.

Preliminary analysis of the Copan valley test pitting program (Fash 1980, this volume) indicates that the population during Stage V (represented by the Late Acbi ceramic phase) was probably as numerous in the valley bottomlands (the *vegas*) as it was during the Late Classic Coner phase. But the population density in the foothill zone (the *falda*) was considerably less. The filling of this zone would mean a good-sized population increase during the Late Classic; however, it is unlikely that it could have been as much as 500%. Populations can double within the 75-year-long time period being discussed but more than two doublings is extremely unlikely. Another possible source of population increase and, therefore, an increased labor pool is the area outside the Copan pocket itself. Recent survey by Webster during the second stage of the Copan Archaeological Project indicates that the densities here are comparable to those in the foothill zone in the Copan valley. These communities may have come under closer control by the rulers of Copan during the Late Classic. The Copan-style hieroglyphic monuments at the site of Los Higos along the upper Rio Chamelecon, 80 km east of Copan, provide support for the idea that Copan was expanding its sphere of influence in the Late Classic. The absolute size of the population in outlying areas is unknown since the survey is unfinished, but it could have provided a large increment to the labor force.

Innovations in agricultural technology could have provided surplus, devoted to supporting an increased construction program. However there is no physical indication that this occurred at Copan. The few features that could be interpreted as agricultural terraces (Turner 1979) are too few to have made an impact on the productive capacity. Irrigation also does not seem feasible given the topography of the valley.

Of the various means for raising the size of the labor pool, the incorporation or colonization of land outside the Copan pocket in conjunction with a more intensive exploitation of the faldas could have increased the labor pool sufficiently to approximate the large increase in effort at the Main Group.

In summary, it is obvious from the various settlement surveys undertaken in the valley and the surrounding regions that population peaked in the Late Classic, and that it had grown by some unknown factor over that of the Middle Classic. It also seems likely that surrounding groups were incorporated into the Copan polity at the same time. Perhaps when the final counts for the population estimates are in, it will be found that the increase in the labor pool available for construction at Copan would be sufficient to build the Late Classic Main Group without any increase in the level of taxation. However, I do not think so. The data suggest that the increase in the rate of effort is greater than the rate of population increase whether by natural increase or by incorporation. Thus the rulers at Copan seem to have increased the tax burden on their peasant populations. Whether this was sufficient to cause them excessive stress will not be known until actual figures of the amount of labor involved are computed and until final population figures are available. Until then, the application of quantified construction data to studying the Late Classic construction boom at Copan will remain profitable insofar as it has suggested the possibility of changed political relationships between the populace of the Copan pocket and the surrounding territory, and the elite. It should also bring to our attention the importance of comparing the growth of population to the growth in the material subsystems of a society.

Copan and Quirigua

Another problem that occurred in the Late Classic can be investigated by reference to the construction events in the Main Plaza: the effect of the hypothesized "capture" of a Copan ruler, 18 Rabbit, by a ruler of Quirigua, Two-Legged Sky (also called "Cauac Sky"; Ashmore and Sharer 1978, Marcus 1976, Sharer 1978a). The scenario is as follows: Two-Legged Sky of Quirigua successfully declared his city's political and economic independence from Copan, to which Quirigua may previously have been subject. One outcome of the declaration was the capture of 18 Rabbit, the thirteenth ruler of Copan, at 9.15.6.14.6, possibly as the result of a battle. This interpretation follows from certain texts on Quirigua stelae. At Copan there is a 20 year gap in dated stelae between 9.15.5.0.0 (Stela D, A.D. 736), and 9.16.5.0.0 (Stela M, A.D. 756). Although none of the authors cited above specify a connection between the "capture" and the gap in stela erection at Copan, the two events are juxtaposed in their texts in such a manner as to imply that the "capture" is in some way responsible for the gap.

It is possible that the "capture" of 18 Rabbit and the political and economic separation of Quirigua from Copan affected the internal organization of Copan enough that it had an impact on the elite activity at the site. Any such impact would be localized either in the chain of command among the elite or in the interruption of the flow of trade into and/or through the valley of Copan. Either of these phenomena would affect the ability of the elite to operate as efficiently as they had previously. Cessation of the erection of stelae could be one result; a slowdown in elite construction would be another. The latter would be even more probable since it is more labor intensive, and therefore more "expensive" and requires better organization than stela carving and erection. Thus, if there were an effect it should be reflected in the building activity in the Main Group, provided the construction events are dated precisely enough. Although the time period in question is rather short, it is possible to examine this matter with the construction data since most of the Late Classic structures are fairly closely dated and can be assigned to specific rulers.

The ruler 18 Rabbit was responsible for a large amount of construction prior to his capture, including the entire north sector of the Main Plaza (called by Morely [1920] the Great Plaza), as well as the eastern boundary of the Main Plaza. Additionally, 18 Rabbit's name has been identified on the central marker of Ball Court II (Riese, personal communication, 1979), an indication that he may have been responsible for its construction.

Structures 10L-26-1st and Ball Court III can also be assigned to his reign. Of the possible dates expressed on the glyph bands on the playing benches of Ball Court III, the ones that fit the stratigraphic evidence the best are between A.D. 722 and 733. Since the ballcourt was moved north in this phase, leaving the earlier ballcourt exposed, the earlier court had to be either leveled to the plaza surface or covered with another structure to eliminate the resulting eyesore. It was not leveled, since there are large segments of it still existing inside Str. 10L-26. This implies that the latter structure was built at essentially the same time as Ball Court III and therefore at least the first phase of Str. 10L-26-1st, -1stB, was built, or at least started, by 18 Rabbit.

Fewer structures were built in the period after 18 Rabbit's "capture," which occurred in the middle of phase 4 in Stage IIIb. The Hieroglyphic Staircase is the primary event; if it had been started earlier it was certainly finished after 18 Rabbit was no longer ruler, sometime after A.D. 743 (Riese, personal communication). Riese (this volume) has remarked that the Hieroglyphic Staircase is equivalent to 30 stelae of Copan size and quality. Associated with the construction of the Hieroglyphic Staircase must have been a partial rebuilding of Str. 10L-26-1st, for a corner of the ballcourt is covered by the later modification. Other less precise structural information suggests that Str. 10L-11-2nd may have been built during the gap in stelae erection. This structure was not as tall as the later 11-1st with the monumental staircase, but was substantially taller and larger than 10L-11-3rd, and was given a weight of 10. Although the data on the Acropolis have not been quantified, some information is available from the profile cut by the Copan river, as studied by Becker and Guillemin. The profile of the cut shows that there were at least eight structures built at one locus between the time the north Acropolis platform (Pl. 2-2nd) was built (Phase 6) and the time the Acropolis was raised to its present level during the reign of the sixteenth ruler of Copan, Madrugada (Phase 3). Some of these were probably built during the period in question.

Although the level of effort expended on the structures built during the 20 year gap in stela production is high, the frequency of construction drops significantly in the Main Plaza. We must consider that by the end of the reign of 18 Rabbit the Main Plaza was essentially a finished architectural entity to which no major additions or alterations were made for the remainder of its use life. Construction in Stage II at the Main Group continued to be massive but was concentrated in the Acropolis, not in the completed Main Plaza. Thus the fact that there was a slowdown might not be significant. The continuity in building activity and hieroglyphic texts, if not stelae, indicates little if any disruption of the power structure. Thus it seems that the political and/or economic impact of the "capture" and the independence of Quirigua either was slight at Copan, or that the break between the two sites was not as strong as has been recently proposed.

Summary

Excavations in the Main Plaza at Copan revealed a series of nine successive cultural stages. There is no evidence in the Main Plaza for extensive Early Classic or earlier occupation. However, at least by

A.D. 300, major construction was started in the Main Group with a stuccoed courtyard, a large unstuccoed plaza, and a ballcourt. Construction and expansion continued throughout the Middle Classic. There is a break in the Main Plaza architectural record between A.D. 600 and 675. After this there was a major expansion and continued construction in the plaza through the rule of the thirteenth, fourteenth, and fifteenth rulers of Copan. With the start of the reign of the last known ruler, most construction shifted to the Acropolis where building ended shortly after A.D. 800.

The construction sequence in the Main Plaza of the Main Group at Copan was utilized to examine a series of problems or situations common to other Maya sites, and how Copan responded to these situations. Considered were the relationship between construction activity and other cultural activity at Copan at three points in its history: the hiatus, Late Classic development, and, in the Late Classic, a time of potential stress for the society. It was found that Copan either was not exposed to, or did not respond in the same way to, the processes that brought about the Classic lowland hiatus. It seemed, however, to respond to events in the highlands. The temporal distribution of stelae was also examined and did not seem to be very sensitive to the same forces affecting the construction activities.

Secondly, the relationship between the growth of construction and the growth of the population was examined. It was concluded that although the Late Classic population did increase substantially, through both local growth and incorporation of other populations, the construction activity grew faster. This suggests that an organizational change took place at Copan at the beginning of the Late Classic which enabled the rulers to demand more labor from their subjects.

The last section examined the question of whether or not elite activity at Copan suffered a setback with the postulated capture of 18 Rabbit by the ruler of Quirigua. The answer to this question was somewhat ambiguous. Construction did decline in the Main Plaza immediately following this event but not by much and one could argue, as I have, that the lack of construction here was due at least partly to the fact that it was a completed architectural entity at this time; construction then shifted to the Acropolis, which remains largely unexcavated.

This paper has been concerned with both methodological and substantive issues. It has addressed the problems and utility of exploiting construction data to answer developmental questions concerning the Maya. It has also presented some tentative answers to certain broader problems as expressed at Copan. However, the study is not finished. To obtain a complete picture of the energy devoted to public construction at Copan much more work needs to be done on the Acropolis and in the two large platforms on the north edge of the Main Plaza. It will also be useful to get more precise data on the costs of different kinds of fills which characterize different construction stages (see Cheek 1983). In summary, it can be said that in the continuing effort of Mayanists to specify the values of the variables involved in the evolution of Maya society, construction data can prove very useful.

Note

1. Structures 10L-21 and -22 on fig. 1 are omitted from the calculations since they are on the Acropolis and do not even face the Main Plaza unlike Strs. 10L-11 and -26 which face on, and are integrated into, the Main Plaza.

WILLIAM L. FASH, JR.

6

History and Characteristics of Settlement in the Copan Valley, and Some Comparisons with Quirigua

A number of similarities exist in the physiographic and ecological settings of the lower Motagua and Copan valleys. In both valleys, a large fertile zone of floodplain and river terraces is delimited by foothills (*faldas*), which in turn give way to steeper slopes (*montañas*) higher up. Although the bottomlands of the lower Motagua valley can be considered more "mature" in the geological sense, the Copan River was, and continues to be, fairly active in terms of changing its course within the valley bottom. At both Copan and Quirigua the Late Classic "epicenters" were located in those sections of their respective valleys which had the widest expanse of floodplains and river terraces. Both sites were also built next to their respective rivers, and the two share a number of characteristics in their layout and internal structuring. In Copan, the fertile, constantly renewed soils on the bottomlands or *vegas* were densely occupied in Late Classic times by residences of all sizes. While the same is true for the settlement around Quirigua, the evidence in terms of currently visible archaeological sites tends to indicate that the Late Classic population there was not as dense as that which flourished at Copan.

The First Phase of the Proyecto Arqueologico Copan (P.A.C.) has involved a continuation and expansion of the mapping project begun by Gordon Willey to include the recording of all visible sites in the valley, as well as a much more extensive test-pitting program. Here we will be concerned primarily with the results of the valley survey and sampling program of test excavations which have a bearing on the subject of the history of settlement within the valley, and the implications of these data within the larger regional and socio-political framework.

The Rio Copan cuts through a region of rolling hills and mountains, forming a series of small valleys or pockets along its length in Honduras and eastern Guatemala, before draining into the Rio Motagua just north of Zacapa. Of these small valleys, the most ecologically rich and diverse from an agricultural society's point of view is the Copan valley. The Copan pocket offers both the largest expanse of river bottomlands (low terraces as well as floodplain), and the most extensive zone of foothills of any of the pockets which the Copan River forms (fig. 1). This double advantage is bolstered by the fact that the lands of this pocket are well-drained and constantly renewed, a circumstance still recognized and taken advantage of today. While the most densely settled area of the valley in Late Classic times was the low terrace north of the river, this need not always have been the case. The P.A.C. program set out to test all ecological zones in equal proportions in order to demonstrate or refute this hypothesis on the basis of an unbiased sample.

Space does not permit a detailed explication of the mechanics of the sampling program; this can be found elsewhere (Fash 1983a; Kurjack 1978). Briefly, we endeavored to obtain a representative excavation sample of the different ecological zones identified by B. L. Turner II and his associates, with an initial target size of 1%. Areas of gently rolling or flat terrain were gridded off into squares measuring 52 m on a side; and 2 by 2 m excavation units were located within them both systematically, with one test-pit in each of the square's four quadrants, and randomly, the location within the quadrant being determined by random number selection. These 52 by 52 m squares constituted the sample grain size within the west end of the valley, the alluvial bottomlands in the east half of the valley, and parts of the east pocket foothills. In more rugged areas, such as the foothills and upper slopes of the valley, a larger grain size, consisting of squares measuring 500 m on a side (25 ha in area), was used to obviate problems of locating sample units in such steep or rocky terrain. The choice of excavation locations within these units was determined by the investigator based on his/her perceptions of where the most likely places for occupation would have been. A 2 by 2 m test pit was dug within each hectare of the 500 by 500 m squares wherever this was not precluded by the steep nature of the terrain. The selection of particular study blocks for investigation (52 by 52 m and 500 by 500 m) was accomplished by first stratifying the sample by ecological area and then randomly choosing study units from

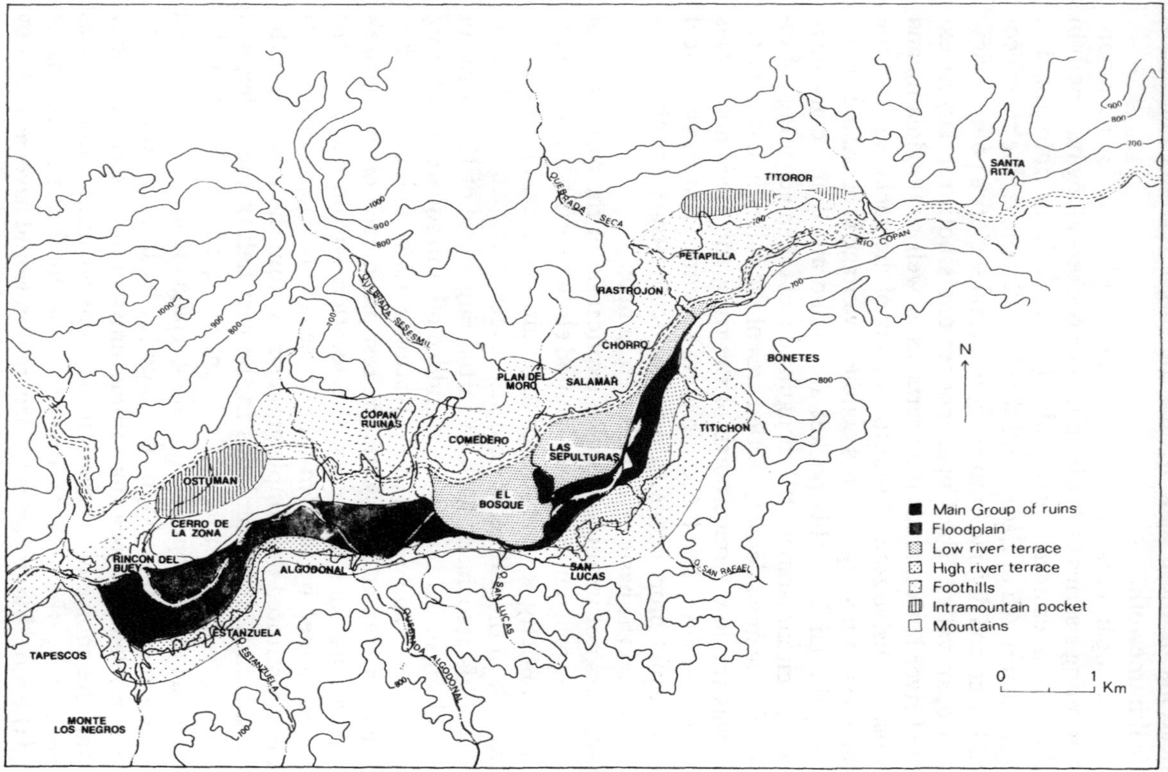

Figure 1. Map showing distribution of major environmental zones within the Copan valley as mentioned in the text.

within the blocks of 100 such units up to the proportion desired for each ecological zone (at minimum, 1%).

The 1% area sample was achieved with the completion of the 1978 season; moreover, in selected zones deemed of greater importance, the test-pitting sample was expanded to a coverage of 4% during the 1979 season. Emphasis was placed on sampling space, rather than testing only the visible mounds and plaza groupings. This was due to the fact that the primary goal of the test-pitting program was to obtain information on the history of settlement of the valley, with the hope that an unbiased sample of space would yield representative proportions of material from each time period manifested in the archaeological record. Previous investigations by the Harvard team indicated that most, if not all, visible architectural remains dated to the Late Classic era, and for this reason during the first season, 1978, primacy was given to the areas outside and between the visible structures. This emphasis on the "invisible universe" was continued during the second season, 1979, but augmented by direct sampling of visible structures. This latter program was undertaken to test the hypotheses that all visible architecture dates to the Late Classic and that the larger groups possessed the longest histories of in situ development, and to investigate the problem of the variability in Late Classic societal and settlement characteristics within and between ecological zones. Two sampling strategies were used to sample the visible architecture. First, 1% of all the mounds which were instrument-mapped in the 24 km^2 of the Copan pocket were tested by means of a 2 by 2 m pit on the back side of the mound. The mounds were selected in a systematic, stratified method (1 of each 100 within adjacent map quads), without regard to their height or position with relation to other mounds. The back of the mound was investigated in order to procure good midden samples and collapse debris which would allow inferences on the materials and quality of building construction. Second, a series of large sites (mostly Types 3 and 4, but resorting to some Type 2 in outlying areas) were selected for purposive testing. Here the locus of investigation was the center of the largest plaza of each site, since there was less likely to be disturbances of earlier strata in that area by Late Classic fill procurement or other activities. In all in the course of these investigations, 11 sites were tested by 2 by 2 m test pits placed purposively within their plazas. Information derived from other suboperations fills out the sample on five other large sites, while data secured at five more sites by the Harvard test-pitting program provides additional information. Based on a preliminary sorting of the ceramics recovered from all sub-operations (supervised by Viel), we can now present some tentative results of the test-pitting program.

I shall proceed by time period, beginning with the earliest manifestations, and tracing the development on up through the Late Classic and Postclassic periods. At the time of the First Phase Proyecto Arqueologico Copan investigations, the earliest-known ceramic tradition was the bottle and flat-bottom bowl complex discovered by G. B. Gordon in the caves of the Quebrada Sesesmil (Gordon 1898a). This assemblage has been designated the Gordon subcomplex of the Middle Preclassic Uir phase. These finds have recently been augmented by that of another burial ground dating to the same period, encountered beneath the plaza of a large architectural compound in the bottomlands east of the Principal Group. Subsequent investigations at this site (Group 9N-8, originally designated "CV-36" by Willey, Leventhal, and Fash 1978) revealed domestic remains in association with the burials found in my original (1978) sounding, and domestic features associated with a yet earlier ceramic complex (the Rayo phase, dated 1100–900 B.C.) underlying the Gordon remains (Fash 1982). A few sherds which may represent pieces of bottles from the Gordon funerary ceramic subcomplex have also been found in excavations near the Main Group and in two units in the foothills south of the river.

The faldas in general do seem to have been utilized for settlement during the Middle Preclassic Uir phase. A few sherds of Uir material were found in secondary contexts in the foothills both north and south of the river, indicating that these areas and perhaps others nearby were in use at this time. The bottomlands of the intramountain basin of Ostuman, ecologically equivalent to the foothills of the Copan pocket proper, also have produced Uir sherds (Suboperations 4 and 5).

Uir material has been found in primary contexts in the bottomlands, and in the case of the midden deposit encountered by Agurcia in Suboperation 82, in sufficient quantity to indicate sedentary settlement nearby. More primary contexts have been encountered in other units in the low terrace north of the river, indicating that this zone may have been the site of several Uir phase settlements or activity areas. These primary context materials are augmented by those found in secondary deposits in other suboperations in the low terrace north of the river. The evidence at present argues for a denser habitation of the bottomlands than the foothills, but it should be kept in mind that the sample size is larger in the former than the latter.

In the succeeding Late Preclassic (Chabij) phase, we have a drastic

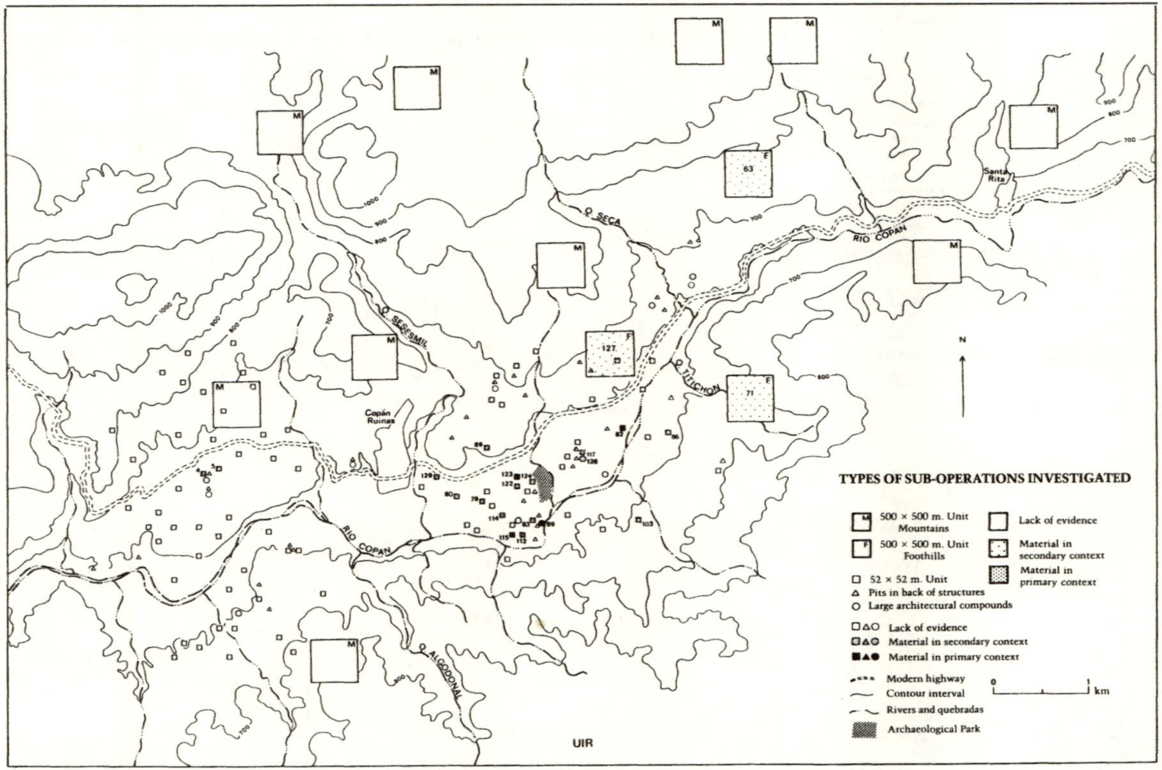

Figure 2. Map showing the distribution of settlement for the Middle Preclassic Uir Phase.

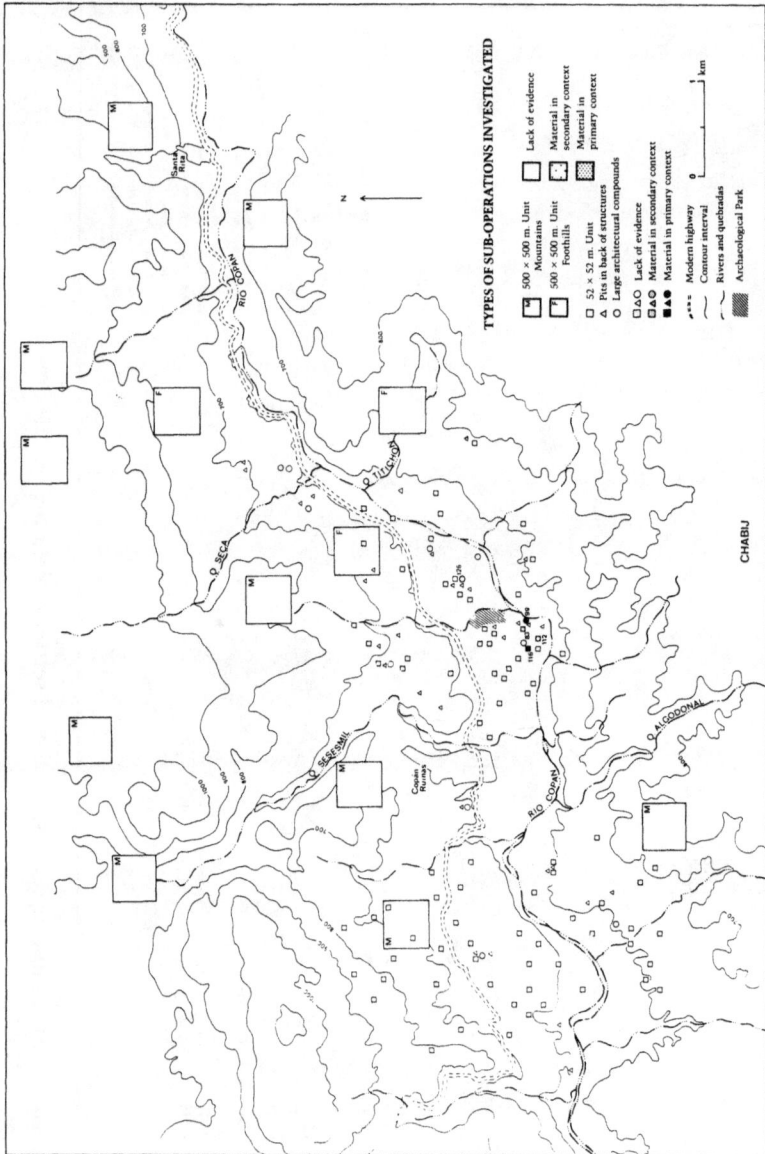

Figure 3. Map showing the distribution of settlement in the Late Preclassic Chabij Phase.

reduction in the number of suboperations yielding material. Only two units in the bottomlands (99, 116) have yielded pottery in primary context, with three others producing a handful of sherds from secondary contexts. The mountain units produced no Chabij pottery, and the foothills to date have only yielded two possible Late Preclassic sherds, hardly convincing evidence for sedentary settlements. Even the two primary deposits that have been found appear to represent a relatively short occupation—perhaps 100 years or less (Viel, personal communication). The number and distribution of excavations realized seems to preclude sampling as an explanation for the paucity of Late Preclassic material in the valley. Rather, there seems to have been a drastic reduction in the size of the population occupying the valley, which stands in contrast to developments taking place at many sites in the Peten and northern Belize during this time.

In the Early Classic (Bijac phase), there is an upswing in the number of units represented, and in the proportions of units yielding primary deposits. For the first time, a mountain unit is represented, with Suboperation 77 southwest of Santa Rita producing a few sherds of Bijac pottery in primary context. The foothills are again utilized (if not occupied in all cases), as evidenced by pottery recovered from units 63, 71, 89, and 127. The promontory on which the modern village of Copan is located was certainly inhabited at this time, as salvage and illicit excavations are constantly reaffirming. The bottomlands are also well represented, with eight suboperations yielding primary deposits, and another nine producing Bijac pottery in secondary depositional contexts. The total number of units nonetheless has increased only slightly over that recorded for the Uir phase, and although the number of sherds recovered may be somewhat greater, we still do not appear to be dealing with more than a limited population. For the first time, however, we find ceramics in association with stone architecture, in at least two loci (111 and 124).

The transition from Bijac to Acbi (Middle Classic) also sees a reduction in the number of units represented, but this may be a function of the relatively short amount of time which is represented. The distribution of the reduced number of units is approximately the same as that recorded for the Bijac phase, with the exception of the mountain square near Santa Rita. This unit is no longer represented, but its place is taken by unit 59, where the site of Cerro de las Mesas is found. The early hieroglyphic monuments recovered in the village of Copan also date to this time, and make for an interesting comparison with Quirigua. There are at least two loci lying outside of

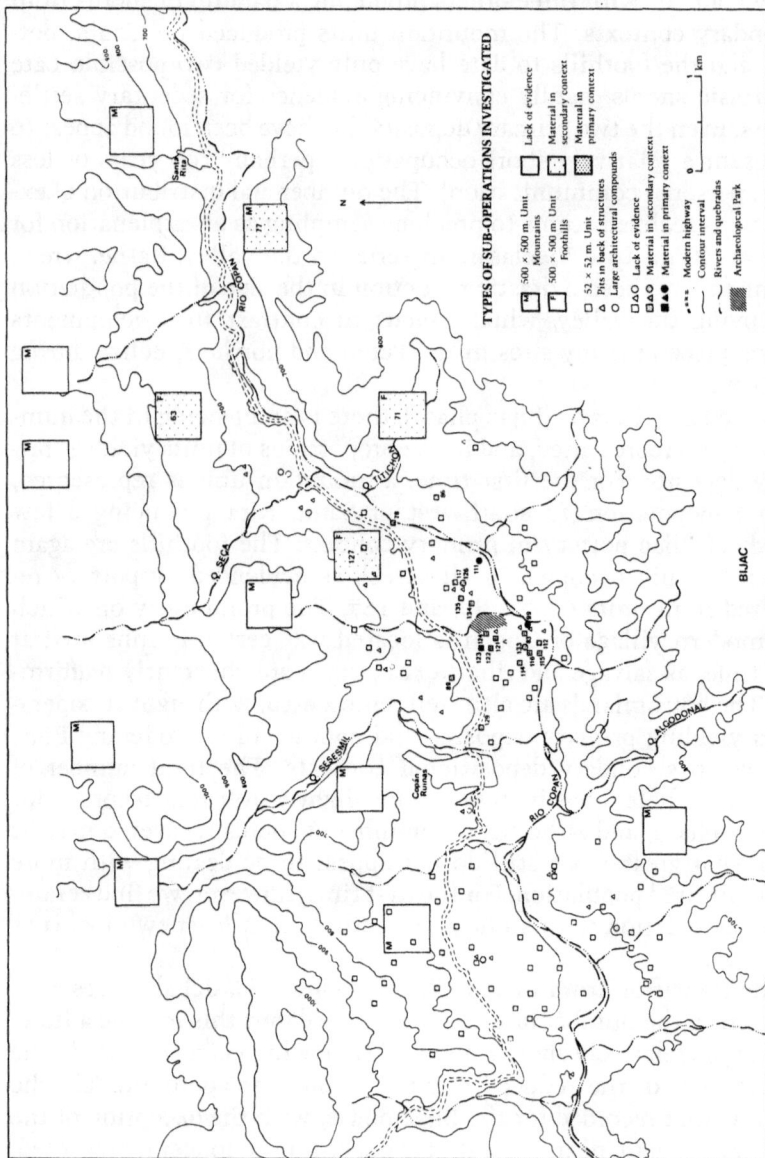

Figure 4. Map showing the distribution of settlement in the Early Classic Bijac Phase.

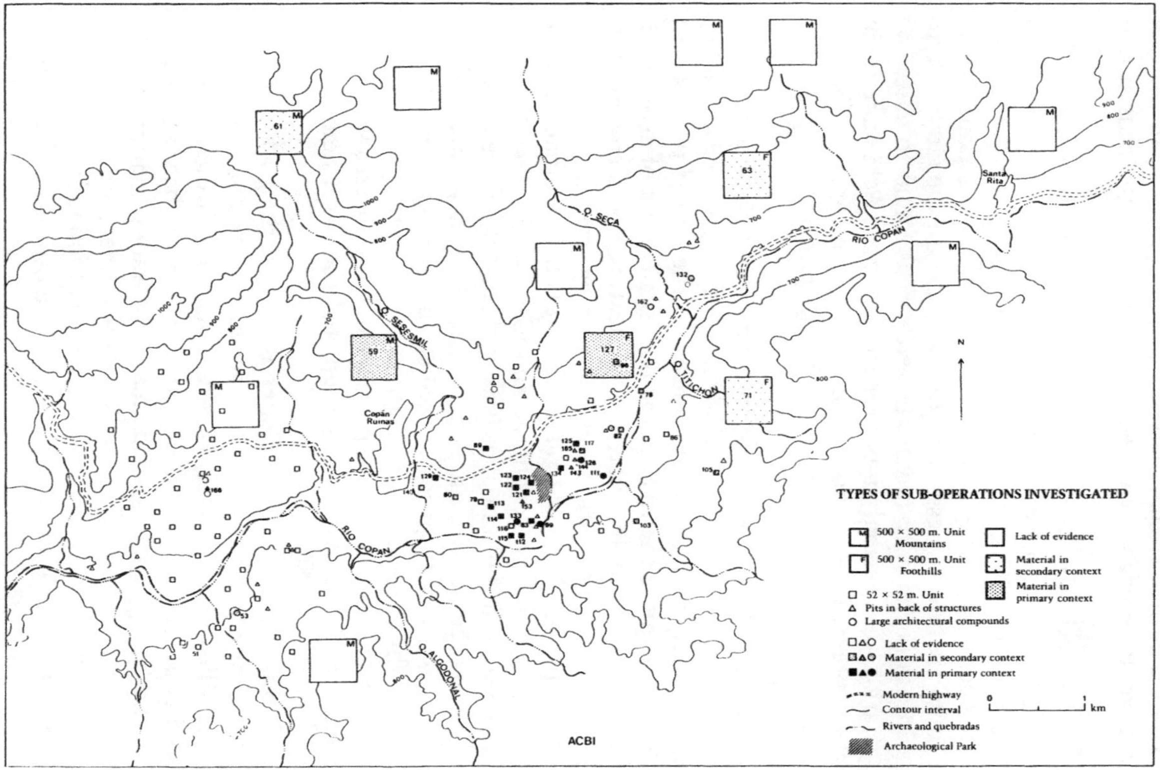

TYPES OF SUB-OPERATIONS INVESTIGATED

☐	500 × 500 m. Unit Mountains	☐	Lack of evidence
☐	500 × 500 m. Unit Foothills	☐ ▨	Material in secondary context
		▨	Material in primary context

☐ 52 × 52 m. Unit
△ Pits in back of structures
○ Large architectural compounds

☐△○ Lack of evidence
☐▲◑ Material in secondary context
■▲● Material in primary context

▪▪▪ Modern highway
— Contour interval
⟋ Rivers and quebradas
▨ Archaeological Park

Figure 5. Map showing the distribution of settlement in the Middle Classic Acbi Phase.

the area that was to become the site core of Quirigua in the Late Classic period which have produced monuments dating to the same period as the earliest stelae found in the village of Copan; neither area appears to have consolidated all power in a single locus at that time.

During the full Middle Classic (Acbi phase), there is a large increase in the number of units represented, and in the amount of material recovered. This is true especially of the faldas and vegas, particularly the latter, and to a lesser degree of the mountains, where three units are now represented. However, the hilltop site of Cerro de las Mesas is the only mountain settlement found to date, and Suboperation 59 is the only mountain unit to yield Acbi material in primary context. This anomaly is all the more intriguing when we realize that the Acbi phase seems to be the primary component of this large, hilltop center.

During the Middle Classic, the number of units producing material in primary context is double that from any of the preceding phases, indicating a significant increase in the size of the resident population. Many of the Acbi phase deposits consist of dense middens and/or fills of mixed materials, indicating that a considerable amount of land modification was being undertaken at various loci during this period. Of considerable interest is the fact that all of the large ("Type 4"; Willey, Leventhal, and Fash 1978) residential complexes tested in the bottomlands have yielded Acbi phase materials, as did the large center of Cerro de las Mesas. This may indicate that a number of competing polities existed at this time, an apparant continuation of the political fragmentation evident in the previous transitional period as seen in the importance of both the area which was to become the Copan Principal Group, and the site where modern Copan is now.

It is during the Late Classic Coner phase that the gradual expansion of outlying land use reaches its apogee; the bottomlands moreover, are filled-in completely. Every single unit which produced pottery in our sample yielded at least some Coner phase sherds. Although the most densely settled area of the valley continued to be the low river terrace north of the Rio Copan, there are zones in the foothills which rival the density of settlement found in the bottomlands. All of the 25 hectare squares in the foothills and mountains produced Coner pottery, and the majority of the 52 by 52 meter squares in the same areas did as well. All of the pits dug in the low terrace north of the river produced Late Classic ceramics, and all of the 32 mounds thus far tested in the 1% mound sample were constructed in Coner times. Perhaps the most impressive demographic

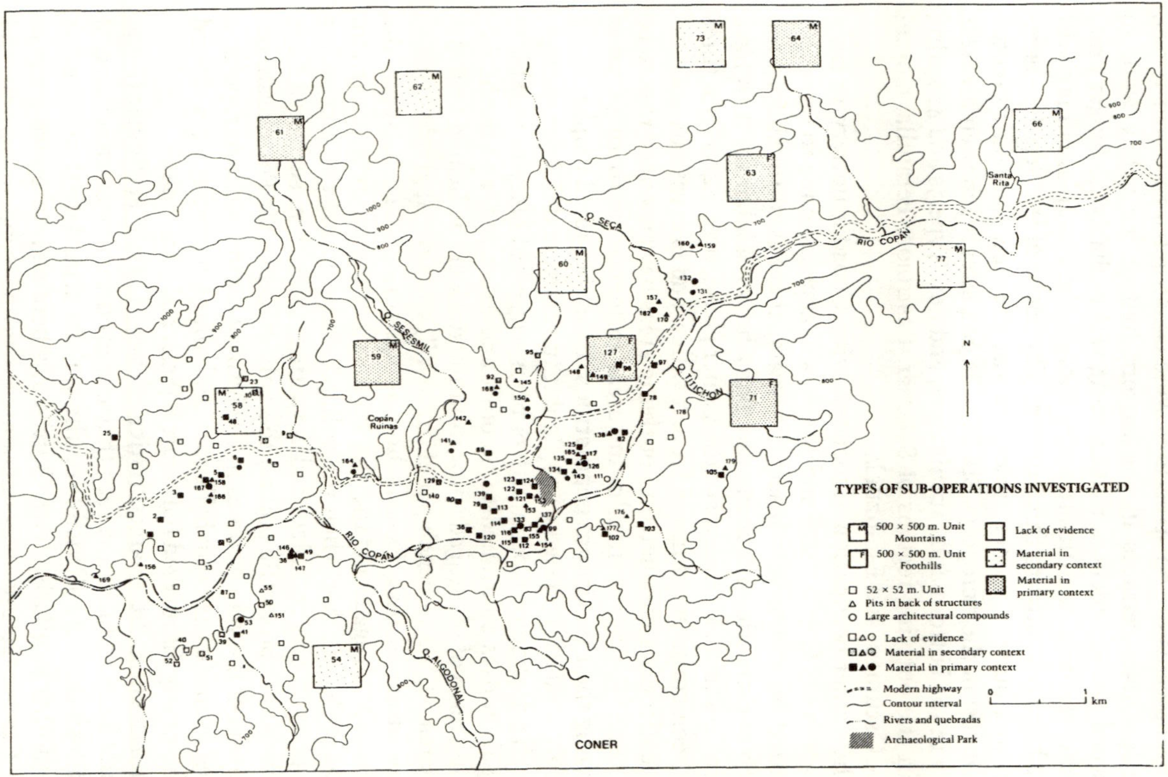

Figure 6. Map showing the distribution of settlement in the Late Classic Coner Phase.

growth is the western end of the valley, where only scattered secondary deposits datable to the Uir and Acbi phases had been found, but
where upwards of 500 structures were constructed in Coner times.
The low river terraces in the eastern half of the valley were so
crowded with residences that farming was probably no longer practiced there on a significant scale, though the floodplains may still
have been relegated to this purpose. The sacbe of the Sepulturas region was built in Coner times, as was the new ballcourt erected
southwest of the Acropolis. Six large Type 4 sites reach their greatest
glory in the bottomlands at this time, and new Type 3s and 4s spring
up in the outlying regions of Salamar, Rastrojon, Petapilla, Comedero, Ostuman, and Estanzuela.

The Coner occupation associated with Copador pottery is truly
the apogee of Copan's size and power, and appears to me to represent
a period of, at the very least, 100 years; there is quite simply too
much construction requiring too many hours of labor for it to have
taken less time. By the end of the Coner phase, over 3,400 structures
had been constructed in the Copan valley, and excavations and surface collections conducted in outlying areas have revealed this to be
the time of Copan's maximum areal influence, with these areas
reaching their maximum populations. It can be stated emphatically
that the end of the reign of 18 Rabbit in this period did not precipi-
tate the decline of Copan as has been suggested elsewhere (Sharer
1978a): houses continued to be built and expanded, and in the following reign of Madrugada new monuments were dedicated at outlying sites—CV-43's bench panel, Altar W', and several glyphic incensarios attest to this. Exactly how much time passed between the
death of Madrugada and the abandonment of the valley is uncertain.
What is clear is that when the collapse came during the succeeding
Ejar phase it was complete and devasting: aside from scattered finds
of diagnostic projectile points, the only evidence for Postclassic occupation of the valley comes in the form of tombs in the Acropolis, a
vessel found in the main ballcourt, and some superficial refuse found
at the newly discovered Ballcourt B (Fash and Lane 1983).

In assessing the characteristics of Late Classic settlement, one
should keep in mind the fact that not even the latest architectural
manifestations are all visible on the surface in modern times. Here is
yet another similarity with Quirigua, where an impressive array of
Late Classic features was encountered in independent commercial
trenching of the bottomlands (cf. Ashmore 1980c). Contrary to ex-
pectations, Preclassic and Early Classic materials were not the only
ones to have been covered over by subsequent soil deposition: several
cases of Late Classic constructions and features buried to a consider-

able depth were encountered in both valleys. Several of the most sobering instances of this at Copan resulted from the investigation of two seemingly, humble low platforms in Suboperation 165, one of which was buried to a depth of three meters, with the other extending 2.1 meters below the current ground surface. Nearby, in Suboperation 125, various artifacts and a number of Copador sherds were found directly on top of a cobblestone floor, buried two meters below the surface. Another Late Classic cobble construction was found buried at a depth of 1.8 meters in Suboperation IV/135. Suboperation 97 also produced a buried Coner phase floor at a depth of over a meter, and in 111 the remains of a perishable Late Classic structure were found at a depth of 1.6 m below the surface.

Even more sobering is the fact that this "invisible universe" between visible structures is not confined to the bottomlands: several examples of deep soil deposition were also encountered in the faldas. Excavation undertaken as part of the investigation of Suboperation 127 yielded subsurface architectural features, and Suboperation 148 revealed a structure that stood 2.3 m (rather than only 30 cm) high. Likewise the 1.5 m of soil which had accumulated in back of the foothill structure investigated in Suboperation 152 obscured not only the rear wall of the building, but an entire separate structure was found in back of the former which was not visible on the surface. The same situation occurred behind a structure tested by Suboperation 151, where another superficially "invisible" construction was encountered in back of the mound being investigated. These data should be kept firmly in mind when one examines the settlement patterns visible on the surface; in Copan and Quirigua, at least, what you see is not always what you get! A further complicating factor is that the river is known to have changed course several times even in this century, and the entire floodplain is devoid of any archaeological deposits which could conceivably have been laid down in the fertile alluvium next to the river.

Now let us turn to a consideration of the distribution of visible architectural remains. This discussion is based on the 3,441 mounds which were instrument-mapped by the Harvard team and the P.A.C. within the confines of the 24 km^2 covered by the mapping program in the Copan pocket (Fash and Long 1983; numerous others were mapped along the periphery of the grid borders as well).

In terms of the distribution of settlements within the pocket, the map allows us to define with precision their extent in each physiographic zone. Table 1 shows the sizes of the different physiographic zones and the numbers and kinds of settlements occurring on their surfaces within the 24 km^2 study area. Within the different zones,

Table 1. Settlement Data by Ecological Zone within 24 km^2
Mapped by the Proyecto Arqueologico Copan

Ecological Zone	Size (ha.)	Area Occupied (ha.)	% of Total Area Occupied within Zone Valley	Number of Groups
I. West End of Pack (Quadrangles monte los Negros-Yaragua, 15C–9H)				
A. North of the River				
Vega	1.8	0.04	2.2	.01	1
H.R.T.	21.3	1.16	5.4	.31	9
Falda	272.5	6.40	2.3	1.73	20
I.P.	64.9	4.76	7.3	1.29	26
(Ostuman)				
Montana	9.6	0	0	0	0
Floodplain comprises 162.3 ha.				
B. South of the River				
Vega	22.9	0.32	1.4	0.12	5
H.R.T.	76.8	5.36	7.0	2.62	37
Falda	167.5	0.76	0.5	0.28	18
Montana	0.4	0	0	0	0
II. East Pocket (Quadrangles El Pueblo/El Puente-Titoror)				
A. North of the River				
Vega	161.4	44.22	27.4	5.09	148
T.A.R.	19.4	0.68	3.5	0.08	4
Falda	563.9	31.96	5.7	3.68	196
B.E.M.	24.1	0.88	3.7	0.10	9
(Pepatilla)				
Montana	99.3	1.0	1.0	0.12	8
B. South of the River				
Vega	49.75	2.36	4.7	0.17	43
T.A.R.	60.10	3.96	6.6	0.68	36
Falda	422.55	7.52	1.8	1.28	55
Montana	53.80	0.36	0.6	.06	6
(Floodplain comprises 146 ha.)				
Totals	24 km^2	111.74		4.66	591

Note: H.R.T. = high river terrace; I.P. = intramountain pocket;
I.M. = isolated mounds; I.G. = irregular groups.

Types					Plazas	Plazas with Subsidiary Mounds	I.G.	Total Number Mounds	% of Total Number Mounds in Valley
1	2	3	4	I.M.					
1	—	—	—	—	—	—	1	2	0.06
9	—	—	—	4	6	2	3	38	1.10
17	3	—	—	5	6	3	7	80	2.32
21	2	2	1	9	21	7	11	150	4.36
—	—	—	—	—	—	—	—	—	—
5	—	—	—	—	5	1	—	18	0.52
31	4	2	—	21	25	8	16	183	5.32
17	1	—	—	7	12	2	7	74	2.18
—	—	—	—	—	—	—	—	—	—
89	33	13	11	34	201	58	40	1,180	34.29
4	—	—	1	3	3	2	1	20	0.58
133	50	9	4	79	157	48	76	1,086	31.56
7	2	—	—	—	7	3	2	40	1.16
6	2	—	—	10	3	1	6	38	1.1
10	3	—	—	22	7	2	6	66	1.92
34	2	—	—	17	15	6	21	147	4.27
46	9	—	—	52	36	11	22	300	8.72
6	—	—	—	—	—	—	6	18	0.52
436	111	26	17	263	504	154	205	3,441	100.00

the minimum surface area of the groups and isolated mounds was measured to the nearest 0.04 ha. I emphasize "minimum" because this represents only the area covered by the visible mounds and does not include buried or "invisible" structures or other activity or boundary feature areas not presently discernible on the modern ground surface. The proportions of areas covered by settlements, as seen in the table, show certain clear patterns. The density of settlements can be broken down into four levels:

1) The vega north of the river (east pocket), with a density far exceeding that of any of the other physiographic zones. 2) Physiographic zones with greater than 5% of their surface area covered by settlement, i.e., the high river terrace north of the river in the west end of the pocket, the high river terrace south of the river in both the west end and east pocket, the falda north of the river in the east pocket, and the intra-mountain pocket of Ostuman. 3) Physiographic zones whose surfaces were covered in proportions greater than 1% but less than 5%, i.e., the intra-mountain pocket of Petapilla, the falda north of the river in the west end of the pocket, the vega south of the river in both the west end and east pocket, the high river terrace in the east pocket, and the falda south of the river. 4) Physiographic zones whose surfaces were covered in proportions of 1% or less by Coner phase settlements, i.e., the faldas south of the river in the west end, and all the montaña zones.

The gradation is clearly from the most level land north of the river (always the prime focus of settlement in the valley), to the outlying foothill zones and the vega south of the river, and finally to the upper slopes which have thin soils and a tendency to pine and oak forest (cf. Turner *et al.* 1983). The one exception in this gradation is the high terrace north of the river in the east pocket. The oldest residents recall that when the modern village of Copan was founded, the most important settlement determinant was the distribution of mounds: these covered the area so completely that one had to search well for a level tract of land upon which to build. Morley's emphasis on the importance of the ancient settlement located there was based in part on the ruins still extant during his visits to Copan in 1912–1919 (Morley 1920). Originally, the density of settlements on this spur of land would probably have placed it at the second defined level, rather than the third. The fact that the vega south of the river is only at the third level of density can be explained I believe by a need for intensive cultivation in this zone, plus other logistical reasons to be discussed below.

According to the data in this table, settlement outside the vega north of the river was not particularly dense, but such appearances are deceiving. The condensed data do not take into account several important facts. First, there is differential density of occupation within the different sectors of each physiographic zone, e.g., the vega north of the river is much less densely settled in the swampy areas west of the *bosque* than in the remainder of its surface, and the falda north of the river is quite densely settled from Comedero to Chorro, but much less thickly occupied to the east of Chorro. Second, there were, no doubt, extensive activity areas, and we know there are significant numbers of structures, which escape surface detection—I would estimate that all the "area occupied" figures within each zone could be revised upwards by at least 2–5%. Third, within all the zones outside the vega there were large areas which could not possibly be utilized for the purpose of human settlement location due to steep slope, bedrock outcrops, stream cuts, etc. Only about 90% of the zones defined as high river terrace were actually level enough to support settlement, with about 80% of the foothill zones, and perhaps only 50–60% of the montaña, being adequate for the placement of human settlements. Finally, beyond all of these problems is the question of relative soil fertility. The limestone outcrops found in several sectors of the falda zones (Titichon, Chorro, Rastrojon, Petapilla) produce quite adequate soils for maize agriculture, but the tuff and siltstone substrates found in most other areas are notably less productive. Clay sources, and areas with either good limestone for the manufacture of cal or tuff for building stone, were most likely exploited for their resources, but such zones might not have strongly attracted human settlements. It seems more likely that land fertility, and at a later date, political concerns, were the most important determinants of settlement locations.

A revealing example of this is to be found in the vega and high river terrace south of the river. The high terrace is itself premier agricultural land, but in fact it was rather densely covered with settlements by the end of the Late Classic. The reason for this probably lies in the fact that the even-more-fertile low terrace and floodplain just below were left virtually unsettled and used for intensive agriculture. The settlements on the high terrace probably represent the quarters of people engaged in the cultivation of the vega; with time and in situ population growth, these high terrace settlements expanded considerably, while the vega itself was still, for the most part, devoted to agriculture rather than occupation. In the east pocket, where the high terrace south of the river fades out near the Quebrada Titichon, the vega settlements in fact increase in size and density as a result.

Socio-political reasons for settlement concentrations can be subsumed under the idea of the increasing "drawing power" or attraction of the residents of the larger structure groups and residential zones through time. The settlements in the foothills north of the river (east pocket) seem to have virtually merged with that of the vega north of the river in terms of the density of occupation (Willey and Leventhal 1979: 87). Most of the terrain in this adjacent foothill zone is fairly level, and the soil fertility is reasonably good, but the placement of settlements on other than level tracts of falda signals a cultural need for proximity to other groups in the area. As noted by Willey and Leventhal, this "drawing power" is noticeable even in the rather distant sectors of Ostuman and Estanzuela, where settlements cluster around a Type 4 and Type 3 site, respectively (*Ibid.*: 88; note that their assesment of the main group of Estanzuela, 14F-1, as a Type 4 was made prior to instrument mapping). Models derived from ethnographic studies of modern Maya groups see the larger groups as the result of the gradual expansion of a single extended family, with neighboring smaller groups perhaps representing the quarters of nuclear families of sons (or daughters) who have married and fissioned off from the larger extended family grouping. Whatever their social composition, "successful" groups as measured by the size and complexity of their visible architecture, seem to have been strong attractions to settlement to new groups. In situ population growth may very well have been bolstered by influxes of people from the margins of the pocket or outside it. Such a process is taking place in the west end of the pocket today, where immigrants from eastern Guatemala—motivated by political tensions and land pressure in their own area, and by the prospect of new economic opportunities in the fast-growing village of Copan—have moved in, in gradual waves, resulting in a rather sizeable increase in the size of the aldea of Rincon del Buey. Such influxes would help explain the rather rapid (in some cases, virtually exclusively Coner phase) growth of settlements in some of the outlying valley sectors.

As noted, socio-political concerns in terms of the drawing power of the main community in the vega north of the river crosscut the topographic division between that physiographic zone and the falda immediately adjacent to it. This community or subcommunity "cross-cutting" of physiographic zones is to a degree present in other areas within the pocket, but in fact numerous sub-communities can be shown to occupy discrete physiographic units. These sub-communities correspond to the divisions noted by Kurjack (1974; Kurjack and Garza T. 1981) in Dzibilchaltun and termed barrios or neighborhoods. In the Copan pocket, they were noted early-on in the P.A.C. surveys. The clearest examples are the settlements in the intra-mountain pockets of Ostuman and Petapilla, where the limits of the basins clearly also correspond with the limits of the sub-communities or neighborhoods. Very clear sub-communities are also definable on the large tracts of high river terrace in Algodonal and Estanzuela in the west end of the pocket, south of the river. Although for these two sub-communities a few scattered groups are found in the falda and low terrace immediately adjacent to the high terrace, the vast majority of their settlements occur on the high terrace itself. Another such high terrace community existed north of the river at the locus of the modern village of Copan (actually an alluvial fan of the Quebrada Sesesmil: Turner *et al.* 1983), although precious little of this has survived to the present day. In the vega north of the river in the east pocket, two sub-communities can be defined, one to the east and north of the Main Group (Las Sepulturas) and the other to the west and south (El Bosque). Another very clear barrio can be defined on a table-like configuration of gently rolling terrain called the Petapilla Mesa. Other divisions in the valley settlement are somewhat more difficult to isolate (cf. Kurjack 1974: 80, where the problem is discussed for the Dzibilchaltun settlements), but to my mind they may be discerned. All in all, some 20 sub-communities or barrios (besides the Main Group) can be defined for the 24 km² of the valley thus far instrument-mapped (Fash 1983a).

A general model for the explanation of the Late Classic settlement patterns in the Copan pocket can be presented at this point, based on the combined results of the excavations and survey conducted to date. The settlements in the vega north of the river have been shown to be the most extensive in the pocket throughout its occupational history. By the end of the Acbi phase the density of settlements in this sector must have been quite high. The strong socio-political control exerted by the royal lineage occupying the Main Group came to replace purely agricultural concerns as the principal reason for settling in this zone, making increased cultivation of the adjacent falda north of the river (and the vega south of the river) more and more necessary. As population pressure grew due to the increasing success of the Copan socio-political system, these vega settlements north of the river expanded northward. Increasing control of the floodplain and still-unoccupied low river terrace available for intensive agriculture (probably including double-cropping) by the dominant families made cultivation and settlement of the adjacent falda the most attractive option. Meanwhile, the falda settlements which we know existed prior to that time were also expanding, which, combined with the newly-founded settlements, came to result in a dense occupation of this zone. In time, to judge from the density and internal diversification of the groups found in this falda sector, it had reached the point of forming part of the urban core of the site of Copan. The presence of a sacbe system, as well as three Type 4 and numerous Type 3 sites in this area, attest to this inclusion. Furthermore, zones which had previously supported scattered hamlets or isolated residences took on increasing importance in terms of agricultural production. The older lineage segments in these areas which owned larger or more fertile tracts of land grew bigger and increasingly more powerful as in situ valley population growth was augmented by the arrival of at least some immigrants from the margins of the pocket or outside its limits. In some cases, the form and distribution of the settlements in these outlying zones clearly marks their function as dwellings of agriculturalists: the relatively dense concentrations of groups on the high terrace south of the river overlooked the very best agricultural land of the zone, the low terrace and floodplain. This low terrace and floodplain zone south of the river was never, to judge from present evidence, very densely occupied. I believe that its value as a food producing area over-shadowed its attraction for settlement. Doxiadis (1970) and Kurjack (1974: 94) suggest that people form their communities so as to facilitate safe access to culturally-determined parts of their habitat. The settlements south of the river in the east half of the pocket would perforce be less easy of access for large numbers of people and in fact somewhat "out of sync" in terms of communication and interchange in general with those clustered around the Main Group, located north of the river. As a result, the rich alluvial soils of this sector were devoted almost exclusively to intensive agriculture.

Sub-communities which were located even in relatively isolated areas such as the intra-mountain pockets of Ostuman and Petapilla Mesa became increasingly larger and internally diversified not only as a result of in situ population growth over the span of the Coner phase, but probably also due to the greater "buying power" which their agricultural produce (and possibly access to such raw materials as limestone for cal and tuff for building stone) gave them as more and more agricultural land in the vega and falda north of the river was taken up by residences. In the end, agriculture in the urban core was probably restricted to "kitchen gardens" (Willey, Leventhal, and Fash 1978: 36), following exactly the "infield-outfield" system predicted by Sanders (1981) based on analogy with sub-Saharan African kingdoms.

The even more dispersed groups and isolated mounds found in the upper slopes of the falda and montaña zones would, in this model, represent the dwellings of agriculturalists who were literally "pushed

to the brink" by demographic pressure. It is to be noted that the proportions of isolated mounds—some of which may in fact be only
field-houses rather than year-round residences of the people who
farmed the adjacent fields—increase with altitude, with one notable
exception. This exception is the vega south of the river near the confluence of the Quebrada Titichon and the Rio Copan. As noted
above, the placement of a settlement here was at least in part due
to the lack of an adjacent strip of high terrace for occupation; the
fact that a good number of these mounds are in actuality isolated
lends credence to the idea that this was basically a hamlet of agriculturalists.

In summary, we have documented a gradual rise in complexity and
density of settlement from the Early Preclassic up through the Late
Classic Period, and a drastic decline thereafter. The mountainous
terrain has been shown to have been intensively utilized and sparsely
occupied only in the Coner phase. The foothill or piedmont zones
(the faldas), one of considerable ecological and topographic complexity, were utilized by inhabitants of all time periods, though it has not
yet been adequately demonstrated what forms such utilization took,
except for the Late Classic Period. The river bottomlands in the eastern half of the valley were the locus of sedentary settlements from at
least the Uir phase onwards. However, the density of settlement
even here did not become significant until the Middle Classic. At
that time, several competing polities would appear to have existed,
one at what was to subsequently become the Main Group, one at the
spot upon which the modern village of Copan stands, another at the
hilltop site of Cerro de las Mesas, and at least three other loci on the
low terrace north of the river. Expanding use of the foothills appears
to coincide with the increases in population size and social complexity occurring at this time, with an increasing need for agricultural
land and wood for construction and fuel being possible motivations
for this trend. This pattern culminates in the Coner phase of the
Late Classic Period, when population and socio-political control
reach their peak, and the largest amount of terrain is under cultivation and used for sedentary settlements. At this time the residents of
the pocket proper may have been relying on at least some importation of foodstuffs from outlying areas, since the amount of land
available for cultivation was being reduced by the constantly expanding number of settlements. During the reign of Copan's last great
ruler, Madrugada, the Copan pocket may well have had a population
of somewhere around 15,000 to 20,000 people; it is precisely during
this Copador-related occupation that the settlement in the Copan
valley was most impressive, and most dynamic.

Late Classic Relationship between Copan and Quirigua: Some Epigraphic Evidence

Background

Prehispanic relations between Copan and Quirigua have been deduced in very general terms from similarities of the sculptured monuments and in more specific terms from parallel passages in hieroglyphic inscriptions.

The fact that Copan displays a greater abundance of Early Classic monuments than Quirigua is a main argument for considering Copan the source, and Quirigua the recipient, in this relation network. A hiatus in the sculptural record at Quirigua from about 9.3.0.0.0 to 9.12.0.0.0 (A.D. 495−672)[1] argues, according to Heinrich Berlin (1977: 89−90), for a subsequent recolonization of Quirigua from Copan, thus establishing the Late Classic splendor of the city.

David Kelley argued that Monument 5 (E)[2] at Quirigua, which mentions Copan ruler 18 Rabbit and Quirigua ruler Two-Legged Sky,[3] contains a kinship relation glyph (fig. 1: D79), defining the Copan ruler as father, or uncle, or something similar, of the Quirigua ruler. This interpretation was subsequently narrowed down by Kelley (1976: 226) to the sole interpretation of father. Joyce Marcus (1976: 135) and following her Robert Sharer (1978: 67) object to this interpretation because the glyph joining 18 Rabbit's and Two-Legged Sky's names on Monument 5 (E, fig. 1: D19) has to be interpreted as "captor," thus referring to a hostile encounter of the two rulers in

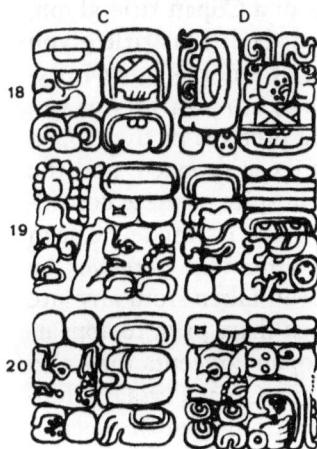

Figure 1

Figure 2

Figure 1. Quirigua Monument 5 (E): C18–D20.

Figure 2. Quirigua Monument 5 (E): A12–A13.

which Two-Legged Sky subdued 18 Rabbit. This captor statement or its equivalent capture statement (fig. 2: B12,1) is consistently repeated on other monuments in connection with the two rulers' names. Sharer pushes this interpretation further, stating that after this event there was a significant drop in building and sculptural activity in Copan, thus implying that this war had major disruptive effects on the Copan polity (Sharer 1978: 17; Ashmore and Sharer 1978: 14).

I will reevaluate these partially conflicting statements and arguments in the light of epigraphic evidence at Copan and Quirigua.

The Late Classic ruler Two-Legged Sky begins his reign in Quirigua at 9.14.13.4.17 12 Caban 5 Kayab (A.D. 724)[4] when he is twenty-eight years of age (Riese 1980: 164). Except for a deviant group of three monuments, 12 (L), 17 (Q), and 18 (R), there is no Late Classic sculpture at Quirigua prior to the first dated monument, 13 (M), of his reign at 9.15.0.0.0 (A.D. 731). On the basis of these data it can be argued that Two-Legged Sky initiates a renaissance in Quirigua, after a little over two hundred years of scarcely any sculptural activity.[5]

The study of Two-Legged Sky's first monument, 13 (M), makes clear that he had already adopted central concepts of royalty from neighboring Copan. Of these I want to point out two: Two-Legged Sky's extensive use of the Copan emblem glyph in his own name clause (fig. 1: C19, D20), and his adaptation of a Copan title glyph, employing it as his own emblem glyph (fig. 3: H8). This title glyph was in fairly common use during the reigns of Smoke-Jaguar-Imix-Monster and 18 Rabbit in Copan, from 9.9.0.0.0 to 9.14.19.5.0 (A.D. 613–731; Monuments 6, 7, 12, F, H, I). The prefixes of the Copan title glyph are partially changed, the kin infix is dropped, and the glyph itself is turned 90 degrees (fig. 3: H8). In spite of these considerable changes which distinguish it clearly from its model, Copan no longer made use of the original glyph after this takeover by Quirigua scribes. Both glyphs cannot have been taken from any site other than Copan, as they are exclusively used there prior to appearing at Quirigua. Some further copying of Copan concepts may also date from this time: the layout of the Quirigua Great Plaza, including stela placement therein, the size and positioning of the second ballcourt, and so forth.[6] I cannot otherwise than suspect a leading role for Copan in the creation of this apparently epigonal realm at Quirigua. Although Kelley's argument of kinship relations between the two centers is based on erroneous interpretations of the "captor" glyphs and others, the best tentative hypothesis to explain the Quirigua renaissance, as long as we do not have more direct evidence, is to assume some kind of dynastic kinship ties.

At 9.15.6.14.6 6 Cimi 4 Zec (A.D. 736), Two-Legged Sky captured, during battle, Copan ruler 18 Rabbit. The glyphic expression of this event is twofold. Glyph 1 always and exclusively follows immediately upon the date 6 Cimi 4 Zec (fig. 2: B12, right). Glyph 2 is always embedded into the nominal phrase of Two-Legged Sky (fig. 1: D19, left). Thus glyph 1 should correspond to a verb, glyph 2 to a noun. Glyph 2 is indeed almost exactly the same as the one Tatiana Proskouriakoff interpreted as meaning "captor" in Yaxchilan (Proskouriakoff 1963). From this it follows that glyph 1 should have the meaning "capturing" or "was captured." There are only five known cases of this glyph, three from Quirigua, one from Aguateca, Stela 2, and one from Dos Pilas, Stela 16 (fig. 4: D2). The two cases outside of Quirigua contextually suggest the same meaning.

The date 6 Cimi 4 Zec is recorded in Quirigua on Monuments 5 (E), 6 (F), 10 (J), and 7 (G) (fig. 1: A12–B12), but only twice in Copan (Hieroglyphic Stairway, Dates 23 and 23a). As references to 18 Rabbit stop abruptly at this date in Copan,[7] we might conclude that this event did indeed bring his rule to an end, disrupting Copan society, were it not for two other important facts: another ruler, Ruler XIV, had already assumed the throne in Copan at 9.15.5.10.10 12 Oc 12 Pop, a year before the capture of 18 Rabbit; further, the event at 6 Cimi 4 Zec does not cause a hiatus in Copan's sculptural and artis-

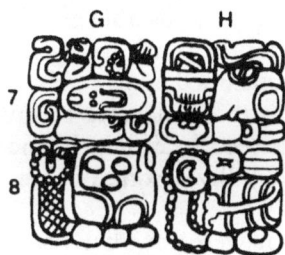

Figure 3

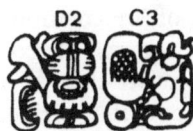

Figure 4

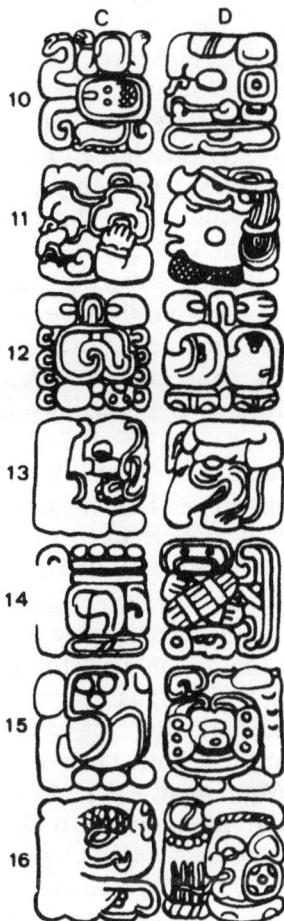

Figure 5

Figure 6

Figure 3. Quirigua Monument 10 (J): G7–H8.

Figure 4. Dos Pilas Stela 16: D2–C3.

Figure 5. Quirigua Monument 10 (J): C10–D16.

Figure 6. Copan Stela B:B11–B13.

tic activity as suggested by Sharer.[8] These are two puzzling and yet unresolved facts contrasting with the capture statements.

Presumably only after this puzzling victory over Copan did Two-Legged Sky dare to call himself the fourteenth ruler on Monuments 5 (E) and 10 (J) (fig. 5: C14), thus implying that he was a direct successor to 18 Rabbit, who had declared himself thirteenth ruler of Copan on Stela B in the Great Plaza (fig. 6: B11). A possible earlier dynastic count at Quirigua is discontinued after the ninth ruler over 250 years before and could hardly have been continued by 18 Rabbit.[9] Nevertheless, Copan remained unimpressed by this audacious claim and continued its proper sequence with a fourteenth, fifteenth, and sixteenth ruler without regarding Two-Legged Sky as one of their own.

Apparently relations between the two centers were not totally severed and lasted until the end of Copan's inscriptional and architectural activity, at or shortly after 9.18.10.0.0 (A.D. 800), the construction of the last dated building, Structure 18. Quirigua keeps referring to Copan, especially Copan's last and greatest ruler, Madrugada (Sun-at-Horizon). A possible contemporaneous reference is found on Monument 7 (G), and a surely posthumous reference is found on Structure 1-B-1 (fig. 7). Quirigua also continues to copy fancy Copan inventions, for example the mat-pattern design of inscriptions, manifest on Copan Stela J and copied in less intricate and elegant style on Quirigua Monument 8 (H).[10] Other imitations are the use of bench-panel inscriptions, common in Copan and copied in Quirigua Structure 1-B-1; frieze inscriptions, not very common at both sites (Copan, Temple 26; Quirigua, Structure 1-B-1); and wall decoration in mosaic technique, found commonly in the Copan Acropolis and

Figure 7

Figure 8

Figure 7. Quirigua Structure 1:o'-o'.

Figure 8. Copan fragment from the Hieroglyphic Stairway.

copied in several late Quirigua buildings, such as Structures 1-B-1, 1-B-2, 1-B-3, and 1-B-4. On the other hand, Copan does not really bother about its southern neighbor, mentioning Quirigua but once, on a loose fragment from the Hieroglyphic Stairway (fig. 8), a monument erected immediately after the reign of 18 Rabbit. I can think of only one innovation flowing from Quirigua to Copan, namely title glyph 115-761-59, first used by Two-Legged Sky (fig. 3: H7) and later incorporated in Madrugada's name clause at Copan.

Final Remarks

Epigraphic and sculptural evidence from Copan and Quirigua indicates that there was an initial intellectual and artistic influx at about A.D. 725 from Copan into Quirigua, through unknown channels, possibly dynastic kinship relations. A conflict between these two Maya centers culminated in the capture of 18 Rabbit, ruler of Copan, by Two-Legged Sky, ruler of Quirigua, at A.D. 737. The effects at Copan of this capture were apparently minimal, as measured by the large amounts of effort which continued to be invested in the production of sculpture and glyphic inscriptions at the site. This and other conflicting facts surrounding the capture of 18 Rabbit still need explanation. Despite the period of hostility, relations between the two cities were never cut off completely, and ideas continued to flow between them until the end of the epigraphic record, occurring at A.D. 800 in Copan and twenty years later in Quirigua. As was the case before the capture of 18 Rabbit, Copan seems to have been the initiator of these ideas and innovations and Quirigua, primarily, the recipient.

Epigraphic studies now allow us to reconstruct a more precise and detailed picture of relationships between Copan and Quirigua during the last century of their Classic splendor, which is more adequate, at least, than previously published work, but still far from reliable. To arrive at a fully adequate picture and resolve remaining puzzles, a more holistic approach and a more sophisticated model of interactions, integrating all archaeological evidence, will be necessary.

Acknowledgments

This paper is a revised version of one originally presented at the 45th Annual Meeting of the Society of American Archaeology, April 30 through May 5, 1980, in Philadelphia. Thanks are due to Claude F. Baudez, director of the Copan Archaeological Project Phase II, for financial, technical, and intellectual assistance, to Robert Sharer, Wendy Ashmore, and Christopher Jones of the Quirigua Project for sharing their ideas in talks, letters, and prepublication copies of papers, and to Karl Friedrich von Flemming, who brought to my notice Jones and Sharer's most recent paper, which reflects discussion during the meeting. All figures in this paper have been drawn by the author.

Notes

1. Christian dates are according to the GMT correlation.
2. Nomenclature of Quirigua monuments is in accord with the Quirigua Project. Pre-1978 nomenclature is included in parentheses.
3. Most rulers have been called by different names. Two-Legged Sky is also called "Cauac Sky" by the Quirigua Project and "Ruler I" by different authors. I stick to the scientific rule calling for preservation of the name a ruler has been first referred to in the scholarly literature. The only exception to this rule, I admit, occurs when a decipherment for the ruler's name glyph is proposed. Then, this deciphered name should supplant earlier conventionally given names. This is the case with "18 Jog," originally named by Kelley (1962), who is now renamed "18 Rabbit" according to the meaning of his semantically deciphered name glyph.
4. Stated on Monuments 5 (E), 6 (F), and 7 (G) (see Shaw 1977: 140).
5. According to Satterthwaite (1979: 39) and Morley (1935: 151–152), Altars L, Q, and R (now called Monuments 12, 17, and 18) are similar in form, size, and design, and according to the date of Altar L (9.12.0.0.0 or A.D. 672) fall into this period. I suspect that they were originally carved as three markers for ballcourt 1-B-Sub. 4. Altar L, which is slightly greater in diameter than Altars Q and R, would have been the central marker. Before this ballcourt was buried in the course of further construction work in the acropolis, the markers could have been taken out and two of them reset at the entrance of Structure 6, the third one in an unknown location. This hypothesis would explain the uniqueness, number, and similarity of these sculptures in the overall context of Quirigua art. Although the date (A.D. 720–740) given originally to the ballcourt by the Quirigua Project does not agree with Satterthwaite's date for Altar L, the date for this ballcourt has been revised and published by the Quirigua Project (Jones and Sharer 1980), after the epigraphic and locational evidence for these sculptures was discussed at the 1980 Society for American Archaeology meeting. The revised dating accommodates the epigraphic date of Altar L.

6. Suggested by Claude Baudez. Compare the maps of Copan ball-courts in Stromsvik 1952.

7. Dates 23B and 26/28 of the Hieroglyphic Stairway at Copan, both at 9.15.6.16.5 6 Chicchan 3 Yaxkin (A.D. 737), are connected with 18 Rabbit's capture date and thus may also refer to him, although the following noncalendrical glyphs are not preserved. This later date could be the death of 18 Rabbit, conceivably sacrificed by Quirigua ruler Two-Legged Sky.

8. His presumed hiatus is probably a misinterpretation of shifting activity in Copan, away from stela carving to erection of the Structure 26 Hieroglyphic Stairway, which amounts to the equivalent of about 30 stelae of Copan size and quality. This feat was accomplished in the two decades following 18 Rabbit's reign.

9. Recorded on Quirigua Monuments 3 (C) and 26 (see Jones and Sharer 1980; Jones 1983).

10. During the 1980 Society for American Archaeology meeting, Cancuen Stela 3 was suggested as a more probable model for the pattern on Quirigua Monument 8 (H), and this argument has since been repeated in print (Jones and Sharer 1980: 18). To my knowledge, Cancuen Stela 3 is undated and thus does not offer proof in any conclusive way. Instead one may still consider Copan Stela J as the original model from which Quirigua Monument 8 (H) derived its pattern and from which, in turn, Cancuen Stela 3 was copied.

DAVID T. VLCEK AND
WILLIAM L. FASH, JR.

8

Survey in the Outlying Areas of the Copan Region, and the Copan-Quirigua "Connection"

A walking survey of wide areal coverage, entailing sketch mapping and surface collecting of visible sites, was conducted by the senior author over a span of three months during the 1978 field season of the Copan project. This survey resulted in the discovery or re-location of some 97 archaeological sites in the region, over an area of roughly 300 km². It should be emphasized, however, that the survey was not intended to be exhaustive; priority was given to following out the river and quebrada drainages, with a nearly complete cover-age of all of the bottomlands and the foothills and steeper slopes bordering them. The intermontane valleys were also covered thor-oughly, and a number of other sites located in the more rugged mountainous terrain were also visited. Some transects were also walked during passage between sites, but future workers would do well to increase the coverage of the mountainous terrain, as more sites do certainly exist there. The 1978 survey has been supple-mented by limited excavations by the junior author at two sites, and detailed instrument mapping of three of the larger sites by Kurt Long of the Proyecto Arqueologico Copan (P.A.C.). We now have some idea of the broad outlines of the characteristics of settlement in the Copan region, and can set forth some tentative hypotheses regarding the "rules" which generated the patterns observed (see fig. 1 for the location of sites mentioned in the text).

Thanks to the efforts of B. L. Turner and his associates, we have a good basis for interpreting the observed settlement patterns within

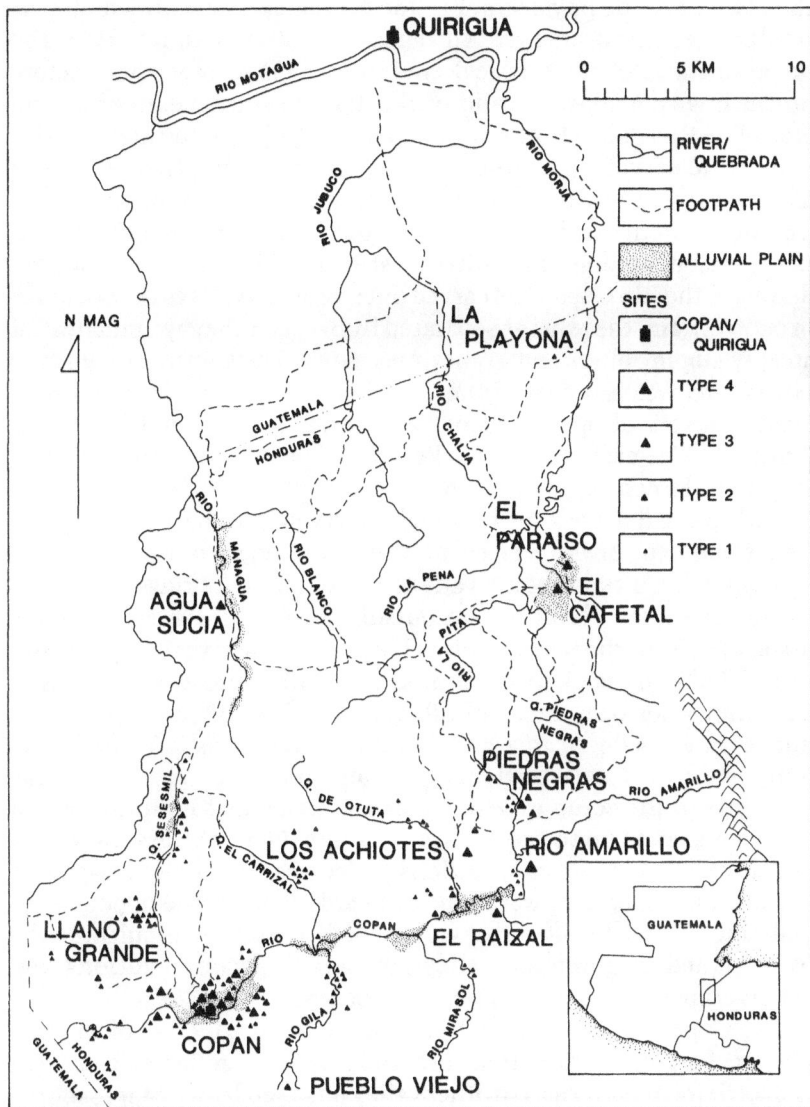

Figure 1. Map of sites mentioned in the text.

the context of the physiographic and ecological zones in which particular sites are located (cf. Turner *et al.* 1983). A summary of the
broad outlines of the physical environment is in order here before
proceeding to a consideration of the ancient settlements of the region. The Rio Copan begins on the western slopes of the Sierra Gallinero, which divides the Copan drainage system from that of the Rio
Chamelecon. The Copan winds approximately 38 km before reaching the Guatemalan border, along which course it is fed by numerous permanent and intermittent streams. Within its Honduran
drainage, the Rio Copan has carved out five small valleys or "pockets"
of open terrain, these being separated from each other by "pinches" of
steeply sloping bluffs and, sometimes, cliffs. The Copan valley is the
largest and westernmost of these pockets; to the east of it are three
small pockets of open terrain: Santa Rita, El Jaral, and lower Rio
Amarillo. The easternmost pocket, the upper Rio Amarillo, is large
enough to be considered a valley.

Within the five pockets, four major terrain types have been identified: floodplain, river terraces, foothills, and ridges or higher slopes.
Occasionally, intermontane valleys are found in the ridge lands, but
for the most part, level terrain outside the Copan River pockets is
associated with the narrow valley bottoms of the river's larger tributaries. Tributary pockets are similar to their riverine counterparts in
that they offer open areas of alluvial soil, but differ in that these
pockets are smaller in area, and the alluvium is not as well developed.
Soil fertility within a particular physiographic/ecological zone may
vary, due to the complex geology of the region and its influence on
local soils, and due to precipitation factors. Nevertheless, there is a
tendency for cultivation conditions to decrease in quality away from
the Rio Copan, both upwards and outwards. That is, the upper slopes
and ridges tend to offer the worst conditions for agriculture; the
foothills and intermontane valleys, moderate to good conditions; and
the riverine and tributary valleys, the best.

The Copan valley is far and away the most productive of the five
pockets for prehistoric agriculture, and this fact is reflected clearly in
the settlement patterns. No other valley has a settlement approaching
the density of that found in the Copan pocket, nor an organizational
center nearly as impressive as the Main Group.

In our discussion of the outlying settlements, we shall proceed
from west to east, beginning with the intermontane basin of Hacienda Grande. This small valley was first reported on by G. B. Gordon (1898a), who noted "a stela within a walled enclosure." The
stela (19) is associated with a small Late Classic settlement, and a
larger site (a Type 2 within the Willey-Leventhal [1979] typology) is

located within 500 m of it. Both of these sites are set on slight rises in the center of the basin, with no settlements having yet been located on the foothills or higher slopes which define the valley's limits. The small bit of architecture exposed in a preliminary investigation of the Type 2 site is of high quality, and the recovery of Copador and Ulua-Yojoa polychrome sherds attests to the relatively high social standing of the site in question, and its close ties to the Copan valley.

Copador polychrome was also encountered in surface collections from several small sites located near the Guatemalan boundary along the foothills and river terraces bordering the Rio Copan. This seems to indicate that these sites, too, were tied into the Copan polity, and that further surveys on the Guatemalan side of the border may net other settlements of the same affiliation. The small intermontane valley of El Salto was the locus of at least two small Late Classic sites, which also yielded Copador pottery and domestic wares indistinguishable from those found in the Copan pocket proper; these settlements also appear to be closely connected with Copan.

To the northwest, in the intermontane basin of Llano Grande, a cluster of sites has been located. The majority of these are small settlements ringing the edges of the bottomlands, which with one exception do not appear to have been loci of Precolumbian settlements. The largest site in the area is a hilltop center consisting of two fairly large mounds, with a commanding view of the bottomlands and north slopes of the basin (fig. 2). Surface pottery collected from several sites is again indistinguishable from that found in the Copan valley, indicating that the visible settlements (Late Classic in their majority if not totality) were probably an offshoot of the Copan pocket community.

The eastern end of Llano Grande opens out on a constricted portion of the Quebrada Sesesmil, where sites are for the most part nonexistent. Farther upstream, however, the steep slopes give way to open areas of alluvial soils, and a number of sites were located in proximity to these patches of bottomlands. Double-cropping is currently practiced in this area, and the number of sites indicates that the pattern may have been current during the Late Classic, as well. The majority of the sites in the Sesesmil Primero-Segundo area are located on high river terraces bordering the bottomlands, rather than on the prime farming land itself. One Type 2 site (Sesesmil Segundo #1, fig. 3) has a layout similar to that of similarly proportioned sites in the Copan valley, and the surface ceramics also show great similarities to their Copanec counterparts.

In the middle reaches of the Rio Managua sites appear again, lo-

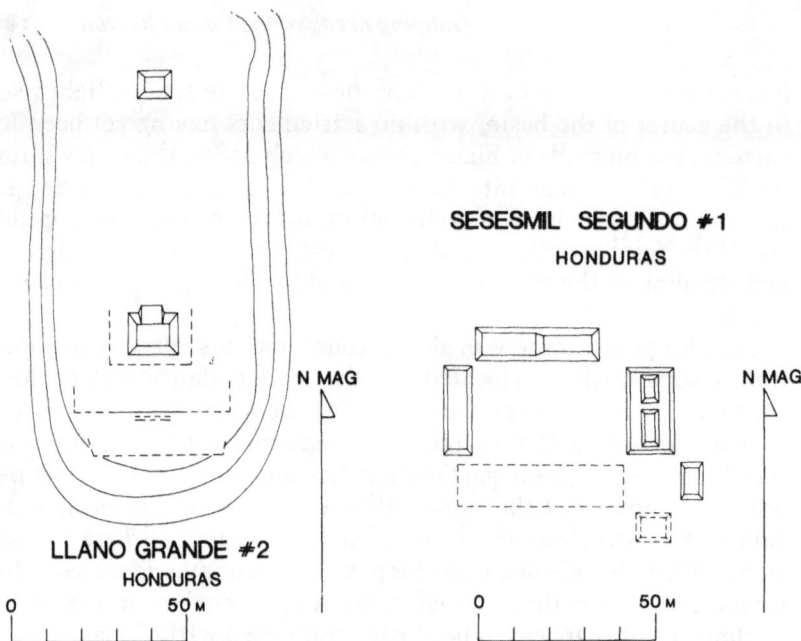

Figure 2. Dominant hilltop center, intermontane basin of Llano Grande.

Figure 3. Sesesmil Segundo site, Sesesmil Primero-Segundo area.

cated in close proximity to fairly large pockets of alluvial bottom-lands. The largest of these settlements is a Type 3 site (Agua Sucia, fig. 4) situated on the top of a large terraced hill, the total complex evidencing a considerable amount of coordination and effort. This site's placement, overlooking the largest tract of alluvial bottom-lands, would hardly seem fortuitous. A nearby site, located on a foothill spur east of the bottomlands, was investigated in a rapid fashion in 1978, and contained pottery and architectural features closely akin to those found in the Copan valley. The pottery included both typical Copan domestic wares (Casaca, Masica, Lorenzo, and Cementerio), as well as a number of Copador sherds, and one sherd of Ulua-Yojoa polychrome. It should be noted that the site of Agua Sucia lies at a distance from Copan which can be walked in one day, and that the Sesesmil-Managua route was probably the fastest over-land passage from Copan to Quirigua. Mountain trails lead from the termination of the alluvial bottomlands under discussion to the modern village of Los Amates, and the journey from Copan could conceivably have been made in as little as two days. We are certain

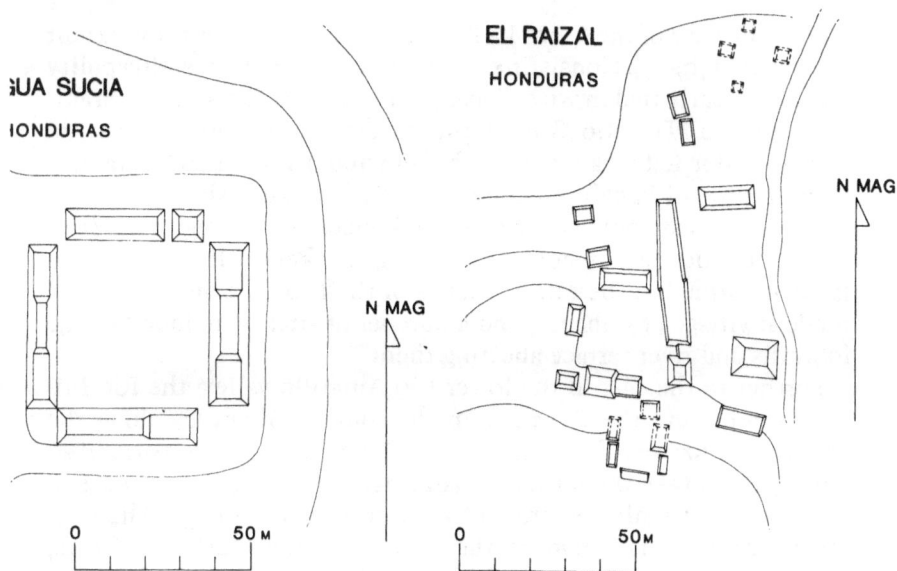

Figure 4. Agua Sucia site, middle Rio Managua drainage.

Figure 5. Cerro La Butaca community of sites, Quebrada El Carrizal drainage.

that all of the settlements on the Honduran side of the border along this route were firmly within the Copan orbit.

The first major site upriver from the Copan valley, that is, east of the Copan pocket proper is that of Santa Rita, now largely destroyed as a result of modern building activities. Two hieroglyphic monuments are known from this site, and Morley (1920) suggested that some of the construction was of considerable size. These data take on some interest when one realizes that the site is located near the confluence of two major tributary drainages, the Quebrada El Carrizal to the north and the Rio Gila to the south. In addition, it overlooks a fairly good-sized parcel of river terraces and floodplain, double cropped in tobacco and maize today. The combination of these physical features could help explain the presence of carved monuments and high-quality architecture; future investigations might reveal a considerable time-depth of occupation in the area.

The Quebrada El Carrizal has its origins in the intermontane valley of La Reforma, a medium-sized basin which had at least two Late Classic settlements. Farther downstream, on a massive natural terrace at the base of the Cerro La Butaca, a community of some extent was located (fig. 5). Consisting of a number of small sites, this polity was also clearly tied in with Copan, to judge from the surface ceramics collected. The Rio Gila originates far to the south of the Rio Copan, and is fed by a large number of tributaries. Surface ceramics from the site of Pueblo Viejo included Early Classic sherds, indicating that at least some occupation took place in this region prior to the Coner phase expansion. A fairly large pocket of alluvial bottomlands is formed in the lower reaches of the Rio Gila just below the modern village of Cabanas, and a number of sites were found in the foothills and river terrace abutting them.

Further to the east in the lower Rio Amarillo valley, the Rio Mirasol drains into the Copan from the south, and survey along the former has located three small sites. Like their counterparts elsewhere, these take the form of small settlements ringing the edge of patches of bottomlands formed by the tributary drainage. The next major tributary is found to the northeast: the Quebrada Otuta, which drains into the upper Rio Amarillo at the point where the bottomlands of the latter reach their widest expanse. This stream is fed by a number of tributaries, all of which have small associated settlements. Of particular interest is the site of Los Achiotes, the "controlling" or organization center of the region. Like the site of Agua Sucia, Los Achiotes sits atop a large terraced hillside, next to a stretch of rich bottomlands. The terraces upon which the site sits rise to a height of 25 meters, and reflect considerable effort and planning. In their visit to the site, Vlcek and Sandoval noted two long, parallel mounds, which may possibly represent a ballcourt. Between the site proper and the surrounding bottomlands, hillsides, and ridgetops, a total of perhaps 70–80 mounds was observed, indicating that at its peak the site was probably a rather large community.

At the confluence of the Quebrada Otuta and the Rio Amarillo, one Type 2 and one Type 1 site have been located. To the east of these is the intersection of the Quebrada El Raiza and the Rio Amarillo, where another small site was encountered. The Quebrada El Raiza boasts a fairly extensive site of the same name, at the point where it widens out and produces a small patch of alluvial soil. This site is very similar in layout to other Type 3's in the Copan valley, and like those, would appear to have grown by accretion, with subsidiary plazas being added a number of years after the initial establishment of the site.

A number of small sites are found upriver on the terrace bordering the floodplain. The northernmost of these is in close proximity to Rio Amarillo, a major Late Classic site. The Rio Amarillo site itself is built into the side of a hill, overlooking a small stream which drains into the Rio Amarillo. No complete map of the site has yet been published, and during a visit there the authors were unable to assess the size or extent of the site, other than to see that it was fairly extensive, and had one structure (visible on Morley's map, 1920) in the neighborhood of 7 m in height. Morley discovered two hieroglyphic altars at the site, and Pahl and his colleagues found numerous fragments of a sculptured mosaic architectural frieze or panel, indicating that the site housed individuals of high social standing. The excavations at this site produced Copador polychrome, but no Ulua-Yojoa.

Draining into the Rio Amarillo just west of the site of the same name is the Rio Blanco. This tributary boasts a number of sites in its middle course, particularly at the junction of the Quebradas del Gobiado and Piedras Negras. There are two Type 2 sites in this area, and a Type 3, named after the Quebrada Piedras Negras (fig. 6). This site, like Agua Sucia and Los Achiotes, is built on top of a natural rise, overlooking an area of rich bottomlands. In similarity to both sites, it exhibits evidence of formal planning, and it has a large plaza similar to Agua Sucia's. This site and Los Achiotes, however, are both out of the range of variation of site layout and planning of anything found in the Copan valley, and appear to reflect distinct con-

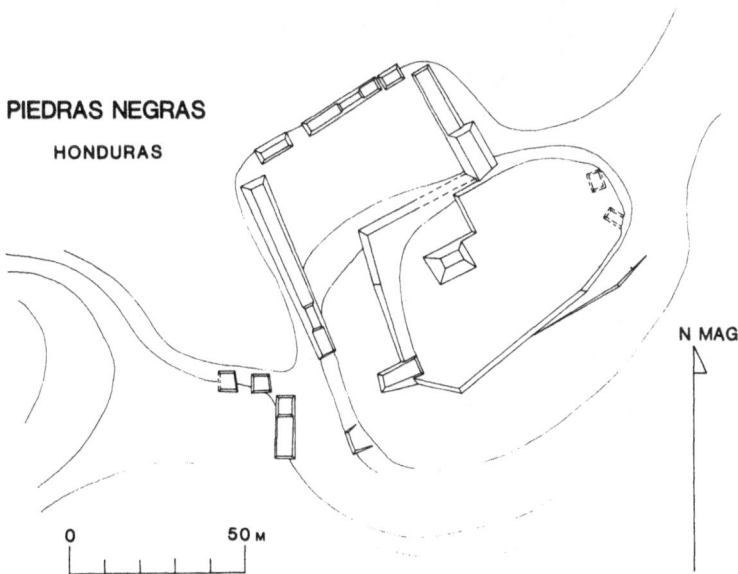

Figure 6. Piedras Negras site, junction of Quebradas de Gobiado and Piedras Negras.

ceptualizations of space as well as direct responses to local ecological conditions (in this case, the poor drainage of the bottomlands).

A consideration of the settlements and trade connections of the upper Rio Chamelecon drainage, which lies outside the range of our survey, is beyond the scope of this paper. We do have data, however, on the Rio Morja drainage, which begins west of the Sierra Gallinero, and empties into the Motagua west of Quirigua. The largest site in the region, El Paraiso, is located where the modern village of the same name stands today. This site comprises a number of plazas and at least one large pyramidal structure; portions of the site are still preserved. Lunardi (1948: 296) mentions a possible ballcourt at the site, and carved sculptures were found both by Sapper (1895) and Yde (1938). None of these visitors, however, seems to have seen the large architectural compound which we will call the "El Cafetal Group" (fig. 7), located approximately 1 km south-southeast of the "Main Group." Although the northern segment of the site has been cut by a stream, the extant portion exhibits a number of large structures, grouped around an immense open plaza. Compared to outlying sites in the Copan valley, this site is bigger in bulk and distinctive in layout; together with the other group located in the vicinity of the modern village, they comprise a major organizational center.

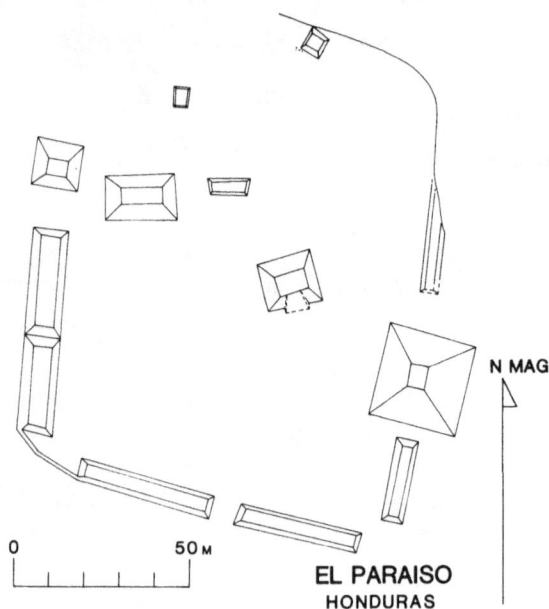

Figure 7. El Paraiso site, El Cafetal Group, Rio Morja drainage.

This should not come as too much of a surprise, since these sites are located in a valley which boasts alluvial bottomlands much larger than those of either the upper Rio Amarillo or Copan valleys. Elevation and precipitation factors are such that double-cropping is feasible in some parts of this valley, and a range of ecological variation can be found in the valley's immediate environs. This region is in particular need of intensive survey; certainly the area just west of the "El Cafetal Group" is crowded with visible structures for the 0.5 km² which was rapidly surveyed. A test pit in the plaza of the large complex yielded evidence of long-term occupation: hundreds of Late Preclassic materials mixed with a few Early and Middle Classic sherds in a secondary deposit. A pit in back of one of the long structures on the west side of the plaza yielded Coner phase ceramics which can be included in the Casaca, Cementerio, Raul/Masica, and Lorenzo domestic ceramic groups found in the Copan valley. Underneath a stone floor which runs out from the base of the building, several sherds of Copador were recovered, indicating that this structure (and possibly most of the other structures in the main compound) was constructed in the Coner phase. Rene Viel informs us that the pastes of the Copador and Caterpillar polychromes excavated from this test pit are visually identical to those of the same wares found in the Copan valley, further evidence for the close connection between the two sites. Also of interest is the recovery of a rim sherd of an imported basal-flanged polychrome, and several sherds of Ulua-Yojoa, indicating that El Paraiso's outside contacts were not limited to Copan. Downstream from El Paraiso are found the ruins of La Playona, a small site on a foothill spur south of the Guatemalan border. Although a surface collection was made here, Viel found the material too eroded to classify, and we are at present unable to make any assessments as to the cultural affiliation of this site. It could certainly have served as a way station for anyone traveling from Paraiso to Quirigua, being slightly less than a full day's walk from the former. If we posit an overland route running east and then north from Copan, it would be at least an eight-hour walk from Copan to any of the larger sites in the upper Rio Amarillo valley or the Rio Blanco drainage. El Paraiso could conceivably be reached the same day, but probably not by anyone carrying much in the way of cargo. From El Paraiso one could arrive at Quirigua in a day's time. This route would thus appear to have taken in the neighborhood of two-and-a-half to three days to traverse, only slightly longer than the proposed Sesesmil-Managua passage.

To sum up, settlement in the outlying reaches of the Copan valley tends to cluster on the borders of the tracts of fertile bottomlands formed by the Rio Copan and its tributaries. In some cases the sites are located on adjacent river terraces, but most of the large sites are found on terraced hills overlooking the bottomlands. Although a heavy bias exists in the survey data toward river and stream drainages, it seems unlikely that any major sites will be found in the mountainous terrain not yet surveyed. Scattered settlements do exist in the mountains, however, and there is one case (Cerro La Butaca) of a community of respectable extent. With the exception of Pueblo Viejo, all sites which produced surface collections had sherds of the Coner phase, and if the pattern which exists in the Copan valley is any indication, most, if not all, of the currently visible sites date to this period. At present we hypothesize a late expansion into the outlying regions, by people related, or at least closely tied by commerce and culture, to the people inhabiting the Copan valley. Not surprisingly, the strongest concentrations of sites cluster around the richest agricultural lands, and especially in those areas where dry season and/or double-cropping are feasible. The sites are generally situated on the upper borders of the alluvial tracts, both so that these could be devoted totally to agriculture and because in many areas drainage and seasonal inundation create problems for the placement of houses in the bottomlands.

We tentatively suggest that an exchange system existed wherein agricultural surpluses from the outlying intermontane and tributary valleys were exchanged for pottery and other goods and services from the Copan valley, where the prime agricultural lands were increasingly being given over to residential use (see Fash, this volume). The ceramic data tend to support this hypothesis, in that the same types are represented in the surface collections thus far recovered, and with the exceptions of Pueblo Viejo and El Paraiso, are all Late Classic in date. Future sampling may indicate that certain types are sensitive indicators of relative prestige or "closeness" with the Copan polity, but for the moment we advise caution on this matter; the presence of Ulua-Yojoa polychromes in a small outlying settlement such as the Rio Managua site, and at Hacienda Grande, indicates that its absence in the collections thus far obtained from the large site of Rio Amarillo may be fortuitous rather than real.

In this vein, the question of Copador at Quirigua and other lower Motagua valley sites merits consideration. It seems clear that Copan "controlled" or participated in exchange with all of the sites thus far located on the Honduran side of the border (although La Playona needs to be tested). It is also clear that transport to Quirigua from Copan was theoretically a very simple matter, with a number of possible way-stations along at least two alternative routes; but a whole series of mountain trails has yet to be surveyed. The fact that Copador was not found in high frequencies at Quirigua or any of the other lower Motagua valley sites indicates that it probably was not traded into the area in significant quantities; however, the Peten wares are not particularly well-represented at Quirigua either. We lean toward selectiveness on the part of the Quirigua-lower Motagua valley polity in the procurement of imported ceramics as an explanation of both of these phenomena. The hypothesized severing of trade from the Peten to Copan by the elite of Quirigua does not appear to us to have caused particular stress in Copan. The fact of the matter is that Peten ceramics never made up more than 1–2% of the Copan assemblage at any time during the sequence. On the contrary, it appears that Copan did better than ever during the Copador phase, with a tremendous population growth occurring, and expansion into outlying areas reaching an unprecedented level (see Fash, this volume). Copan seems to have done very well for itself without a strong Peten trade, and its "inward turn" may be as much deliberate as enforced from the outside.

EDWARD M. SCHORTMAN **9**

Interaction between the Maya and Non-Maya along the Late Classic Southeast Maya Periphery: The View from the Lower Motagua Valley, Guatemala

The Problem

The boundary of the Southeastern Periphery of the lowland Classic Maya culture area is traditionally drawn somewhere within the general area of northeastern Guatemala, western Honduras and western El Salvador (Longyear 1947; Lothrop 1939; Thompson 1970). It is primarily defined by the distribution of certain material items whose conjunction reflects a unitary phenomenon known as "Maya Culture" (see Table 1; also Marquina 1964: 511). While the existence of such a periphery has long been assumed little effort has been directed towards more precisely defining it or, more importantly, trying to understand the behavioral significance of the observed distribution of the defining Maya traits. Recently, several researchers have called for an explicit consideration of the processes behind the formation, maintenance, and changes within the Southeastern Maya Periphery in the Classic period (Helms 1976; Lange 1976, 1979) but little study has, as yet, been devoted to these problems (see, however, Fox 1981 for a consideration of cultural processes operating in the Late Postclassic southeastern area).

The lower Motagua valley, in northeastern Guatemala, provides an excellent opportunity to consider questions of the placement and the behavioral significance of the Classic Maya periphery. It is situated within the traditionally-defined periphery zone and, in the Late Classic period (A.D. 600–900), was marked by a clear distinction in the distribution of Maya-related items. Quirigua and the large centers located within a 5 km radius of that center (see Ashmore, this volume, and 1981a) possessed the hallmarks of Maya civilization (Table 1) while the nine sizable sites found beyond this radius to the northeast were almost totally devoid of them. The central focus of this essay, therefore, is the determination of the factors which lay behind the exclusive distribution of material items between the two sets of monumental centers within the Late Classic lower Motagua valley. The focus of this paper is on sites within the valley with monumental construction, as it is in terms of this class of centers that the Maya pattern was originally defined. Monumental architecture is defined here as those structures whose size and complexity suggest that the individuals for whom they were built had a control of labor and managerial expertise well beyond the means of the common householder (Adams 1981). Monumental construction, therefore, is associated with centers of administrative and economic power. From the outset, certain factors can be eliminated as determinants of material distribution within the Late Classic valley. Physical barriers to communication do not exist within the broad, flat floodplain of the Rio Motagua. Similarly, the established contemporaneity of the monumental sites in the Quirigua area and those to the northeast within the wider valley and the short distances separating them (see fig. 1) would argue for the presence of much greater material similarities than have been found to exist. As a result, any model developed to explain the observed differences must concentrate on the intangible aspects of the interactions which took place in the valley in the period from A.D. 600–900, in particular, the content of the cultural systems in contact, the differing environments they occupied, and the general circumstances of their intercourse. Such a model is presented below after a brief description of the general patterns apparent in the data from the wider valley monumental sites. Following the exposition of the model and its application to the lower Motagua valley situation, the utility of this general approach to the study of the Southeast Maya Periphery and the study of any area peripheral to centers of major cultural developments is considered.

Table 1. Characteristics of Major Lowland Classic Period Maya Sites

Architecture

Substructure Platforms
  Cut block masonry
  Plastered
  Broad staircases, usually only one on a structure

Superstructures
  Cut block masonry
  Plastered
  Temple, palace, and shrine forms
  Decoration in stucco or stone with the use of paint frequent
  Roof combs
  Stone vault
  Often burials and caches associated with construction; burials also
    found under the floors of residential structures.

Special structures
  Ball courts and ball court markers
  Terraces

Special Feature
  Superimposed construction

Monuments

Nature
  Carved stelae and associated altars, often with glyphs
  Associated with dedicatory caches

Location
  In plazas

Artifacts

Ceramics
  Decorated polychromes with "traditional Maya" designs

Obsidian
  Polyhedral cores and their associated prismatic blades

Table 1. (*continued*)

Site Morphology

Appearance
  Orthogonal site plans

Structure groupings
  Temple groups
  Palace groups
  Acropolis
  Quadrangles

References: G. F. Andrews 1975: 1–78; Coe 1965; Hardoy 1973: 206–209, 222, 229, 233; Longyear 1947; Marquina 1964: 506–516; Pollock 1965; Proskouriakoff 1963b; xi–xii, xv–xvii; Ruz 1965; Smith 1950; Thompson 1966: 60–65, 68, 70–71, 73, 77–80; 1970.

Data Summary

The material patterns pertinent to Quirigua and the large sites in its immediate area have been described in detail in several publications (e.g., Sharer 1978a; Jones, Ashmore, and Sharer 1983; Ashmore 1981a). For present purposes it is simply noted that these centers generally possessed those material hallmarks of Maya civilization listed in Table 1. In addition, these researchers have reconstructed a complex, hierarchically arranged socio-economic system with wide-ranging external contacts centered on the powerful ruling dynasty of Quirigua itself (Sharer 1978a, 1979; Jones and Sharer, this volume; Ashmore 1981a, and this volume). Such a reconstruction is fully consonant with similar socio-economic systems reconstructed for other major Maya centers. The lower Motagua valley, itself, is situated within the tropical lowlands of Guatemala between the point where the Motagua valley widens out near Quirigua and the Caribbean coast (see fig. 1). The valley comprises 1800 km² of broad, flat, and agriculturally-rich floodplain (West and Augelli 1976) bounded on the northwest and southeast by the high slopes of the Sierras de las Minas and Espiritu Santo respectively. While the wider valley

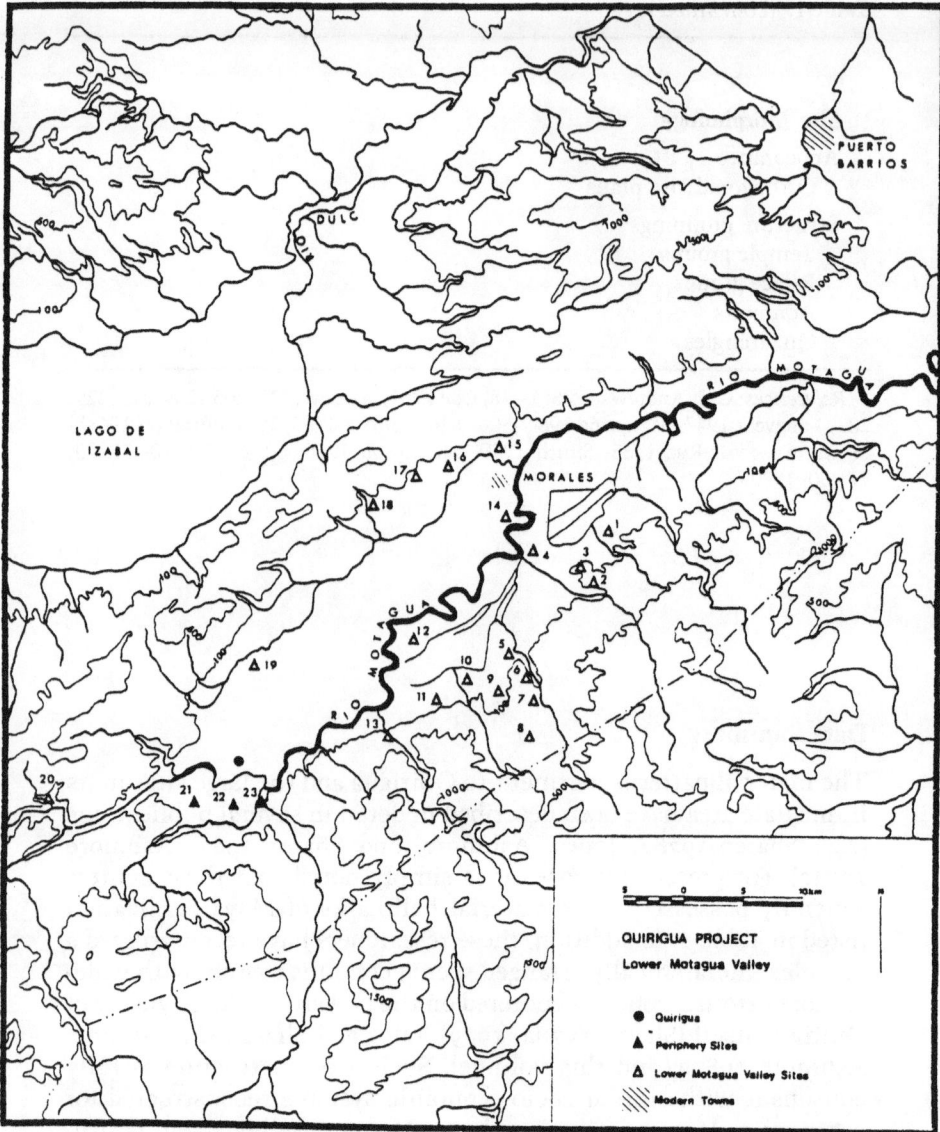

Figure 1. Map showing distribution of major sites mentioned in the text
within the lower Motagua valley: 1) Quebrada Grande; 2) Las Quebradas;
3) Los Cerritos; 4) Bobos; 5) Playitas; 6) Los Limones; 7) Los Vitales;
8) Mojanales; 9) La Coroza; 10) Choco; 11) Araphahoe Viejo; 12) Comanche
Farm; 13) Juyama; 14) Oneida; 15) Cruce de Morales; 16) Monterrey;
17) Fca. America; 18) Puente de Virginia; 19) Cristina; 20) Juan de Paz;
21) Chapulco; 22) Jubuco; 23) Morja.

northeast of Quirigua has long been a focus of intermittent archaeological research, initiated by Karl Sapper in the late nineteenth century (1895, 1897), little has ever been known about it in detail. Timothy Nowak was the first person in recent years to attempt to remedy this situation (1973, 1975). On the basis of his extensive reconnaissance of the valley a concentration of large sites with monumental constructions was noted within a restricted segment in the southern portion of the wider valley. This 180 km² area is defined by the Rio Motagua and the Sierra de Espiritu Santo on the northwest and southeast and the Rios Quebrada Grande and Tepemechines on the northeast and southwest. Following up on Nowak's original work, the author directed a program of survey and test excavations within this area over the course of three field seasons (1977–1979). This program, a part of the general Quirigua Archaeological Project, was designed to record more fully, date, and determine the extensiveness of monumental construction within this subsection of the wider valley. In all, 13 sites were recorded in this area, nine of which contained monumental architecture. A brief survey outside of this zone discovered seven additional sites which, though some were quite large (up to 81 structures), did not contain large-scale constructions. The following discussion will deal primarily with those nine sites containing monumental constructions (see Schortman 1984 for a detailed description of the wider valley work).

Excavated and surface remains indicate that the nine wider valley monumental sites were occupied during a very limited portion of the Late Classic period, from A.D. 700–850 (Quirigua's Hewett and early Morley Phases). It is quite likely, in fact, that most, if not all, of the visible construction at these centers dates to this period as well. All of this points to a remarkably rapid expansion of monumental construction within the southern survey zone. Some evidence of earlier occupation dating back to the Protoclassic and Early Classic periods (50 B.C.–A.D. 500) has been found sporadically within the surveyed zone though the possibility remains that much of·this earlier occupation lies undetected beneath the alluvial silts of the Motagua floodplain as was the case at Quirigua (Ashmore 1980b). To date, however, there is no good evidence to indicate the presence of sites with monumental construction in the research area prior to A.D. 700.

The general material patterns which characterize the nine monumental valley sites will be considered within four principal categories corresponding to those listed in Table 1: site planning, architecture, monuments, and artifacts. In site planning, the wider valley centers show considerable variation in size but not overall configuration (Table 2). Each contains at least one principal monumental

Table 2. Sizes of Monumental Sites within the Surveyed Area
of the Lower Motagua Valley

Site Name	Number of Court Groups	Number of Structures	Number of Disturbed Features[a]
Playitas	4[b]	194	41
Las Quebradas	3	279	11
Quebrada Grande	4	49	0
Choco	1	84	0
Comanche Farm	1	23	0
Juyama	2	109	0
Bobos	1	24	0
Mojanales	1	7	0
Arapahoe Viejo	1	23	0

[a]Disturbed features are concentrations of construction and/or artifactual debris which may represent now-destroyed structures.

[b]One of the Playitas quadrangles is not contemporary with the remaining three; it dates to A.D. 700–750, while the remainder were occupied between A.D. 750 and 850.

group composed of four large substructure platforms 2 to 8 m high, arranged orthogonally around a central court which they enclose on all sides. At least two of the corners providing potential access to the interior court are closed by construction linking adjacent structures and, more commonly, all four corners are sealed in this fashion. The enclosed courts range in area from 920 to 5330 m^2. At the three recorded multi-court sites, Las Quebradas, Playitas, and Quebrada Grande, there is a ranking of contemporary major courts by sizes of component structures, total area covered, and overall complexity. These large sites are dominated by a single court complex composed of two or three adjoining courts of nearly identical form sharing a common structure(s) between them; the remaining courts are much smaller and simpler. The other six monumental sites are much smaller than the three multi-court centers and contain only one or at most two simple courts. Whatever their sizes, excavation and surface data indicate that the wider valley monumental courts served primarily as residences for the local elites.

Surrounding these major architectural foci are smaller structures which appear either singly or, more commonly, in aggregates averaging 3–6 constructions arranged into regular or irregular plaza groups. Structure heights here are generally 1 m or less. On the basis of excavated data and surface configurations these groups appear to have served as residences and loci for the performance of domestic activities for the non-elite segment of the population. The density of these small structures drops off gradually away from the monumental constructions around which they cluster. In multi-court sites, the greatest concentration of smaller structures is found around the largest court unit while each successively smaller and simpler court complex has correspondingly fewer, more dispersed surrounding structures.

In general, there is an absence of structural diversity at all recorded monumental wider valley sites. There are none of the large temple or palace groups found so commonly at large Maya sites (see Andrews 1975) and even the ubiquitous ballcourt has not been securely recognized in the survey zone. Rather, each site is composed of a redundant set of structure configurations which bear a general resemblance to only two Maya architectural groupings: the quadrangle for monumental constructions and the domestic plaza group for smaller ones (Table 1). In the category of architecture, the investigated structures (20 excavated), no matter what their dimensions, are built almost exclusively without the use of cut block masonry. The most common method employed in raising the large substructure platforms of the monumental courts involves the use of unmodified river cobbles, packed round with chinking stones and mud, to construct long, low vertical terrace walls. Surmounting these cobble walls are horizontally-laid schist stone slabs which run back to and under the next ascending terrace wall, forming the ca. 40 cm wide terrace treads. This procedure was often carried all the way to the structure's summit producing substructures composed of a number of narrow terraces which extend the length of the structure and gradually step up in 35 to 40 cm increments. The interdigitation of slab treads and cobble walls coupled with the low height of the terrace risers makes for a very stable construction. Only one example of plastered terrace surfaces was recorded, this at the largest structure at Playitas, Str. 200-77. Evidence for stucco or carved stone architectural ornaments was also restricted to Str. 200-77 at Playitas where Berlin recorded the former presence of stone tenoned heads (1952).

The superstructures topping these monumental platforms were constructed of perishable materials, primarily adobe or bajareque; no standing stone masonry was noted. Excavation suggests that these perishable walls were often set on low stone foundations and there is even some evidence at most of the major sites to indicate the use of pillar bases built of cobbles in the superstructures. The courts which these structures faced were either unpaved or surfaced with a thin level of small pebbles.

The more modest constructions found around the major courts also eschew the use of faced masonry. Two principal construction styles are noted for these small constructions (five excavated examples). In two cases, one each at Playitas and Choco, the basal platform facing stood vertically 60 cm to 1 m high and was built of horizontal courses of river cobbles, packed round with chinking stones, which enclosed a packed earth fill. In the last three situations, all at Las Quebradas, low cobble and chinking stone walls served as risers for broad earthen terraces which stepped up to the summit. In both cases superstructures were made of adobe or bajareque walls, at least some of which were set on a stone footing.

Given the sculptural florescence for which Quirigua is famous, it is somewhat surprising that carved monuments with glyphic texts are absent from the survey zone. While eight monuments were recorded by this project, seven at Las Quebradas and one at Arapahoe Viejo, they consist of one roughly-shaped column (Las Quebradas), one massive, unmodified slab (Las Quebradas), three unmodified white quartz boulders (Las Quebradas) and three pecked stone spheres (two at Las Quebradas and one at Arapahoe Viejo). In contradiction to the very open and accessible locations of the Quirigua monuments in the Great Plaza, and of most Maya monuments in general, these wider valley stones are secluded in the centers of the large enclosed courts. Because of the large percentages of incensario sherds found directly associated with these monuments it appears that they served as foci of ritual activity, perhaps performed by the residents of the surrounding massive structures.

These distinctive wider valley patterns in site plan, architecture, and monuments stand in contrast to the remarkable similarity in pottery exhibited by both Quirigua and wider valley assemblages. By-and-large, only minor differences, most at the varietal level, were noted between Late Classic Quirigua and the wider valley ceramic collections. This suggests the existence in the area of an active regional ceramic tradition at this time. As at Quirigua, the bulk of the pottery recovered from survey and excavation, no matter what the contexts, is composed of utilitarian wares with imported polychromes almost nonexistent. The same likeness of type and form is noted for the incensarios with only one out of the six recorded wider valley types having no counterpart at Quirigua (Benyo 1979).

The wider valley chipped stone assemblages, primarily obsidian, represent both blade-core and flake-core industries (Sheets 1983). The former depended on high-quality imported polyhedral cores and required sufficient skill to suggest the presence of at least part-time specialists in blade manufacture. Flake tools, produced by the simple percussive removal of chips from small obsidian nodules found locally in the river bed of the Motagua, may have been produced on a more informal basis by a larger segment of the society (*Ibid.*). This pattern of stone tool use and manufacture is essentially the same as that noted at Late Classic Quirigua though there may have been more effort devoted at Quirigua to the exclusion of the products of the flake-core tradition from the monumental site core (Sheets 1983; Ashmore 1981a). It seems very likely that much, if not all, of the obsidian needed for blade manufacture came into the research zone through Quirigua which controlled the crucial northeast-southwest route along the Motagua valley into the Guatemalan Highlands and the vast Ixtepeque source zone (Hammond 1972). Beyond ceramics and obsidian, the material remains from the wider valley are very sparse. There is a total absence to date of such elite-associated status items as jade, flint and obsidian eccentrics, carved shell, and so forth. On the level of social integration it now appears that the segment of the valley intensively studied was divided into at least four independent polities each dominated by one large center: Las Quebradas, Playitas, Quebrada Grande, and Choco. The first three are multiple court sites while the single court complex at Choco measures 165 by 95 m overall and is the largest such unit recorded anywhere in the valley. Based on the large and roughly equivalent sizes of these centers, the amounts of labor invested in their monumental constructions, and their fairly regular spacing, on average 5.9 km apart, it is presumed that they served as the seats of the most powerful Late Classic period elites resident in the study area. As noted earlier, the massive court complexes seem to have served as residences and, most probably, the administrative foci of these elites. Presumably the ranking of court groups by size and complexity within multi-court centers reflects the amount of labor their residents could call on for their building projects and, hence, their relative power and prestige. If this correlation is valid, then there is evidence of internal stratification within the elites occupying these largest centers. The area dominated by each of these four sites averaged 57.5 km² (Schortman 1984). In addition to the socially integrative functions served by these four centers they may have played an important economic role as well. Las Quebradas and Playitas specifically are located at strategic control points on two of the few passes to pierce the Sierra de Espiritu Santo mountains heading southeast towards Honduras: those cut by the Rios Bobos and Chinamito respectively. This implies an interest in the control of any commerce which flowed along these routes by the residents of these sites; they may, in fact, have served as important distribution centers for goods entering the valley via these passes. Quirigua's control of a greater number of verifiably important lines of communication, those leading down the Rio Morja towards Copan and the southwest-northeast route along the valley of the Motagua from the Guatemalan Highlands to the Caribbean, probably gave that center greater control over the bulk of valley imports, however (Ashmore 1981a). Subsidiary to these four major centers were those with one or two small court groups: Comanche Farm and Juyama within the Choco district; Mojanales in the Playitas sector; and Bobos in the Las Quebradas area. No center subsidiary to Quebrada Grande has yet been found. Arapahoe Viejo, because of certain site planning peculiarities and its possession of a monument, does not fit in this scheme. At present, it is thought to represent a special-purpose settlement which existed outside the socio-economic hierarchy postulated for the rest of the survey zone (Schortman 1984). The presence of the court complex form at these second level sites on a smaller scale than that found at the major centers indicates the presence of a resident elite group subsidiary to that occupying the closest larger center. Presumably, these second order monumental sites served as local points for the collection of tribute, the distribution of goods, and as small-scale administrative nodes. Surrounding these low-level centers is a series of sites without monumental constructions. The distribution of these loci is poorly known as they were not intensively sought in the survey. Four were found in the study area, ranging from two to eleven structures in size. The organization of constructions here into regular and irregular plaza groupings is similar to that characteristic of the smaller structures surrounding the monumental courts at larger centers. It seems likely that both served the same domestic and residential functions. While at least four hierarchically-arranged independent polities have been recognized within the survey area, each appears to have been characterized by a level of central authority weaker than that characteristic of Maya centers, including Quirigua. All evidence indicates that the elites resident at the wider valley monumental sites performed a restricted range of specialized services for their dependents and, in turn, could exercise only limited control over their labor. This interpretation is based on three lines of reasoning. First, none of the typical luxury items associated with the Classic period Maya elite, e.g., jade and eccentric flints, have been found at the wider valley monumental centers. This implies that the local elites, in addition to not controlling the necessary long-distance trading networks, also possessed insufficient wealth to enable procurement of these items. Second, there is the redundancy of the monumental structure arrangements found at the investigated major sites, marked by the single, double, or triple court group, a mere combination and repetition of the same basic forms. This implies a relatively low level of elite specialization in different activities which, in turn, required specific physical facilities. Most major Maya centers, in contrast, are distinguished not only by the large sizes of their structures but also by the variety of their forms and combinations into groups (Andrews 1975; Shook 1950: 70–93). Insofar as monumental structures were designed and built as the physical facilities for particular elite-level functions, diversity of structure forms and their combinations should grossly reflect the level of complexity and segregation of different elite activities within a particular society. It appears, therefore, that the elite residents within the survey area were less complexly organized than their Maya counterparts, with a less rigid spatial separation of their various activities: in fact, most of their functions may have been dispatched in and around the court complexes in which they lived.

Finally, the multi-court sites have a very segmented appearance: each court unit is surrounded by a cluster of smaller structures whose density decreases towards the fringes of its distribution. This gives the impression of a series of three or four elite residences, each with its own set of immediate adherents, separated from each other by a sparsely inhabited area. Such segmentation may well reflect the absence of a powerful overarching authority capable of organizing these largest of the known centers according to a coherent, centrally focused plan. Ultimately, all the residents of a multi-court site may have owed allegiance to the occupants of the largest court complex and participated in its construction, as its larger size and complexity suggests. Still, the different elite groups in each site appear to have maintained a considerable degree of autonomy as reflected in the spatial separation of their massive residences.

The Model

In order to interpret the distribution of Maya elite items within the lower Motagua valley an attempt must be made to place them in their behavioral contexts (cf. Hodder 1978b: 102, 104, 110; Lange 1976: 180). As has been noted in the specific case of ceramics (Ball 1983), until the cultural roles of artifacts have been inferred, little behavioral information can be gleaned from plotting their distributions (cf. Binford 1962; Haaland 1977: 1–3; Hodder 1978a: 24). One of the analytical weaknesses of the trait-list approach is its combination of the products of a number of different behavioral spheres into a single, monolithic entity, an archaeological culture, on the basis of which comparisons are made and whose significance is assumed, not stated (cf. Shennan 1978: 114–118, 135). A first step, therefore, involves the specification of the behavioral significance of the Maya trait list. It is postulated here that the items listed in Table 1 reflect the existence of a Late Classic Maya elite interaction sphere (Caldwell 1970; Streuver and Houart 1972) or ethnic status (e.g., Barth 1969; Cohen 1978; Shibutani and Kwan 1965) which linked social elites throughout the southern lowlands. The second postulate is that three general factors controlled the spread of these material items within the survey area: local environmental differences, the contents of the cultural systems in contact (the local and Maya elites), and the circumstances in which the interaction took place (cf. Wells 1980). A corollary of this second statement follows from the need to divide the proposed Maya elite subculture into four behavioral subsystems within which the items listed in Table 1 are believed to have functioned. It is only in this way that the behavioral implications of the distribution of any material trait can be understood and the differences in content between cultures in any interac-

Table 3. Characteristics of Major Classic Period Lowland Maya Sites Arranged by Behavioral Categories

Technological

Architecture

Substructure Platforms
  Cut block masonry
  Plaster
  Broad staircases, usually only one on a structure

Superstructures
  Cut block masonry
  Plaster
  Decorations in stucco or stone with the frequent use of paint
  Roof combs
  Stone vault

Special Feature
  Superimposed construction

Artifacts

Ceramics
  Decorated polychromes with "traditional Maya" designs
Obsidian
  Polyhedral cores with their associated prismatic blades

Table 3. (*continued*)

Proxemic
Special Structures
  Terraces
Site Morphology

Appearance
  Orthogonal site plans
Structure Groupings
  Temple groups
  Palace groups
  Acropolises
  Quadrangles

Monuments
Location
  In plazas

Ideological
Architecture

Superstructures
  Temple and shrine forms
  Burials and caches associated with construction; burials also found
    beneath the floors of residential structures
Special Structures
  Ball courts and ball court markers

Monuments
Nature
  Carved stelae and associated altars, often with glyphs
  Associated with dedicatory caches
Location
  In plazas
Structure Groupings
  Temple group

Social
Architecture

Superstructures
  Temple, palace and shrine forms
Site Morphology
  Temple groups
  Palace groups
  Acropolises
  Quadrangles

tion measured. The four postulated subsystems are the technological, proxemic, social, and ideological.

We turn first to the definition of the four behavioral subdivisions. Table 3 illustrates how the items within the Maya trait list (Table 1) are distributed among the proposed cultural subsystems.

The technological class consists of those material traits which reflect a society's methods of construction and production. Their dissemination depends on the mastery of a set of mechanical skills, access to the appropriate raw materials, and an acquired taste for the item involved (Haaland 1977: 16). The distribution of these items is primarily controlled by environmental factors. The one complicating exception involves the factor of "acquired taste." Reina and Hill (1978) have recently pointed out the importance of the consumer's conception of what makes a "good pot" to the current distribution of types of ceramic vessels within the Guatemalan Highlands. This *costumbre* (*Ibid.*), or traditional conception of appropriateness, limits both the range of variation a producer can introduce and the marketing strategy of the trader who transports the vessels. The result is a coherent pattern in the spatial distribution of ceramic styles and forms. It is on this point of acquired taste or "standards of appropriateness" that the technological and ideological realms overlap to some extent.

The proxemic category includes those elements which reflect a society's conception of the proper use of space (e.g., Hall 1973). In Table 3, the fact that Temple Groups are associated with open plazas while Palace and Quadrangle Groups are not suggests that certain religious ceremonies associated with the first structure group were meant to be observed by large audiences while elite residential activities carried out in the last two contexts were intended to remain private.

The ideological realm includes those features which reflect something of the belief structure of a group, both its religious views and the underlying rationalizations for the social system. Maya glyphic inscriptions fit well in this class as they enjoyed a complex and extensive relationship to both cosmological (calendrics) and political (dynastic histories) aspects of elite Maya life. Religious structures and signs of ritual performance also fit in this category as does interment of the dead, insofar as it reflects a conception of the afterlife and the relation of the dead to the living.

Finally, within the social category are objects suggesting the range of activities carried out at a site which involve the articulation of individuals within a coherent interacting group. The importance of these activities and the extent to which they required special facilities for their performance are all factors which are included in this category. As noted earlier, the assumption here is that the larger and more complexly organized a society is, the more diversified and specialized will be the activities carried out to articulate all segments of it. This should find material expression in the size of public architecture, its diversity of form and groupings, and the sizes and numbers of residences built to house the governing social segment. The structure forms listed in Table 3 fall within this class as do the structure groupings.

The factors controlling the dissemination of elements which functioned within the last three categories are social, relating more to the cultural contents of the groups in contact than to any environmental factors.

The list presented in Table 3 is probably incomplete. Further, more detailed study of Maya monumental centers would assuredly reveal other, more subtle, material similarities which could be related to these four behavior classes. It is also inevitable that there will be some overlap between any set of proposed behavioral categories; elements included in one might well be found in others as well. The reason for this is that behavioral typologies divide what had been a coherent cultural system into a number of subdivisions for the purposes of analysis. In reality, however, any one material item, say the Temple Group in this case, is formed by a number of different factors and, hence, reflects those factors to some degree. In the case of the Temple Group, the arrangement of these massive structures owes something to the Maya concept of the proper use of space (proxemics), to their system of religious beliefs (ideology), and, further, reflects the complex nature of the society which built and was integrated through these special structures (social). Despite these problems, the proposed classification provides an initial basis for understanding why certain elements of the Maya elite material pattern did not spread widely within the Late Classic lower Motagua valley. It does this by specifying more precisely the content of the Maya elite cultural pattern that came into contact with that possessed by the wider valley elite and by requiring that an explanation of the distribution of the material elements in each behavioral class be phrased in terms of a set of factors relevant to that particular class (Binford 1962; Cohen 1978: 383). The traditional Maya trait list, in short, is not a single monolithic entity whose distribution reflects the operation of one set of factors. Given this interpretive scheme, we can now turn to what the traditional Maya trait list may reflect in behavioral terms.

The concept of the interaction sphere, first developed to account for the widespread occurrence of the Hopewell phenomenon in eastern North America (Caldwell 1970), presumes the existence of spatially extensive, regularly used lines of communication along which information and material pertaining to a limited range of behaviors are transferred. Outside of these similarities the inter-communicating groups maintain distinct material patterns pertaining to those behavioral spheres which are not shared. An ethnic status, on the other hand, refers to a self-conciously distinct social unit within which a great number of basic assumptions, value orientations, and standards of evaluating proper behavior are shared (Barth 1969: 13–15; Cohen 1978: 383, 397–398; Fishman 1977: 16, 22–24, Shibutani and Kwan 1965). This social group is linked to other similarly-organized segments within a larger society by a limited range of shared assumptions which guide mutually intelligible behaviors in an equally limited range of standardized interaction situations (*Ibid.*).

The material correlates of an interaction sphere are the distribution of a limited set of material items found in similar associations/ contexts which functioned in one behavioral sphere but in a number of otherwise distinct local cultures. An ethnic status, however, is recognized by the existence of a number of spatially limited and distinct aggregates of material items associated with the full range of behavioral spheres within one reconstructed society. To be sure, the mere existence of shared aspects of material culture does not necessarily indicate the presence of a distinct ethnic unit (Barth 1969: 13–15). The ethnographic recognition of these "subcultures" places primary emphasis on how the participants categorize themselves rather than on the distribution of distinctive material features, variation in some of which at least may be due as much to ecological as social factors (*Ibid.*). In trying to determine the former existence of ethnic groups, therefore, emphasis must be placed on the recognition of distinct associations of artifacts which functioned in those behavioral spheres which are most likely to reflect a group's basic assumptions, value orientations, and standards of evaluation. Within the present formulation, the relevant behavioral spheres are the proxemic, social, and ideological. This is based on the assumption that embedded in these categories are those core beliefs which determine how a group perceives itself, the social and physical world around it, and the propriety of individual behaviors. Variation in elements related to the technological realm is less significant in defining ethnic groups as the distribution of these items is more likely to be controlled by non-cultural, environmental forces than those which pertain to the other three categories.

The Late Classic lowland Maya phenomenon is defined on the

basis of a coherent association of material traits which represent the full range of proposed behavioral systems and yet are distributed over a very wide area. It seems, therefore, that the Late Classic Maya partook of elements of the interaction sphere in the extensiveness of their spatial distribution and ethnic group in the comprehensiveness of their shared elements reflecting a wide range of shared assumptions/beliefs. I propose, therefore, that by the Late Classic all of the sites traditionally defined as Maya in the southern lowlands, including Quirigua, were occupied by participants in a large-scale, intercommunicating ethnic network. This system incorporated elite segments residing in what may otherwise have been distinct local cultures who saw themselves as a group apart with their own pan-Maya identity and shared concerns. They maintained a basic set of assumptions and standards for evaluating "proper Maya" behavior as reflected by the distribution of artifacts which operated within the proxemic, social, and ideological spheres. Ties between the dispersed Maya elite might well have been initiated and maintained through various sorts of exchanges: economic, e.g., trading (Rathje 1972); ceremonial (Adams 1971); and social, e.g., marriage alliances (Molloy and Rathje 1974). Perhaps Freidel's concept of an elite Maya "ethos" (1979) might best be applied to this situation rather than either the interaction sphere or the ethnic group. This elite ethos had become established by the Early Classic over most of the southern lowlands and may have had its genesis in the Late Preclassic (Freidel 1979).

Having outlined the model with its basic set of assumptions the following section is devoted to applying it to the specific case of the Late Classic lower Motagua valley.

Interpretation

Given that the Maya resident at Late Classic Quirigua were participants in the elite Maya ethos, we can now consider why the elites in the wider valley were not members as well. As stated in the second postulate of the model, this explanation is phrased in terms of differences in the environments occupied by the elite at Quirigua and the wider valley, differences in their cultural contents and the nature of their interaction.

Differences in Environment

The presence of elements of the Maya technological sphere at Quirigua and its immediate neighbors and their absence at wider valley

sites reflects no more than the differential distribution of the necessary raw materials. It is obvious from even a casual examination that
river cobbles, the most common building material in the survey
area, are abundant near most of the wider valley monumental centers. Similarly, easily worked sandstone and rhyolite are found close-
by Quirigua. While detailed geological surveys have not been carried
out within the wider valley, no sandstone or rhyolite outcrops were
seen during the survey or were reported by informants. While there
is undoubtedly an element of the aesthetic here, a view that the
technological traits listed in Table 3 were important elements in a
Maya structure, their distribution within the lower Motagua valley
must owe something to such prosaic aspects as ready access to appropriate resources. There would certainly be no advantage in learn-
ing the techniques of, say, cut block masonry or acquiring a taste for
it if it were impractical to use in construction. As noted earlier, the
absence of staircases in the research zone probably owes much to
another technological factor: the manner of building in low step-
terraces removes the need for any formalized means of summit
access.

Differences in Culture Content

On the basis of first principles, traits related to the proxemic category should not spread easily from one cultural system to another.
This is primarily because concepts on the proper use of space are
learned "out-of-awareness" and, hence, form assumptions which are
crucial to daily life and perceptions and are rarely consciously considered (Hall 1973: 162–185). As a result, the presence of a similar
structure arrangement, the quadrangle, associated with the same set
of elite residential/administrative functions at Quirigua (the Acropolis and Group 3C-2; Ashmore 1981a, this volume; Sharer 1978a)
and the monumental wider valley centers suggests the existence of a
widespread set of underlying shared proxemic assumptions. The distribution of the quadrangle within the known portion of the valley
may be due to the existence of a broad, ancient, valley-wide tradition
of structure arrangement. The absence of any pre-A.D. 700 wider valley monumental centers in which this form might have functioned
calls this view into question. Another, more plausible, view holds
that the ubiquity of this form results from its having been borrowed
wholesale from the residents of Quirigua by the newly developing
wider valley elite. If the absence of earlier wider valley monumental
structures is not merely a result of sampling error and alluvial burial, it would seem that the local elites did not have a long tradition of

hierarchic social organization and the construction of facilities associated with its functions. As a result, they may have had no model for their large-scale constructions other than that provided by the Maya at Quirigua. As the residents of the wider valley had no pre-existing notions of how to organize "elite space" any such proxemic conceptions from Quirigua could have been readily accepted as they did not conflict with existing proxemic assumptions. Only further work in the valley will be able to untangle this problem. At present, in this segment of the proxemic level, there is similarity in culture content between Quirigua and the large wider valley sites.

The cultural differences between Quirigua and its surrounding area on the one hand and the wider valley on the other are most marked in the social and ideological realms. The absence of diverse Maya structural forms and groups in the survey area most likely reflects the lack of any need for them there. As noted earlier, it is probable that the societies integrated through these monumental sites were neither sufficiently large nor complexly enough segmented to warrant the investment of labor in the construction of special facilities for different elite-level activities. The social systems focused on the wider valley centers were much simpler than those of the Classic Maya lowlands and probably did not require a set of specialized, large-scale activities to integrate them into a cohesive unit.

Just as Maya structure groupings and types could not easily spread to societies where the level of complexity did not require them, so too would elements associated with their ideological system be limited. The glyphic inscriptions which filled roles in both the religion (calendrics) and social justification (dynastic histories) of Maya society could not be easily transferred to areas where these complex conditions did not already exist (cf. Hodder 1977: 247). Coupled with this limitation is the tremendous body of knowledge the recipient group would have had to master before they could read or write in this script. As a result, the absence of glyphic inscriptions in the simpler social systems of the wider valley is not at all surprising. Further, what is currently known about wider valley religious practices, with their ceremonial foci (the monuments) hidden away in inaccessible portions of the sites, conflicts with what is known from the Classic period southern Maya lowlands. The latter seem to have performed at least some of their rituals for large audiences, hence the open nature of the Temple Groups. If these religious differences were significant and widespread there would have been little incentive, and perhaps much resistance, to adopt elite Maya religious practices and their material manifestations.

Nature of the Interaction

The points that are of relevance here are self-conscious exclusiveness on the part of the Maya elite at Quirigua and competition between centers over land and trade. The protagonists were the Maya elite at Quirigua and the wider valley elites.

The Maya at Quirigua may well have consciously striven to restrict access to those traits which defined their participation in the Maya elite ethos. If, as seems plausible, the Late Classic rulers of Quirigua were an intrusive element in the valley (Kelley 1962; Morley 1935; Sharer 1978a) they may well have wished to maintain their self-esteem through their distinctiveness as a non-local group whose ties lay towards other "high prestige" zones, i.e., the southern Peten or Copan. It may also have been to the elite group's material benefit to maintain their exclusive participation in the Maya ethos in order to play an important role in any long-distance trading which involved other major Maya centers. If Late Classic commerce in the southern Maya lowlands were elite controlled (e.g., Rathje 1972) it may have been crucial to Quirigua's economic position to maintain the symbols and, hence, membership in that elite group. If these symbols and the knowledge of their use were allowed to spread throughout the valley then other centers might have been in a better position to compete with Quirigua for control of that trade.

The last point brings up the question of intra-valley competition. Ethnographic (Barth, ed., 1969; Cohen 1978: 396–397; Collins 1975: 70–72; Despres 1975: Fishman 1977: 26–27; Hodder 1977, 1979; Knutsson 1969: 90–95, 99) and archaeological (Brose 1979) research has pointed out that one element which contributes to the exclusive distribution of material culture between two adjoining ethnic groups is competition for the same set of resources. Under this condition, various cultural features, material and non-material, which distinguish one group from another are emphasized as symbols of the corporate will to compete (Shibutani and Kwan 1965: 220, 465). They also act to facilitate the identification of group members and provide an unambiguous means of assigning rights of access to the available resources (Barth 1969: 25–26; Brose 1979; Haaland 1969: 71; Shibutani and Kwan 1965: 577). As a result, competition, active and unresolved or traditionally resolved through the allocation of specific resources to particular ethnic groups, places a premium on the participants' ability to clearly assign each individual to a particular social/ethnic unit. This, in turn, results in the proliferation of social symbols. Within the Late Classic lower Motagua valley, competition between all monumental sites, including Quirigua, may have been over both local resources and external trade routes. Some evidence has appeared to suggest that cash-cropping, possibly of cacao, was important to the Late Classic economy of the region (Ashmore 1981a; Schortman 1984). Competition over land suitable for growing this crop may, therefore, have played a role in relations between the Maya and the non-Maya segments of the valley. More obvious is the location of three of the largest valley sites, Quirigua, Las Quebradas, and Playitas, along potential routes of communication leading out of the region. This distribution suggests the importance of inter-regional commerce to their residents and there may well have been some contesting for its control. Quirigua, therefore, would have maintained its distinctive material elements and striven to restrict their dissemination.

At the same time, within the survey area the two sites which controlled passes out of the valley, Playitas and Las Quebradas, also maintained material differences as they too competed to control the flow of goods into the valley. The latter interaction involved fewer imperishable material symbols than those distinguishing Quirigua from the wider valley centers in general. The Playitas-Las Quebradas distinction is reflected in some differences in site morphology: Las Quebradas has two large open plazas incorporated into two of its court complexes, each with one side devoid of a structure, while Playitas does not; and the presence of monuments at Las Quebradas and their absence at Playitas. These factors are related to the proxemic and ideological realms of behavior respectively and hint at significant differences in the nonmaterial value orientations of both societies. This difference suggests that the wider valley elite may not have comprised as homogeneous an ethnic unit as was first presumed. More work and detailed analysis may indicate that even within this restricted zone there was some variation in shared assumptions and perceptions which are manifest in slight divergences in material patterns. Whatever these differences are, however, it seems secure that within the research area the elite still shared a great number of basic values and assumptions as reflected by the distribution of material items which functioned in the proxemic, social, and ideological realms of behavior. They certainly shared far more assumptions with each other than they did with their Maya counterparts at Quirigua.

Continued Contact

Inter-site competition and a desire to maintain exclusive knowledge did not preclude regular interaction between the different Late Clas-

sic social systems within the valley. Such exclusion is not necessarily the case ethnographically in competitive situations (Barth
1969: 10; Hodder 1977, 1979). The very existence of distinct ethnic
groups may depend on some degree of opposition and contact between them (e.g., Cohen 1978; Shibutani and Kwan 1965). The great
similarities in the ceramic assemblages of Quirigua and the other
monumental Late Classic valley centers would certainly argue
against all cessation of intercourse. Further, if, as has been argued
here and elsewhere (Schortman 1984; Sharer 1979) Quirigua were
the principal middleman for the valley's supply of imported goods,
especially obsidian, some inter-site commerce would have been
essential.

Summary

A set of factors which together played important roles in determining the differential distribution of Maya elite traits within the Late
Classic lower Motagua valley has been presented. They fall within
three major categories: the physical environments of the interacting
groups, differences in their respective culture contents, and the circumstances of their interaction. The fact that all of these factors
seem to have played a role in patterning the observed distribution
probably accounts for the depth of the material differences between
Quirigua and the wider valley. It is far from certain, however, that all
of the relevant factors have been identified. In fact, this interpretation and the model on which it is based should be treated as tentative and subject to further testing and revision. Despite these lingering uncertainties, however, I believe that this preliminary effort has
some merit in providing a means of looking at, and extracting information from, the distribution of material traits in this portion of the
Southeast Maya Periphery. Its true utility, however, can only be
gauged when it has been tested in the lower Motagua valley and
applied to other areas along the periphery.

General Application and Problems

Ultimately, a greater body of information about the Classic period
Maya lowlands themselves will be required before the full behavioral
implications of the distribution of elite Maya material traits along
the Southeast Mesoamerican Periphery can be obtained. Variations
in the elite Maya pattern from site to site must be outlined to determine, first, if the general homogeneity attributed the "Maya culture" of the southern lowlands is borne out and, second, whether

slight differences in that pattern might conform to regional "sub-cultures." Quirigua, itself, with its paucity of large ritual structures (temples) and deposits (caches and burials) does not fully conform to the general Maya pattern at the ideological level and may not be unique in this divergence. A greater understanding must also be obtained of the total range of Classic lowland Maya material culture and its relation to different behavioral spheres. This requires data gathered at both major centers and small residential loci. Only in this way can it be determined whether there was a degree of cultural homogeneity in the general Maya lowlands that parallels that postulated for the Maya elite alone. Finally, more information is needed on the full range of settlement and material culture of the societies that existed along the southern Maya periphery. Beginnings are being made along these lines (e.g., Agurcia 1980, this volume; Ashmore, ed., 1981; Robinson, this volume; Urban, this volume). It is only against this background that more detailed comparisons of Maya society and the groups they contacted in the southeast can be made.

In a broader sense, the approach advocated here may have some general utility for the study of all areas peripheral to zones of major cultural developments. It is pointless to ask in these situations whether a given site is a member of a particular cultural tradition, like the Maya, or not. Rather, the question which should be asked is why certain material items, and their behavioral correlates, were accepted by a peripheral society and others rejected. Along the edges of any complex cultural development there are bound to be a number of local social systems with different cultural contents, occupying different environments, and interacting with different segments of the more complex culture under a variety of circumstances for different purposes. The result is that a number of different complex forces will act to pattern the distribution of material items associated with the complex culture along the periphery. A corollary of this position is that as these conditioning elements change, environment, cultural content, and circumstances of contact, the nature and location of the periphery as defined by artifact patterns will also shift. Such a complex peripheral situation has recently been discussed by Wells (1980) for the contact between the classical Mediterranean world and central European elites in the period from 600–400 B.C. and is certainly not uncommon. As a result, a great deal of information on the structure of the societies involved and the circumstances of their interaction is embodied in the patterning of material items along the peripheries of complex cultures and remains to be retrieved. The model proposed here is but a suggestion towards accomplishing this goal.

A Reexamination of Stela Caches at Copan: New Dates for Copador

The Late Classic center of Copan produced, in its final florescence, a polychrome type of pottery called Copador. In the past, Copador has often been dated to roughly A.D. 650–700. The evidence for this dating developed from the excavation of substela caches at Copan by the Carnegie Institution of Washington during the 1930s and 1940s. Four of these caches produced Copador material. A closer examination of the caches and their monuments, however, does not substantiate this previously accepted dating and consequently our dating of Copan's last period of occupation is altered.

Stela A Cache

Stela A is dated to 9.15.0.0.0 (A.D. 731). As is common at Copan, the cruciform chamber below the stela is covered with a large cylindrical stone which also serves as a base for the stela butt (fig. 1). This cache, located on the floor of the chamber, consisted of a disk of Copador pottery and a probable Copador sherd. A rodent pelvis and two chips of white igneous rock may have been part of the deposit. In this instance, the association of Copador material and the stela is indisputable.

Stela I Cache

Stela I is dated to 9.12.5.0.0 (A.D. 685). Stromsvik (1941) identified two chambers associated with this monument (fig. 2). One was located directly under the stela and was an integral part of the stela foundation. The second chamber was located west of, and abutting, the first. Stromsvik speculates that this second chamber was associated with the stela's altar, located further to the west. The chamber directly below the stela contained a variety of artifacts including three small red cache jars. The second chamber contained several Copador vessels.

The association between the dated Stela I and the substela cache is clear. However, the connection between the monument and the second chamber remains clouded. In fact, the location of this chamber may indicate that it was constructed at some date following the erection of the stela for example as a part of a rededication ceremony for the monument. Thus, Copador vessels found within the chamber can not be dated to A.D. 685, as previously hypothesized.

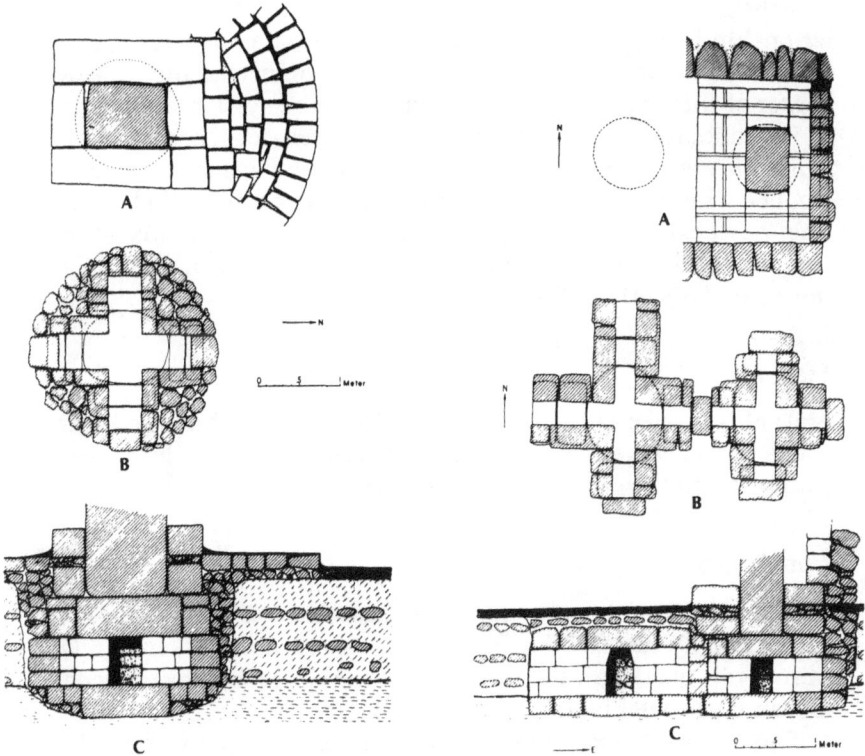

Figure 1. Copan, Stela A setting and cache chamber (from Stromsvik 1941: Fig. 1).

Figure 2. Copan, Stela I setting and cache chambers (from Stromsvik 1941: Fig. 3).

Stela J Cache

Stela J is dated to 9.13.10.0.0 (A.D. 700). Directly below this monument was a cache chamber of the common Copan cruciform shape. Five cache vessels and a buff, handled jar were found within this cache. Another chamber was discovered underneath the southeast corner of an altar located in front of Stela J. This small chamber was constructed of three tiers of roughly cut masonry with the top course slightly beveled to produce an arch-like shape. Twenty-one vessels were located within this cache chamber, including two Copador pots. Stromsvik (1941) stated that the "corner of the structure at the junction of the south and west arms was torn out in ancient times, apparently to make room for the large number of pottery vessels in the cache."

Although the altar is located directly in front of the stela, the relationship between the two monuments remains unclear. Even if, however, the two monuments are contemporaneous, the destroyed corner of the altar cache chamber brings into question the integrity of its contents. The chamber may have been reopened in ancient times during a rededication ceremony and new ceramic vessels introduced, thereby mixing vessels from different time periods. Therefore, any chance of applying an absolute date to the material from this altar cache has been destroyed. Again, the Copador material can not be tied directly to Stela J.

Stela M Cache

Stela M is dated 9.16.5.0.0 (A.D. 756). The contents of this dedicatory cache include several Copador vessels. Here there is a clear association between the cache and the dated stela.

Conclusions

This reexamination, showing a direct association of Copador material with only two dated monuments, Stela A (A.D. 731) and Stela M (A.D. 756), may indicate that this pottery was not introduced to Copan until roughly A.D. 730.

This theory is strengthened by other data from the rest of the southeast Maya area. Quirigua, the second major site within this region, was also occupied during the Late and Terminal Late Classic periods. The relationship between the cities of Copan and Quirigua remains unclear. Quirigua was apparently greatly influenced, and maybe even controlled, by Copan during the early part of the Late

Table 1. Copador Found within Copan Stela Caches

---

1. **Stela A (9.15.0.0.0)**
   Copador sherd, reworked as a disk

2. **Stela I (9.12.5.0.0)**
   2 chambers
   1. Stela chamber: no Copador
   2. Chamber to west: 2 Copador cylinders
                      1 Copador bowl
                      1 small Copador jar
                      2 Copador jars

3. **Stela J (9.13.10.0.0)**
   2 chambers
   1. Stela chamber: no Copador
   2. Altar chamber: 1 Copador cylinder
                   1 Copador effigy jar
                   1 Copador two-handled jar

4. **Stela M (9.16.5.0.0)**
   1 tall concave-walled Copador vase
   1 Copador vase

Classic. Site layout and hieroglyphic similarities indicate that the two centers were closely related. At both sites, a long, low, major plaza area, filled with tall, carved monuments of the rulers, sharply contrasts with a massive towering acropolis to the south. At both Copan and Quirigua, the transition from the plaza to the acropolis is achieved through the ballcourt and the adjoining structures. Recent archaeological work at both sites indicates that this similarity extends to the regions around the center where elite residential areas are connected to the center by a large sacbe. However, during the recent major excavation program of the University of Pennsylvania at Quirigua, virtually no Copador pottery was recovered (Sharer 1978a). This difference in the Late Classic polychromes of Copan and Quirigua supports the often discussed hypothesis of a political schism between these two major cities. Epigraphers have recently argued that Copan and Quirigua broke political and economic connections at roughly 9.15.6.14.6. or A.D. 737 (see Jones and Sharer, this volume; Reise, this volume). It appears that Quirigua waged war with Copan, perhaps captured or killed the Copan ruler 18 Rabbit, and then claimed its independence. Copan was therefore no longer the center of power within this southern area, and may have been cut off from contact with the Guatemalan highlands and the southern lowlands.

The new examination of the substela caches shows that it is at this time that Copador appears at Copan. At about A.D. 735, Copan was forced to turn its priorities away from the highlands and southern lowlands and shift its attention to the south (western and central El Salvador) and to the east (central Honduras). During this time, Copador, or an antecedent such as Arambala, was probably a minor local ceramic type within western El Salvador. Copan, cut off from its sources for elite pottery from the highlands and southern lowlands, probably adopted Copador as its own and began to manufacture it as its primary polychrome type. This A.D. 730 date for the arrival of Copador at Copan explains the lack of this ceramic style at Quirigua.

Such a model of shifting allegiances within the southeast may also suggest the reasons for Copan's early demise shortly after A.D. 800. Prior to its defeat and break with Quirigua, Copan may have functioned as a funnel for goods and ideas moving between the northern regions of the Guatemalan highlands and southern lowlands and the southern areas of the frontier zone of Central America. However, Copan's break with Quirigua changed its relations not only with the southern lowlands, but also with the areas to the east and south. Although it may have remained one of the most important and powerful cities within this frontier zone, Copan was not part of the Maya cultural sphere to the north and could not derive its power as an intermediary for the southern lowlands. It was no longer located at a central economic node, but was now on the outer edge of the frontier zone. Its original reasons for preeminence were eliminated. After a brief hundred years, Copan was no longer the controlling power of the Maya southeast frontier region.

RONALD L. BISHOP, MARILYN P. BEAUDRY, RICHARD M. LEVENTHAL, AND ROBERT J. SHARER

11

Compositional Analysis of Copador and Related Pottery in the Southeast Maya Area

Background of the Project

The Late Classic period in the southeast Maya area was the time of flourishing economic and administrative centers like Copan and Quirigua. Available data suggest considerable communication and trade during this period both within this general region and beyond. One of the ceramic indicators for this era is Copador, a highly distinctive cream paste ware found with varying frequencies throughout the southeast region. A standardized and limited design repertoire has been judged as being evidence of specialized production. From the "criterion of abundance" Copador's place of manufacture has been postulated as being centered in the Copan area. Its distribution, then, is thought to have been the result of trade from the manufacturing zone of Copan.

This reconstruction of Copador's specialized production in a restricted geographic area with distribution to the various known proveniences has been used by archaeologists for some time as a working hypothesis but has never been subjected to detailed investigation. If accurate, it would lead to several test implications which can be empirically assessed:

1. Centralized production in one area would result in the utilization of clays from a similarly restricted geographic area. Clays from the same procurement zone often tend to be quite similar in their

trace elemental composition (cf. Brooks *et al.* 1974, Bishop 1980). Thus, if Copador is the product of this type of resource procurement and production, specimens should show very similar chemical paste compositional characteristics regardless of their provenience.

2. Centralized production of Copador in the Copan area would result in corresponding trace elemental composition of clays used for Copador and for other similar ceramic wares judged to be indigenous to the Copan valley. Some variability might be engendered due to a temper-clay interaction effect if the "local" wares were heavily tempered since the "fine" Copador ware was not. Nevertheless, a basic correspondence would be expected if Copador had been manufactured in the Copan valley.

Other ceramic components from the southeast Maya area also raise questions about production and trade which can benefit from empirical study. For example, other cream paste ceramics, Chilanga Red-Painted Usulutan and Gualpopa Polychrome, are found in approximately the same distribution area as Copador. One of these, Chilanga, appears to be temporally earlier than Copador. Questions arise about these ceramic types *vis-a-vis* Copador. Do the various components of the southeast Maya cream paste tradition all represent products of a similar type of an economic subsystem or can differences in the pattern of utilization and production be detected among the types? Does production-related data about Chilanga give any insight into the development and spread of the more recent Copador (and, secondarily, of Gualpopa)?

A polychrome type, Arambala—not illustrated here—stylistically related to Copador and seemingly coeval with it, is also of interest because of its occurrence within the general Copador distribution area; Arambala, however, is not a part of the cream paste tradition, having been made of red-firing clays. As such, it is not compositionally germane to the present investigation. Stylistically, however, questions arise about its role during the Late Classic period in the southeast area. Was it perhaps a substitute for Copador? Can centers of Arambala production be distinguished from that of Copador? We cannot, at present, answer these questions but the stylistic similarity, which crosscuts very different wares, is important for a synthesis of Late Classic ceramic traditions in the southeast area.

In order to investigate aspects of regional ceramic production and distribution, a cooperative effort was initiated to examine the three primary fine paste, cream ceramic wares—Copador, Gualpopa, and Chilanga. Pottery for the study came from a number of field projects recently conducted in the southeast Maya area (fig. 1). Three different geographic zones—western Honduras, western and west-central

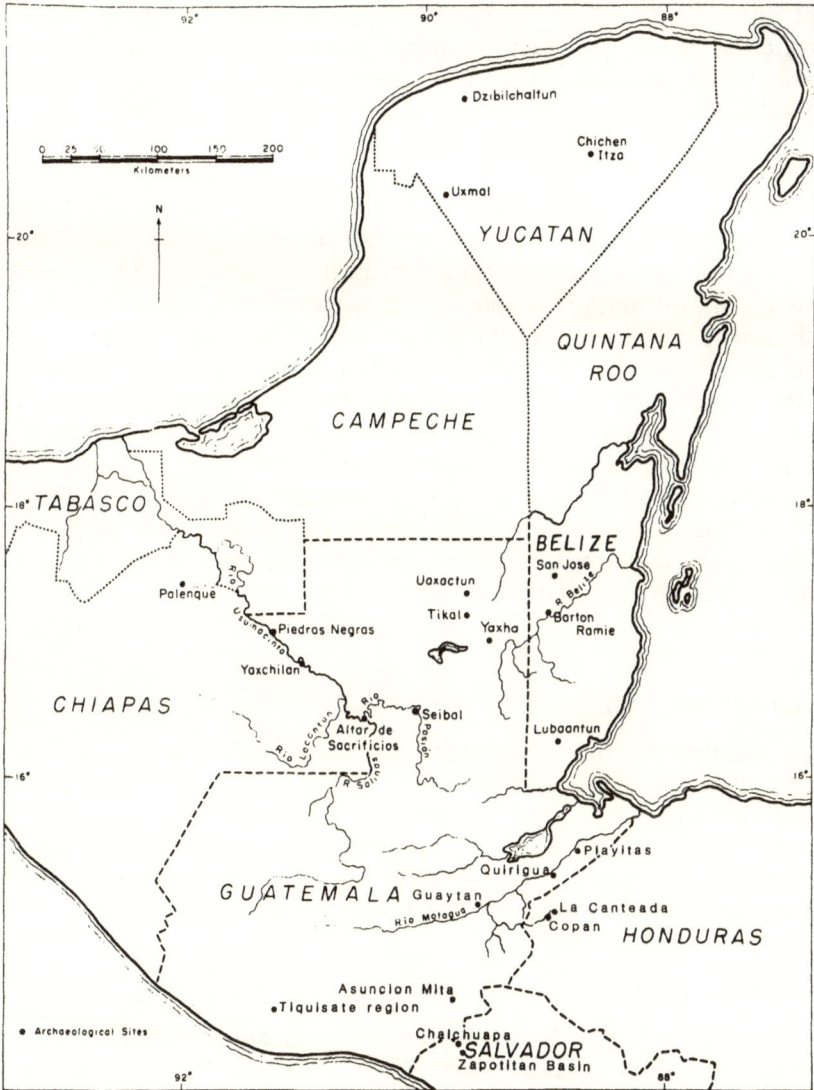

Figure 1. Map of the Maya area including sites or regions referred to in text.

El Salvador, the middle and lower Motagua valley of Guatemala—were the foci of these investigations. Additional materials collected from other sources added to the data base and widened the geographic scope of the compositional analysis.[1]

Overview of the Methodology

Since a major objective was the attribution of the ceramics to their production zone, our approach utilized chemical compositional analysis. This method enables the investigator to assess the level of similarity or difference in the trace element patterning of samples of ceramic materials. Conclusions can then be reached about the probable resource procurement and production zone(s) of the vessels. Specifically, Instrumental Neutron Activation Analysis for chemical trace element characterization was the method applied. X-ray diffraction, petrographic examination, and mineralogical separation were utilized to evaluate the mineralogical composition of a subsample of the pottery. The elemental information generated by the activation process was then subjected to multivariate statistical analysis.

Natural Environment of the Study Area

As mentioned, three different subregions of the southeastern Maya area were the focus for the current investigation. Each zone has a unique natural and cultural setting within which ceramic compositional data must be assessed. This section will provide a geographic and geologic perspective of the environments. The next section will describe the archaeological sites in each of the zones.

Rio Copan Zone, Western Honduras

The ruins of Copan lie in the western part of Honduras within a small valley carved by the Copan River. The Copan River flows westward into the Motagua drainage through the Central American highlands, some of the most rugged terrain of the region. The river forms a series of small valleys or pockets which are, from west to east, the Copan valley, Santa Rita, El Jaral, the lower Rio Amarillo, and the upper Rio Amarillo. Turner *et al.* (1983) have defined four principal physiographic zones of these valleys: 1) the floodplain; 2) the river terraces; 3) the foothills; and 4) the ridge slopes. The pockets of Santa Rita, El Jaral, and the lower Rio Amarillo are all extremely small, and combined make up an area of less than 4 km^2 of valley bottomlands. The upper Rio Amarillo forms a much larger pocket with almost 9 km² of bottomlands. The main ruins of Rio Amarillo are located along the southern edge of the bottomlands.

The westernmost pocket, the Copan valley, is the largest along the Copan River system. The entire valley measures about 10 to 12 km east-west and averages about 2.5 km north-south, creating an area of between 25 to 30 km². Approximately half of this area consists of well watered bottomlands, extremely good for agriculture. The floodplain, of varying width, is a fairly small part of the bottomlands. Terraces ranging in height from 5 to 10 m above the river, dominate the bottomlands. Foothills gradually rise upward from the river terraces and merge into steep, rugged upper ridge slopes.

Middle and Lower Motagua Valley, Guatemala

The Motagua river and its tributaries provide the major drainage from the Guatemalan highlands eastwards, emptying into the Caribbean at the Gulf of Amatique. For most of its length the valley coincides with the Motagua fault, a major rift forming the margin of two continental plates (see Plafker 1976). The mountainous margins of the valley are composed of a great variety of geological formations, mostly of metamorphic (serpentine and schist/gneiss with quartz, mica, and feldspars) and sedimentary (sandstones and, near the Caribbean, limestone) origins (West 1964). In the lower Motagua valley, defined by an active flood plain that begins just west of Quirigua, there are narrow bands of igneous (rhyolite) materials. Volcanic deposits overlay many of these deposits, especially in the middle portion of the valley.

Western and West-Central El Salvador

The country can be divided into four major topographic units based on structure, age, and origin (Daugherty 1969). These are the coastal plain, the coastal mountains, the interior structural trough, and the northern mountains. Of particular interest to this project is the interior trough which is ringed with Late Pleistocene and Recent volcanoes along its southern edge and has occasional earlier volcanoes along its northern edge.

Chalchuapa, in western El Salvador, is situated in this trough, in a broad basin drained by the Rio Paz and its tributaries, some 700 m above sea level. Climate and environmental conditions are best described as transitional between lowland (coastal) and highland types (Vivo Escoto 1964). The entire region is dominated by recent volcanic activity (West 1964). The Sierra Lamatepeque y Apaneca, including the extinct volcano Santa Ana and the recently active cone of Izalco, bounds the valley of the Rio Paz to the southeast. Overlooking Chalchuapa to the northwest is the dissected cone of Chingo volcano. The valley floor is composed of recent volcanic and alluvial deposits, revealed by the downcutting of the Rio Pampe immediately north of the site.

The Zapotitan valley, in the west-central part of El Salvador, spreads between the Santa Ana and San Salvador volcanic complexes. It is drained by the Rio Sucio and the southern end is formed by the coastal mountains. The basin is a remnant of the interior structural trough, hemmed in on the east and west by geologically recent volcanic activity which created the interior mountains. This zone, having been formed by the erosion and deposition of mountain sediments in the restricted area, is rich and fertile.

Cultural Settings of the Study Area

Rio Copan Zone

Copan Valley. The ancient Maya site of Copan has been the center of archaeological research for the past 90 years. Expeditions led by the Peabody Museum, Harvard University, in the 1890s and the Carnegie Institution of Washington in the 1930s and 1940s focused primarily upon the monuments and major architecture within Copan's central zone. However, several projects over the past eight years have begun to examine the entire Copan valley as a single settlement area.

The main center of Copan is located on a river terrace within the central area of the Copan valley. It consists of a major acropolis area, towering upwards some 30 m, and a large open expanse of plaza which is studded with various carved monuments. Extremely dense settlement extends to the east into the Sepulturas section of the valley and to the south-southwest into the Bosque section. These are apparently elite residential areas. Large, multiple plaza groups are located throughout these two areas (see Fash, this volume).

The northeast section of the valley, comprised of mostly low foothills, is also fairly densely occupied, but with a greater number of smaller groups than in the bottomland areas mentioned above. Scattered household groups are found within the remaining portions of the valley. It is clear that although there is occupation outside of the valley area itself, the steep upper slopes which demarcate the valley proper also demarcate the main focus of ancient settlement.

There is evidence of some sort of occupation within the valley which extends as far back in time as the Preclassic. However, it is hard to pinpoint the extent of this early occupation. The earliest monument, recovered by the Proyecto Arqueologico Copan, dates to approximately 8.19.0.0.0–9.0.0.0.0 (A.D. 416–435). At this time, settlement seems to have been concentrated at several points, primarily within the bottomlands. One family, located at the site of the present Main Group, was able to somehow consolidate power within its own hands and found the lineage which controlled Copan until its collapse around A.D. 800.

Settlement became more extensive during the Late Acbi and Cueva phases. However, it is particularly around the time of the end of the Cueva phase and beginning of the Coner phase (marked by the appearance of Copador at Copan) when there was a population explosion within the valley. Almost all sections of the valley were occupied and the central areas were built up with a concentrated population.

Rio Amarillo. This part of the zone has been less thoroughly investigated than the Copan valley. Nevertheless it appears to have sustained a sizeable population at least during the Cueva and Coner phases. The Rio Amarillo site consists of several large plaza groups with architectural sculpture and carved altars. While the nature of its relationship with Copan has not been precisely established, it seems probable that the site functioned as a secondary center in the social hierarchy of the Coner phase of occupation. The ceramic assemblage, as presently known, contains the major components of the Copan valley sequence.

Middle and Lower Motagua Valley

Quirigua. The recently completed archaeological research at Quirigua (1974–1979) comprised excavations in the site core (Jones and Sharer 1980, this volume) and both survey and excavations in the surrounding 95 km² site periphery (Ashmore 1980a, 1981a). These investigations indicate that peak occupation in both areas of the site occurred during the Late and Terminal Classic period. Traces of a smaller Early to Middle Classic occupation were found in several areas of the site periphery (Ashmore 1980b, 1981a). The available evidence indicates that Quirigua was founded in the fifth century

A.D., probably as a colony from the central Peten (Jones and Sharer 1980, this volume), although there are sparse and deeply buried remains datable to the Protoclassic and Late Preclassic eras beneath the present water table and therefore essentially inaccessible (Ashmore 1980b).

Lower Motagua Sites. Reconnaissance and survey were conducted in the lower Motagua valley as part of the Quirigua Project in 1973–74 (Nowak 1973,1975), and again in 1977–79 (Schortman 1980, 1984, this volume). In the most intensively studied sample area (180 km²) along the southern margins of the valley, Schortman's research located and mapped 19 sites, all dating to the Late and Terminal Classic. Nine of these are monumental in size, three comparable to (or larger than) the contemporary site of Quirigua (Las Quebradas, Playitas, and Quebrada Grande). Although none duplicate all the Classic Maya hallmarks found at Quirigua (such as sculptured monuments and hieroglyphic texts), these sites do share a considerable range of material culture, including ceramics, with Quirigua (Schortman, this volume). Excavations indicate a range of interactions between all the Late Classic lower Motagua sites, and suggest that these centers rose and fell in synchronization with Quirigua (Schortman 1984).

Western and West-Central El Salvador

Chalchuapa. The most comprehensive archaeological investigations at Chalchuapa were conducted from 1967 to 1970 (Sharer, ed., 1978). The earliest remains at the site are datable to the end of the Early Preclassic era. Occupation appears continuous, and it expanded for the next millenium, peaking in both size and complexity during the Late and Terminal Preclassic. Cessation of construction and drastic decline in occupation accompanied the Ilopango eruption in ca. A.D. 250, detectable at Chalchuapa by a distinctive level of volcanic ash. Occupation at Chalchuapa gradually recovered thereafter and peaked again in the Late Classic-Early Postclassic eras. In the Late Postclassic-Conquest period, Chalchuapa was occupied by Pokoman Maya, according to ethnohistoric sources (Miles 1957).

Zapotitan Basin. This area has been systematically investigated through a stratified random sample survey combined with excavation at several sites (Sheets, ed. in press). The survey revealed 54 sites ranging from isolated residences through villages to secondary and primary regional centers. From surface evidence, the majority of the sites were occupied during the Late Classic period. A lack of

Early Classic settlement seemed to indicate abandonment due to the infertile layer of Ilopango ash. Preclassic settlements in the region seem to be few in number but that may be circumstantial since they would be hidden beneath thick volcanic deposits. Postclassic occupation was light. Settlement appears to have clustered on the high plains west and north of the basin and along permanent water sources in the basin itself (Black 1979).

Description of Fine Paste Ceramics

Having established the natural and cultural settings in the various sub-regions, we will now give a brief description of each of the fine paste ceramics included in the investigation.

The terminology for the ceramic groups in this investigation is that used by Sharer in the Chalchuapa ceramic report (Sharer 1978c). The report was the first instance in which the type-variety system was applied in a standardized manner to those particular ceramic materials. An abbreviated format, patterned after the Chalchuapa presentation, will be followed here. The descriptions list for the major site in each subregion the ceramic complex in which the group occurs. (Table 1 presents the ceramic group names and their equivalences for the sequences at Copan, Quirigua, and Chalchuapa). Next in the description are given the main identifying attributes which distinguish the group; the vessel forms in general order of frequency then follow. The final part of each description specifies the known distribution of the ceramic group along with a summary statement of the approximate magnitude of its occurrence, where known.

A more complete description of the pastes and surface finishes along with the decorative details can be found in Sharer 1978c.

Copador Polychrome (fig. 2)

Ceramic Complexes
Copan—Coner
Quirigua—Hewett
Chalchuapa—Paya

Identifying attributes
1. Specular hematite or deep purple-red, black and usually orange paint on a cream or orange-tinted slipped background. 2. Glyphic,
human, and bird, or geometric motifs. 3. Fine cream to light buff paste, soft in texture.

Forms
1. Convex-wall bowls with direct rim. 2. Composite-wall bowls with direct or slightly everted rims. 3. Faceted-flanged com-

Table 1. Complex Names and Equivalences

			Chalchuapa	Quirigua	Copan
Post Classic	E				
Classic	E. M. L.	900	Matzin	Morley	Ejar
		625	Payu	Hewett	Coner
		400	Xocco	Maudslay (late)	Cueva
		200	Vec	Maudslay (early)	Acbi II Acbi I
Preclassic	Late	0	Caynac (late)	Catherwood	Bijac
		200	Caynac (early)		Chabij

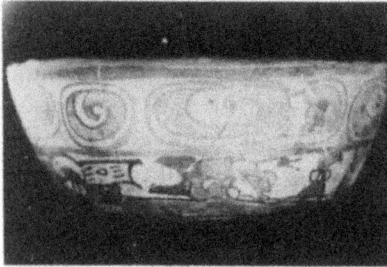

A   B

C   D

Figure 2. Examples of Copador pottery.

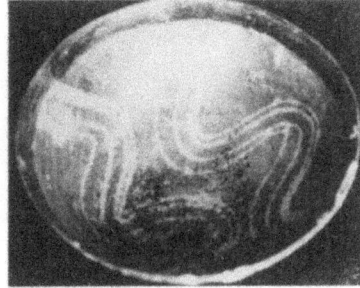

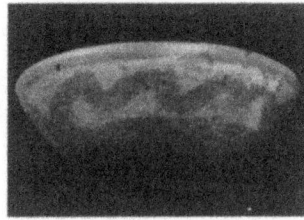

Figure 3. Examples of Gualpopa (a, b) and Chilanga (c, d) pottery.

posite-wall bowls with direct rims. 4. Vertical wall cylinders. 5. Low (less than 10 cm) vertical wall cups. 6. Small restricted-neck jars with direct rims.

Distribution
Copan—predominant polychrome type
Chalchuapa—predominant

Zapotitan—dominant
Quirigua—practically absent
Other observations (frequency not known)— Playitas (lower Motagua); Guaytan (middle Motagua); Asuncion Mita (Guatemala—El Salvador border); Tiquisate region (south coast, Guatemala)

Chilanga Red-Painted Usulutan (fig. 3)

Ceramic Complexes
Copan—Cueva
Quirigua—Maudslay (early and late)
Chalchuapa—Vec

Identifying attributes
1. Red-paint along with Usulutan technique decoration over an

orange slip. 2. Simple animal and geometric motifs. 3. Fine cream to buff paste. 4. Convex-wall (hemi-spherical) bowl shape dominant. 5. Interior usually plain.

Distribution
Copan—frequent
Chalchuapa—frequent

Quirigua—frequent
Other observations (frequency not
known)— Lower Motagua;
Guaytan; Asuncion Mita.
Not present—Zapotitan

Forms
1. Convex-wall (hemispherical)
bowls with direct rims, sometimes
with ring base. 2. Composite-wall
bowls with direct rims.

Gualpopa Polychrome (fig. 3)

Ceramic complexes
Copan—Acbi II and III (Cueva)
Quirigua—Maudslay (early and
late)
Chalchuapa—Xocco and Payu

Identifying attributes
1. Red and black paint on an
orange to orange-cream slipped
background. 2. Simple animal and
geometric motifs (similar to
Chilanga with additional black
paint used as an outline or fill).
3. Fine cream to light buff paste.
4. Convex-wall (hemispherical)
bowl as the dominant shape. 5. Interior often plain.

Distribution
Copan—frequent
Chalchuapa—frequent
Zapotitan—frequent
Other observations (frequency not
known)— lower Motagua;
Guaytan; Asuncion Mita

Forms
1. Convex-wall (hemispherical)
bowls with direct rims, may have
slightly restricted orifices.
2. Composite-wall bowls with direct rims. 3. Vertical-wall bowls
with direct rims, may have
slightly recurved walls and
slightly restricted orifices.

Elemental Analysis

Following the usual Brookhaven National Laboratory procedures
(Bishop, Harbottle, and Sayre 1982) samples and standards were bom-
barded for 18 hours at a thermal neutron flux of 1×10^{14} n/cm^2 sec.
or its equivalent. The activated samples were transferred to counting
vials and placed in an automatic sample changer. The counting configuration consisted of a Princeton Gammatech Ge-Li detector
(35 cm crystal with a better than 1.8 keV resolution on ^{60}Co) which
was coupled to an ND-2400 4096 channel analyzer and magnetic
tape readout. The resulting gamma spectra were processed by the
BRUTAL program on the Brookhaven CDC 7600 computer. Final
elemental concentrations were obtained by use of the in-house programs ELCALC and SAMPCALC. The present investigation utilized
the elemental abundances of the following: Sc, La, Ce, Eu, Lu, Hf,
Th, Cr, Fe, Co, Sm, Yb, Rb, Cs, and Ba. Full analytical data on the
fine paste cream wares will be published in the Peabody memoirs as
part of a more extensive investigation of Copan area ceramics.

Table 2. Correlation Matrix for the Copan-Focus Reference Group

	LA	CE	EU	LU	SM	YB	SC	TH	CR	FE	CO	HF	RB	CS	BA
LA	1.000														
CE	.949	1.000													
EU	.858	.898	1.000												
LU	.815	.800	.875	1.000											
SM	.890	.925	.967	.888	1.000										
YB	.788	.807	.899	.936	.916	1.000									
SC	.417	.383	.430	.530	.402	.422	1.000								
TH	.390	.378	.334	.499	.416	.408	.441	1.000							
CR	.298	.302	.397	.259	.295	.242	.350	-.148	1.000						
FE	.258	.214	.225	.298	.197	.223	.752	.225	.412	1.000					
CO	-.046	-.060	-.064	-.116	-.119	.079	.001	-.236	.264	.176	1.000				
HF	.404	.367	.389	.560	.397	.446	.648	.721	.011	.439	-.161	1.000			
RB	-.028	-.029	-.146	-.074	-.037	-.051	-.239	.316	-.218	-.278	-.201	-.062	1.000		
CS	.105	.102	.032	.083	.125	.139	.060	.293	.014	-.017	-.009	.054	.579	1.000	
BA	-.208	-.212	-.174	-.229	-.158	-.204	-.173	-.198	-.018	-.167	-.214	-.262	.285	.013	1.000
	LA	CE	EU	LU	SM	YB	SC	TH	CR	FE	CO	HF	RB	CS	BA

Data Analysis

This section will summarize the various steps in the analysis of the data. Before setting forth the various procedures, mention should be made of the problem of selecting the specific elements used in the analysis. Basically it is necessary to ascertain which, from among the full suite of elements determined, are the most likely to provide interpretable patterned results, as opposed to those engendering "spurious" variation. This is equivalent to problems associated with distinguishing the "signal" from the "noise." The reasoning as to which are the "best" elements to use in a particular situation can become rather circular and represents one of the most difficult aspects to consider during the synthesis of ceramic compositional data. If the membership in a group is known, the selection of variables to be used to summarize that group's characteristics is relatively simple. In the absence of such knowledge—the usual situation—some insights can be gleaned from a consideration of the mineralogical composition of the pottery.

The pottery under investigation is found in an area of volcanic-derived soils and clays. In fact, although the pottery could be characterized as having a temperless texture, volcanic glass particles in the paste are not uncommon. There is a correlation between barium concentration and the amount of volcanic glass in other Maya pottery (Bishop and Rands 1982) and the negative correlation of barium with most of the other determined elements (Table 2) suggested that a similar situation occurred in the cream paste pottery. For this reason, we decided not to include barium during the stage of initial group formation as expressed by chemical similarity. In a like manner, rubidium, somewhat less negatively correlated with the other elements, can substitute in similar crystal loci as barium (cf. Bishop 1980), and might also be related to varying amounts of volcanic glass.

Successive attempts at the determination of "natural" clusters in the ceramic analytical data employing different combinations of elements revealed that typological or distributional patterning was more pronounced when cesium, hafnium, and cobalt were excluded; that is, the inclusion of these elements resulted in greater variation within groups that were otherwise "more compact." Once a trial reference group was formed however, the full range of determined elemental abundances and elemental intercorrelations were employed.

Once a subset of the elements had been selected, the following steps were carried out: preliminary group formation, single group evaluation, and multiple group comparison.

Step 1: Trial Group Formation
Excluding the concentrations of Ba, Cs, Hf, and Co, an Euclidian distance matrix expressing the similarity (or dissimilarity) of each data point relative to all other data points was employed. More similar samples were then joined using average linkage cluster analysis, with the results summarized in a dendrogram (Sneath and Sokal 1973: 124, 228–230). Several small (more homogeneous) clusters were formed; three closely similar groups were of special interest for of the 56 data points included, 29 were of Copador pottery having a Copan provenience. These three groups were subsequently merged to form a trial reference unit, presumably representing a characteristic chemical profile for Copador pottery occurring at Copan.

Step 2: Reference Group Evaluation
Under the assumption that a group is a statistically random sample drawn from an infinite, multivariately normal population, the probability of an individual data point belonging to that group can be calculated. To do this, we first determine the Mahalanobis distance which is the squared, standardized, Euclidian distance from a group centroid to a data point, divided by the group standard deviation in that direction. Based on these distances, the probability of a sample belonging to a given group is expressed by Hotelling's T, a multivariate extension of the more familiar Student's t statistic. In this way, numerous specimens occurring in other clusters were found to have greater than 10% probability of belonging to the same population from which the trial reference unit was drawn—many with a very high likelihood of group membership.

Part of the reason for this apparent initial group fragmentation undoubtedly is due to the nature of the clustering algorithm and the role played by elemental intercorrelation. It has been well documented by Rohlf (1967) that the presence of correlated variables tends to distort the relationships between cases, especially when the data are subjected to clustering of the Euclidean distances between cases (Blackith and Reyment 1971: 11). With strong intercorrelation the data are "stretched out" along the directions of correlation and they form an ellipsoidal distribution. Clustering techniques such as average linkage of Euclidean distances fail to adequately cope with such data. While points in the denser areas may be grouped together, points at the two ends are frequently forced into separate groups. Inspection of the trial reference group correlation matrix revealed a pattern similar to that of Table 2 with very high correlations existing among the rare earth elements: La, Ce, Eu, Lu, Sm, and Yb. The pattern of elemental correlations can be quite characteristic for a given clay procurement region. In order to more realistically reflect the multivariate relationships present in the data matrix during the cluster analysis, some normalization of the data was required.

A convenient transformation of the data involves their normalization relative to the variance-covariance matrix of the trial reference group. From this matrix, standardized characteristic vectors (eigen vectors) were obtained which constituted a new set of uncorrelated axes. Sample coordinate positions were defined by projection onto these axes, maintaining the relative positions of the data points (Sayre 1973; Bishop, Demarest, and Sharer n.d.a). Variable loadings comprising the vector associated with the greatest amount of variation in the data set were found to be of the same sign suggesting that this vector (vector 1) might be attributable to "size-related" variability in the data (Rao 1964; Sneath and Sokal 1973: 172). Such variation might result from a non-determined component, such as silica, introduced by varying amounts of volcanic particles. Since a chemical profile of pottery is a weighted expression of all components, the presence of a material lacking the elements of interest would lower the absolute concentration but would not alter the sample to sample proportional similarity. The negative correlation of barium with most of the other elements discussed earlier tends to support the assumption that elemental ranges were being affected by non-clay components of the pottery. To the extent that this interpretation is correct, sample similarity based on absolute elemental concentration, would tend to distort the "natural" (usually fewer) number of groups present in the data set.

Step 3: New Trial Group Formation and Evaluation

Average-linkage cluster analysis was carried out as before but now employing the sample loadings on the characteristic vectors as the variables. In order to reduce the potential size-related variation, the first vector was not included. The resulting dendrogram revealed one large and two smaller clusters of samples as well as a considerable number of samples which showed little tendency to form compact or homogeneous groups. The large clustering was of particular interest for it contained the earlier trial reference group samples as well as additional Copador and Gualpopa pottery.

Using the newly obtained cluster as our reference unit, Mahalanobis distances and probabilities of group membership were again calculated. Those specimens, not in the large cluster but having a membership probability of greater than 10%, were added to the group; any group member which fell below 10% probability was removed. Statistical evaluation and specimen addition or subtraction continued until no further samples fell within the chosen 90% confidence interval. The sample membership within this enlarged and refined reference group is summarized according to typological assignment and site provenience in Table 3. Due to the predominance of pottery of a Copan provenience, we will refer to this chemically derived compositional unit as the Copan-Focus reference group.

Step 4: Multiple Group Comparison
The derivation of the Copan-Focus reference group represents the most refined level of our data analysis. Utilizing variance and co-variance elemental relationships within the particular group, and under the stated series of statistical assumptions, the probability of an individual sample's membership in that group has been determined. We also needed to determine what relationship, if any, this large group had to other clusterings of samples appearing in the dendrogram. The two smaller groups were of interest due to their site- or region-specific nature; one was comprised of only samples from El Salvador (n=22) while the other was made up of pottery from sites in the valley of the Motagua River (n=15).

The two small groups and the Copan-Focus reference group were submitted to discriminant analysis, employing the full set of elemental variables. Using the classification options within the discriminant analysis program (Nie *et al.* 1975) five samples, all from sites in El Salvador, were judged to be misclassified in the Copan-Focus reference group, belonging instead to the El Salvador provenience cluster. Subsequent rerunning of the discriminant analysis showed all samples to be correctly classified and all groups separable at a statistically significant level (p < 0.001). Group membership is summarized in Table 4. The separation of the groups from each other is illustrated with reference to the two discriminant axes in Figure 4, and variable loadings on the derived discriminant functions are given in Table 5. Inspection of the group elemental means and standard deviations (Table 6) reveals considerable overlap of concentrations at one standard deviation with the notable exception of chromium.

The Motagua-focused group was too small to subject to the more rigorous statistical evaluation given to the Copan-Focus reference groups. However, the group with the Salvadoran samples was larger. When its pattern of elemental variances and co-variances were considered and the Mahalanobis distances calculated, it was found that 40 of the 135 Copan-Focus reference group had projected probabilities of group membership exceeding the 10% threshold. If these samples were then added to the El Salvador group and the membership probabilities recalculated, additional samples would obtain high probabilities of belonging to the group.

In summation, a large chemically defined compositional group, weighted heavily toward Copador pottery having a Copan provenience, has been determined. A small group of cream paste pottery found at sites in the valley of the Motagua River is distinct, differing primarily due to its higher chromium value. A group comprised of specimens from sites in El Salvador is more similar to each other in

Table 3. Sample Membership in the Copan-Focus Reference Group

	Copador	Gualpopa	Chilanga	Totals
Copan	43 (11)	9 (3)	4 (8)	78
Rio Amarillo	5 (3)	0 (10)	8 (4)	30
Chalchuapa	14 (9)	9 (5)	1 (1)	42
Ceren	1 (4)	2 (6)	—	13
Cambio	5 (5)	4 (6)	—	20
Quirigua	0 (4)	0 (6)	1 (3)	14
Lower Motagua	0 (4)	—	—	4
San Agustin Acasaguastlan	2 (5)	6 (2)	2 (0)	17
Naco Valley	—	—	0 (4)	4
Asuncion Mita	1	1	1	3
Pusilha	10 (9)	—	—	19
Column totals	135	69	40	244

Note: Numbers in parentheses represent samples not belonging to the group.

Table 4. Composition of Reference Groups and Provenience of Cream Ware Sherds

| | In Reference Group | | | | |
Provenience	Copan Focus	Motagua	El Salvador	Not Grouped	Total
Western Honduras					
Copan Valley	43/9 5			11/3 8	78
Rio Amarillo	5/0 8			3/10 4	30
Western and West-Central El Salvador					
Chalchuapa	14/8 1		6/4 5	3/1 0	42
Zapotitan Valley	6/6		3/9 0	6/3	33
Motagua Focus, Guatemala					
Quirigua	0/0 1	4/5 2		0/0 1	14
Lower Motagua sites	0/0	2/0 0		2/0 0	4
Middle Motagua sites	2/6 2	0/1		5/1 0	17
Comparison Loci					
Naco Valley, Honduras	—	0/0 1		0/0 3	4
Asuncion Mita, Guatemala	1/1 1			0 0	3
Pusilha, Belize	10/1			9/0 0	19

Note: Membership is as determined by the classification statistics of SPSS multiple discriminate analysis. The number of samples in the Copan-Focus reference group is not the same as in Table 3, for some samples have been reallocated to the El Salvador group. First number in column is Copador membership followed by a slash and then the number of Gualpopa samples. To the right of these numbers is the number of Chilanga specimens in a given group.

Table 5. Standardized Discrimination Function Coefficients

Element	Function 1	Function 2
Rb	0.52	0.24
Cs	0.18	0.33
Ba	−0.21	0.07
Sc	−0.18	−1.20
La	−0.87	−1.35
Ce	0.79	1.15
Eu	0.89	0.15
Lu	0.30	2.25
Th	−0.67	−0.45
Cr	−1.19	0.24
Fe	0.65	0.97
Co	0.11	−0.25
Sm	0.18	−1.12
Yb	−0.84	−0.65
Eigenvalue	4.85	1.46
Percentage of Discriminatory Power	76.9	23.1

Table 6. Major Group Mean Concentration

	Copan-Focus Reference Group n = 127		El Salvadoran-Focus Reference Group n = 26		Motagua-Focus Reference Group n = 14	
La	24.10	(6.60)	21.60	(7.50)	23.00	(6.10)
Ce	51.80	(15.30)	50.60	(18.40)	44.50	(12.80)
Eu	1.16	(0.36)	1.16	(0.45)	0.97	(0.25)
Lu	0.50	(0.12)	0.55	(0.15)	0.50	(0.10)
Sm	5.28	(1.76)	5.28	(2.04)	4.40	(1.25)
Yb	2.94	(0.74)	3.11	(0.98)	2.83	(0.63)
Sc	18.20	(2.28)	15.90	(2.21)	18.10	(2.09)
Th	9.34	(1.34)	9.00	(2.10)	9.17	(1.54)
Cr	13.90	(3.10)	8.84	(2.20)	35.60	(9.90)
Fe	2.81%	(0.33)	2.89%	(0.49)	3.22%	(0.66)
Co	6.37	(4.90)	4.94	(2.50)	8.48	(11.20)
Hf	5.13	(0.64)	5.06	(0.88)	5.05	(0.37)
Rb	59.20	(15.60)	81.20	(24.60)	57.50	(21.60)
Cs	3.80	(1.26)	4.70	(1.51)	3.48	(1.23)
Ba	1,360.00	(327.00)	1,490.00	(338.00)	1,570.00	(324.00)

Note: Concentrations expressed as oxides in parts per million except for iron, which is in percent. Numbers in parentheses represent one standard deviation.

the group than to other samples. It is separable from the other groups when discriminant functions are calculated to achieve maximum group separation. However, considerable overlap between the El Salvadoran group and the Copan-Focus reference group is noted when the groups are viewed relative to the variance-covariance pattern of the El Salvadoran specimens.

Discussion

Given the analytical data at hand, what may be inferred about the nature of Copador production and distribution? Of the Copan cases, 78% of the analyzed Copador and Gualpopa samples fall into the Copan-Focus reference group; this included samples from the site center as well as from excavations in the valley. There are no verifiable compositional differences noted between form classes. For example, the cylindrical forms cannot be distinguished from the bowls although several of the cylinders occupy a peripheral position in the

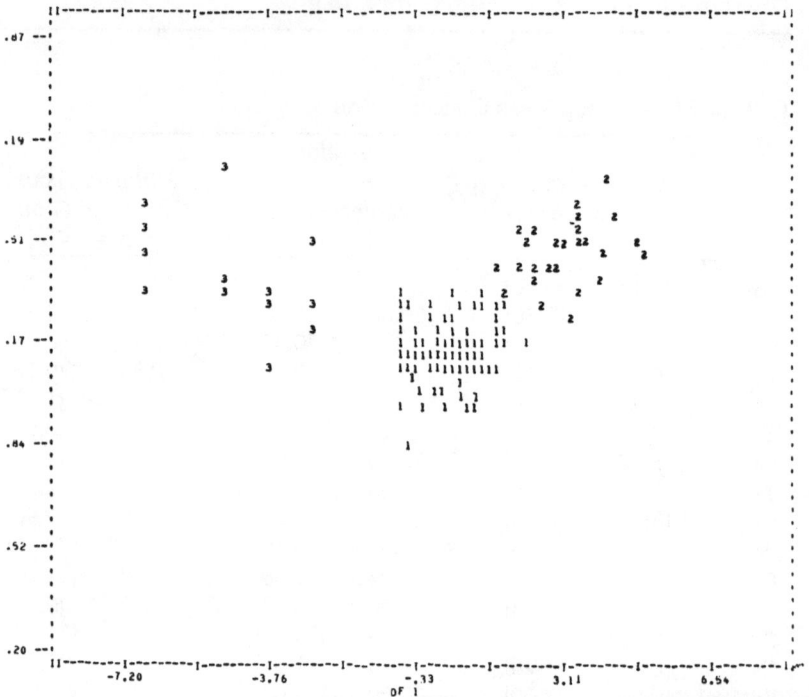

Figure 4. Plot of the three primary compositional groups relative to derived discriminant axes. Symbols: 1) Copan-Focus reference group; 2) El Salvador reference group; 3) Motagua reference group.

reference group. Of the non-fitting Chilanga specimens, there is no tendency for patterned variation such as might be expected if a particular clay resource were being exploited.

The lack of patterned variation is most noticeable for the Gualpopa samples from Rio Amarillo, the site near Copan. None of these cases obtained membership in the Copan-Focus reference group. While a few of the Gualpopa samples exhibit greater iron concentrations relative to the Copan-Focus reference group, other elemental concentrations vary unvariately, again negating hypotheses of a single, specific source. For virtually all types at each of the sites considered, the inclusion of some specimens in our Copan-Focus reference group, while others are excluded, presents a baffling picture quite at variance to the sharper demarcations between resource procurement regions elsewhere in the Maya area (cf. Bishop, Rands, and Harbottle 1982; Rands and Bishop 1980; Bishop, Demarest, and Sharer, n.d.a).

A specific source for the Copador and other cream paste pottery is difficult to interpret directly. On the basis of its published occurrence, Copan and the Copan valley would appear to be likely candidates. In an earlier paper, we attempted to seek those compositional similarities that might exist between the cream paste and non-cream paste ceramics at Copan (Bishop *et al.* n.d.). At that time, our information regarding compositional variability was limited and our level of comparison too generalized. Subsequent analyses have served to demonstrate statistically significant chemical differences between the local Copan pottery and the cream paste ceramics; these distinctions are verified by the determination of the clay mineralogical differences.

Mineralogical information was gained by the X-ray diffraction of pottery from the Copan valley which, due to its abundance or duration in the ceramic sequence, is presumed to be of local manufacture. When pottery is fired, there is a loss of water in the crystal lattice and an accompanying loss of crystal structure. Maya pottery tends to be low-fired well below the vitrification point and, over time can rehydrate (Grim and Bradley 1948). Rehydration appears to be easier for some clay minerals such as illite and montmorillonite than for others like kaolinite. X-ray diffraction scans of the locally-made Copan pottery revealed the presence of montmorillonite and mixed layer montmorillonite-illite clay minerals. Similar scans of Copador, Gualpopa, and Chilanga pottery failed to reveal any peaks. These data, combined with the low iron concentrations of the cream paste pottery, are consistent with the hypothesis that a kaolinite clay was used.

Since the trace-element pattern primarily reflects the clay composition, differences in the basic underlying mineralogy would preclude finding closely similar ceramic profiles. In the absence of similar ceramic wares believed to be of local manufacture, we are forced to rely on the Criterion of Abundance (cf. Bishop, Rands, and Holley 1982). Therefore, given the percentage of pottery of a Copan provenience in the Copan-Focus reference group, for the present, we must heuristically regard that group as representing pottery made from raw materials obtained in the Copan valley area.

If we accept the above judgement, how can we interpret the separation of the three derived groups and the non-fitting specimens?

One should bear in mind that the concentrations for the three derived groups are not greatly different. Some explanation for the compositional variation in the data set may be gleaned from a consideration of the nature of the clay deposits in the Copan valley. Clays formed in the valley are derived from various lithological features including limestones and sandstones as well as from units derived from volcanic activity. Some clays tend to be washed off the valley slope and deposited in low-lying, flat areas. Other clays which are suitable for pottery are noted as occurring in isolated patches (Turner *et al.* 1983). These isolated pockets of clay would be subjected to differential depositional history and weathering. Thus, the valley would provide a wide range of ceramic materials including two with rather different clay compositions—those formed from volcanic tuffs and those of sedimentary origins. The presence of quartz phenocrysts in some of the Copan valley pottery, including the cream paste pottery, attests to the volcanic derivation of the raw materials. Additionally, Turner and associates note observing varying amounts of phenocrysts in contemporary pottery of the Copan valley, another suggestion of similarity to the ceramic material under study. Consequently, it seems logical to postulate the geological possibility for a Copador clay source in the Copan valley. The varying amounts of phenocrysts in different pockets of clay could also explain the fine-level variation in trace element data being observed.

Of our three defined groups, the Copan-Focus reference group is very similar to the El Salvador reference group in the rare earth elements, Th and Fe, but divergent in Rb, Sc, Ba, Cr, and Co. The differences are small but significant, as verified by the discriminant analysis described earlier. It will be recalled, however, that when samples of the Copan-Focus reference group were evaluated relative to the variance-covariance pattern of the El Salvadoran group, overlapping membership was indicated. From the perspective of extensive analysis of Maya pottery, it is difficult to conclude that the respective raw material procurement sources for the two groups are too distant from one another.

The Motagua reference group consisting of Copador, Gualpopa, and Chilanga specimens from Quirigua as well as Copador samples from San Agustin Acasaguastlan and the lower Motagua survey appears to be quite divergent from the Copan-Focus reference group and the El Salvador reference group. Although not presented in this paper, the locally made Quirigua pottery, when projected onto the two discriminant axes, diverges in the same direction only more strongly. A separate source for the Motagua cream-paste wares is indicated.

The compositional variability observed in the pottery from the Belize site of Pusilha is difficult to evaluate. Approximately one half of the Copador samples fall near the centroid of the Copan-Focus reference group. However, the remaining samples diverge dramatically and without consistent pattern. Our analyses of these samples were carried out on drilled powder supplied by the British Museum, thus we have not been able to seek a mineralogical basis for the divergent compositions.

Compositional analysis of Late Classic period fine cream paste pottery has been carried out to obtain data relevant for an investigation of southeast Maya ceramic production and exchange. Chemical variation in the pottery, engendered, in part, by varying amounts of naturally occurring non-plastic volcanic material, and the lack of potentially important white firing clays from the Copan valley, render data interpretation difficult. Nevertheless, sufficient distributional and typological patterning can be discerned to allow inferences to be made regarding Copan and related cream ware production.

Pottery from the western Honduras sites of Copan and Rio Amarillo either fall within the main Copan-Focus reference group or are not grouped at all. This contrasts to compositional data for pottery from El Salvador where group membership is split between the Copan and El Salvador reference units. Although based on more limited sampling, the samples from the Motagua valley also appear to divide between two reference groups but with a noted tendency for distributional patterning. That is, pottery from Quirigua forms a major component of the Motagua group with the exception of one Copador sherd that is placed in the Copan-Focus reference group. On the other hand, the pottery from the middle Motagua site of San Agustin Acasaguastlan is grouped predominantly within the group weighted toward Copan. The presence of Copador and related pottery from differing sources of raw material are indicated for sites along the Motagua River.

Given the extent of chemical similarity between the pottery of the Copan-Focus reference group and the El Salvador-Focus reference group, it appears that different specific clay resources were exploited but were contained within a restricted region; on the basis of the abundance of fine cream paste pottery found at Copan, such a region was probably the Copan valley. The ungrouped pottery from the Western Honduras sites could represent, therefore, smaller scale exploitation from different pockets of cream-firing clay deposits within the valley system.

Within this interpretation, differing patterns of resource utilization and production can be inferred. Producers of, especially, the Copador and Gualpopa pottery which constitute the Copan-Focus reference group were exploiting a restricted resource area both for internal consumption at Copan and export to El Salvador, San Agustin Acasaguastlan, Asuncion Mita, and Pusilha. A different source, although not too distant, was utilized by producers of pottery that was exported to El Salvador. Such directed production and distribution was apparently in response to the needs of Chalchuapa, a conspicuous consumer of Copador and Gualpopa pottery. Yet another source is indicated for the pottery constituting the Motagua reference group. At present, we cannot suggest where a likely resource area for this pottery was located. Wherever the location, given the low occurrence of Copador or Gualpopa ceramics at Quirigua and the lower or middle Motagua sites, the production center for this pottery was of secondary importance in comparison to the region producing the pottery of the Copan-Focus reference group.

Any interpretation of the patterns of ceramic production must acknowledge the numerous fine cream paste specimens which were not placed in any of the three groups and failed to demonstrate close similarity to other ungrouped samples. Although the analytical data for a few of the specimens demonstrated marked divergence such as those from Pusilha, many were just outside the chosen 90% confidence interval surrounding a particular group centroid.

Taken together, the data are not inconsistent with an interpretation of a major center of Copador and Gualpopa ceramic production probably located in the Copan valley. There is no obvious covariation of vessel form or decorative motifs with compositional patterning. Only limited inferences regarding ceramic craft specialization can be drawn from the separation of a compositionally similar group of pottery, all with El Salvadoran site provenience, and may represent production for export to that area. The lack of patterned variation of the non-grouped specimens might be the result of small, even family level, producers employing available clays which would mimic the white-paste ceramic tradition. In the future, we plan to carry out compositional analyses on samples from many pockets of white clays occurring in the Copan valley; these analyses should provide needed information on mineralogical and elemental variability. For the present, the extent of observed chemical variation seems to argue against as high a level of craft specialization as developed for elite pottery at other Maya centers.[2] Against this conclusion, assumptions of elite ties between Maya centers based on the presence of Copador or Gualpopa pottery would be oversimplified.

Notes

1. The projects participating within this research program include, in Honduras, the Copan Valley Project, Harvard University (Willey, Leventhal, and Fash 1978; Willey and Leventhal 1974) and the Rio Amarillo (La Canteada) Project, U.C.L.A. (Beaudry 1977); in El Salvador, the Zapotitan Protoclassic Project, University of Colorado, (Sheets 1979a; Sheets, ed., in press) and the Chalchuapa Project, University of Pennsylvania (Sharer, ed., 1978); in Guatemala, the Quirigua Project, University of Pennsylvania (Sharer 1978a); and the Maya Jade and Ceramics Project of the Museum of Fine Arts, Boston, with funding provided by Mr. Landon T. Clay and in collaboration with Brookhaven National Laboratory. Material from the Tiquisate region of Guatemala and from the site of Asuncion Mita and Guaytan were made available through the courtesy of the Museo Nacional de Guatemala, and pottery from San Agustin Acasaguastlan was submitted by Gary R. Walters. Research at Brookhaven National Laboratory is conducted under contract with the U. S. Department of Energy and supported by its Office of Basic Energy Sciences.

2. For many ceramic manufacturing centers in the Maya lowlands and highlands, developed craft specialization is inferred from reduced compositional variability observed in more elite pottery (figurines, incensarios, figural painted polychrome, etc.) as compared to domestic ceramics. This is seen in smaller elemental concentration means and standard deviations as well as sharply defined characteristic chemical profiles for a group of pottery. Such reduced variation results from a combination of cultural and natural factors involving patterned (controlled?) stages of ceramic production utilizing a specific clay resource. This interrelationship between specialized ceramic production and compositional variation will be discussed in the future as part of the summary publications of the Maya Jade and Ceramics Project.

Copan, Quirigua, and the Southeast Maya Zone: A Summary View

The papers of this symposium have ranged over a variety of topics —hieroglyphic texts, sculptural art, ceremonial center layout and architecture, settlement patterns, and ceramics. From these the authors have offered us historical and processual interpretations concerning the rise and fall of dynasties, the impingement of "foreign elites" on humbler local populations, trade relations, and other themes. In my overview, I shall not attempt to treat these several articles individually and serially, but, instead, I shall opt for an easier way out—easier for myself and the reader—and attempt to put together a culture-historical summary that will incorporate some of the results described and analyzed in the symposium presentations.

Recent, as well as earlier, findings on Copan and Quirigua indicate that these two great sites of the Southeastern Lowland Maya Zone became a part of the Classic Maya world—as this "world" is defined by stelae texts, sculptural arts, and architectural styles—by the beginning of the fifth century A.D. if not before. We have long known of early Cycle 9 dates from Copan. To these we may add the discovery, reported by Claude Baudez in his paper, of a fragment of a sculptured monument from there which bears close stylistic resemblances to the Leyden Plate, with implications of a Long Count date of 8.19.0.0.0 to 9.0.0.0.0. This piece was discovered in architectural fill, rather than in a dedicatory placement, but presumably it had been transported from such an earlier position. From Quirigua, Christopher Jones and Robert Sharer also refer to recently discovered early Cycle 9 monuments. As the stylistic affinities of the Leyden Plate, the early Copan fragment, and the other early Copan and Quirigua monuments are very definitely with the northeast Peten, it seems reasonable to infer that the Early Classic "colonization" of Copan, Quirigua, and the Southeastern Zone may have come from this assumed lowland Maya heartland and, quite possibly, from the premier site of that region, Tikal. Such a line of argument might be further advanced by incorporating Wendy Ashmore's statement that the Copan and Quirigua ceremonial center and architectural layouts reflect the plans of sites of the Peten.

If we assume that a Peten hearth was the source for the implantation of Classic lowland Maya culture at Quirigua and Copan, what was the nature of this intrusion? What forces and what processes were involved? I have already led with the processually loaded term "colonization." How apt might this be? To begin with, we know that Classic Maya elite culture was not carried into unoccupied territory in the Southeast Zone. For both Copan and Quirigua there is a record of resident Preclassic period populations. These resident populations, who may or may not have been of Maya speech, participated in southern Mesoamerican ceramic traditions. At Copan, those of the Middle Preclassic Uir phase had pottery which, as described by William Fash, relates to early Middle Preclassic complexes in several southern Mesoamerican regions. Subsequently, in the Late Preclassic, Copan ceramics appear to be a part of a Usulutan resist-painting pottery tradition, one which is primarily associated with the Guatemalan-Salvadoran Highlands, rather than the Peten lowlands. Were all of these Preclassic Copan and Quirigua populations simple village farmers? Fash, on the basis of his considerable experience with Copan valley settlement patterns, concludes that the Preclassic Copanecos were, and this would seem to confirm Longyear's (1952) opinion of a good many years ago. Neither Fash nor Longyear report anything in the way of public buildings associated with their Preclassic sites and levels. I am puzzled by this, for Copan is hardly a location that could be said to have been isolated from southern Mesoamerican Preclassic communications. Chalchuapa and Kaminaljuyu, both with imposing Late Preclassic ceremonial constructions, lie no great distance to the south, and at Los Naranjos, not far to the east in Honduras, the Late Preclassic was the time of considerable ceremonial or public building. The matter is an important one as we attempt to frame hypotheses about the processes of Classic Maya "colonization," or whatever, in the Southeast Zone. Was Classic Maya civilization moving into an area of egalitarian farming societies or into one where a non-egalitarian social order was already on the rise? If the former situation obtained, direct conquest by an invading Maya elite seems a likely formula for what happened; if the latter, then Kent Flannery's (1968) oft-cited processual model of trade contacts, imitation of a foreign elite by local chieftains, and subsequent intermarriages of, say, Tikal royal daughters to Copan "barbarians" might be closer to the mark.

But to go on to the Classic Period, both Copan and Quirigua were probably sizable and important places in Early Classic times. For Copan, this refers to both its main center of public architecture and to outlying settlements in the Copan valley. Charles Cheek has discussed the main center in some detail. An interesting observation which he makes is that the Classic Maya hiatus, which is usually dated at 9.5.0.0.0 to 9.8.0.0.0, or from A.D. 534 to 593, is not registered in the Copan data. There is neither a slackening of major constructional activity nor a cessation of stelae dedications during this time at Copan. Instead, Copan's hiatus, or halt in such elite activities comes later, from about A.D. 580 to 660. Cheek's speculations about this are interesting and certainly worthy of further examination. They can be summarized as follows.

If the Peten hiatus were occasioned by the breaking off of Teotihuacan trade connections—as I once suggested (Willey 1974)—then it may be that Copan did not suffer this same rupture at this same time. Cheek notes that Kaminaljuyu, in the Guatemalan Highlands, continued its Teotihuacan contacts all during the sixth century A.D. If Copan were probably as much within Kaminaljuyu's trading sphere as within, say, Tikal's, Copan prosperity could have continued, through its Teotihuacan-Kaminaljuyu connections, while that of the Peten and Tikal suffered a decline. Subsequently, in the seventh century, there appears to have been a break in Kaminaljuyu-Teotihuacan relations; and, perhaps significantly, it is at this latter time that Cheek observes the constructional-stelae hiatus at Copan. Cheek puts this forward with the caution that economic prosperity might not be the only correlate to such an activity as stelae carving—and I would certainly agree; nevertheless, he has raised a very interesting point and has made us aware that the hiatus phenomenon was not as chronologically uniform as once we thought.

William Fash's settlement results from the Copan valley give us some idea of population sizes there through time. There are indications of Middle, and even Early, Preclassic residences in the valley. There is then the curious Late Preclassic decline—a decline so inconsistent with other parts of the Maya lowlands or highlands. Some populations did continue there, however, for in addition to the limited amount of evidence which Fash details we know that Longyear's Preclassic findings were those of Late Preclassic ceramics. In the Early-to-Middle Classic, from about A.D. 450 to 700, there was at least a doubling of the Copan Valley "house mound" populations. This period corresponds, it will be noted, to the main center constructional era that we have just been referring to through Cheek's work. I should think that it will be of interest to see if Cheek's seventh century Copan building and dedicatory hiatus is in any way reflected in the residential data. As yet, Copan archaeologists working with outlying settlement patterns and related ceramics (among whom I must include myself) have nothing to say on this score. Obviously, what is needed is a refinement in ceramic chronology to intervals of a century or less. With our ceramic sequence charts, we pretend that we can do this, but I think most of us have our misgivings. We can only hope that after the current intensive spate of research at Copan is completed this may be done.

Whether Quirigua was as big and as important a place as Copan in the Early and Early-to-Middle Classic periods remains unknown. For a long time we have thought that it did not amount to much then, achieving its greatness only in the Late Classic and then with a fatherly assist from Copan. Jones and Sharer are at pains to set the record straight on this, and we have already referred to Early Classic beginnings in the Quirigua site zone. Quirigua was no parvenu establishment but has beginnings as old and as aristocratic as Copan's. After about 9.5.0.0.0 (A.D. 534) the Quirigua stelae and, major constructional record is silent, however, with these activities not being resumed until about 9.15.0.0.0 (A.D. 731). The first part of this "silent" period corresponds, of course, to the standard Peten hiatus interval of A.D. 534–593, and it may be that Quirigua was hard hit by the causes behind this phenomenon. Following Cheek's suggestion, might this have been because Quirigua, in its geographical position, was more a part of the Peten-related orbit of trade and other interaction than was the case with Copan with its Kaminaljuyu-highland connections? This is a possibility; but, at the same time, it must be remembered that there is a sampling problem at Quirigua, not present at Copan. Much of the Motagua valley floor is covered with a thick layer of alluvium. It was only through agricultural ditching operations of the last few years that the Early Classic monuments and structures which Jones and Sharer describe were brought to light. The alluvium cover has also hampered Ashmore's settlement pattern work. Thus, it could well be that Quirigua continued with more vigor through the 200 years from 9.5.0.0.0 to 9.15.0.0.0 than it now appears on present available evidence.

After A.D. 700, which carries us into the full Late Classic period, both Copan and Quirigua enjoyed their greatest florescences. These are measured in ceremonial center constructions, stelae dedications, and population concentrations. At Copan this last dimension can be appraised by "house-mound" count in the 12 by 4 km valley pocket surrounding the center, as well as inferred from the size and magnificence of the Late Classic center itself. At Quirigua house platform counting has been made difficult by the aforementioned alluviation problem, but the size, grandeur, and hieroglyphic texts of the main center provide a basis for an inference of great population concentrations. At both sites this cultural zenith was maintained until A.D. 800, or a little after, when Copan was abandoned and Quirigua entered upon a Postclassic phase of its history marked by a general reduction of activities.

During this eighth-century peak in their fortunes Copan and Quirigua both must have had high status within the Classic Maya world and constant contacts and communication with it. There are some hints that Copan's contacts and cosmopolitanism may have been more wide-reaching and sophisticated than Quirigua's. Baudez calls attention to Teotihuacan-influenced pottery in Copan Early and Middle Classic contexts. To what extent is this matched at Quirigua? If the latter part of the Early Classic and the Middle Classic are weak or absent at Quirigua, this might explain the absence of such influence there. This would be consistent with Cheek's hypothesis about Copan's continued Teotihuacan contacts via Kaminaljuyu in the sixth century A.D. Baudez also mentions what he refers to as derived-Teotihuacanoid traits at Copan in the sculptural art of the brief period of A.D. 706–731. Among these are Tlaloc figures and turbanned figures. Could such ideas have reached Copan via the Guatemalan highlands? I think we can only raise questions about such things now. There are, as Baudez states, resemblances to Campeche and Yucatan although in this central-to-northern Maya lowland context I would think of such traits as being Terminal Classic (ca. A.D. 800–900) rather than early eighth century. No one in the symposium group addressed such matters with reference to Quirigua. If derived-Teotihuacanoid or Late Classic Mexicanoid traits are present there it would have a bearing on how they might have arrived at Copan.

Our concern here with the interrelationship between Copan and Quirigua has been implicit in all that we have been saying up to this point; with the Late Classic period it becomes fully explicit. It is a subject which has received some previous attention. Some years back, David Kelley (1962), in his studies of hieroglyphic inscriptions, assigned Copan the leading or "parental" role in the relationship. He argued that a junior member of Copan's ruling dynasty was the founder, or at least the instigator, of Quirigua's Late Classic period greatness. Since then, this opinion has been challenged, and in the present paper Jones and Sharer have given us something of the counter-case against the Kelley interpretation. Their arguments rely upon Quirigua's claim to Early Classic beginnings, to which we have already referred, and also upon other readings of the Copan texts which cast doubt on the "father-son" relationship between the two sites. Instead of such a relationship, they believe that the texts refer to a conquest and capture of the ruler of Copan of the early eighth century, one 18 Rabbit (or Jog), by the ruler of Quirigua, Cauac Sky (or Two-Legged Sky). Thereafter, according to this interpretation, Cauac Sky reigned over both Copan and Quirigua for a time.

Berthold Riese steers something of a middle course between these two interpretations. In his opinion, 18 Rabbit and Cauac Sky probably had some sort of familial or lineage relationship although not necessarily that of father and son. He accepts the more recent reading that indicates a war between the two cities and the capture of 18 Rabbit by Cauac Sky, an event that took place in 9.15.6.14.6 or A.D. 737; but he does not go along with the historical truth of the Quirigua inscription that is read as saying that Cauac Sky became the new ruler of Copan. On the contrary, Riese argues that the Copan inscriptions dating after the event of the capture continue to indicate a list of local Copan kings which does not include Cauac Sky. Thus, 18 Rabbit may have been captured in battle on the said date, but this did not end Copan's independence. That Copan continued to thrive, in Riese's view, is attested by continued great activity in the Main Group. The famed Hieroglyphic Stairway was constructed in this post-defeat era; and Riese estimates that this was an undertaking, in labor, skill, and intellectual effort, equivalent to the carving of 30 stelae.

That such matters of history can even be discussed is a testimony to the advances that have been made in Maya hieroglyphic research in the last 20 years. The Copan-Quirigua controversy is by no means settled, but we are "surrounding" the problem, coming at it from many different sides, supplementing hieroglyphic textual information with data from other sources. This is what Riese means in his paper when he refers to an "holistic" approach.

Two papers dealt with aspects of regional, as opposed to the more localized Copan and Quirigua, settlement patterns. One of these, by David Vlcek and William Fash, is concerned with the territory between Copan and Quirigua. These two big sites are 55 km apart. Halfway between them is a sizable center, El Paraiso, one which in the Southeast Zone regional scale of things could be called a "secondary center." Halfway between Copan and El Paraiso is the smaller center of Rio Amarillo. It is of a size to be called "tertiary." In the other direction, halfway between El Paraiso and Quirigua, is another "tertiary center," La Playona. And there are still other smaller mound sites dotted intermittently all along the way between these centers. The Southeast Zone, like other parts of the Maya Lowlands, was, obviously, densely settled. Regional settlement pattern studies in the Maya lowlands are in their infancy; however, the continuity of settlement, and the sizes and spacings of centers, in this Copan-Quirigua situation is consistent with settlement hierarchies and spacings elsewhere in the area (Willey 1981). Vlcek and Fash are of the opinion that the regional settlement pattern which they have observed most probably goes back to Late Preclassic times; however, they also emphasize that the numbers of sites involved and the sizes of these sites were probably at a maximum in the eighth century A.D. An interesting side-light on all this, which demands speculation, is that it must tell us something about the relationships between Copan and Quirigua. Whether these great sites existed in enmity or friendship, or, as is more likely, alternated between these two conditions, their communications must have been very close. Such continuity in occupation over the intervening landscape demands it.

The other regional settlement pattern paper raises some fascinating questions of another sort. Edward Schortman has surveyed a large part of the lower Motagua valley, beyond Quirigua to the north. Here he has found a number of large sites. Some of the multiple plaza ones he describes as being volumetrically (in their constructional materials) as large or larger than Quirigua. These largest sites would appear to be at the top of a site hierarchy which descends through "secondary" and "tertiary" establishments and ordinary small "house-mound" residences. The associated pottery and other minor artifacts that have been found around these sites are largely similar to that of Late Classic period Quirigua. The larger of these sites have boulder masonry and plain monuments. There is, however, no evidence of Maya hieroglyphic inscriptions or Classic Maya style stone sculptures.

What is the significance of these lower Motagua sites? What are their affiliations? Were they, perhaps, built by non-Mayans? Situated as they are on what is the northeastern periphery of the Maya world—and given the great size of some of them—it is difficult to see them as simply outlying residential units tributary to Quirigua. Do we have here the remains of peoples who were only partially assimilated to Classic Maya traditions, sharing some traits, such as pottery, but not participating in the things of the Classic elite order? This seems the best explanation for the present. We recall our observations at the beginning of this commentary about the Classic Maya hierarchic culture being intruded into an earlier, Late Preclassic type of life in the Southeast Zone. The unstated implications of this interpretation were that a full Classic-type acculturation eventually took place. This may have been the case within certain perimeters, but it looks as though Schortman has pushed beyond those perimeters, going into territory that was not fully Classic Maya-acculturated, into communities that were just undergoing such acculturation, and then in an only marginal way, as late as the Late Classic period. These are sites—and problems—that demand large-scale excavations and extensive study. The results should throw much light on the nature of frontiers and the processes of culture change that characterized them.

To return again to the heart of things—to Copan and Quirigua relationships—there are some ceramic findings which bear upon these, especially during the Late Classic. One of the most important Copan pottery types is Copador Polychrome. From his study of stelae cache associations, Richard Leventhal has said that Copador Polychrome at Copan dates no earlier than A.D. 737. This may, or may not, be attempting too fine a shading of the dating, but there cannot be much doubt that the type is primarily an eighth century one. Ronald Bishop and his associates, from compositional and trace element studies, have made out a strong case for Copador's manufacture only at Copan or at some place within the Copan valley. Interestingly, while it occurs as trade to the south, in El Salvador, it does not appear at Quirigua. Was trade, at least in some items, cut off between Copan and Quirigua as a result of the A.D. 737 conflict between 18 Rabbit and Cauac Sky? Several of us (Willey *et al.*, 1980) have argued that it is at about this time that Copan seems to turn away from exchange with the north—much of which, presumably, had been mediated via Quirigua—and to become more caught-up in trading patterns involving Salvador and the highlands to the south. In so doing, the people of Copan would have been returning to old Preclassic period associations.

PART II

The Greater Southeast

13

NEDENIA C. KENNEDY

The Periphery Problem and
Playa de los Muertos: A Test Case

Introduction

Selected ceramics from Playa de los Muertos have been compared since their discovery (Popenoe 1934; Strong, Kidder and Paul 1938) with Early, Middle, and Late Formative (or Preclassic) ceramics ranging from Tlatilco in Central Mexico (Porter 1953) to Valdivia in Ecuador (Lathrap 1974). Considering the status of Formative period studies, postulation of such far-flung affiliations was reasonable, if not always insightful, through the 1950s. However, while many other Formative sequences from Mesoamerica were either established or updated following 1960, continued reference to Playa de los Muertos (Green and Lowe 1967; Coe 1961; Stone 1972) served primarily to point up the inadequacy of the available record.

In order to promote more precise evaluation of Playa de los Muertos with respect to sites beyond and within the Southeast Periphery and southern Mesoamerica, I returned to and reopened the site in 1975. Due to circumstances beyond my control the excavations carried out at this time were exploratory in extent. Nevertheless, analysis of the data recovered from tightly stratified deposits culminated in the preparation of a three-phase ceramic sequence and an extensively revised comparative study (Kennedy 1981).

Based on this, a number of outstanding questions concerning Playa de los Muertos have been or may now be readdressed. Since, however, it has been presumed in the past that Formative period developments in this portion of the Southeast Periphery were peripheral or retarded, and because prior investigations in this zone have not served to clarify this point, in my opinion an overriding issue is whether or not these terms apply. In other words, although a number of authors have recognized this problem (Willey 1969; Baudez 1976; Kennedy 1981), it has not been subjected to rigorous testing.

In this paper I shall therefore review the revised ceramic sequence from Playa de los Muertos as a case in point, along with selected comparative data. This record will then be examined against previous references to Playa de los Muertos in order to illuminate the degree to which prior assumptions regarding peripherality inhibited objective assessment of the site. In conclusion, I shall contend that whether or not the labels "periphery" or "frontier" still apply to Playa de los Muertos, objective appraisal of this and related issues concerning the Southeastern Periphery will only be achieved by giving alternative hypotheses an at least equal chance.

The Ceramic Analysis

The ceramic assemblages described below were recovered from vertically stratified deposits at Playa de los Muertos which is located immediately to the east of the Ulua River in the Department of Yoro,

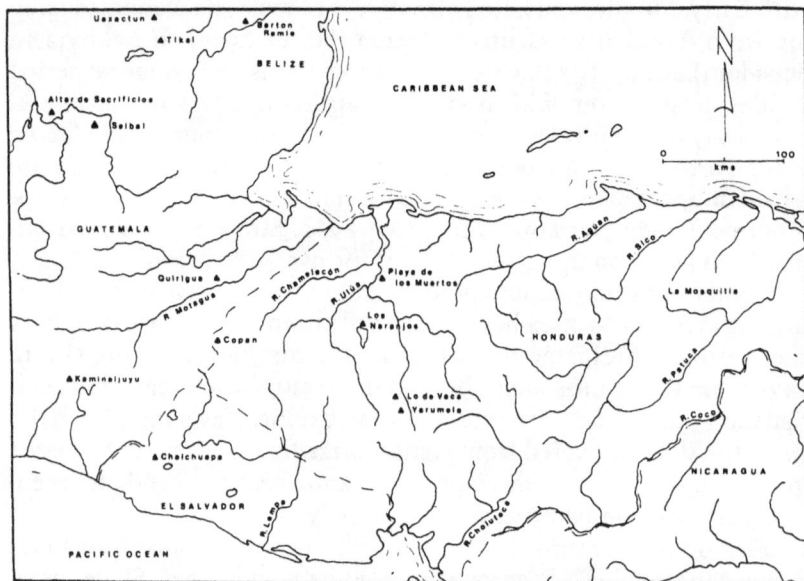

Figure 1. Map of Honduras showing location of major archaeological sites mentioned in the text.

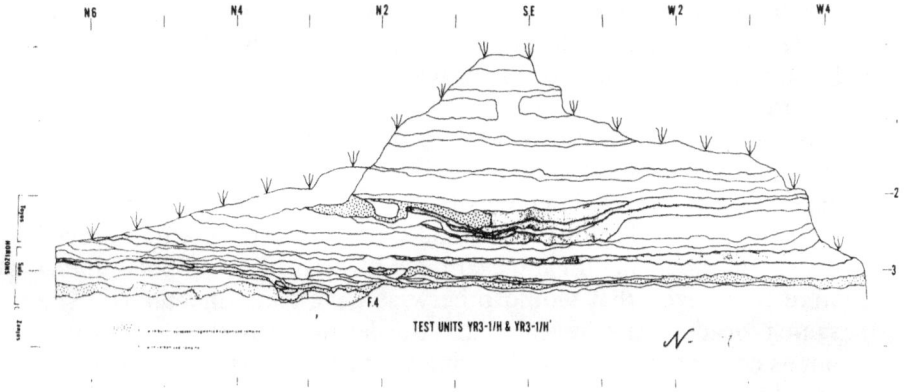

Figure 2. The east and south profiles of Units YR3-1/H and YR3-1/H1.

Honduras (fig. 1). Since the primary refuse concentrations sampled were separated by relatively sterile layers of alluvial fill, inspection of these deposits suggested from the beginning that at least two, and possibly three or four, cultural horizons had been exposed (fig. 2). In spite of this, ceramic analysis was structured from the outset to permit complex discrimination as well as complex definition, since it could not be assumed that these deposits had not been disturbed by prior transgressions of the river.

To achieve these goals, frequencies of directly observable paste, form, and decoration attributes were plotted at the outset on distribution graphs by excavation levels. However, it soon became apparent that more in-depth analysis would be required just to isolate each complex, since most of the attributes selected for this purpose were represented in all of the levels sampled, or in each of the postulated cultural horizons. Therefore a modal analysis was carried out according to procedures described by Rouse (1939) and Lathrap (1962). This analysis culminated with the definition of paste, form, size, finish, and design modes for each of nine ceramic lots, which were plotted again in bar graph form to expose differential distribution patterns. Unfortunately, this approach proved as inconclusive as the preceding since the majority of modes discerned were represented in each of the cultural horizons observed in the stratigraphic record.

At this point a form of cluster analysis was initiated after an approach advocated by Spaulding (1960), which resulted in the successful discrimination of significant combinations or clusters of paste, form, size, and decoration modes for each of nine levels. When the frequencies of the respective combinations, later defined as types, were plotted by levels in bar graph form, distribution curves finally emerged that conformed respectably with the stratigraphic record.

Before proceeding further, the graphs were checked against the stratigraphic record in order to clarify whether irregularities that did appear in the curves reflected significant instances of slopewash or redeposition (cf. Phillips, Ford, and Griffin 1951). This test proved insightful since significant examples of both of these phenomena were recognized that would otherwise have gone undetected. The same procedures also revealed that the developmental trajectory was not as continuous or smooth as suggested by the distribution graphs and thus permitted tighter definition of the respective ceramic complexes. To any who would argue that the benefits of combined modal and cluster analysis are outweighed by labor costs, I would therefore repeat that standard classificatory procedures failed to expose several major depositional events in this instance, much less the sequence reviewed below.

With this in mind I would also add that the analytical procedures reviewed above conform with principles of deductive logic to a greater degree than those employed by type-variety analysts. For example, following attribute identification and postulation of hypothetical vessel forms, I deduced that aperture size, aperture angles, and/or neck heights would scatter nonrandomly if they were modal forms. In many instances, scattergram preparation revealed this to be the case, or led to revised specification of forms. Following this, I deduced that the hypothetical forms and vessel sizes should also cluster with attributes of decoration, and proceeded to test this by means of rudimentary cluster analysis. Where this was the case, attributes and clusters, respectively, were elevated to the status of modes and hypothetical types.

In contrast, type-variety analysts appear to assign type, variety, and even mode designations to inductively generated features or attribute clusters. That is, I am aware of comparatively little revision of type or variety specifications carried out in the laboratory or mentioned in the literature that was based upon deductive testing procedures.

Since the same analysts have become increasingly sensitive to such scientific procedures where lithic, paleozoological, paleobotanical, or settlement system data are concerned, I find this ironical. Indeed, to my mind this explains what I have perceived as a developing disinterest in ceramic analysis and data among students of the skeptical variety.

The Ceramic Sequence

Although discontinuities are emphasized in this presentation, through time as much bifurcation and merging of modal clusters are indicated in this ceramic sequence as total replacement of types. It must therefore be stressed that the ceramic inventory from Playa de los Muertos in its entirety comprises a well-integrated tradition (figs. 3, 4, 5, 6, and 7).

The Zanjos Complex

The earliest complex defined encompasses a comparatively limited inventory of types, and has been named the Zanjos complex. Among these, fine and coarse paste flaring neck jar types with unmodified or outturned rims were most prevalent. The respective form variants were finished in red-on-buff, in the first instance, and in matte red slip in the second. Red-on-buff or red rim painting was also employed on incurved wall bowls with upturned rims.

The most distinctive Zanjos type is comprised of shallow flaring wall bowls whose exterior walls were both painted in fugitive red and incised. The incised designs were placed below circumferential lip incisions, and consisted of sine curve elements combined in a variety of layouts.

Since radiocarbon samples were not recovered from Zanjos strata, its age was estimated with reference to comparative data. Unfortunately, though, the comparative record proved unilluminating in this case because the types concerned compare to varying degrees with both Early and Middle Formative types from southern Mesoamerica. For example, whereas the flaring wall jars resemble both Achiotes Unslipped and Abelino Red types of the Xe ceramic sphere (Adams 1971; Sabloff 1975), the flaring wall bowls compare with types assigned to both the Jaral complex of Los Naranjos (Baudez and Becquelin 1973) and the Tok complex of Chalchuapa (Sharer 1978c).

Because of this I originally, and it appears overeagerly, hypothesized that the Zanjos complex dated to the end of the Early Formative period (Kennedy 1978). However, with combined reference to four radiocarbon dates from overlying deposits and internal comparative data, it later became apparent that alignment with the Los Naranjos Jaral phase (Baudez and Becquelin 1973) was most appropriate. Therefore the occupation is now bracketed between 650 and 450 B.C. (Kennedy 1981).

Aside from this, it remains noteworthy that the Zanjos complex incorporates almost all of the features that Lowe (1978) has ascribed

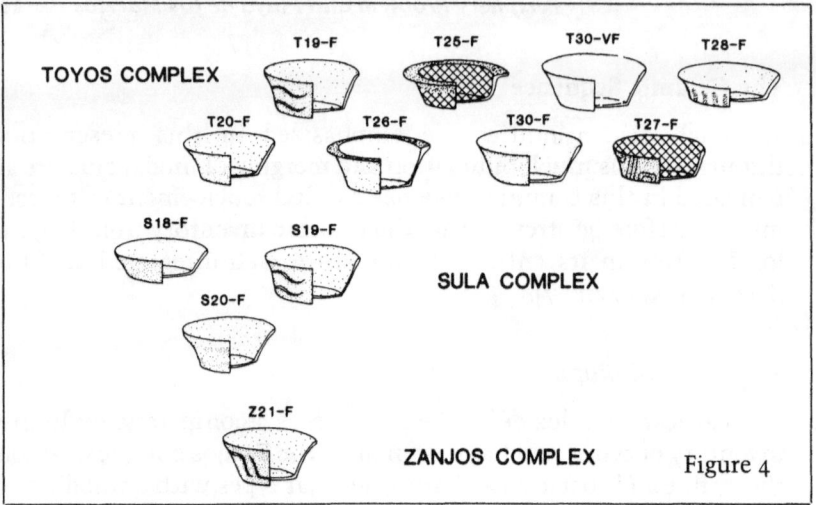

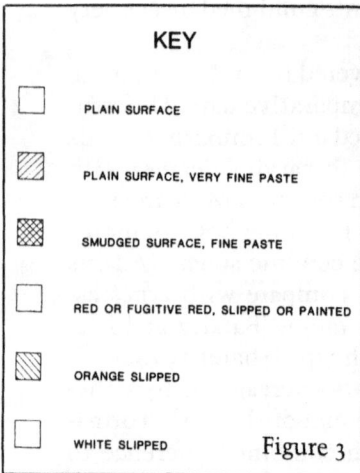

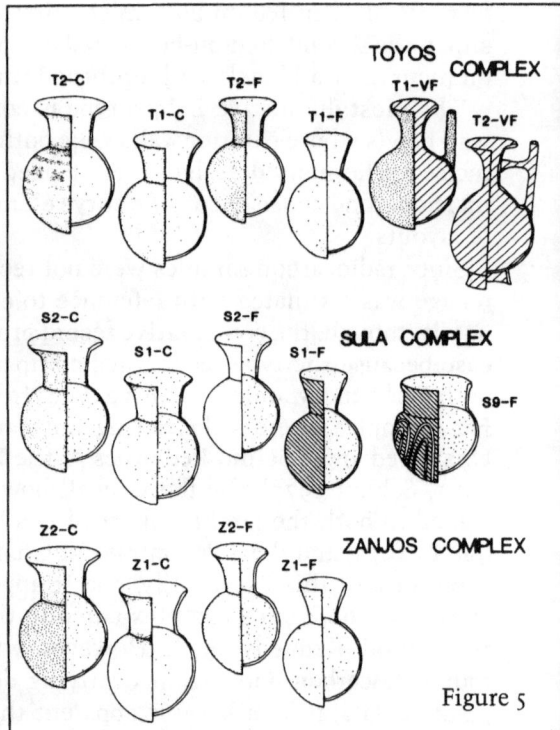

Figure 3. Key to Figures 4 through 7.

Figure 4. Sequence of flaring-wall bowl, trapezoidal bowl, and dish types.

Figure 5. Sequence of flaring-wall jar types.

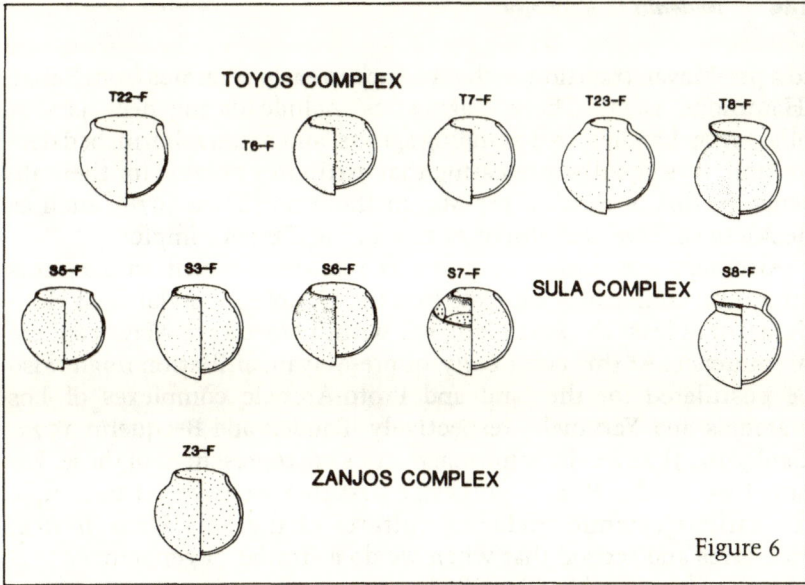

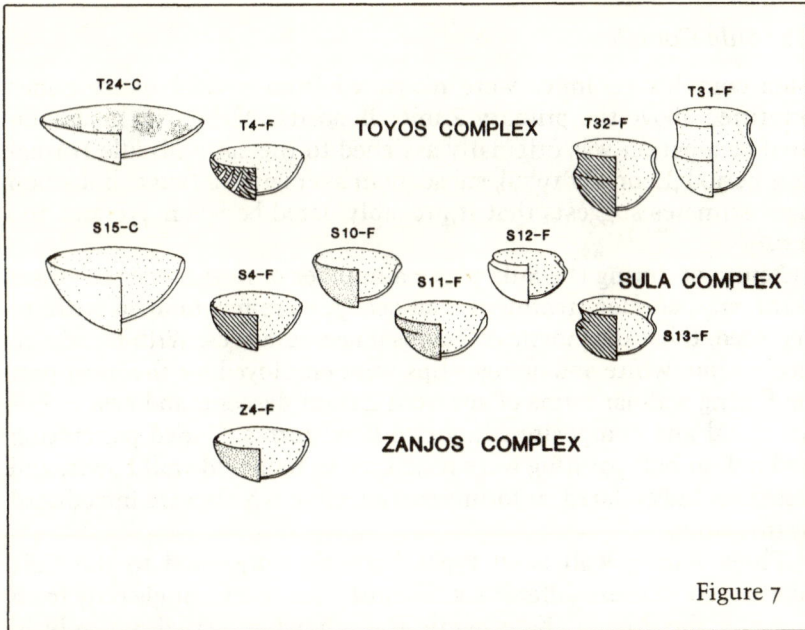

Figure 6. Sequence of incurved-wall bowl, neckless jar, and collared jar types.

Figure 7. Sequence of sub-hemispherical and composite-silhouette bowl types.

to a pre-Mayan tradition with reference to early ceramics from Belize (Hammond 1977). These diagnostics include flaring neck jars or ollas, strap handles, free-standing spouts, and pattern-burnished decoration. It is equally interesting that attributes notable for their absence in this postulated pre-Mayan tradition (Lowe 1978), such as neckless jars, are also absent or rare in the Zanjos complex.

Although the Zanjos complex is relatively recent in age, this structural conformity suggests that the Caribbean lowlands of Honduras, or at least the Sula Plain, fell within Lowe's pre-Mayan sphere of influence. At this point early, or pre-Mayan, affiliation might also be postulated for the Jaral and Proto-Archaic complexes of Los Naranjos and Yarumela, respectively (Baudez and Becquelin 1973; Canby 1949), since the same diagnostics are represented in these. For now I would therefore hypothesize first that we have yet to sample the earliest ceramic-producing cultures of the Sula Plain or west Honduras and second that when we do a similar or generalized pre-Mayan pattern will be identified.

The Sula Complex

Sula complex ceramics were recovered from several refuse zones stratified above the primary Zanjos deposits. Although the associated occupation was originally assigned to the early Middle Formative period (Kennedy 1978), subsequent averaging of two radiocarbon age estimates suggests that it probably dated between 450 and 300 B.C.

Before or during the Sula phase a number of new modes of vessel form, size, surface treatment, and design were recombined with, or replaced, those diagnostic of Zanjos phase ceramics. With respect to decoration, white and orange slips were employed for the most part on flaring wall jar forms of apparent Zanjos descent, and new hemispherical and composite-silhouette bowl forms. Zoned punctation and red-on-buff painting were restricted to incurved wall bowls, and neckless and collared jar form variants, all of which were introduced at this time.

Three flaring wall bowl types have been assigned to the Sula phase. One of these differed significantly in aperture angle only from those of the Zanjos phase, while the other two varied not only in depth and aperture angle, but also in decoration. The most notable finishing innovation was application of fugitive red paint to exterior walls in narrow parallel circumferential bands.

Most of the innovations referred to above recall Middle Formative diagnostics of Conchas 1 in Soconusco (Coe 1961), Real Xe at Seibal (Sabloff 1975), Colos and Kal at Chalchuapa (Sharer 1978c), and Jaral and Eden 1 at Los Naranjos (Baudez and Becquelin 1973). However, the diagnostic modal clusters, as opposed to individual modes, compare with Early or Middle Formative types defined at Chalchuapa and Los Naranjos to a much greater degree than those of either Mexico or Guatemala. It therefore appears most likely that the introduction of at least white and orange slipping, zoned punctation, and neckless jars at Playa de los Muertos was stimulated by contacts with a number of diagnostic Early and Middle Formative Isthmian types, the complex as a whole compares more precisely with variants of these that appear to have evolved in the southeastern highlands.

Since the Sula complex shares as many structural features with the contemporary Eden 1 complex of Los Naranjos as with either the Kal or Colos complexes of Chalchuapa, this set of relationships merits further mention. Specifically, the influences referred to may have been channeled to the Sula Plain from or through the southeastern highlands by way of sites such as Los Naranjos, because white slipping and other Sula diagnostics characterized the earlier Jaral phases there as well as Eden 1 (Baudez and Becquelin 1973). Since composite-silhouette bowls at both Los Naranjos and Chalchuapa were regularly decorated in Usulutan resist as well as orange slip, it appears that Playa de los Muertos was also further along some receiving line than Los Naranjos with respect to this technology (cf. Baudez and Becquelin 1973; Sharer 1978c).

The Toyos Complex

Ceramics assigned to the Toyos complex were recovered from several layers of fill associated with a well-defined pit house. Because the ceramics associated with the floor of the house differ from those that accumulated above it, up to a hundred years may have elapsed between these depositional events. However, since circumstances have, to date, prohibited proper differentiation of these remains, the associated ceramics are considered below as a single assemblage.

A variety of intrusive and modified Sula modes of paste, form, and decoration distinguish the Toyos complex. An unusually fine or homogeneous paste that sustained a high polish was first employed at this time in the manufacture of specialized jar and bowl forms. The former included tall single-spout and bridge bottles with markedly flaring or trumpet necks, low pedestal bases, and fine applique or incised decoration. The latter included forms with out-turned rims, the upper surfaces of which were incised with single or paired line layouts. In some instances these rim incisions were terminated on small lugs, tabs, or rim adornos.

In the Toyos phase flange rim bowls and trapezoidal bowls were also introduced. Most of these were intentionally smudged or under-fired to contrast with fugitive-red painted panels that were zoned and decorated with engraved lines. The latter, which were often filled with white paint, were confined to bowl flanges and the exterior of trapezoidal bowls. The designs comprise a discrete class character-ized by the use of nested rectangle, triangle, and stepped-line elements.

Well-polished red slipped and red-on-white painted vessels are also characteristic of the Toyos phase. Red slip, in this instance, was em-ployed on neckless and collared jars, incurved wall bowls, and simple flaring wall bowls, or on forms that had previously been decorated in red-on-buff or by zoned punctation. Red-on-white paint was utilized on small trapezoidal bowls and coarse paste flaring neck jars.

Many of the modes referred to above closely resemble or are even identical to Sula modes. Nevertheless, it is possible that external contacts catalyzed the respective type transformations or mode re-combinations, since the Toyos complex (300–100 B.C.) is contempo-rary with or postdates those with which it best compares. For ex-ample, the complex as a whole recalls not only a number of late Middle Formative complexes of the southeastern highlands and the Maya lowlands, but also an early Late Formative complex from Los Naranjos.

After Baudez and Becquelin (1973), it therefore appears that ce-ramic development in Honduras was increasingly conditioned, at least towards the end of the Formative period, by stylistic trends in Mesoamerica proper. Nevertheless, for the following reasons I would not follow Baudez and Becquelin's (1973) lead to the extent of pin-pointing the Maya lowlands as the source of such stimuli. First, al-though Toyos red slipped ceramics resemble types assigned to the San Felix (Sabloff 1975), Escoba (Adams 1971), Jenny Creek, and Bar-ton Creek (Gifford 1976) complexes, they compare just as well with earlier and contemporary complexes from Chalchuapa and Kaminal-juyu (Sharer 1978c). Second, the very fine paste Toyos bowl types with out-turned and incised rims are as comparable to earlier Isth-mian types as they are to contemporary Mayan types. Third, while the unusual zoned-textured flange rim bowls are similar to types defined at Mirador and Izapa (Peterson 1963), the infamous stirrup spout jars recall forms associated not only with Tlatilco (Porter 1953) but also the Gulf Coast (Lowe 1978).

In sum, if external contact is to be invoked in this instance, it appears that eclectic borrowing and recombination of modes or ideas are represented as opposed to input from a single source. I would therefore hypothesize first, that by the Toyos phase Playa de los Muertos was hooked up to an extensive ethnic trade network spanning portions of both highland and lowland Mesoamerica as well as western Honduras and points east and south; second, that Isthmian notions of right form prevailed over strictly Mayan standards up to and into the Late Formative period; and third, that receptivity to particular innovations along the line and at Playa de los Muertos was dictated by local preference or precedent.

Finally, with reference to Tlatilco it now appears that any connection that existed with Playa de los Muertos must be reexamined with reference to the spread of greater Olmec, west Mexican, or Isthmian cultural modes. It also seems that a relationship of common ancestry is more probable in this case than one of direct contact, since Toyos specialty wares recall South American traditions to as great or to a greater degree than either Tlatilco or Olmec ceramics. I would therefore postulate that whether or not Tlatilco conventions directly impacted ceramic evolution at Playa de los Muertos, there was a long-term, if indirect, connection of at least equal significance between the Sula Plain, or the eastern lowland corridor of Central America, and northern South America.

Previous Investigations Reconsidered

The preceding comparative discussion may appear conservative as compared with previous assessments of Playa de los Muertos, which dealt to a much greater degree with possible long-distance contacts as opposed to relationships within the Southeast Periphery of southern Mesoamerica. Although the relevant discrepancies reflect prior errors of omission as much as commission, they are reviewed below because they illustrate the degree to which presumption of peripherality has biased the record.

To begin with, when Popenoe (1934) prepared her preliminary report describing the burials she uncovered at Playa de los Muertos, she was unable to determine their relative age. Her illustrations taken together with Vaillant's (1934) comparative analysis revealed that the associated ceramic remains dated to the Preclassic or Formative Period, but that was about all.

When Strong, Kidder, and Paul (1938) returned to the site, they sampled two refuse deposits of cultural horizons that were separated by a thick bed of alluvial fill. After defining five tentative ceramic groupings, they noted that the relative frequency of sherds assigned to the respective classes varied significantly between the two deposits, which they had named Cultural Horizons A and B. It is probable that this report would have proven more informative if they had had an opportunity to refine the analysis. However, since they did not other scholars have had to refer to Playa de los Muertos, for the most part, as a single complex or cultural tradition (cf. Stone 1972; Coe 1961).

In retrospect it appears that Strong, Kidder, and Paul failed to proceed further than they did because analytical difficulties comparable to those described in a previous section of this report were encountered. In other words, significant variations between the horizons they observed may have been obscured by significant continuities. This claim seems reasonable since their ceramic horizons do conform respectably with the Sula and Toyos complexes described above (Table 1).

At this point it should also be noted that Strong, Kidder, and Paul (1938) dwelled on description and illustration of specialty wares in their report, such as stirrup-spouted jars or embossed bottles, to what appears to have been an exaggerated degree. Because of this, other dimensions of variability were overlooked that were subsequently recognized as Early and Middle Formative diagnostics. For example, it is now well known that red-rimmed neckless jars, bowls with out-turned or flange rims, zoned punctation, and a variety of

Table 1. Juxtaposition of Strong, Kidder, and Paul's Subtypes with Their Groupings, and the Complexes Reviewed in This Report

Strong, Kidder, and Paul Subtypes	Strong, Kidder, and Paul Horizon Affiliations	Kennedy Complex Affiliations
1. Coarse ware	B and C	Zanjos and Sula
2. Red-orange ware	*B*[a] and C	*Toyos* and Sula
3. Gray-to-buff ware	B and *C*	Toyos and *Sula*
4. Dark-gray ware	B and C	Toyos
5. White ware	B and *C*	Sula
6. Painted ware		
Red-and-black	B	Toyos
Red-on-buff	C	Sula
White-on-red	B	Toyos

[a] Several of the subtypes were represented in both horizons or complexes. Those in which they were predominant are italicized.

incised design layouts are diagnostic of Formative period ceramics. If these features had been clearly illustrated and described by Strong, Kidder, and Paul I believe that Playa de los Muertos would have found a home in the Mesoamerican Formative at a much earlier date.

In sum, descriptive adjectives appended at the outset to delineations of Playa de los Muertos ceramics, such as "preliminary" and "tentative," were subtly displaced over the years by adjectives such as "peripheral" and "retarded." If the pertinence of these labels had been adequately tested earlier on, this problem might not have arisen. As it happened, the labels "periphery" and "frontier" provided an on-going excuse to give low priority to continued investigations in this region, and thus the terms became more firmly entrenched than ever.

Discussion

The periphery problem was aggravated in the 1950s as investigators came, unintentionally in many cases, to assume, in effect, that cultural spacing achieved prior to that time was as absolute as their new radiocarbon record. Since it soon became evident that the radiocarbon record was not all that absolute, these age estimates were fairly promptly recognized as such and tested against one another and other indices of age. However, independent verification was not as carefully sought with respect to the bounding of space with the result that the Southeastern Periphery and other similar spatial-cultural frames became more firmly entrenched than ever.

If the hypothetical nature of these boundaries had been recognized and examined systematically against independent measures of cultural variability across space this might have been avoided. Instead, and although archaeologists became ever more attentive to sampling prerequisites within some cultural and geographic regions, the fact that each of the culture areas concerned also merited an equal chance was often, in practice, overlooked. In other words, if one is counting investigations carried out or energies invested in random sampling of or within postulated culture areas as opposed to regions, the Southeastern Periphery was inadequately sampled.

Because of this, the boundaries concerned should probably have been erased for the duration, and, for lack of attention, it might be argued that to some degree they were. However, both the area frame and the labels "periphery" and "frontier" lingered in the literature. The latter was the more inappropriate, because its use implied that the area concerned was bounded through time by a culture area that was relatively central, focal, pivotal, or nuclear.

With respect to lowland Maya cultural development in the Classic period and contemporary developments in the Southeast Periphery, such a claim of peripherality can be substantiated to some degree. However, as we move back into the Formative period it becomes increasingly difficult with available data to demonstrate that cultural development within the Maya lowlands or the supposed Periphery was any more or less focal. Ironically though, just this notion was perpetuated by inattention to the Southeast Periphery or by what I would label "area centric" tendencies. Specifically, those engaged in research in southern Mesoamerica proper as opposed to the Periphery all too naturally or subconsciously tended to assume that those areas with which they were already and increasingly familiar were not only distinct but also central or focal.

To those engaged in, or planning, research not only in the Southeastern Periphery but also in southern Mesoamerica, I therefore offer the following thoughts as a means by which the objective appraisal and ranking of cultural variation across space could be furthered in the future. First, if spatial frames are to serve as structural devices that assist in the detection and explanation of cultural exchange both within and beyond geographical regions or areas, I believe they should be labeled as such and nothing more. In other words, such loaded terms as "peripheral" and "frontier" should be deleted unless they can be qualified. Alternatively, such a term as "ethnotone" might be employed in their place, with the latter being defined as an ethnic transition zone or as a cultural equivalent of an ecotone. I would opt for a label such as this because the cultural boundaries with which we are concerned, at least in Mesoamerica, are more akin to ethnic interfaces than they are to classic frontiers (cf. Fox 1981).

Second, collection of a data base amenable to such evaluation or classification is still required. This tactic is not as obvious as it may appear. As our knowledge of previously unknown zones in southern Mesoamerica improves, as is now the case for the Sula plain, Lake Yojoa, and portions of central Honduras, and as these areas appear not to be as peripheral as was previously supposed, we should not succumb to the temptation of simply displacing the frontier further east. This would serve only to box off, or to contain, another zone of ignorance, or to further prejudice the record, when what is called for now is extension of our sampling universe to include just this zone.

Third, if the latter is to be avoided I feel we should carefully define qualitative and quantitative cultural indices that measure degrees of centrality as well as peripherality (Lattimore 1962). Along these lines, increased efforts might be directed at organization and presentation of ceramic data in a manner permitting or encouraging independent evaluation of the movement of raw materials and manufacturing processes as well as finished products. To some extent this has been attempted or achieved in the past, at least on a regional level. However, to the degree that prior practice has reinforced comparison of relatively arbitrary types in comparative analyses and synthetic statements, as opposed to the methods advocated here, differential or cross-cutting distribution patterns or systems have been partially obscured.

In conclusion, with reference to the revised Formative ceramic sequence from Playa de los Muertos, I have attempted in this paper to demonstrate that an area formerly recognized as a cultural frontier was then, and remains to a large degree, a frontier of knowledge. I have also suggested that this frontier will only be penetrated if the barrier this notion has become is at least temporarily dismantled, or if sites such as Playa de los Muertos are sprung from the peripheral bag.

ARTHUR A. DEMAREST AND ROBERT J. SHARER

14

Late Preclassic Ceramic Spheres, Culture Areas, and Cultural Evolution in the Southeastern Highlands of Mesoamerica

Introduction

In the past decade, Mesoamericanists have shown an increasing interest in the archaeology of the highlands of El Salvador and Guatemala. Recent excavations in western El Salvador (Demarest 1981; Sharer, ed., 1978; Sheets 1976) have belied that region's traditional designation as "peripheral" to the mainstream of Mesoamerican cultural evolution. Indeed, the new evidence indicates that during the Preclassic period, western El Salvador was a populous, innovative region contributing key traits to the increasingly complex material culture of southern Mesoamerica (cf. Demarest and Sharer 1982; Sharer and Gifford 1970; Sheets 1979a). Meanwhile, archaeological researches in the adjacent highlands and Pacific coast of Guatemala (fig. 1) have confirmed that area's critical role in the formation of Mayan civilization (see, for example, Graham 1976, 1978; Lowe 1978; Sedat and Sharer 1972).

This intensified archaeological activity in the southeastern highlands has consisted of independent projects with a minimum of inter-project coordination of research or results. In the published reports, interregional comparisons have identified important connections with distant areas such as Central Mexico (e.g., Parsons 1969; Sanders and Michels, eds., 1977) and the Maya lowlands (e.g.,

Figure 1. The Late Preclassic Southeast Highland Ceramic Spheres.

Dahlin 1979; Sharer and Gifford 1970; Sheets 1976, 1979a). Yet inter-site connections within the highlands themselves have remained rather ill-defined.

The Chalchuapa report (Sharer, ed., 1978) took the first steps toward establishing a more systematic framework for intersite comparison within the southeastern highlands. In this site's ceramic study, Sharer (1978c) noted that the two great Late Preclassic centers of the southeastern highlands, Chalchuapa and Kaminaljuyu, shared several major ceramic types as well as many attributes of both vessel form and surface decoration. Sharer summarized this important pattern of similarities in his concluding observations on Chalchuapa's Chul and Caynac complexes of the Late Preclassic:

> In many ways the Chul Complex is a near duplicate of the Miraflores Phase at Kaminaljuyu. There are regional (local) variations, and the internal Chalchuapa pottery traditions remain viable, but there are undeniably strong ceramic ties to Kaminaljuyu. The Caynac Ceramic Complex (Early Facet) demonstrates a con-

tinuation and elaboration of the intimate ceramic ties to Kaminaljuyu first expressed during the Chul Complex (Sharer
1978c: 126).

While the Chalchuapa project was in progress, a large-scale program
of excavations and settlement pattern studies was undertaken at Kaminaljuyu itself (Sanders and Michels, eds., 1977; Wetherington
1978; Michels 1979a, 1979b). The problem orientations of this Pennsylvania State University Kaminaljuyu Project were quite specific:
on the one hand, the excavators focused on the evolution of intra-
regional exchange networks and social systems and, on the other, on
the nature of long distance contact with Central Mexico. In the published reports to date, there has been little discussion of interregional interaction within the highlands themselves, e.g., connections between Middle to Late Preclassic Kaminaljuyu and centers
such as Chalchuapa, Izapa, Monte Alto, and Bilbao. The ceramic reports on Kaminaljuyu also have quite specific problem orientations,
while the descriptions of the ceramics (Wetherington 1978) use a
new taxonomic system (stressing wares) with ceramic classes which
are not easily compared with more conventional type-variety units,
such as those defined at Chalchuapa. While the problem-specific
orientation of the Kaminaljuyu reports is their greatest strength, it
does leave us with the important task of more precisely defining
Kaminaljuyu-Chalchuapa relations in the Middle to Late Preclassic,
as well as the overall nature of interregional networks within the
southeastern highlands.

Recent Comparative Research

The Santa Leticia Project (Demarest 1981, in press) has undertaken
the first steps toward this goal by attempting to systematically compare and align the Preclassic highland assemblages. The ceramics of
the Preclassic village and ceremonial center at Santa Leticia, a highland site in the Department of Ahuachapan (see fig. 1), are a provincial variant of the Chul and Early Caynac complexes, showing close
similarities to both the Chalchuapa assemblage and those of the
Guatemalan sites to the west. Furthermore, Santa Leticia ceramic
mode and classificatory tabulations were designed to generate sets of
descriptive statistics directly comparable to both Wetherington's
(1978) taxonomic approach at Kaminaljuyu (based on rim sherds and
emphasizing modes) and Sharer's (1978c) methodology at Chalchuapa (using total sherd counts and stressing type-variety classes).
Thus, the Santa Leticia analysis served as an interface between the

TRADITIONAL KAMINALJUYU CHRONOLOGY (Borhegyi 1965a: Table 1)	REVISED KAMINALJUYU CHRONOLOGY (Wetherington 1978)	ORIGINAL CHALCHUAPA CHRONOLOGY (Sharer 1978c)	SANTA LETICIA CHRONOLOGY FOLLOWED IN THIS REPORT	
			VEC	— 300 A.D.
SANTA CLARA	AURORA	VEC		— 200 A.D.
			CAYNAC (Late Facet)	
	ARENAL	CAYNAC (Late Facet)		— 100 A.D.
MIRAFLORES			CAYNAC (Early Facet)	— 0
	VERBENA	CAYNAC (Early Facet)		— 100 B.C.
				— 200 B.C.
			CHUL	
	PROVIDENCIA	CHUL		— 300 B.C.
PROVIDENCIA				
		KAL	KAL	— 400 B.C.
LAS CHARCAS	LAS CHARCAS			— 500 B.C.

Figure 2. Chronologies of the southeastern highlands.

Chalchuapa and Kaminaljuyu taxonomies, allowing reassessment of both typologies. In turn, these reassessments required modification and refinement of the western Salvadoran chronology (see fig. 2) and type-variety taxonomy (Demarest 1981; Demarest and Sharer 1982).

A second stage in these researches involved actual reexamination of previously excavated collections from southeastern Mesoamerica, beginning with the Kaminaljuyu collections from the Carnegie Institution excavations of the 1930s and 1940s (Kidder, Jennings, and Shook 1946; Shook and Kidder 1952). We also reexamined the type collections from the Pennsylvania State University excavations at Kaminaljuyu (with the generous assistance and advice of their analyst, R. K. Wetherington).

Comparison to southeast highland complexes was extended to Monte Alto by a brief comparison of materials and subsequent discussion between A. Demarest and the analysts of the Monte Alto ceramics, E. Shook and M. Hatch. Looking further to the north, direct comparisons to the ceramics of the Salama valley sites were made by Sharer and Sedat, co-directors of the valley project. Examination of a "rediscovered" collection from Wolfgang Haberland's test excavations at Atiquisaya, near Chalchuapa, identified materials as familiar Salvadoran Late Preclassic Chul and Caynac complex types. At the present time, comparisons to Bilbao are based only on the published monograph (Parsons 1967).

The patterning in the southeast highland materials was confirmed by study of Late Preclassic collections from less closely related southeastern Mesoamerican sites including Quelepa (eastern El Salvador), Rio Grande and El Perical (central El Salvador), Quirigua (southeastern Guatemala), Copan (western Honduras), and Yarumela (southcentral Honduras). Discussions and comparisons with the pottery of even more distant regions, for example, central Chiapas and Belize, provided a broader context for interpretations.

Problems in Taxonomy and Terminology

As detailed below, these comparative studies revealed that many of the ceramic assemblages of the southeastern highland sites (Kaminaljuyu, Chalchuapa, Santa Leticia, Monte Alto, Atiquisaya, Bilbao) are virtually identical. Nonetheless, the actual type-by-type correlation of the ceramic classes of these sites proved to be a frustrating problem due to widely differing classificatory schemes applied by the original analysts. Indeed, it now seems apparent that such differences in taxonomic methodology have largely obscured the unity now seen in the ceramic assemblages of southeast highland sites.

The most important example of these confusing misalignments was found in attempts to compare the ceramic taxonomies of Kaminaljuyu and Chalchuapa—the two largest centers of the southeastern highland region. As mentioned above, the Kaminaljuyu (Wetherington 1978) and Chalchuapa (Sharer 1978c) reports used non-comparable classificatory schemes to describe the ceramics of the two sites. The Chalchuapa Project used a conventional "type-variety" methodology emphasizing surface treatment and decorative modes (Gifford 1976). In contrast, the Kaminaljuyu ceramic report used a classification stressing broadly-defined and long-lived "wares," based principally on paste characteristics. These methodological differences obscured some of the most significant ceramic connections between these sites. It should be noted, however, that a series of ceramic traditions was also defined at Chalchuapa, based upon general continuity through time in major ceramic groups (Sharer 1978c: 115–118). Several of these traditions do seem to correspond to "ware" units defined at Kaminaljuyu.

A comparison of the Chalchuapa and Kaminaljuyu black-brown ware taxonomies illustrates the differing logic used to classify all of the other types at the two sites (see fig. 3). At Chalchuapa, the black-brown types were defined by specific decorative modes (plain, coarse-incised, red-filled) according to standard type-variety procedures, while taxonomy at Kaminaljuyu divided such material into black-brown (matte surfaced) and polished black wares. Another difference is that at Chalchuapa this same long-lived, black-brown tradition was divided into a chronological sequence of ceramic "groups" (Jinuapa, Pinos, and Chiquihuat), whose diagnostic traits were isolated in the stratigraphy of Chalchuapa's Laguna Cuzcachapa midden (B. Anderson 1978). In contrast, ceramic groups were not used at Kaminaljuyu. Instead, Wetherington's (1978) two wares, Miraflores Black-Brown and Miraflores Polished Black, were more inclusive categories running from the Middle Preclassic beginnings to the Postclassic end of the sequence. Chronological division of the Kaminaljuyu black-brown ceramics was accomplished by studies of vessel form and other modes, but few chronologically restricted types were defined.

A more serious problem in the existing classifications and interpretations is the taxonomic quagmire surrounding the important "Aguacate Orange" group. The presence of Aguacate Orange has often been considered one of the most significant features of the Caynac Complex at Chalchuapa. Not only is Aguacate Orange one of the major groups defining the complex, but it is also a key element in controversies concerning Salvadoran influence on the Maya

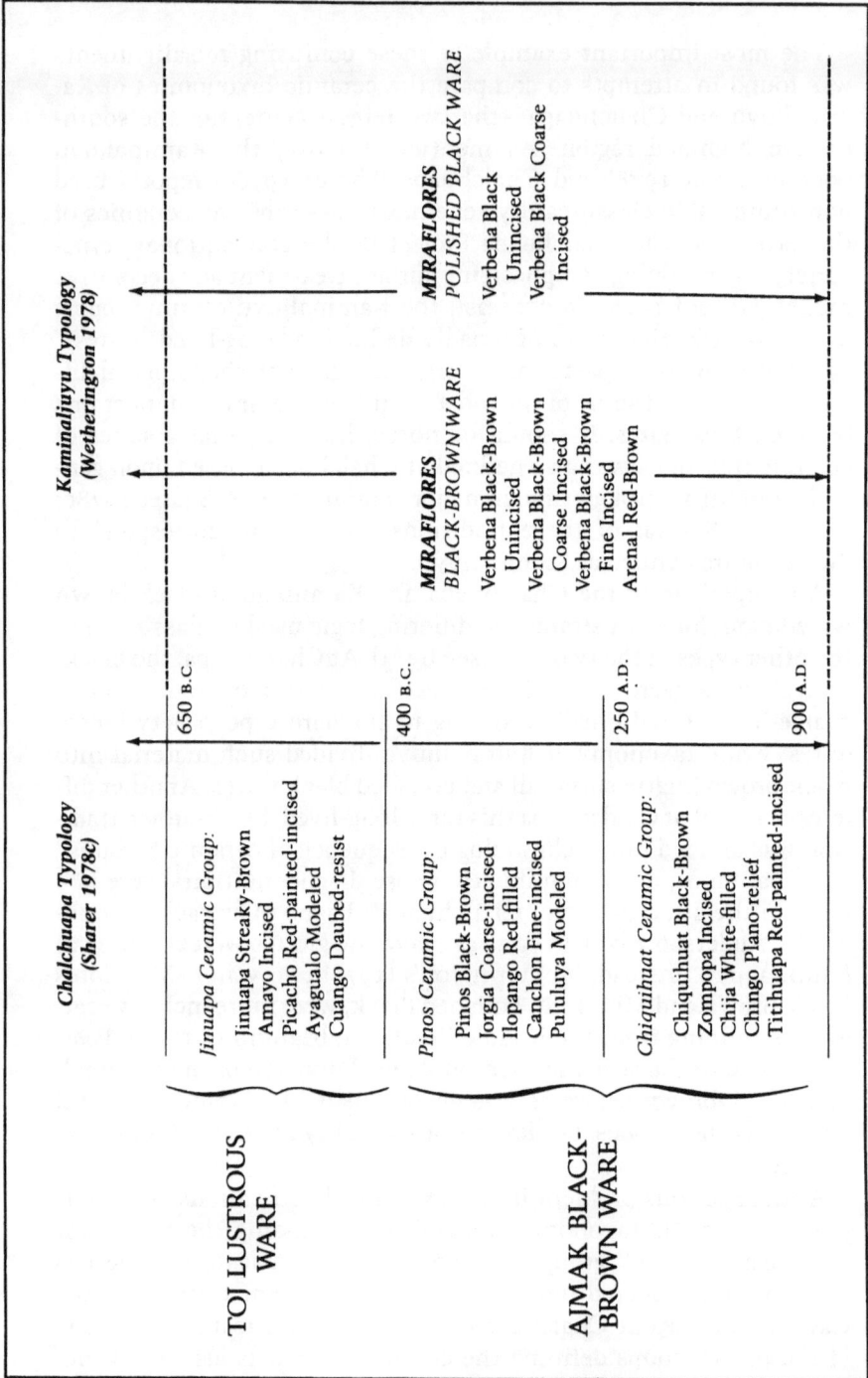

Figure 3. Contrasting classifications of identical southeast highland black-brown ceramics.

lowlands, the hypothesized "Protoclassic Intrusion" into Belize, and the processes leading to the rise of Maya civilization (Gifford 1976; Sharer and Gifford 1970; Sharer 1978c; Sheets 1976, 1979a). An unexpected discovery of our recent reanalyses was that the Carnegie excavation collections (Peabody Museum) from Kaminaljuyu include large quantities of heavy-walled sherds strikingly similar to "Aguacate Orange: Atecozol variety" as defined at Chalchuapa. Examination of other Kaminaljuyu collections have confirmed that the coarse, cache bowl variants of this red-orange ceramic were shared by the Terminal Preclassic assemblages at Kaminaljuyu (Verbena and Arenal Complexes) and Chalchuapa (Caynac and Vec Complexes).

However, such sherds (dating to the Verbena and Arenal phases) have been tabulated by the Pennsylvania State Kaminaljuyu project within the Villalobos Red Ware (Wetherington 1978: 80). This ware also includes other material (with the same general paste characteristics) which is quite different from the Atecozol variety ceramics of Chalchuapa, lacking the specific surface characteristics used to define this class there. The Kaminaljuyu Villalobos Red Ware types into which these sherds were classified are less restricted than Chalchuapa's Aguacate Orange: Atecozol variety in both their diagnostic characteristics and chronological placement. Thus, although Chalchuapa's Aguacate Orange: Atecozol variety of the Caynac Complex had a close counterpart at Kaminaljuyu in the coeval Verbena and Arenal complexes, it is impossible to express this culturally significant fact in terms of a one-to-one correspondence of types or other ceramic classes.

The highland Aguacate Orange situation is further complicated by our reassessment of the typological link between the original "Aguacate Orange" ceramic group first defined in Belize (Gifford 1976) and these heavy-walled red-orange highland types. Our recent researches have led us to question the original definition (Gifford 1976; Sharer and Gifford 1970) of these highland ceramics as a variant and ancestor of the Maya lowland Aguacate group. As detailed elsewhere (Demarest 1981) sherd-to-sherd comparisons using the wider range of materials available in both the eastern lowlands and southeast highlands can no longer be said to support type- or even group-level connections between the respective Late Preclassic heavy pasted red-orange ceramics of these two regions. Similarities are found in associated modes (such as mamiform tetrapod supports) but typological correspondences are limited to their general color and some paste characteristics. We have tentatively proposed (Demarest 1981: 301–309) that Aguacate Orange: Atecozol variety and the similar ceramics at Kaminaljuyu and other southeast highland sites be designated a single Atecozol Ceramic Group only distantly related to the Aguacate Orange ceramics of Belize. Thus again we see that reassessment of previous taxonomic categories reveals the closer ties between southeast highland assemblages (e.g., Atecozol Group), while deemphasizing earlier arguments for long-distance connections.

Other examples of confusing non-comparable taxonomic divisions of identical materials shared by Kaminaljuyu, Chalchuapa, and other southeast highland sites include the Usulutan-decorated ceramics. Though three of the four major Usulutan-decorated types at Kaminaljuyu have identical correlates in the ceramics of Chalchuapa, the appropriate taxonomic and terminological connections had not been made—again, due to the differing logic of the respective classificatory schemes (Wetherington 1978; Sharer 1978) applied at the two sites. Modal, rather than typological, treatment of Usulutan designs at Santa Leticia has facilitated the revision of the taxonomy of the Usulutans (see Demarest 1981; Demarest and Sharer 1982), aligning the differing classifications of the identical Usulutan ceramics at the two sites.

The correction of all of these distortive factors through direct comparisons of southeast highland collections, reassessment of taxonomic logic, and reclassifications have supported and greatly extended the earlier suggestions of ceramic ties between some southeast highland centers (Sharer 1978c: 125–127; 1974: 170–171). Indeed, reevaluation and alignment of the red and black monochromes, the Atecozol group ceramics (alias Aguacate Orange), and the Usulutans reveal the virtual uniformity of ceramic assemblages of the southeast highlands in the Late Preclassic period.

Preclassic Ceramic Unity in the Southeastern Highlands: An Overview

The general conclusion of all of these comparative studies is that southeast highland sites—including Chalchuapa, Santa Leticia, Atiquisaya, Kaminaljuyu, and Monte Alto—share remarkably similar ceramic assemblages during the late Middle to Terminal Preclassic periods. New evidence has confirmed and increased the list of types and modes shared by Kaminaljuyu and Chalchuapa and has shown that this pattern extended to other sites in the region, thus demonstrating essential ceramic unity of an area extending across the highlands of southeastern Guatemala and western El Salvador (see fig. 1).

This unity can be defined in terms of most of the major types of the Late Preclassic period. The basic monochrome groups of the Chul and Caynac complexes in western El Salvador are identical to

Providencia and Verbena-Arenal complex monochromes at Kaminaljuyu; the Salvadoran fine red (Santa Tecla), orange (Olocuitla), and black-brown (Pinos) ceramic groups are shared by the Kaminaljuyu and Monte Alto assemblages, with the same paste and surface characteristics, vessel forms, and decorative modes.

The similarity of the assemblages is especially striking if one considers the extreme degree of decorative manipulation characteristic of these Late Preclassic ceramic groups: shared types are defined by quite distinctive and complex modal clusters. For example, the Santa Tecla Red Group, defined by its distinctive fine paste and deep-red slip, is often found in western El Salvador with scalloped-flanged open bowls with double circumferential grooves above the flanges— sometimes with graphite paint in the grooves. The fine red wares at Kaminaljuyu include exactly this same combination of paste, slip, form, and decorative modes. Another example of the complexity of linked types is seen in the Jorgia Coarse Incised type of the Pinos Black Group, defined for western El Salvador, but part of the basic black ceramic tradition of the highlands. This deeply incised or carved ware is not only similar in paste and identical in slip and form traits to the Kaminaljuyu and Monte Alto equivalent "Verbena Black-Brown Coarse Incised," but precisely the same corpus of complex geometric designs is found on both types. Indeed, after mixing sherds of the Jorgia and Verbena Coarse Incised collections now in Harvard's Peabody Museum, it was only possible to separate them by catalog number.

Similarly, the varied "Usulutan" types found at Chalchuapa (Sharer 1978c) and Santa Leticia (Demarest and Sharer 1982) are also shared by Kaminaljuyu and Monte Alto. As detailed below, three of the four major Late Preclassic Usulutan types defined by Wetherington (1978) at Kaminaljuyu are identical to the major Usulutan types in western El Salvador, both in terms of standard taxonomic criteria of surface treatment and ware and also in the specific motifs, appearance, and (presumably) techniques of the "negative-effect" Usulutan designs themselves (Demarest and Sharer 1982).

In all, more than a dozen major types (see below) defining the western Salvadoran Chul complex (400 to 100 B.C.) are indistinguishable from the ceramics of Kaminaljuyu's Providencia assemblage (presently dated to 500–200 B.C.; Wetherington 1978). The preliminary comparisons to Monte Alto's unpublished collection indicated the duplication of most of these types in the Late Preclassic ceramics of Monte Alto. Almost all of these early Late Preclassic types continue to be diagnostic of the subsequent Terminal Preclassic Verbena and Arenal complexes at Kaminaljuyu and the Caynac Complex at Chalchuapa (which is now dated from 100 B.C. to A.D. 250). These Terminal Preclassic complexes differ from the preceding Chul-Providencia assemblages only in the addition of new modes and ceramic groups. At Chalchuapa, these new ceramic groups were the (unslipped) Izalco Usulutan Group, the Mizata Buff Group, Tepecoyo Usulutan Group, and the minor Pajonal Cream, Soyapango White-on-Orange, and Finquita Red groups. Again, except for one minor group (Soypango), these ceramics were identical to cognates in the diagnostic ceramics of the Verbena and Arenal Complexes at Kaminaljuyu. Finally, as suggested above, it appears that even the important "Aguacate Orange" of Sharer's Caynac Complex is linked to Kaminaljuyu and other southeast highland types where large numbers of such sherds are found. This last critical link completes the picture of ceramic unity in the southeast highlands. The strength and potential significance of this pattern in the Preclassic archaeological record justify the definition of a new set of ceramic spheres.

The Late Preclassic Southeast Highland Ceramic Spheres

The Ceramic Spheres

In 1965, The Guatemala City Conference on Lowland Maya Ceramics defined "ceramic spheres" for the Maya lowlands (Willey, Culbert, and Adams 1967). The organizational framework and standardization of terminology provided by the conference have proven to be critical to interproject comparability of results and to the identification and description of ceramic patterning in the archaeological record. Indeed, the groundwork laid by that conference has been a major factor contributing to the past decade's great progress in elucidating culture history and process in the Maya lowlands.

Even the brief comparative review given above demonstrates that both the Chul-Providencia (ca. 400–100 B.C.) and Caynac-Miraflores (Verbena/Arenal; ca. 100 B.C.–250 A.D.) equivalences now justify the definition of two new sequential "ceramic spheres" in the highlands of southeast Mesoamerica. Despite the lack of a perfect one-to-one correspondence between taxonomic classes, most sherds from any coeval Late Preclassic context over a wide area of the southeast highlands (see fig. 1) are virtually identical. Such a pattern of shared types (listed in figs. 4 and 5) fits the accepted definition of ceramic spheres:

> The concept of ceramic sphere was defined to emphasize a high degree of content similarity between complexes. A ceramic

PROVIDENCIA CERAMIC SPHERE

(ca. 400–100 B.C.)

(Western Salvadoran Terminology)	*(Kaminaljuyu Terminology)*
AJMAK BLACK-BROWN WARE	**MIRAFLORES BLACK-BROWN AND POLISHED BLACK WARES**
Pinos Black-brown: Pinos Variety	Verbena Black-Brown Unincised and Verbena Black Unincised
Jorgia Coarse-incised and Ilopango Red-filled	Verbena Black-Brown Coarse Incised and Verbena Black Coarse Incised
AJPUJ FINE HARD WARE	**MIRADOR RED WARE**
Santa Tecla Red (plain), Miramonte Grooved, Tacuba Incised, Coatepeque Modeled	Verbena Fine Red: Verbena Variety (types 290–298: plain, grooved, incised, modeled)
Copinula Graphite-painted	Mulato Graphite-painted
Olocuitla Orange, Opico Grooved, Tecoluca Incised, Acachapa Modeled	Verbena Red-Orange (types 280–289: plain, grooved, incised, modeled)
Providencia Purple-on-Fine-Red	Providencia Purple-on-Fine-Red

USULUTAN DECORATED TYPES

Jicalapa Usulutan (also some Puxtla and Tepecoyo Usulutan)	Usulutan Cream Slipped
Olocuitla Orange Usulutan	Verbena Red-Orange: Usulutan Variety
Izalco Usulutan	Usulutan Unslipped

[Diagnostic of the later Caynac-Miraflores period, but appears earlier in these Chul-Providencia complexes]

CENSER WARE

Cara Sucia Ceramic Group	Censers within Baul Reddish Brown Paste Ware

[Correspondence of surface treatment, vessel forms, and decorative modes]

RED-ON-BUFF JARS

(Tijox Buff Ware)	(Velarde Buff Paste Ware)
Guaymango Red-on-Buff (Guaymango, Talnique, and Elena Varieties)	Arenal Polished and Arenal Matte: Red Painted Variety (Also some Embudo Buff Ware, Prado Red-on-Buff type)

[Ceramics designated by Shook and Hatch (1978) as "Sacatepequez Polished Red on Unpolished Buff" (KJ) and "Monte Alto Red on Buff" are very similar to Guaymango Red-on-Buff]

CHAM RED WARE	**CANCHON RED WARE**
Lolotique Red, Curaren Incised, Lolotique Thin, Anguiatu Incised	Las Charcas Pallid Red (types 260–269: plain and incised)

[Similarity of materials classified within these red post-slip incised types. They are diagnostic of the earlier Kal-Las Charcas period but continue in reduced frequency in Chul-Providencia complexes]

Figure 4. The Providencia ceramic sphere (ca. 400–100 B.C.).

MIRAFLORES CERAMIC SPHERE
(ca. 100 B.C.–A.D. 250)

(Western Salvadoran Terminology)	(Kaminaljuyu Terminology)
AJMAK BLACK-BROWN WARE	**MIRAFLORES BLACK-BROWN AND POLISHED BLACK WARES**
Pinos Black-brown: Pinos Variety ◄─►	Verbena Black-Brown Unincised and Verbena Black Unincised
Jorgia Coarse-incised and Ilopango Red-filled ───	Verbena Black-Brown Coarse Incised and Verbena Black Coarse Incised
Canchon Fine-incised: Varieties Unspecified (minor at Chalchuapa) ───	Verbena Black-Brown Fine Incised: several varieties
AJPUJ FINE HARD WARE	**MIRADOR RED WARE**
Santa Tecla Red (plain), Miramonte Grooved, Tacuba Incised, Coatepeque Modeled ───	Verbena Fine Red: Verbena Variety (types 290–298: plain, grooved, incised, modeled)
Olocuitla Orange, Opico Grooved, Tecoluca Incised, Acachapa Modeled ───	Verbena Red-Orange (types 280–289: plain, grooved, incised, modeled)

Proposed

KAN HEAVY WARE	**[ATECOZAL GROUP]**	**VILLALOBOS RED WARE**
Aguacate Orange: Atecozal Variety ◄··►	Arenal Red: Dull Variety (also some of Arenal Red: Polished Variety)	

KAT UNSLIPPED WARE	**OSUNA COARSE WARE**
Mizata Buff Orange and Conchalio Coarse-incised ───	Arenal Coarse Incised: Buff Paste Variety

USULUTAN DECORATED TYPES

Izalco Usulutan ◄─►	Usulutan Unslipped
Olocuitla Orange Usulutan ◄─►	Verbena Red-Orange: Usulutan Variety
Jicalapa Usulutan ◄─►	Usulutan Cream Slipped

[Continues in reduced frequency into Miraflores complexes]

Olocuitla Red-rimmed Usulutan ◄─►	Verbena Red-Orange Red-rimmed Usulutan

[minor type]

CENSER WARE

Cara Sucia Group and Topozoco Group ──►	"Incensarios" largely within Baul Reddish Brown Paste Ware

[Correspondence of surface treatment, vessel forms, and decorative modes]

Types Appearing in the Latter Part of Miraflores Sphere Phases

Pajonal Cream and Apaneca Incised ◄─►	Verbena White Incised

[Same surface treatment but dissimilar pastes]

Finquita Red and Tapagua Modeled ◄··►	Type 460: "Face Necks" (body sherds mostly placed in types of the Velarde Buff Paste Ware)

Figure 5. The Miraflores ceramic sphere (ca. 100 B.C.–A.D. 250).

sphere exists when two or more complexes share a majority of their most common types. Whereas the horizon need imply no more than a few connections at the modal level, the sphere implies high content similarity at the typological level (Willey, Culbert, and Adams 1967: 306).

The content of a ceramic sphere is the sum total of all the types and modes of its member complexes. The diagnostic content of the sphere consists of those elements shared by all or some of the complexes upon which decisions about membership in a sphere are based. (*Ibid.:* 307; see also Gifford 1976: 1–20, 323–330)

Based on these prehistoric ceramic similarities, but with an awareness of the modern taxonomic incongruencies, it is now possible to define such ceramic spheres uniting the Preclassic ceramic assemblages of the highlands of southeastern Guatemala and western El Salvador (see fig. 1). We propose ceramic spheres and complexes having the following designations in Table 1.

These designations follow the procedure established by the 1965 Guatemala City Conference (Willey, Culbert, and Adams 1967). The names of the ceramic spheres were adopted from the Kaminaljuyu phase names (see fig. 2). Retention of local phase-specific ceramic complexes is justified by consistent regional variations between the

Table 1. Late Preclassic Ceramic Spheres and Complexes of the Southeastern Highlands

Providencia Ceramic Sphere	
(ca. 400–100 B.C.)	
(Western El Salvador)	(Valley of Guatemala)
Chul Providencia Complex	Providencia Providencia Complex
Miraflores Ceramic Sphere	
(ca. 100 B.C.–A.D. 250)	
(Western El Salvador)	(Valley of Guatemala)
Caynac Miraflores Complex	Verbena Miraflores Complex
(Early Facet)	
Caynac Miraflores Complex	Arenales Miraflores Complex
(Late Facet)	

highland assemblages. At this time it seems likely that Monte Alto's assemblages will also warrant a separate complex designation within each sphere, when the analysis of its ceramics is completed.

Figures 4 and 5 list the diagnostic types of the Providencia and Miraflores ceramic spheres. The left hand side of the figures gives the type-variety designations for the Salvadoran wares and types while the right hand side gives the names of the wares and types within which identical ceramics are found in the Kaminaljuyu collection. Solid-line connections between the two columns indicate identity of ceramic material at the type or group level. Dotted-line connections signify similarity of the ceramic classes and/or sharing of a large number of complex modes, but with the precise degree of difference and appropriate taxonomy still uncertain. As discussed above, in no case is there a perfect one-to-one correspondence of types since the Kaminaljuyu type definitions are generally broader, different in their taxonomic logic, and usually include material from most periods in the long Kaminaljuyu sequence. As seen in the black-brown types, while the ceramics are often identical, the exact relationships of the previously-established taxonomic categories are extremely complex. Type descriptions and illustrations of the ceramic classes listed in the figures can be found in the ceramic reports on Santa Leticia (Demarest 1981: Chapter 4), Chalchuapa (Sharer 1978c), and Kaminaljuyu (Wetherington 1978).

Additionally, important to future comparative research is the standardization of type names and definitions of identical ceramics shared by the sphere sites. In general, the Salvadoran type definitions are more period-specific: the original Chalchuapa sequence was derived from finely stratified midden deposits (B. Anderson 1978; Sharer 1978c) and this typology was further refined based on the pure Chul phase domestic deposits of the Santa Leticia village. These sets of contexts were well-dated by stratigraphic associations and consistent series of C^{14} dates (Demarest, Switser, and Berger 1982; Sharer 1978c). Since the Salvadoran taxonomic classes are more period-specific and are defined in conventional type-variety terms, the Salvadoran class names given in the left column should generally be used to designate identical material from Kaminaljuyu and other sites (at least for intersite comparisons and characterization of ceramic sphere patterns). Pending the final results of ongoing neutron activation analyses, different variety names should be applied to the types at each site.

In summary, the sharing of over a dozen red, orange, and black-brown monochromes and the several Usulutan-decorated types securely unites the assemblages of the southeast highlands during both periods. These shared monochromes and Usulutan types con- stitute the bulk of the early Late Preclassic ceramics of Kaminal- juyu, Chalchuapa, Santa Leticia, Atiquisaya, and Monte Alto. In the Terminal Preclassic Miraflores sphere, the inventory of types shared by these sites is augmented by the proposed Atecozol Group and the distinctive coarse-incised "flower-pot" shaped vessels of the Mizata Ceramic Group (Arenal Coarse Incised in the Kaminaljuyu termi- nology). These connections in identical ceramic material are further reinforced by similarities in the censer wares and red-on-buff, buff, and red ollas. A great number of shared decorative modes, design elements, and unusual vessel forms further unites the ceramic spheres. At all sites in the spheres, shared modes cluster in the same complex patterns and appear at the same chronological positions in the sequence.

Intra-Sphere Variation

Major regional differences within the ceramic spheres can be briefly summarized. The most consistent regional differences relate to two features limited to the Guatemalan sites: the use of purple paint and characteristic Guatemalan fine white pastes (see Rice 1977, 1978). At Kaminaljuyu, the combination of these two regional traits re- sulted in several major types characteristic of the Guatemalan Pro- videncia, Verbena, and Arenal complexes. In the Providencia com- plex, the distinctive purple-on-white Providencia Purple Painted type is common at Kaminaljuyu and present only as a very minor (trade?) ceramic in western El Salvador. The fine white-pasted Ver- bena Ivory in several varieties, including an Usulutan variety, is an- other important type which is unique to the southeastern Guatema- lan complexes. These regional differences based on the valley of Guatemala's fine white pastes and purple paint last into the subse- quent Miraflores Sphere complexes. Most other regional differences center on local variations on the general southeastern highland red- on-buff jar tradition.

However, note that even the uniquely Guatemalan features define types whose vessel shapes, decorative treatments, and combinations of modes correspond closely with western Salvadoran equivalents. For example, Verbena Purple Painted is a Kaminaljuyu type defined by purple paint on jars of Rinconada White Paste Ware. Yet the com- plex combinations of rim form, vessel form, and painted design ele- ments of Verbena Purple Painted are replicated in the forms and de- signs formed on some of the red-on-buff jar types in western El Salvador. Similarly, though Kaminaljuyu's Verbena Ivory: Usulutan variety is distinguished by its fine white paste, its Usulutan surface treatment, designs, vessel forms, and other features are shared with the Salvadoran Usulutan types.

Another potential key to regional variation may be found in the frequencies of sphere-diagnostic types and modes at different sites. However, here again non-parallel taxonomic methodologies obscure intersite comparisons. Tabulations at Kaminaljuyu were based only on the rim sherds (Wetherington 1978: 5–15) while the Chalchuapa statistics were based on total sherd counts (Sharer 1978c). The Santa Leticia ceramic studies provided a method of comparing the Kaminaljuyu and Chalchuapa counts. Santa Leticia analyses included computer-assisted statistical studies of modes and types, including comparisons of rim, body, and total sherd counts before and after vessel reconstruction (Demarest 1981: 98–108). The results of these comparisons suggest that much intersite variation in type frequencies is caused by the distortive effects of comparing rim counts to total sherd counts. The high relative frequencies of Providencia and Miraflores fine red and black-brown types at Kaminaljuyu is largely due to the fact that these monochromes are found in small low bowls, vessels which have an extremely high rim-to-body ratio. In contrast, the much lower Kaminaljuyu percentages of red-on-buff jars and deep bowls (or their purple-on-white equivalents) are due to the extremely low rim-to-body ratio of such vessel forms.

While the non-comparability of the Kaminaljuyu and Chalchuapa counts cannot be fully corrected, the Santa Leticia statistical studies (Demarest 1981) do provide a general indication as to which frequency variations are methodologically created and which may represent real intra-sphere differences. Preliminary results suggest that, even after discounting methodological exaggeration, there is still a somewhat higher frequency of black-brown types at the Guatemalan sites. One type, Canchon Fine Incised (Wetherington's Verbena Black-Brown Fine Incised), has a much higher frequency at Kaminaljuyu, and may have been an import into western El Salvador. This hypothesis is now being tested by neutron activation studies.

Another regional difference which survives statistical reexamination is the consistently higher frequency of the Usulutan types in western El Salvador. Again, the lower Guatemalan frequencies of sphere-diagnostic Usulutan types are partly due to methodological differences. Nonetheless, while the major Usulutan types are quite common at all Providencia and Miraflores sphere sites, the Salvadoran sites of Chalchuapa, Santa Leticia, and Atiquisaya have extraordinarily high frequencies (up to 40% of all sherds) of the

Providencia-diagnostic cream-slipped Jicalapa Usulutan and the Miraflores-diagnostic unslipped Izalco Usulutan.

It should be noted that despite these frequency variations, the close correspondences of the Salvadoran and Guatemalan Usulutan types are among the strongest ties between sphere sites. The three major Salvadoran Usulutan groups (Jicalapa, Izalco, and Olocuitla) also occur at Kaminaljuyu and Monte Alto in ceramics having the same inventory of decorative attributes, vessel forms, and design motifs. Furthermore, at all sites, the cream-slipped Usulutans (Jicalapa and Puxtla Groups) are more popular during the Providencia sphere, while the unslipped Izalco Usulutan reaches its highest frequency in the subsequent Miraflores sphere complexes. The Usulutan style does appear to have originated in western El Salvador (Demarest and Sharer 1982) and to have much higher frequencies there. However, by late Middle Preclassic times the various, often elaborate, Usulutan variants were common to all assemblages of the Providencia and Miraflores ceramic spheres.

Also note that both surface examination and the ongoing technological analyses at Brookhaven National Laboratory (Demarest and Sharer 1982) indicate that the same methods of producing the Usulutan effect were probably used by all sphere sites. Originally, Sharer (1978c: 134–135) had argued that "differential-firing" was used to create the Usulutan effect, while Wetherington (1978: 101–102) asserted that a "wiping" technique produced the Usulutan designs. However, these are merely contradictory hypotheses about the general problem of Usulutan technology, not assertions of regional variation: both analysts confirm the identity of the surface treatments of the Chalchuapa and Kaminaljuyu Usulutans (Sharer 1978c: 40; Wetherington 1978: 102; personal communication, 1980).

Geographical Boundaries

Even given these intra-sphere variations, the proposed Providencia and Miraflores ceramic spheres form a tightly-knit group of assemblages, as homogeneous as the lowland Preclassic Mamon and Chicanel ceramic spheres and probably more unified than the Classic period Tzakol and Tepeu spheres. Figure 1 shows the minimum extent of the southeastern highland region defined by the sequential Providencia and Miraflores spheres. Chalchuapa, Santa Leticia, Atiquisaya, Kaminaljuyu, and (provisionally) Monte Alto share the diagnostic types of both spheres.

It remains possible, indeed probable, that the sphere's pattern of ceramic similarities extends further to the west and north. Examination of collections of Late Preclassic pottery from Chiapa de Corzo (Warren 1961) indicates several close correspondences in certain specific classes, including fine red, black-brown, and Izalco Usulutan types, but these may all reflect trade wares rather than local manufacture. Preliminary results of the ongoing analyses of the ceramics of Abaj Takalik on the Pacific slope to the west suggest that this site may lie outside the Providencia and Miraflores sphere limits (J. Graham, personal communication, 1979). The published report on the ceramics of Bilbao (Parsons 1967) suggests the presence of many Miraflores sphere traits and types during that site's Late Preclassic Ilusiones complex. Presently, we can only note Bilbao's probable inclusion in the Miraflores sphere, pending direct comparison of sherds and the difficult process of, again, aligning non-comparable taxonomic categories. Preliminary results from ongoing analyses of the Late Preclassic pottery of the Salama valley, to the north, including that from the center of El Porton (Sedat and Sharer 1972), furnish examples of large-scale local production of types closely related to the Olocuitla and Pinos groups, as well as a developed censer-ware tradition nearly identical to that of the Providencia and Miraflores spheres. The Salama valley orange and black-brown types share several familiar modes, including scalloped-flanged rims and double circumferential grooving and incising. One orange type possesses faint resist lines and appears to be related to the Olocuitla Usulutan of western El Salvador. However, the other common Usulutan types (Puxtla, Jicalapa, and Izalco), while present, are relatively rare, and like those found at Chiapa de Corzo, may be trade wares. Pending completion of the Salama valley pottery studies, we can provisionally place this area at or near the northern boundary of the Providencia and Miraflores spheres.

Turning to the east, we find an unusual pattern in the Late Preclassic ceramic collections from Copan, Yarumela, Los Naranjos, and Quelepa. These complexes include some Miraflores-sphere modes and extraordinary frequencies of one major Miraflores type, Izalco Usulutan. However, all of the other sphere-diagnostic types, such as the basic red, orange, and black monochromes, are absent or present only as a handful of sherds. The ceramic complexes of these eastern Salvadoran-western Honduran sites are far more similar to each other than to the contemporaneous western Salvadoran-southeastern Guatemalan Providencia and Miraflores ceramic spheres. In fact, Andrews V (1976: 180–181) has proposed an Uapala Ceramic Sphere (see fig. 1) including the closely-related Late Preclassic ceramic assemblages of Quelepa (Uapala Complex), Copan ("Archaic," now redefined as the

Chabij Complex), Yarumela (Yarumela II Complex), Los Naranjos (Eden I Complex), and Santa Rita (Ulua Bichrome Complex).

Thus, although Izalco Usulutan spread far to the east after its development in western El Salvador (Demarest and Sharer 1982), the overall pattern of the Miraflores and Providencia ceramic spheres ends much further to the west. A more exact placement of the eastern boundary of the two spheres is suggested by review of the Zapotitan Basin Project preliminary reports (Beaudry 1978) and by direct comparison to the Cerron Grande Project ceramic collections from the Upper Lempa Valley. The assemblages collected by these two regional studies share several important types and many diagnostic modes with the Providencia and Miraflores ceramic spheres, but they also include much essentially dissimilar material (see Demarest 1981: 327–335 for more detailed comparisons). It would appear, then, that these ceramic sphere patterns were truly a phenomenon of the highlands, falling off as the volcanic ridge of western El Salvador drops down in the east to the upper Lempa River valley system and in the southeast to the Zapotitan basin.

Remaining Comparative Problems

Clearly, more remains to be done to refine this preliminary definition of Preclassic ceramic spheres in the southeastern highlands. Further comparative study of the Monte Alto material is necessary to precisely identify that site's local variations. Comparative examinations are necessary to confirm Bilbao's position in the two spheres and to identify ceramic connections with other sites to the north and northwest. Furthermore, earlier ceramic patterns in the southeastern highlands warrant investigation. Study of the Kaminaljuyu Las Charcas and Arevalo type collections indicates many similarities to the Colos and Kal complexes (ca. 900–400 B.C.) and some equivalencies of types with the (again, taxonomically unparallel) ceramic classes displayed in Table 2.

While these earlier connections are intriguing, a larger sample of the weakly-defined Guatemalan Arevalo and Las Charcas complexes must be recovered before further conclusions can be drawn. The ongoing analysis of the Monte Alto Late Preclassic ceramics (Shook and Hatch, personal communication) may also shed light on interregional connections in the Early and Middle Preclassic.

Interpretations and Speculations

Above we have proposed a reordering of the archaeological evidence in the southeastern highlands through the definitions of two new

Table 2. Equivalencies between Chalchuapa Ceramic Groups and
Kaminaljuyu Wares

Lamatepeque ceramic group	—Arevalo zoned ware
Lolotique ceramic group	—Canchon red ware
Jinuapa ceramic group	—Canales orange ware
Puxtla ceramic group	—Usulutan cream slipped type
Jocote and Guaymango groups	—Verlarde buff paste ware (red paint varieties)

ceramic spheres for the Late Preclassic (400 B.C.–A.D. 250). We have
defined the diagnostic types and features of each sphere, the regional
variation within each sphere, and the external boundaries of the
shared ceramic patterns defining the spheres. The application of the
sphere concept has helped identify new connections between the
assemblages of these southeastern highland sites. More importantly,
the definition of ceramic spheres should provide a comparative
framework for future analyses of the problems of the development of
complex society in this region.

Determining the cultural significance of these shared ceramic
ideas is, needless to say, a more difficult problem. Such intersite ceramic similarities cannot immediately be associated with any specific cultural phenomenon without an understanding of the broader
nature of the archaeology of the region. Such a broader understanding can be achieved by: 1) comparison of the pattern of intersite
ceramic similarities to the intersite patterning apparent in other aspects of the archaeological record (e.g., figurines, sculpture, settlement patterns, lithics, etc.), and 2) the inductive and deductive exploration of the precise meaning of each of these overlapping patterns in
the ancient remains.

The Archaeological Pattern: The Southeast Highland Culture Area

Initial work on the first step, intersite comparison of non-ceramic
evidence, indicates parallel sets of intersite similarities for the Late
Preclassic sites of southeastern Guatemala and western El Salvador.
Throughout the southeast highland region (fig. 1) strong similarities
can be found in distinctive figurine types, ceramic artifacts, censer
complexes, sculptural styles, lithic assemblages, and site layouts.
Thus, a single, unified archaeological pattern extended across this
part of the southeastern highlands during the Late Preclassic period.

The study of the Chalchuapa figurines (Dahlin 1978) demonstrates the uniformity of Late Preclassic figurine assemblages throughout the southeast highland area. Dahlin (*Ibid.*: 176) asserts that the two major Chalchuapa Late Preclassic figurine types, Alvarez Tri-Punctate-Eye and Nosiglia Heavy-Eyed have duplicates in the major figurine types of Kaminaljuyu and the adjacent highland and piedmont zones. Similarly, Chalchuapa's Terminal Preclassic Busta-mente Long-Faced and Noguera High-Forehead types "show obvious similarities to Late Arenal/Early Santa Clara figurines at Kaminaljuyu, where they occur in profusion" (*Ibid.*). Additional artifactual types in the fired clay and lithic industries are shared by these southeast highland sites (Demarest 1981: 85–95; Sheets 1978).

Another strong link, probably reflecting shared ideological concepts, is seen in the unusual sculptural types of the southeast highland sites. While Late Preclassic boulder figures have a somewhat wider distribution, a distinctive puffy-faced style of potbellied idol (designated by Parsons, 1981, "Monte Alto Style Full-Round Potbelly Sculpture") is found at each site in the ceramic sphere. In fact, individual examples strikingly similar in stylistic detail were found at Kaminaljuyu, Bilbao, Chalchuapa, Monte Alto, and Santa Leticia (Anderson 1978; Demarest, Switsur, and Berger 1982; Lothrop 1926b; Miles 1965; Parsons 1967; Parsons and Jenson 1965). The contextual evidence (Demarest, Switsur, and Berger 1982) places the Santa Leticia potbellies in the Chul or Early Caynac phases (400 B.C.– A.D. 100). Meanwhile, in an independent study relying on stylistic and art-historical arguments, Parsons (1981; personal communication, 1980) arrived at approximately the same temporal placement for the Monte Alto monuments, suggesting a Providencia phase dating for the potbellies.

Another distinctive sculptural style, the so-called "Jaguar Head" first described by Richardson (1940), has a distribution paralleling that of the ceramic spheres, figurine types, and potbellies. Again, nearly identical examples of these squarish, stylized stone faces are found at Santa Leticia, Monte Alto, Kaminaljuyu, and Chalchuapa. As with the potbellies, dozens of "Jaquar Head" monuments have been found at unexcavated sites in southeastern Guatemala and in the Departments of Ahuachapan, Sonsonate, and Santa Ana in far western El Salvador. Again, independent stylistic (Parsons 1981) and contextual (Demarest, Switsur, and Berger 1982) datings place the style in the Late Preclassic period.

The artifactual and sculptural distributions are further supported by parallels in architectural features and layout in both ceremonial centers and domestic zones. "Household cluster" features and arrangements at Santa Leticia's Chul phase village (Demarest 1981) match Borhegyi's descriptions of highland Guatemalan domestic contexts (Borhegyi 1965b). Concerning public architecture, Sharer concluded (1978c: 210) that Chalchuapa's "overall distribution and composition of the structures in this area [site-core] are similar to the Late and Terminal Preclassic architectural patterns at Kaminaljuyu." While the great centers of Kaminaljuyu and Chalchuapa have similar architectural configurations, the excavations at Santa Leticia (Demarest 1981: 61–95) and at Monte Alto (Parsons 1969, 1976) revealed that their smaller ceremonial zones shared an architectural pattern of potbellied idols aligned atop earthen terrace platforms. Indeed, it seems probable that there was a significant congruence between the overall structure of the Monte Alto-Kaminaljuyu and Santa Leticia-Chalchuapa relationships.

Considering all aspects of the archaeological record, it can be hypothesized that there was a late Middle to Late Preclassic southeast highland "culture area," defined by the ceramic spheres and shared figurine, sculptural, and architectural styles. However, the proposal of an archaeologically-defined "culture area" raises both theoretical problems and the question of specific cultural correlates.

The Culture Area Concept

Much, if not most, archaeological interpretation has, implicitly or explicitly, rested upon the concept of the "culture area." Borrowed from ethnography, the culture area concept has been incorporated by archaeologists into their approaches to the fossils of cultures:

> An archaeological culture is an assemblage of artifacts that recurs repeatedly associated together in dwellings of the same kind and with burials of the same rite. The arbitrary peculiarities of all cultural traits are assumed to be concrete expressions of the common social traditions that bind together a culture. Artifacts hold together in assemblages, not only because they were used in the same age, but also because they were used by the same people, made or executed in accordance with techniques, rites or styles prescribed by a social tradition, handed on by precept and example and modifiable in the same way. (Childe 1947: 51)

Despite current rethinking of normative approaches, archaeologists continue to rely (albeit, implicitly) upon this general concept in ordering the artifactual evidence.

However, within ethnography itself the very concept of the culture area has been challenged and criticized since its inception. Even in examining contemporary culture groups, Boas (e.g., 1948) pointed out that such "culture areas" seldom coincide when they are defined on the basis of different categories of culture such as language, technology, social organization, or religious beliefs. Kroeber (1939), a principal champion of the culture area concept, rejected Boas' criticism and argued that while such patterns do often cross cultural boundaries, they more often coincide within the same identifiable areas, otherwise even the concepts of ethnicity and culture would have no validity. The lack of a perfect alignment of all aspects of cultures with specific boundaries does not refute the general utility of the culture area concept.

A more cogent objection is that raised by Harris and others who have, quite correctly, rejected the "culture area" as an *explanatory* device:

Nothing is more obvious than the prospective utility of an ethnographic map which groups tribal entities in relationship to some geographically delineated aspects of the environment. It is quite another matter, however, to suppose that this geographical grouping in and of itself contributes to an understanding of cultural differences and similarities (Harris 1968: 374).

However, while it is true that the trait list and geographical plotting approach obsessed some anthropologists for a few decades (e.g., Wissler 1917, Holmes 1914), Kroeber and others were well aware that the culture area concept was merely a classificatory device—a first step towards more processually oriented analysis:

The second point is to guard against the possible misconception that the determination of culture area is here considered an end in itself. The concept of a cultural area is a means to an end. The end may be the understanding of culture processes as such, or of the historic events of a culture. . .

Ethnology, particularly when concerned with people which, like the native ones of America, have left few or no documentary records, perforce has recourse to spatial classifications such as culture areas. In themselves these yield only a momentary and static organization of knowledge, whereas the purpose of history is genetic. In proportion as the recognition of culture areas becomes an end in itself, it therefore defeats really historic understanding (Kroeber 1939: 1–2).

To the archaeologist, the culture area concept is a valid, indeed, inevitable, initial tool for examination of the patterning in the archaeological record. Patterning in material culture, and the cultural systems which produced it, are often immediately available to the ethnographer. In contemporary ethnography the definition and comparison of such units would indeed be a fairly unenlightening exercise. Yet, to the archaeologist such ethnic units are anything but apparent. The reconstruction of ancient units of close similarity in material assemblages can be an important step towards the analysis of problems of cultural development. While we must remember Kroeber's caveat that it is not an end in itself, the identification of such culture areas can aid in both the structuring and the interpretation of the archaeological record. However, archaeologists must then seek to discover the specific economic, political, and social factors which actually generate these patterns of artifactual homogeneity; i.e., they must explicitly test alternative explanations of these patterns which are phrased in specific cultural terms.

Cultural Correlates: Hypotheses and Ongoing Research

Determining the precise nature of the proposed Late Preclassic "southeast highland culture area" will be a long process involving numerous problem-specific projects. However, the striking degree of similarity in archaeological assemblages suggests a corresponding unity in many aspects of these Preclassic societies. The close affiliation of the societies of the area is most clearly and convincingly seen in the uniformity of the ceramic assemblages of the sites of the Providencia and Miraflores ceramic spheres, as detailed above.

Yet, in response to Harris' and Kroeber's warnings, we must go beyond the identification of such patterns to the specific interpretation of their cultural causes. Does the ceramic sphere pattern result from the overlapping ranges of types produced at specific centers and traded throughout the southeast highland area? Or do the sphere diagnostics represent a shared body of ideas about ceramic manufacture and style? If, as seems likely, the ceramic sphere patterns result from both of these factors, which types, pastes, or slips are spread by long-distance intrasphere trade and which are locally produced according to a shared set of stylistic and technological guidelines?

Compositional analyses of ceramics provide the most promising approach to such questions of specific artifactual connections between sites in the southeastern highlands. Such analyses have the potential to test specific hypotheses on the cultural significance of shared types and groups of the ceramic sphere. Thus, they could eventually allow us to draw conclusions about ancient behavior from the ceramic sphere definitions and the archaeologically-defined culture area which are at present merely comparative taxonomic frameworks.

As an initial step in this direction, neutron activation analysis is being applied to samples of potsherds from sites throughout the ceramic spheres and adjacent areas (Bishop, Demarest, and Sharer n.d.b). Neutron activation is a powerful tool for distinquishing even minute differences in the chemical composition of pastes (Bishop 1980; Bishop, Rands, and Holley 1982; Sayre, Murrerhoff, and Welck 1958). This technique allows the analyst—after rigorous statistical treatment, comparison to the full range of pastes at each site, and cautious interpretation—to distinguish between local and non-local pastes, that is, between the actual importing of vessels and the sharing of ideas about ceramic manufacture and style.

Initial studies already undertaken (Bishop, Demarest, and Sharer n.d.b) included activation of samples from Kaminaljuyu, Chalchuapa, Santa Leticia, Quirigua, and Copan. The first three sites are within the Providencia and Miraflores ceramic spheres, while Quirigua and Copan, Late Preclassic Uapala sphere sites, would provide a non-sphere control sample. These activation studies have also explored specific connections between a smaller village site like Santa Leticia and the major centers. The Late Preclassic samples selected were primarily of the Fine Red (at Kaminaljuyu Verbena Fine Red; at Chalchuapa and Santa Leticia Santa Tecla Red), Fine Orange (Olocuitla Orange in El Salvador; at Kaminaljuyu Verbena Red-Orange), and Black-Brown Groups (Miraflores Black-Brown ware at Kaminaljuyu; Pinos Black-Brown Group in El Salvador). Chemical analysis of these three major monochrome groups was expected to give a preliminary indication of possible paste differences between what are macroscopically identical ceramics found at all of the southeast highland sphere sites. All materials were activated and statistically analyzed at Brookhaven National Laboratory by Ronald Bishop as a part of the Maya Jade and Ceramics Project of the Museum of Fine Arts, Boston, and the Brookhaven Laboratory.

The results of the neutron activation studies of each ceramic group have been detailed elsewhere (Bishop, Demarest, and Sharer n.d.b). However, the general implication of these studies can be succinctly stated: the striking similarity of the Providencia and Miraflores sphere diagnostic types principally reflects shared ideas about ceramic style and technology rather than actual exchange of ceramics from specialized centers. Neutron activation indicated distinct local procurement for each of the sites in the sphere, i.e., each site's

black-brown, red, and orange ceramics had paste chemical compositions indicating different sources. Thus, the identical major fine red
and orange monochromes, black-brown types, Usulutans, and domestic wares appear to be locally produced within each subregion of
the southeast highlands (for example, valley of Guatemala, Chalchuapa basin).

This interpretation, when combined with the parallel patterns described above for other artifactual categories, confirms that the region shows a remarkable uniformity in its material culture. Such a
sharing of ideas in ceramics, sculpture and iconography, figurines,
censer complexes, and so on, suggests that the artifactual patterns
could actually reflect a culturally-unified population in the Late Preclassic period—possibly a single linguistic or ethnic group. This hypothesis of an ethnically and/or linguistically unified southeast
highland culture area is suggested by: 1) close similarities in most
aspects of the artifactual assemblages at each site; 2) clear differences with sites outside of the southeast highland region; and 3) the
negation by activation analysis of the hypothesis that mass production and long-distance trade were the primary causes of the shared
ceramic features. Indeed, if there is any relationship, however imper-
fect, between ethnic or linguistic patterns and material culture, then
the degree of commonality in the material culture of these sites is
sufficient to imply that a single ethnic or even linguistic group occupied the entire region in the Late Preclassic period (cf. Sharer
1974: 15).

Needless to say, a linguistic hypothesis would be difficult to verify
and the identification of the shared language presents an even greater
problem. There has already been heated debate on the possible linguistic affiliation of southeast highland peoples (e.g., *Ibid.*; Andrews V 1972, 1976: 181; Campbell 1976: 167–169; Josserand 1975:
509; Kaufman 1976: 108). Candidates for the language spoken in the
southeast highlands have included Pocom Maya (Kaufman 1976:
108), Cholan and Mam Maya (Josserand 1975: 509), and proto-Xinca-
Lenca ("Xile") (Feldman, cited in Sharer 1974: 175). The problem of
archaeological-linguistic correlations is further complicated by disagreement among linguists concerning the genetic relationship, if
any, of the Xinca, Lenca, and Maya language families (cf. Swadesh
1967; Kaufman 1976; Campbell 1976; Andrews V 1972). Yet the
question of linguistic correlates to the southeast highland "culture
area" is central to theories of migrations from this precocious region
(e.g., Andrews V 1972, 1976: 181, 1977; Sharer 1974) and it warrants
further study by both archaeologists and linguists.

It is also apparent that in addition to general linguistic and ethnic unity the southeast highland region was tied together by ideological, economic, and perhaps even political networks. Regardless of common origins, language, or ethnicity, such strong similarities in culture (and its artifactual fossils) could only be maintained through continual communication and interaction between groups. Long-distance trade in specialized ceramic types was one such channel of communication. Two possible ceramics involved in such trade were the purple-painted red and orange wares and the fine incised complex-design black-brown ceramics. Both of these distinctive ceramics were present at the Salvadoran sites of Chalchuapa, Santa Leticia, and Atiquisaya only in very small numbers (under o.2%) and had been hypothesized (Sharer 1978c, Parsons 1967) to be "trade wares," possibly imported from the valley of Guatemala, where they are far more common (cf. Wetherington 1978). Neutron activation is now being applied to test such specific hypotheses about long-distance trade within the southeast highland culture area (Bishop, Demarest, and Sharer n.d.b). Meanwhile, within subregions of the southeast highland culture area a more substantial flow of ceramics may have united the material culture of local populations while dispersing products and ideas derived from more distant highland sites. Neutron activation and petrographic studies are also testing specific hypotheses concerning ceramic exchange networks within subregions of the southeast highlands.

Another set of economic networks connecting Late Preclassic southeast highland sites involved the exchange of obsidian. Michels (1975, 1976, 1979b) has shown that Kaminaljuyu's control of obsidian sources and networks of manufacture and exchange was crucial to the development of complex society in the valley of Guatemala. Similarly, Sharer (1978c: 209; in press) has suggested that Chalchuapa's access to, perhaps control of, the Ixtepeque obsidian source was a major factor in the development of the Late Preclassic chiefdoms there. It is probable that Chalchuapa controlled trade in obsidian to smaller highland sites, such as Santa Leticia. This speculation is suggested by the typological identity of their obsidian assemblages and by the sourcing of most of the Santa Leticia obsidian to Ixtepeque (Nievens n.d.). However, note that some Santa Leticia obsidian has been sourced by neutron activation to El Chayal in Guatemala. Thus, even a small center such as Santa Leticia, in the highlands above the Chalchuapa zone, has obsidian from both the El Chayal and Ixtepeque sources (Nievens n.d.). As in ceramics, it appears that wider networks of trade and communication crosscut local systems to such a degree that within the southeast highland region geographical and cultural distance were only very loosely correlated.

A further series of hypotheses can also be proposed regarding the "superorganic" aspects of culture in the region. It can be speculated that both a shared ethnic tradition and the networks of exchange hypothesized above helped to maintain a general unity of ideological and political thought throughout the Late Preclassic southeast highland culture area. The sharing of specific religious cults is suggested by the southeast area distribution of "potbelly" and "Jaquar Head" monuments, as well as similarities in the architecture and layout of ceremonial centers. Note the virtual stylistic identity of sculptured monuments and the parallel ceremonial complexes at such distant sites as Monte Alto and Santa Leticia. "Household religion" of the Late Preclassic also appears to be uniform throughout the southeast area, given the identity of distinctive figurine styles (Dahlin 1978; Demarest 1981: 92–95) and specific details of the three-pronged censer complexes found at all sites (cf. Borhegyi 1951a, 1951b, 1965a; Demarest 1981: 246–247; Gonzales and Wetherington 1978; Sharer 1978c: 28–30).

As a final speculation, it can be proposed that political evolution in this southeast highland culture area must be understood both in terms of the increasing interaction and interdependency of the developing highland chiefdoms and their control over long distance and local trade networks. Recent analyses have hypothesized that in the Late Preclassic both Kaminaljuyu and Chalchuapa were the centers of rapidly-evolving chiefdoms each of which controlled networks of exchange and production in obsidian, ceramics, and other materials (Michels 1979b; Rice 1978; Sharer 1975, 1978c). The evidence reviewed above shows that these two proposed chiefdoms and other highland centers shared ceramic and artifactual complexes, ideological systems, and overlapping spheres of economic influence. It would, therefore, seem probable that loosely-knit political alliances between such highland chiefdoms would have resulted from, and in turn reinforced, these growing networks of communication and cooperation.

Clearly, this reconstruction of the Late Preclassic development of complex societies in the southeast highlands is extremely speculative. However, the results of initial neutron activation studies (Bishop, Demarest, and Sharer n.d.b) suggest that these hypotheses are at least worthy of further research and testing. The successful continuation of these material culture studies must be combined with similar detailed analyses and comparative studies of other aspects of the archaeological record for the Late Preclassic highlands—

iconography, architecture, settlement patterns, and so on. Eventually, the completion and comparison of such parallel studies should allow us to derive specific cultural correlates for the observed artifactual patterns. Then the comparative structures provided by the southeast highland "ceramic sphere" and "culture area" concepts can be replaced with specific reconstructions of trade networks, ethnicity, linguistic patterns, political entities, and the transformation of these cultural phenomena through time.

Natural Hazards, Natural Disasters, and Research in the Zapotitan Valley of El Salvador

Introduction

Research directed toward understanding the relationships between people and volcanically active environments has been conducted by staff members of the "Proyecto Protoclasico," University of Colorado, in El Salvador during the past decade. Descriptive, methodological, and theoretical aspects of this research are discussed in a variety of sources (cf. Sheets 1971, 1976, 1979a and b; Sheets, ed., in press; Sheets *et al.* in press; and Zier 1980) and thus need not be repeated here. The explosive eruptions that occurred during the past 2000 years have varied considerably in their magnitude, geochemistry, weathering rates, natural recovery, and, most importantly, cultural and demographic repercussions.

This paper explores part of the theoretical framework within which the Proyecto Protoclasico's multidisciplinary investigations were conducted. These theoretical aspects are here presented as topics, including volcanic impacts on agrarian societies and the processes of recovery from them, settlement patterns and adaptations, and the beneficial and detrimental aspects of living in volcanically hazardous areas. The research design focused on the processes of recovery from the third century Ilopango eruption, and many new data were encountered that bear directly on that topic. As with most archaeological investigations, fortuitous contributions were made to other topics as well. Here we first look at natural hazard theory and

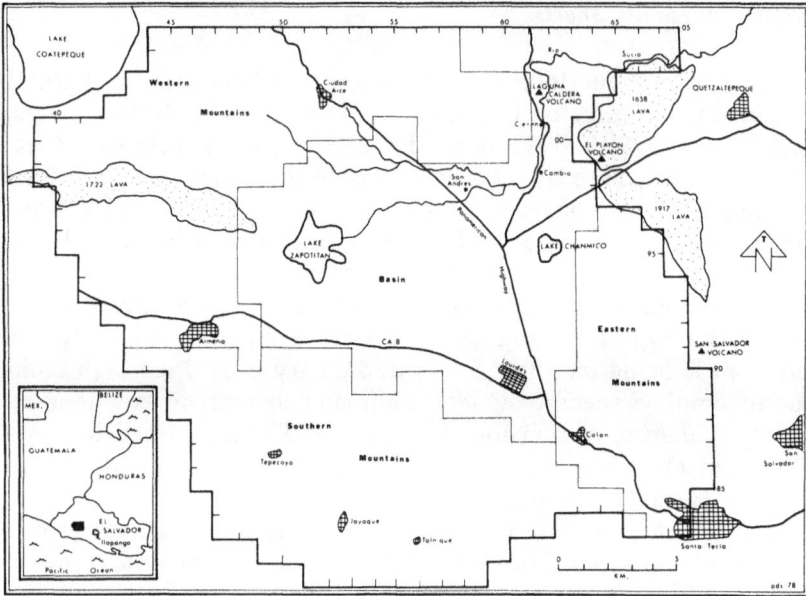

Figure 1. Zapotitan valley, El Salvador.

migration theory, then test three alternative hypotheses regarding the human impact of the Ilopango eruption and the recovery that occurred in the centuries following, and finally look at volcanism in very general terms.

Natural Hazard Research

Natural hazard and disaster research is a subsection of human ecology, the investigation of the dynamic relationships between people and their environments. No environment is entirely constant; mean annual rainfall and temperature figures are statistical abstractions, because no year is exactly average. Because of this, all human societies build flexibility into their adaptive strategies to deal with secular environmental variation. Hazard and disaster researchers investigate the extremes of this continuum, focusing on the mentalistic and behavioral adjustments that people make to major environmental perturbations.

Most hazard and disaster research in the social sciences has been conducted during the past two decades. Research into the Ilopango disaster and other Salvadoran eruptions has exploited the methods, approaches, and generalizations derived from that social science research. For instance, Warrick's (1975) assessment of volcanic hazard research, the volume edited by Haas, Kates, and Bowden (1977) on disaster reconstruction, White's edited work (1974) on natural hazards, the volume on hazardous environments by Burton, Kates, and White (1978), and White and Haas' (1975) assessment of natural hazards research are all key statements on the current methodological and theoretical state of hazard research. One of the field's oft-mentioned shortcomings has been the too-frequent atheoretical context of individual studies (Mileti, Drabek, and Haas 1975: 146) which seldom use social science theory to explain behavior or use alternative hypotheses to explore disaster behavior. Fortunately this problem is being rectified, for contemporary hazard research commonly employs specific models of human behavior; an excellent example is the use of decision theory in the Slovic, Kunreuther, and White article "Decision Processes, Rationality, and Adjustment to Natural Hazards" (White, ed., 1974: 186–205).

Another shortcoming noted by Mileti, Drabek, and Haas (1975: 145), which is avoided in this research, is the narrow time frame of most studies. Most work on disasters concentrates on the immediacy of the disaster and the following post-impact conditions, but some economic studies consider processes in longer time frames. A macro-time frame is built into our research into volcanism and human occupation of the Zapotitan valley in the past two to three millenia.

Warrick (1975) summarized volcanic hazard research. He noted that, at least for most natural hazards, there exists a considerable historic record of their impact on human studies. In contrast, volcanic hazards are notable for the paucity of cases from which hazard-loss relationships can be understood and compared. Warrick (1975: 61) notes that most research on volcanoes has focused on the physical characteristics and their eruptions with the objective of "pure scientific understanding; the quest for knowledge to help man better adjust to the threat of volcanic eruption was, for the most part, a secondary or incidental outcome of research. . . ." Fortunately, he notes (1975:61, 64) that the beginnings of a reversal may be underway. Studies have now appeared specifically focused on volcanic hazards of the Cascade Range of Washington, including Mount Saint Helens, Mount Rainier, and Mount Baker. The general population increase and concentration trends near these volcanoes markedly increase human susceptibility to eruption hazards, and give rise to the question, "Why do people live in known hazardous areas?"

Burton, Kates, and White (1978) isolate four factors affecting the actual human response to hazards; these are directly applicable to the Ilopango and later eruptions. First, the character of the event can vary considerably in duration, frequency, the area affected, and the speed of onset. Experience, the second factor, varies also, in that common events tend to create an awareness of hazard and an inventory of means which can be used by a society to adjust. Resource use is the third factor, with the more intensive resource uses being more susceptible to volcanic damage. Fourth is material wealth, and where material wealth is low, people tend to be aware of the hazard rapidly, but generally are slow to take compensatory action.

An application of these four factors to Salvadoran volcanism helps illuminate the nature of specific eruptions. Because Ilopango erupted suddenly in the third century, following many centuries of quiescence, the surprise factor must have been great. It is unlikely that Protoclassic societies had much knowledge of how to deal with such an event, either based on a direct oral tradition from the last local eruption or garnered from nearby Central American societies who more recently had suffered such a calamity. Resource use at the end of the Protoclassic period was notably intensive, with irrigation and intensive dryland farming practiced across much of the countryside. Other resources, such as obsidian, andesite and basalt, clay, jadeite, and hematite, were exploited intensively as well, thus making the socio-economic system quite vulnerable to disruption. Material wealth is difficult to address in a non-monetary prehistoric society. Viewed internally, wealth can be seen in terms of nature and diversity of material culture and the degree of environmental modification or "improvement." Comparatively, I do not see significant wealth differences in the valley societies prior to each of the four explosive eruptions, but considerable differences in wealth existed within each society, on a synchronic basis.

Migration Theory and Zapotitan Valley Volcanism

The formulations of Burton, Kates, and White (1978) concerning a general theory of human behavioral adjustments to major environmental fluctuations are used here as a context within which to view migration. They categorize responses into four modes of increasing severity: loss absorption, loss acceptance, loss reduction, and radical change (fig. 2). These modes are separated by three different threshold levels: awareness, action, and intolerance.

Loss absorption involves all the incidental adjustments made with no conscious program of change. Loss acceptance involves conscious awareness (crossing the first threshold), and generally the loss of a group of victims is borne by a large group of people. Loss reduction incorporates direct action (crossing the second threshold) by the victims to reduce their losses. However, as the scale of the disaster increases, the third threshold is crossed (toleration) and radical change is undertaken. Such radical action may involve in situ fundamental adaptive changes, or, in the extreme cases where the environmental changes are beyond human technological capacity to adjust, migration occurs. These modes and thresholds apply to the Ilopango-affected Zapotitan valley in the following way. Of the three hypotheses presented below, the first assumes the ability of some highland Maya to be able to make in situ adjustments to cope with their changed circumstances, while the other two hypotheses assume that in situ adjustments were insufficient. Because they were insufficient, emigrations depopulated the devastated areas, and immigration and reconstruction following the disaster had to come from without.

The assumption cannot be made, however, that all societies at the same point of social complexity will react to the same stress by the same adjustments. The condition (or trajectory) of the society and the success of its land and resource use must be taken into account; a society experiencing ecological difficulties likely would react to the same degree of stress by crossing a higher threshold than a comparable society with a more successful adaptation. In this light, the adaptation of the Preclassic highland Maya becomes important. There are no indications, from archaeological or pedological data, that the society before the eruption was undergoing detectable stress or any kind of decline.

Migration may be defined simply as the relatively permanent movement of people over space (Peterson 1968; 286, du Toit 1975: 1). Migrations vary in degree of permanence, number of people, distance traveled, whether they are voluntary or coercive, and their underlying causes. According to du Toit (1975: 6), people tend to migrate to places where they are known and about which they have

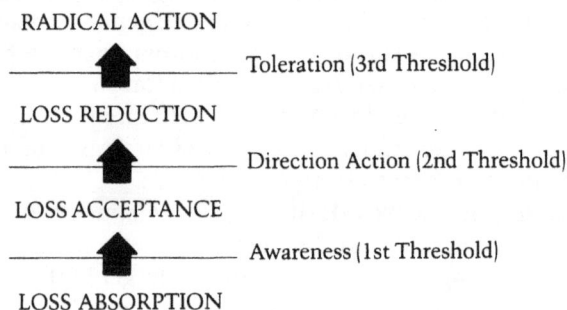

RADICAL ACTION

———————⬆——————— Toleration (3rd Threshold)

LOSS REDUCTION

———————⬆——————— Direction Action (2nd Threshold)

LOSS ACCEPTANCE

———————⬆——————— Awareness (1st Threshold)

LOSS ABSORPTION

Figure 2. Schematic diagram of human behavioral adjustments to extreme environmental changes (from Burton, Kates, and White 1978).

general knowledge or where they already have established fictive or blood kin ties. This general rule may be applicable to the Proto-classic migrations northward to the lowlands immediately following the eruption, but it is of limited utility in investigating the reoccupation of the devastated areas.

Peterson (1968: 289–290) identifies types of migrations by the underlying reasons for the migrants' move. Innovative migrants are those who move to achieve something new (Hypothesis 3 below) while conservative migrants attempt to retain the old way of life by moving to a new location (Hypotheses 1 and 2 below). In either of these cases migration can be forced, depending on circumstances, or it can be a free migration in that the migrants largely retain the power of decision.

As Safa (in Safa and du Toit 1975: 1) and Peterson (1968) have pointed out, the limitations of many previous migration studies have derived from the scale of phenomena examined. Many of these studies assumed or concluded that migrants left because of limited employment opportunities in their areas of origin and hopes of better economic situations elsewhere. Much of migration theory is heavily economic, as it derives from the large nineteenth century migrations of Europeans into North America, and thus it must be used with caution here as a high-level theoretical framework. Safa suggests a wider context than the individual or the family making "economic" decisions, since national and international political and economic factors may be deeply involved.

Three Alternative Hypotheses of Disaster Recovery

The process of recovery from a natural disaster can be generated from outside the disaster zone, e.g., when a government sponsors relief programs, or reconstruction can proceed on an internal, piece-meal basis, with the decisions being made and actions taken by the individuals affected (Haas 1977: 1). Haas (*Ibid.*: 4) notes how research into the issues, problems, and alternatives involved with recovery from disasters has been rare. The following three hypotheses are modified from the disaster and migration literature to make them specifically applicable to reoccupation and recovery from the Ilopango eruption.

Human recovery from the Ilopango disaster involved rebuilding housing and public buildings (pyramids, temples, plazas, and the like) as well as population and agricultural recovery. Kates and Pijawka (1975: 11–17) examined a number of disasters and the recovery from them, and they noticed population recovery was a relatively accurate index to general recovery. They then applied the population recovery index to other data, and discovered that the time for reconstruction appears to be closely connected to the magnitude of a disaster. This demonstrated intercorrelation of disaster magnitude, population recovery, and general reconstruction and recovery provides a research tool for investigating Salvadoran natural disasters. Their approximate estimates of the relationship of population loss during disasters and the time needed for recovery in pre-industrial agricultural societies are as follows: a 10% population loss requires about 15 years to recover, a 50% population loss requires about 50 years, and a 75% loss takes more than 150 years for full recovery. Our data indicate about two centuries were needed for demographic recovery from a thorough depopulation of the Zapotitan valley.

Hypothesis 1: Recovery by Internal Migration

The first of the three alternative hypotheses of reoccupation and recovery holds that remnant populations who were left in hilly areas gradually expanded to reoccupy devastated areas. This is recovery of the internal type, involving Peterson's conservative migrants. It involves loss reduction or radical action, but stops short of abandonment by all valley peoples (cf. fig. 2). Also assumed is that in some areas of El Salvador agricultural communities were able to adjust to their changed circumstances. As Sharer (1974: 172) states for Chalchuapa, "while some continuity of occupation and even agricultural production could have been maintained along the upland slopes and foothills . . . the valley floor itself may have been drastically depopulated." Thus some groups remained in upland areas, where erosional removal of the ash shroud from slopes can be rapid. As chemical weathering and plant colonization recreated in the topographically flatter areas a soil horizon suitable for agriculture people from the remnant communities could gradually reclaim the regenerated lands. Viewed from these small highland communities, the population increases so common within settled, agrarian communities led to population pressures on local productive land, resulting in small-scale migrations into flat-lying land as it slowly became suitable for agricultural production.

Specific test implications were formulated which must be sustained by the data gathered before this internal demographic hypothesis could be accepted as the best explanation. First, communities which did remain in the southeastern Maya highlands after the eruption must be discovered by survey. Second, these highland communities should show continuity of occupation extending from the Preclassic (prior to the eruption) into the Classic period. A cultural continuum must be demonstrable in lithic, ceramic, and other artifacts. Third, the stylistic and technological analyses of artifacts, architecture, and settlement patterns of the Classic communities in the low-lying flat areas should demonstrate more similarities to contemporary nearby highland communities than to the more distant Guatemala highlands, the Maya lowlands, or the Lenca area in eastern El Salvador and Honduras. Geological evidence supportive of the hypothesis would involve rapid removal of the ash layer from hilly areas sufficient to allow some communities to remain.

Hypothesis 2: Gradual Reoccupation by Peripheral Classic Maya

The second hypothesis of recovery, that of a gradual reoccupation of the Salvador area from the southern peripheries of Classic Maya territory, was developed by A. Zier (1976). She noted the lack of artifactual evidence showing that reoccupation could have derived either from the Guatemalan highlands or from the Lenca areas to the east (1976: 2). She then explored the possibility that reoccupation was by small groups of agriculturalists from the Motagua-Ulua areas who were in need of new arable land, beginning about the fifth century A.D. As such, this would fall into Peterson's domain of conservative migrations. One of the pressures driving people out of the occupied Maya area, in addition to the continued population pressures of the Classic (Sanders 1972: 124), was the general unrest of the Middle Classic (Dahlin 1976; Zier 1976: 8). Hypothesis 2 (and number 3, below), of course, involves the most extreme reactions to the disaster, crossing the toleration threshold and requiring abandonment of the area (fig. 2).

The specific test implications of this hypothesis of gradual infiltration of peripheral Classic Maya agriculturalists are:

1. Artifacts (ceramics, lithics, architecture, and sculpture) should be stylistically and technologically derived out of the Maya lowland Classic in the supra-ashfall stratum. 2. Because of its gradual nature and the relative independence of these agricultural groups, initial reoccupation should be low in population density and variable in time and location. 3. Immigrant groups should exhibit minimal intrasite sociocultural diversity, in contrast with the notable disparities of wealth and status of the major Maya centers. 4. Reoccupation would be in a gradual and general southern to southeastern direction along zones with more rapid biotic and soil recovery, and not toward any particular extractive mineral (obsidian) or plant (cotton, balsam, and/or cacao) resource.

Data used to test this hypothesis derive from a variety of sources, involving archaeology, geology, pedology, and palynology. Results sustaining this hypothesis would be greater artifactual similarity to the southeastern Maya lowland area than to the Maya highlands to the west or the Lenca area to the east. The null hypothesis in this case would state no difference or a greater artifactual similarity with one or both of these alternative areas.

Data pertinent to the second test implication are spatial and temporal; the hypothesis is sustained if dated distributions of Classic settlements and artifacts indicate a gradual southward movement in the valley. The third test implication of the gradual Maya reoccupation hypothesis involves the socio-economic complexity of the Classic sites. The hypothesis predicts settlement units of minimal internal heterogeneity. The villages of gradually infiltrating agriculturalists would not be expected to contain ballcourts, large pyramid-plaza units and significant variation in commoner-to-elite housing; or, viewed stratigraphically, the characteristics of ranked or stratified society so apparent prior to the eruption should not be present in the initial settlement of the Early Classic.

The Chalchuapa Project discovered that the Classic period reoccupants built structures on top of the soil of that time without removing the ash blanket (Sharer, ed., 1978), so a soil analysis which controlled for extraneous variables would be able to assess the relative fertility of soils at sites when they were first being reestablished. The agricultural potential of a 1 m thick undisturbed airfall volcanic ash after a decade of weathering, for example, is less than the same thickness of a lahar (eroded ash from a slope with mixed pre-eruption topsoil, deposited as a mudflow).

Hypothesis 3: Recovery by Classic Maya Colonization

The third hypothesis states that the reoccupation and recovery of the southeast highlands was a deliberate colonization by Classic Maya for specific economic objectives. This would be an innovative immigration in Peterson's typology. Viewed from the mode and threshold model (fig. 2), the final threshold had been crossed, that of intolerance, and emigration was necessary. Recovery from the disaster necessarily had to come from beyond the damaged area.

Thompson (1970: 101–102) traced the Early Classic expansion of the Chorti Maya southward from the central lowlands. Copan was established as a functioning elite center by A.D. 495, when stelae with 9.2.10.0.0 long count dates were erected. Thompson extended this migration farther southward:

We can now speak of a Chorti thrust on a broadish front from the Atlantic lowlands right across the highlands along both sides of Guatemala's eastern border, not only in force in El Salvador, north and west of the Lempa River to Lake Guija, but also, it would appear, on the Guatemalan side to south of Lake Ayarza. (1970: 102)

Recent archaeological research extends Chorti expansion deep into western El Salvador (Sharer 1974: 176). Moreover, Hammond (in Sharer 1974: 178) sees the founding of Pusilha and Lubaantun in southern Belize as a component of the general Chol-Chorti expansion of the Middle Classic.

It is unknown to what degree the Chorti expansion southward was initiated by the cultural-economic disruptions of the Middle Classic in the central Peten (assuming, for the sake of argument, this hypothesis is correct). Perhaps the demise of the Teotihuacan-dominated long-distance trade routes in elite and utilitarian goods during the fifth century resulted in severe social and economic dislocations for the Maya. Thus, I suggest that the Chorti southern expansion initiated in the fifth century may have been for economic stabilization; the objective was to establish their own trade network to control the obsidian outcrops of Ixtepeque and Media Cuesta (the fairly small source on the north shore of Lake Ayarza), the middle Motagua jade source, and, probably, to establish access to and control of cotton, balsam, and cacao production.

A number of test implications can be specified to weigh this hypothesis against the others. If colonization were the mechanism of reoccupation instead of gradual infiltration of peripheral agricultural villages, the sites of the earliest immigrants should exhibit indications of socio-economic differentiation. The status indicators of the major lowland sites would have been maintained by the colonists. These include differential wealth in burials and in housing, non-random distribution among the population of high status items, and ballcourts and pyramid-plaza complexes.

If colonization were directed at control of obsidian, then post-fifth century obsidian at consumer sites such as Copan and Quirigua should derive predominantly from sources in Chorti-dominated areas. Sidrys, Andersen, and Marcucci (1976) summarized Maya obsidian sources, and three mentioned by them occur within Thompson's area of Chorti expansion: Ixtepeque, Media Cuesta, and Santa Ana. (The Santa Ana source, according to my own work, was not used by the Maya.) Data required to sustain the obsidian component of the hypothesis would be a predominance of obsidian from one or more of these sources at consuming sites after approximately A.D. 500.

If the second hypothesis is correct—that peripheral farming communities gradually expanded into El Salvador—geographic movement would have been rather slow. On the other hand, if this third hypothesis of deliberate colonization is correct, expansion would have been relatively rapid. According to Thompson, Copan was initiated as a Classic Maya site about A.D. 500. The distance from Copan to the study area is 75 km. It seems unlikely that the gradual expansion of peripheral agricultural communities would cover this amount of territory in less than a century. On the other hand, a state-run colonization operation could yield expansion of this sort within a few years.

Thus, migration in the central and western areas of El Salvador must be viewed in two ways: migration out of the area severely affected by volcanism, and migration into the area as a part of disaster recovery. Comparing the four eruptions in the valley it is important that, to the best of our present knowledge, evidence of migration exists only for the Ilopango eruption, and that includes both emigration and immigration. I interpret the Protoclassic site unit intrusions in the Maya lowlands as evidence of refugees from the southeast Maya area, and the Chorti colonization during the sixth century as the human recovery from the disaster (Sheets 1979a). That we have no evidence of later migrations associated with the Laguna Caldera, Boqueron, or Playon eruptions does not mean migrations did not occur. Almost certainly there were migrations with each, but they were too small, both demographically and geographically, to be detectable in the archaeological record.

Testing the Hypotheses

The first hypothesis is the easiest and clearest to test, based on 1978–1980 data. Despite the efforts to find Early Classic artifacts and sites during survey and excavations, none were found. Thus there is no evidence of remnant populations who survived the Ilopango disaster and stayed in the area, later to supply the population base for demographic recovery in the valley as a whole. Further, the artifacts of the earliest post-Ilopango inhabitants of the valley are not derivative of the Salvadoran Protoclassic, but are clearly from without. None of the test implications were sustained by the data, and this first hypothesis must now be considered the least applicable to the disaster and the recovery process.

The second hypothesis is at least partially supported by our data.

Artifactual analyses, particularly ceramics and lithics, indicate a close affiliation of the Salvadoran immigrants with the Chorti Maya emanating from the central Peten around the fifth and sixth centuries A.D. However, there is no clear evidence either of a slow influx of population into the area, or that the earliest immigrants were a relatively homogeneous population of agriculturalists. The population density was not low, at least in the Ceren area. Thus, the second hypothesis, while more reasonable than the first, is only minimally supported by the data. More detailed data on the sixth century are needed before it can be finally rejected or accepted.

The third hypothesis, that recovery was a planned colonization scheme, has the strongest support from data collected in 1978–80. That is not to say it is proven or demonstrated; rather, its test implications match the data slightly more closely than the second hypothesis. The earliest securely-dated evidence we have of return immigration to the valley is at Ceren. The composite corrected C^{14} date of A.D. 590±90 is for the end of that settlement episode at Ceren, not the initial colonization. The structures were initially constructed prior to that date, and they were refurbished a number of times after that. Numerous agricultural seasons had passed before Laguna Caldera erupted and buried the site. I would guess, based on the extent of remodeling, that the family had lived there a few decades prior to the Laguna Caldera eruption, thus placing the founding of Ceren perhaps early in the sixth century. If this is correct, it would leave very little time between the Chorti founding of Copan and the movement into the valley. This strikes me as much more rapid than one would expect for a gradual expansion of subsistence agriculturalists; instead, it looks more like an organized event.

The Ceren house was not occupied by an economically and socially isolated, subsistence-only oriented family. They participated in far-flung economic networks supplying obsidian, salt, and polychrome ceramics, and they apparently participated in valley-wide exchange or procurement systems for andesite, basalt, clay, hematite, and, probably, other materials. Population density was not low, based on the fairly close spacing of houses on the very young soil.

The survey data indicate a great diversity of settlement types during the Late Classic, with the greatest number and variety of sites that existed in the valley at any time. Although it cannot be demonstrated that they are exactly synchronous with Ceren it is likely that many were contemporaries. The picture is of a complex, stratified society, with a hierarchical settlement system, colonizing the valley. Manufacturing industries, based on occupational specialists evincing considerable skill, are sophisticated from the start.

As mentioned above, the boundaries of Chorti southward expansion include the obsidian sources of Media Cuesta and Ixtepeque. I suspect the economic disruptions for the central Peten Maya caused by Teotihuacan had much to do with the Chorti migrations. The Teotihuacan presence at Kaminaljuyu, increasing during the fifth century and climaxing in the sixth century (Cheek 1977b), gave Teotihuacan considerable influence over El Chayal obsidian. The view from the central Peten must have been one of concern, if not alarm, as it must have appeared that the Teotihuacanos were attempting a monopoly of Mesoamerican obsidian. The Maya faced a loss of control of access to a needed commodity and thus an increase in its cost. I suggest the Chorti southward migrations, beginning in the late fifth century, were motivated at least in part by a need to own some obsidian in order to break the threatened monopoly. Source ownership is more secure if the sources themselves and the zones around them are occupied. Teotihuacan was unable to resist the movement, and tons of Ixtepeque obsidian, largely in the form of macrocores, flowed along Maya-owned and -operated trade routes into Salvador, Honduras, Guatemala, and Belize. Judging by the dating of the beginnings of Teotihuacan withdrawal from Kaminaljuyu (Cheek 1977b), the threat of a Teotihuacan obsidian monopoly had disappeared by about A.D. 600, and possibly as early as A.D. 550. I suggest that the Maya success in exploiting Ixtepeque obsidian directly contributed to the failure of the Teotihuacan presence at Kaminaljuyu.

Volcanic Disasters in General

Using an archaeological approach to study volcanic disasters offers advantages and disadvantages. The disadvantages largely come down to removal, i.e., the event being studied is far removed from us in time, and often in location and in cultural context. Such removal tends to obscure the fine-grained details of the event and its immediate aftermath. In contrast, the social or natural scientist on the scene of a contemporary disaster only hours or days after it occurred can collect highly detailed information on preparedness, scope of physical, biological, and mental damage, and the recovery process. Scientists studying disasters have generally focused on the days or weeks following impact, and they have only recently extended their time frame to "long-term" studies of recovery lasting up to a few years. The broadcast and print media, in reporting natural disasters, consistently emphasize the most drastic and immediate negative impacts.

Inherent to archaeological research is a very long time perspective within which process can be explored and understood. Sites and regions often offer continuous archaeological records which extend for hundreds or thousands of years. Thus, archaeologists could contribute very important insights and comparative conclusions regarding the long-term probable effects of various kinds of natural disasters on human societies and how people adapted in a variety of environments. Archaeologists cannot be expected to contribute much understanding to topics such as post-disaster psychological effects on survivors, or short-term recovery procedures and processes, since phenomena such as these are rarely preserved in the archaeological record.

A sophisticated comparative study of the relationships of variability in societies, volcanism, and environments is not yet possible, principally because of the lack of cases where multidisciplinary data have been collected. For example, not enough is known to be able to specify a type of society and its adaptation to a particular environment, and then predict the long-term effects and plot the expected recovery trajectory from a particular kind of volcanic eruption.

Although it is premature to offer any firm conclusions about volcanic ecology from the archaeological perspective, I will hazard a few general comments. Despite the lack of cases for comparative study, we do have four cases in El Salvador of explosive volcanism and tephra deposits affecting complex societies within a tropical monsoon environment. In addition, about a dozen more eruptions elsewhere in the world have been explored with sufficient detail (Sheets and Grayson 1979) to establish the beginnings of a comparative framework. What is striking to me in attempting to see some sort of patterning in these cases is the remarkable resiliency, in the long run, of human societies in dealing with volcanism. Very few eruptions caused significant cultural-demographic effects which lasted long enough to leave marked effects in the archaeological record. Within this sample, the only eruptions that seem to have caused significant long term culture changes are Thera in the Aegean at about 1500 B.C., and in the Christian era, Ilopango in the third century, and Mount Saint Elias in Alaska-Canada about the eighth century.

Both Thera in the Aegean and Ilopango in El Salvador were of sufficient magnitude to suppress the vitality of stratified, state-level societies, Minoan Crete and the southeast Maya, respectively. The disaster allowed competitive neighbors to take advantage of disruption, allowing for the expansion and supremacy of the mainland Mycenaeans and the Peten Maya. The East Lobe of the White River tephra from Mount Saint Elias severely affected the egalitarian hunting and gathering Athabascans in the Yukon, requiring large-scale migrations out of the area. These may have reached as far south as the United States Southwest, represented today by the Navajo and Apache (Workman 1979).

In contrast, three out of the four explosive eruptions during the past 2000 years in the Zapotitan valley had only minor or nonexistent effects on general cultural evolution. Granted, each was disastrous for the people living near the event when each occurred, but recovery in each case, even on a regional basis, was rapid and thorough. What is impressive in these instances is the resiliency of human societies. Human recovery was effected by people moving back into the devastated areas relatively quickly, and in all cases the material culture, economy, and society after the eruption are much the same as they were before the eruption occurred.

Along the same lines, the bulk of the other cases examined by various authors (Sheets and Grayson 1979) showed rapid recovery to a state very similar to preeruption conditions. What causes such a difference in full versus non-recovery? Certainly one of the major factors is relative scale, i.e., the extent of the volcanic disaster relative to the extent of socioeconomic polities. In the cases where recovery was rapid (on the archaeological time scale, meaning up to a few decades) the extent of the tephra disaster was less than the geographic boundaries of specific socioeconomic units. Thus, with only a segment of a functioning society affected, recovery was facilitated. In contrast, with the three great volcanic disasters, the scale of the disaster exceeded the boundaries of socioeconomic units, leaving no readily available sources of assistance to aid recovery; and, of course, thicker and more extensive tephra blankets take longer to weather and form fertile soils to support floral and faunal recovery.

EUGENIA J. ROBINSON

A Typological Study of Prehistoric Settlement of the Eastern Alluvial Fans, Sula Valley, Honduras: Comparison to Maya Settlement Forms

Introduction

The Sula valley, located on the northwest coast of Honduras, is situated in the southeastern frontier of Mesoamerica, an area which is culturally less sophisticated than that of the bordering Maya zone (fig. 1). In the sixteenth century, the Ulua River served as a boundary between Maya speaking peoples to the west and Jicaque speakers to the east who had cultural traditions relating to those of lower Central America further to the east. Early reports of the archaeology of the Sula valley provided data for a culture area interpretation. The presence of Late Classic polychromes manifesting Maya design principles supported the contention that the Maya were present in the periphery during that epoch. The absence of monumental architecture, elaborately carved stelae and sculptural decoration, painted and carved Maya hieroglyphs and iconographic elements suggested to researchers that the area did not fully participate in Classic Maya lowland civilization. Indeed, stylistic studies linked Sula valley ceramic motifs (Gordon 1898b) and sculpture styles (Lothrop 1921) of the Sula valley to art traditions of lower Central America. It is antici-

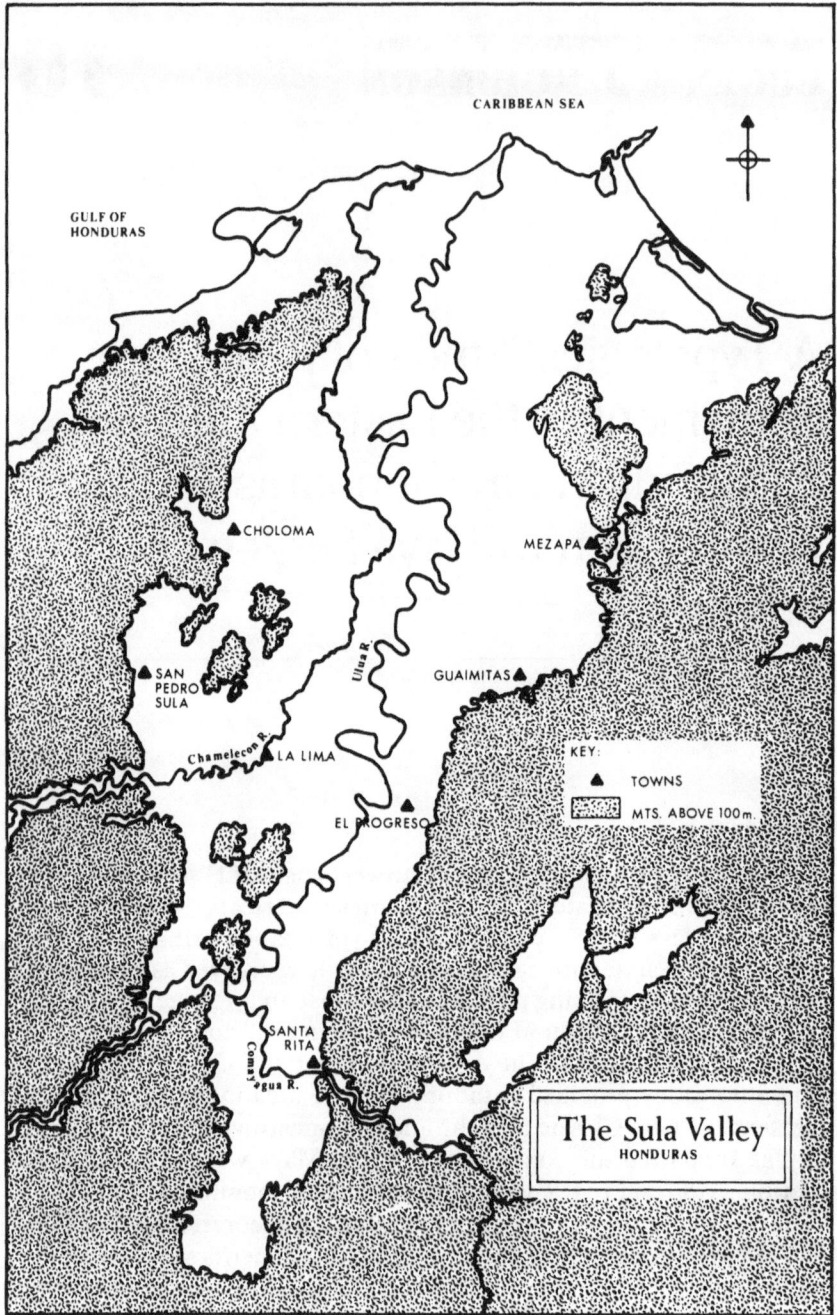

Figure 1. The Sula valley, Honduras.

pated today that the archaeology of the valley is the product of different ethnic groups which participated in socio-political organizations less complex than the state-like developments in the adjacent Maya area.

Prior to the late 1970s, the sum of what was known of the prehistory of the valley derived from non-intensive surveys and infrequent excavations carried out before 1937 (Gordon 1898b; Kramer and Lowe 1940; Popenoe 1934; Steinmayer 1932; Stone 1941; Strong, Kidder and Paul 1938; Yde 1938). In the 1970s, the Instituto Hondureno de Antropologia e Historia (IHAH) recognized the immediate need for a complete survey of the Sula valley; the archaeological resources of the valley were being destroyed by large-scale farming activities, and intensive, often mechanized, looting. In 1979, IHAH initiated the Proyecto Arqueologico Sula co-directed by John S. Henderson of Cornell University and Ricardo Agurcia, Gerente, IHAH. The objectives of the project were to execute a 100% survey and test excavate a representative sample of sites.

As part of the preliminary explorations, I designed a 14% stratified, random, transect sample for the southeastern area of the valley. This zone is an alluvial plain through which flow the Ulua and Comayagua Rivers. The survey area was 224 km^2, bounded on the north and south by arbitrary borders respectively 2 km south of El Progreso and 1 km south of Santa Rita (see fig. 2). Natural features define the east and west boundaries: the Montana de Mico Quemado and Montana de Guanchia form the eastern terminus, and the Cerro La Lima, Cerro La Sirena, and mountains near Potrerillos constitute the western edge.

Several factors contributed to the selection of this area for survey. These were: 1) a high density of previously located prehistoric settlements; 2) the presence of five important published sites—Playa de los Muertos, Travesia, Santa Ana, Santa Rita, and La Guacamaya; 3) components from these sites spanned the Late Middle Formative to Late Classic (600 B.C.–A.D. 1000), all the major time periods known for the Sula valley; and 4) the presence of three linear biotic zones— the alluvial soils of the Ulua and Comayagua Rivers, backlands created by the deposition of flood clays on the right banks of the rivers, and the ecotones of colluvial soils at the base of the mountain slopes. Known settlements were situated along the banks of the rivers and the eastern ecotone suggesting that the prehistoric settlement distribution was linear.

The transect sample was designed to traverse major cultural and ecological zones and to obtain a sample from the north to the south. In order to assure fairly uniform areal coverage of the survey area

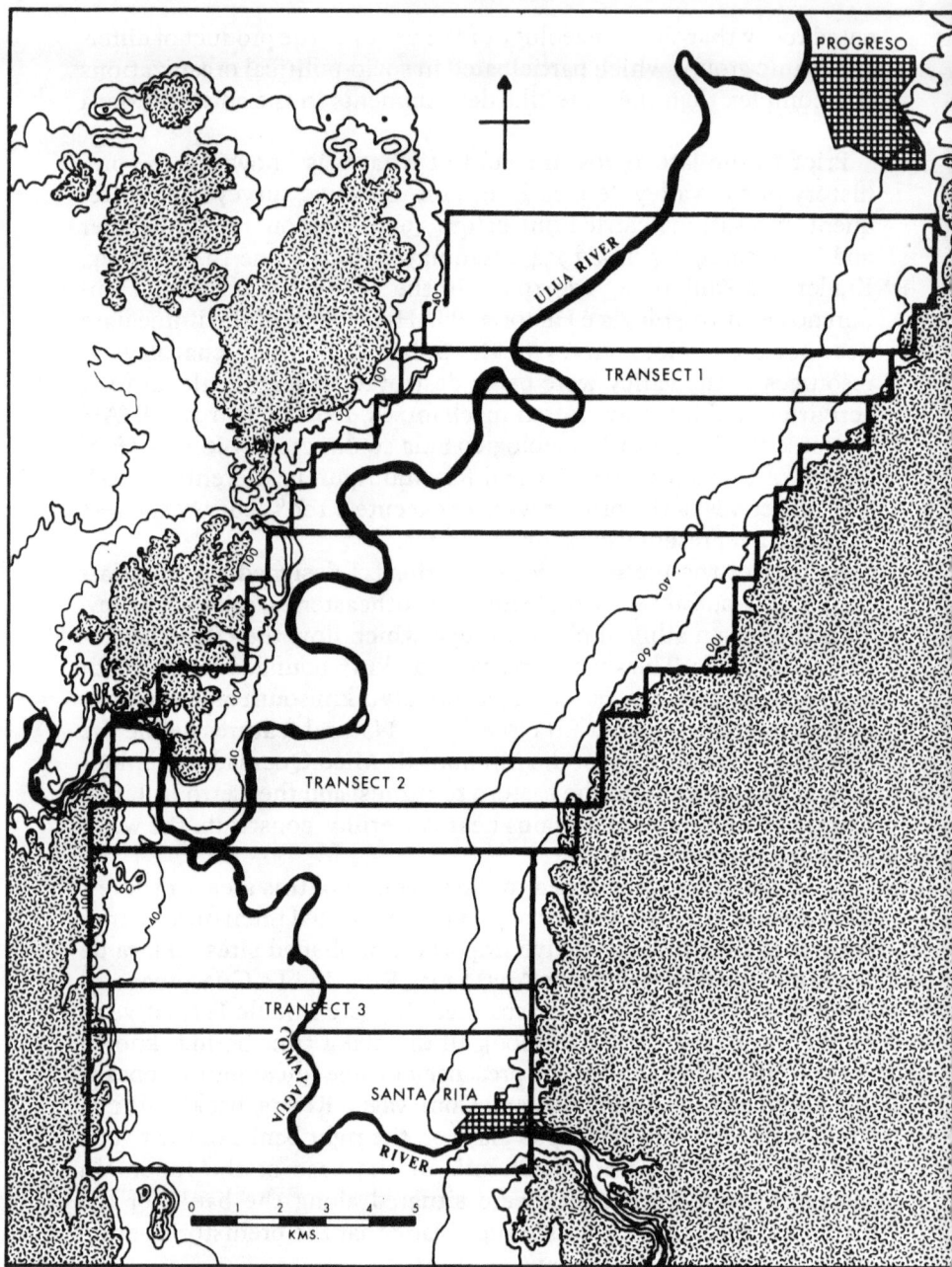

Figure 2. Survey area showing location of transects discussed in the text.

with the transect sample, the survey area was stratified into three units, each 7 km in length (north-south). The transects to be surveyed were determined by random selection of one transect from a stratum of seven. The stratified random selection resulted in the desired spacing of the transects throughout the survey area. Transect 1 (the most northerly) lay 8 km north of Transect 2 and the latter was separated from Transect 3 by 4 km. The length of all of the transects was 1 km, but the widths varied·with the distance between the east and west bordering mountain range: the two most northerly transects measured 11 km and the southerly one was 10 km. A sampling fraction of one-seventh was maintained from each stratum; the transects represent a 14% sample of each stratum and of the survey area as a whole.

The survey objectives were to carry out intensive survey and to locate, record, and map, with brunton and tape at a scale of 1:1000, all visible archaeological remains within each sample transect. The presence of cane and banana plantations in, respectively, the backlands and alluvial plains prohibited systematic survey; instead, we walked major roads and inquired of local people about the situation of archaeological resources. The preservation of archaeological remains is extremely poor in these cultivated areas. In the bananas, infrequent platforms, disturbed sherd scatters and cobble features, and exposed sites in trenches constitute the sample of finds; in cleaned canefields, we located disturbed mound groups and in cultivated fields, in a few instances, preserved platforms. In actuality, intensive reconnaissance was only carried out on the alluvial fans at the eastern edges of the sample units. In this ecotone, land use is pasturage, milpas, and gardens, and the preservation of mound sites was excellent; data from approximately 14% of this zone will be the basis for the ensuing analysis.

Survey work in the southern end of the Sula valley since 1979 suggests that there were sub-regional settlement systems specific to different ecological zones. Sheptak (1981) has discovered, through the study of vertical stereoscopic photographs, a pattern of settlement which appears to be characteristic of the Ulua River and Chasnigua Creek: he could identify large isolated mounds, not organized in plazas, distributed along the water sources. He suggested that Travesia (Stone 1941) (on the west bank of the Ulua River) a site with cut stone masonry, two plazas, and a possible areal spread of 2 km², may have been part of this settlement system. In the intra-valley mountains, west of the Ulua River and between Pimienta and El Porvenir, Joyce (1981) has located and mapped Cerro Palenque, a centralized prehistoric site in a defensible hilltop location, as well as smaller sites at strategic mountain passes. Investigations on the alluvial fans on the east side have found a regular spacing of prehistoric centers in this relatively homogeneous environment. To date, no intensive survey has been executed in the swampy backlands and we do not know how this area was exploited in ancient times. The finding of prehistoric mound sites up to the eastern edges of the swamp, however, suggests that, if there were a population in the swamp, it was operating within a different settlement system than that along the alluvial fans.

Analysis of Settlement Data

In the following sections, a typology of structures, a site typology, and a discussion of the hierarchy of sites on the east side of the Sula valley will be presented.

For this study, analysis was undertaken of 31 located and mapped sites found on the eastern ends of Transects 1, 2, and 3, a 14%

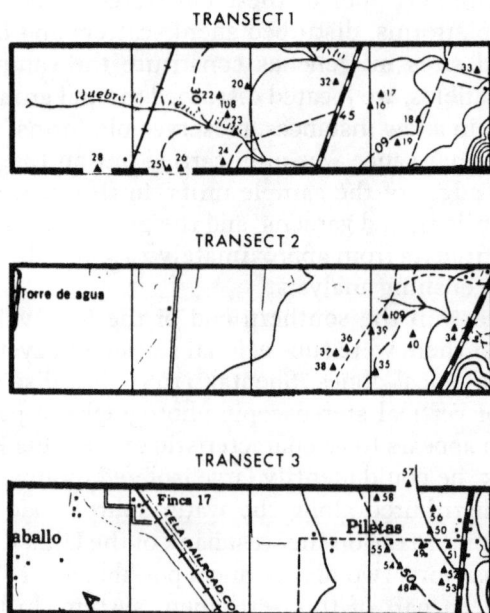

Figure 3. The eastern ends of Transects 1, 2, and 3 showing located sites.

sample of prehistoric settlements on the east side between Progreso and Santa Rita (see fig. 3). These sites are separated, generally, by at least 100 m; they consist of one to 88 earth and cobble platforms. The state of preservation of these prehistoric settlements is variable: several sites had been plowed and the integrity of the mounds destroyed; the forms of others, located near quebradas, have probably been altered by flood water. Due to these factors, 13 small sites have been eliminated; the study sample therefore consisted of 18 sites. These are: YR-16; YR-17; YR-18; YR-19; YR-20; YR-22; YR-24; YR-32; YR-35; YR-48; YR-49; YR-50; YR-52; YR-53; YR-56; YR-57; and YR-58.

The greater part of the area surveyed in the transects was pasture and samples of surface artifacts were difficult to collect; prior to 1981 all the sites in this sample except YR-48, which had a few Late Classic ceramic diagnostics, were undated. A working hypothesis regarding the chronological placement of visible mound sites, based on early excavation in the valley, was that they were Late Classic (A.D. 550–1000). Preliminary analysis of test-excavated ceramic collections and those from surface collecting disturbed mounds located during the 1981 field season (YR-24 in Transect 1 and YR-35 in Transect 2) supported this hypothesis. Test excavations at YR-24 were unsuccessful in recovering diagnostic ceramics; the surface collection of a plowed structure did, however, yield distinctive Late Classic pottery. Ceramic artifacts from a large systematic surface collection from YR-35 confirmed the Late Classic date of this site.

Before turning to the analysis, let me define the terms used below. Other than artifacts and cobble features, the minimal entity encountered on the surface was the substructural platform, referred to here as a structure, platform, or mound. The substructural platforms are aggregated into clusters called sites. Sites, in turn, are parts of entities which I term communities.

The objective of this analysis was to create a site typology which, as one of its goals, summarized site variability. The prehistoric settlements under consideration consisted (almost without exception) of fairly regularly shaped, single-level earthen and cobble platforms which were probably substructures for perishable, perhaps wattle and daub, superstructures. An attempt was made here to create a typology of structures and a typology of sites based on the frequency of occurrence of different types of platforms. This approach tried to 1) clearly delineate types of structures classified by their form and size and allow for the study of their spatial associations from site to site, and, 2) facilitate the rigorous comparative study of the similarities and differences between sites. The spatial arrangement of structures will be dealt with secondarily in this site typology.

Typology of Structure

One hundred and sixty platforms existed in the transect sample. Initial intuitive analysis of the forms and heights of structures did not isolate obvious types. It was noted that platforms varied in their basal proportions from square to very elongated rectangles. In light of this finding, it was thought that the examination of the basal form of mounds and their relative heights might isolate distinct structure categories. For this reason, a quantitative clustering approach was used to construct the typology; the three attributes used in this analysis were the lengths, widths, and heights of platforms measured to one-tenth of a meter. Formal constructional attributes, such as the types of building material or the presence or absence of cut stone, were not used in the creation of this typology. On the east side of the Sula valley, faced stone is a rarity and the construction stone of a site was distinctive in only one instance: at YR-35, a blanched, powdery limestone, local to the Quebrada de Piedras de Afilar just north of the site, was utilized.

The Clustan 1 program (Wishart 1978), using Ward's hierarchical grouping method, with standardized data, created 19 initial taxa (see fig. 4). Inspection of these primary groups found the differences between cases of the groups to be, in some instances, very small: for example, basal lengths and widths differed by only a meter or two between hypothetical types. The study of the sequential, agglomerative clusterings found that nine groups or types of mounds show the variability in the data but do not mask significant differences (fig. 4). Table 1 summarizes data pertaining to the mound types.

Inspection of the nine groups found that there was overlapping in the smaller mound types. For example, a mound with small basal dimensions and low height could have been a member of the Type 7 or 9. I moved several of these cases in order to establish a numerical boundary between the two types on the basis of one variable, area. Ward's clustering technique assesses membership in groups by measuring the total sum of squared deviations of a point from the mean of the cluster to which it might potentially be joined. Fusions are made where there is a minimum increase in the error sum of squares. In essence, for each group there is a measure of central tendency and the groups are defined by their similarity to this central point. This explains why there is overlapping in the categories;

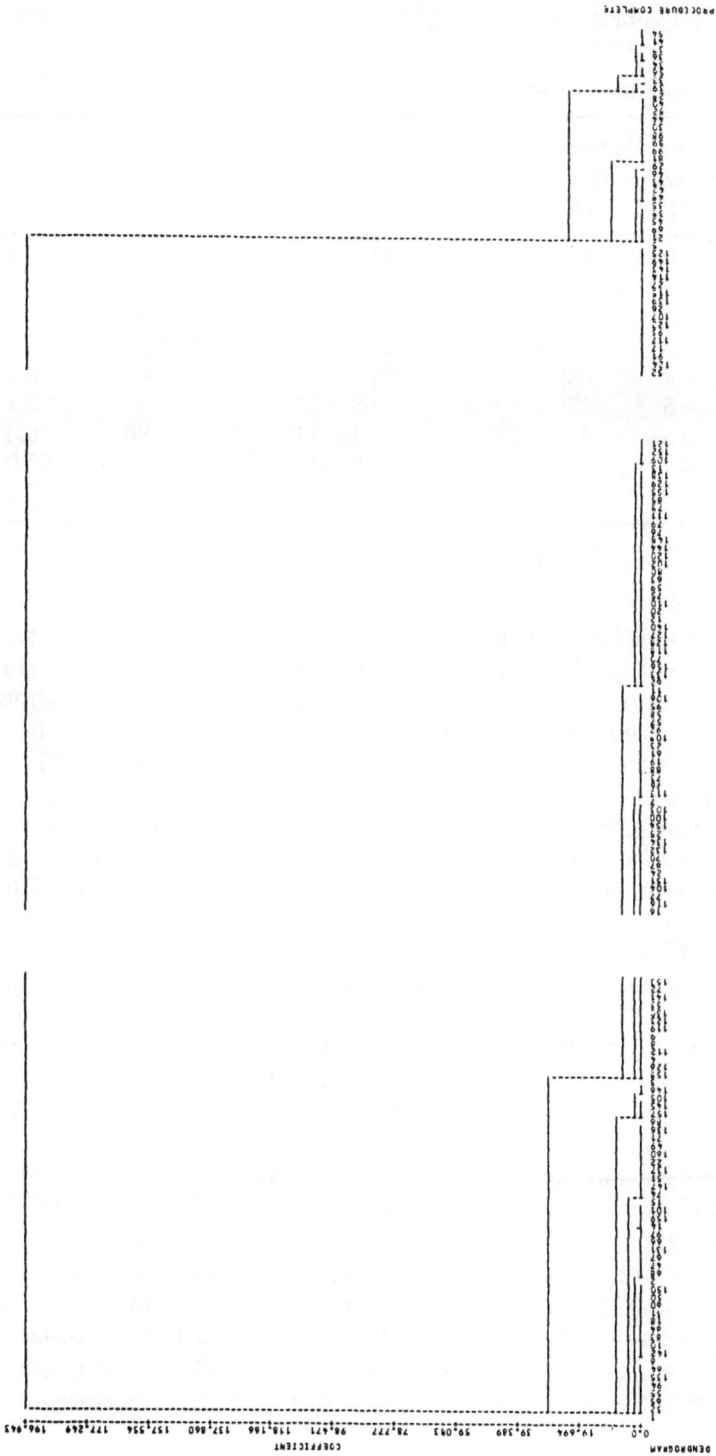

Figure 4. Dendrogram of cluster analysis showing 19 initial clusters.

Table 1. Summary of Criteria Used to Define Mound Types

Type	Fre-quency	Mean Length (m)	Mean Width (m)	Mean Height (m)	Length Range (m)	Height Range (m)	Basal Area Range (m²)
1	2	42.0	14.5	2.9	40.0–44.0	2.50–3.20	480.0–748.0
2	7	23.5	12.9	3.7	19.0–32.0	3.00–4.50	246.0–384.0
3	9	13.3	9.8	3.0	9.5–15.0	2.50–3.50	85.0–165.0
4	10	19.0	9.7	1.7	13.0–23.0	1.20–2.30	116.0–250.0
5	27	8.8	6.2	1.4	6.0–12.5	1.00–2.00	30.0–85.0
6	11	8.5	7.2	.6	6.5–10.0	.30–0.85	52.5–86.5
7	38	5.5	4.3	.5	4.0–09.0	.20–0.90	20.0–46.8
8	5	16.4	4.7	.3	12.5–22.0	.10–0.50	52.0–143.5
9	52	4.2	3.1	.2	3.0–08.0	.05–0.70	5.0–19.5

structures that are at the periphery of their groups and adjacent ones can be almost identical in their dimension. The plot of the two variables, length and height, by the BMDPFM discriminant program illustrates this point. Groups 7 and 9 are tightly clustered (fig. 5); however, the program has established that there are actually two poles of central tendency. The stepwise discriminant analysis, BMDPFM, calculated that 92% of all the structures were correctly classified.

Structure Types 1–3 are the biggest platforms of the sample and appear to function similarly; they all bound, or lie adjacent to, the largest plazas in the survey sample. Type 1 is rectangular in shape and occurs in two situations: 1) as the central structure of the core of the site YR-24 (fig. 7) and; 2) as the obviously dominant structure of YR-22 (fig. 8). The large size of these platforms suggests that they may have had a special function. The Type 2 structures are generally shorter in length than the Type 1, and have, on the average, a greater height. They bound a plaza approximately 100 m long at YR-24 (fig. 7) and at YR-35, the single largest mound of the group is this type (fig. 6). The function of these types of mounds is unknown. We do, however, have some constructional details of the easternmost structure of the large plaza at YR-24, a Type 2 platform. A trench bisecting the mound, initiated to uncover building phase chronology, exposed an interior wall of cobbles in a sand matrix. Excavation of a pit 0.9 m by 1.3 m along the face of the wall and the interior of the mound found clean, undifferentiated sand fill; features similar to this wall and clean fill are known in the Naco valley. Continued excavation to the ground level of a structure along the interior face of

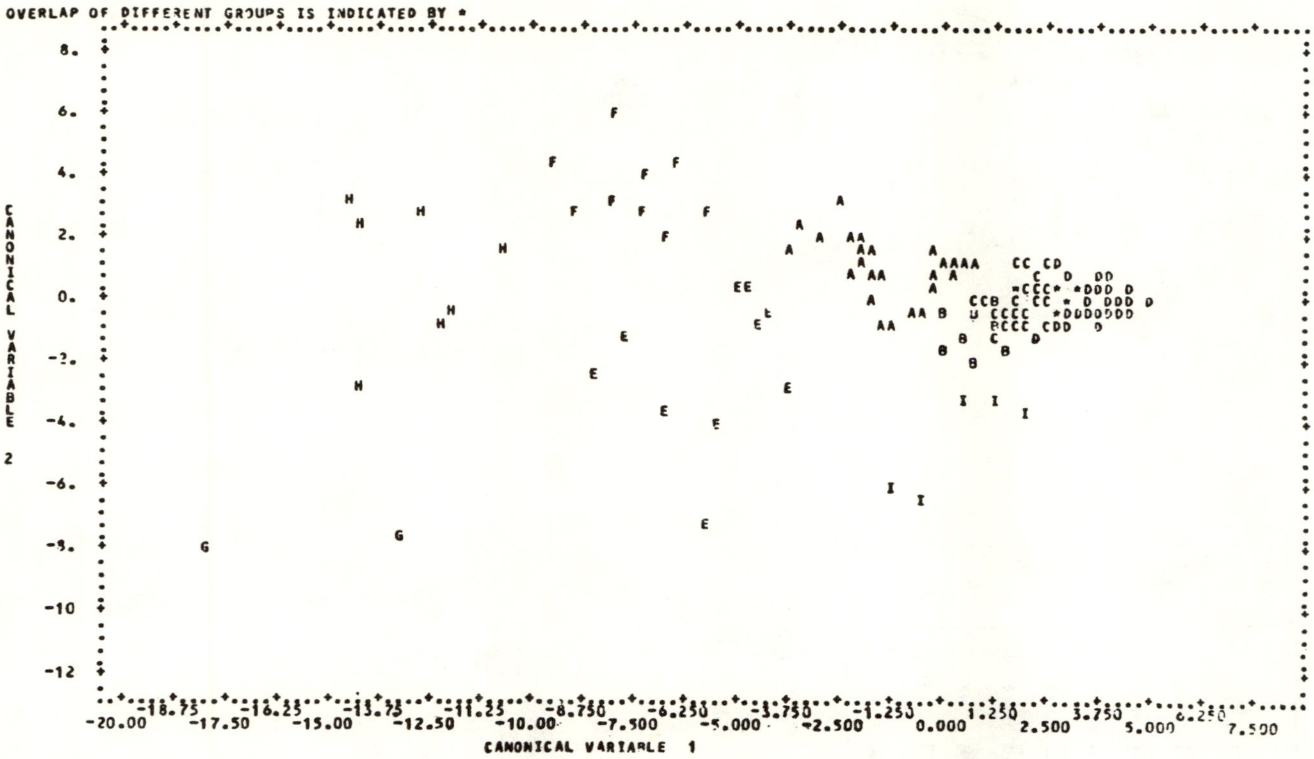

Figure 5. Plot of the variables height (canonical variable 1) and length (canonical variable 2).

KEY : Structure types

type 1
type 2
type 3
type 4
type 5
type 6
type 7
type 8
type 9

Figure 6

Figure 8

Figure 7

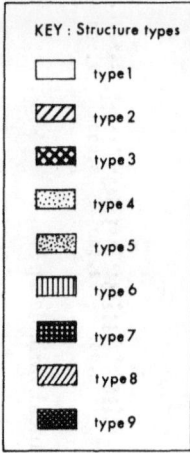

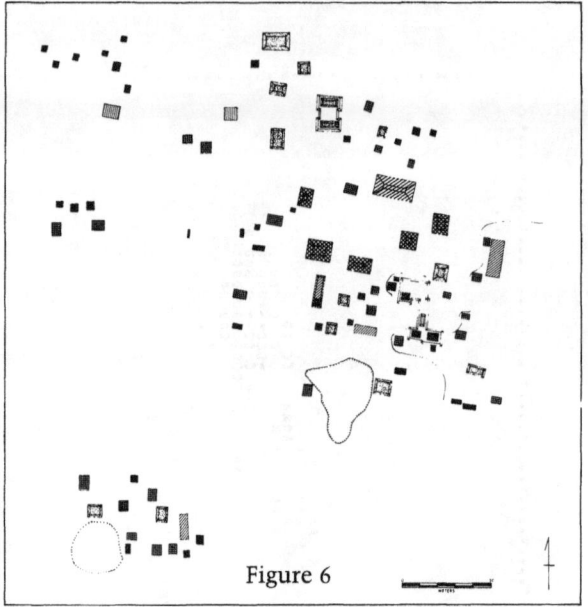

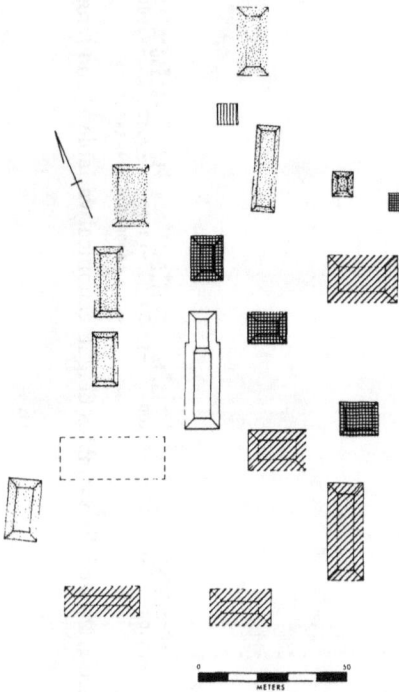

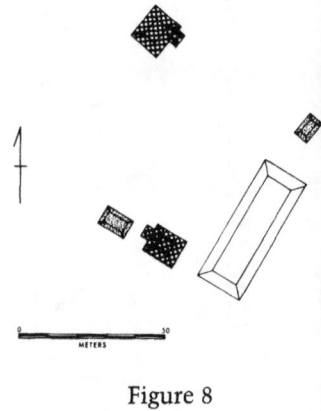

Figure 6. Site YR-35, El Balsamo, Type 4 site.
Figure 7. Site YR-24, Arenas Blancas, Type 4 site.
Figure 8. Site YR-22, Type 3 site.

the wall found no features or artifacts (Joyce, personal communication, 1981).

Type 3 structures are smaller in average length, width, and height than those of Type 2. Their clearest functional setting is at YR-35 where five of them form the major plaza at the site (fig. 6). Clearly prominent in size and height, these mounds also form plaza edges at YR-24 (fig. 7) and YR-22 (fig. 8). Again the functional importance of these structures is unknown; they probably were not burial or cache mounds as the landowner of YR-35 reported that the complete bull-dozing of one of these structures at YR-35 "found nothing in it." Their use as domestic platforms is questionable; plowing to 30 cm in depth of the entire plaza associated with these mounds at YR-35 exposed no artifacts, bones, or features. Areas within and near low platform groups at the same site, however, were littered with building stone, sherds, lithics, ground stone, hearths, and a few pieces of human bone.

Types 4 and 5 are intermediate-sized structures. They range in height from 1.0 to 2.3 m and function in two different contexts. Type 4 platforms, which are rectangular in shape and longer on the average by 8 m than Type 5 ones, are situated primarily in the west and north of YR-24 and are used in conjunction with structures in Types 1, 2, and 3 to form plazas. The Type 5 platforms are rectangular and square in form, and at YR-35 are spatially associated with clusters of low platforms of Types 6, 7, 8, and 9. The function of these two platform types merges in the hamlet settlements at the eastern end of Transect 1. At YR-19 and YR-20 (fig. 9), Types 5 and 4 respectively are the dominant structures of these small groups; they are at least 1 m taller than the associated platforms. Type 5 structures are also associated with low dispersed and clustered platforms where the height is not differentiated significantly from other mounds.

Types 6, 7, 8, and 9 are low platforms less than 90 cm in height. They exist as isolates but are more usually aggregated. Visual examination of the maps of sites has not uncovered any regularity in the spatial association of one type to another. They constitute four groups on the basis of the following characteristics. Types 6 and 7 are structures between 20 and 90 cm in height. Type 6 is distinguished from Type 7 on the basis of its basal area; it ranges in size from 52.5–86.5 m^2, whereas the latter's area falls between 20.0–46.8 m^2. These platforms are square to rectangular in shape and are common to all the groups with three or more mounds; together they have a frequency of 49, 46% of all the small structure types. Type 8 platforms, 50 cm or less in height, are distinctive because of their long narrow form. Examples exist at YR-57 (fig. 11), from Transect 3. The

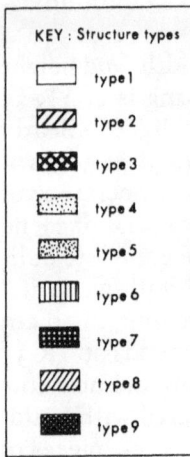

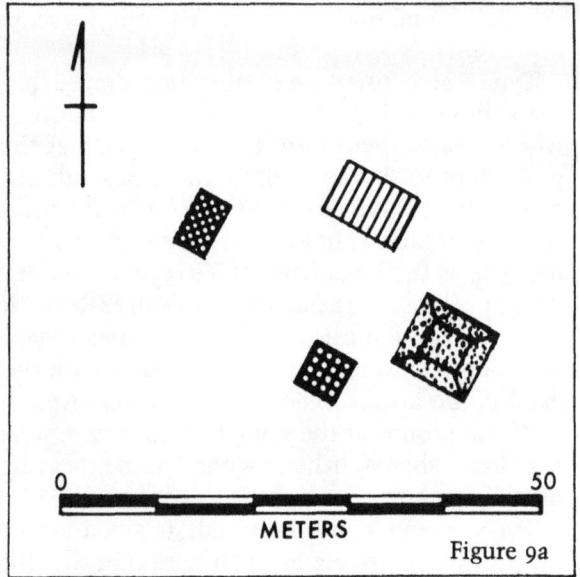

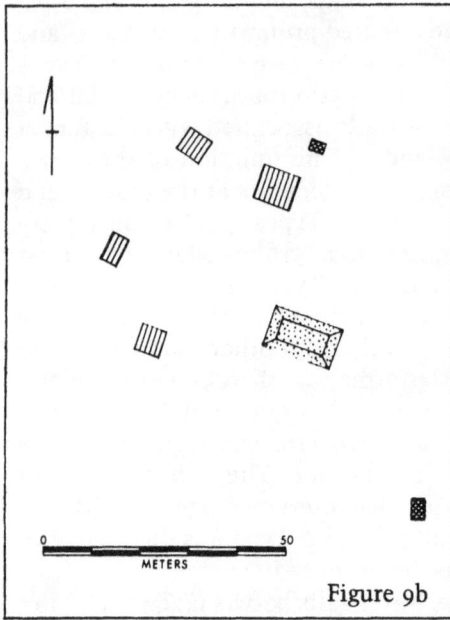

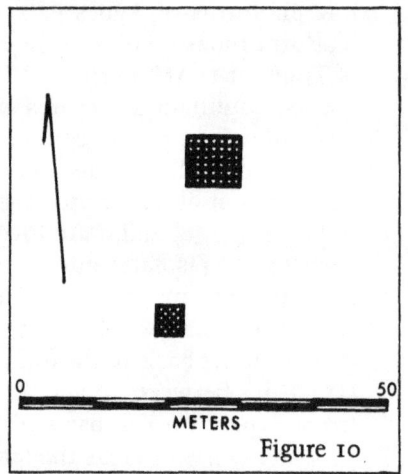

Figure 9a. Site YR-19, Type 2 site.

Figure 9b. Site YR-20, Type 2 site.

Figure 10. Site YR-56, Type 1 site.

platforms are dispersed in space but associated with other, low, un-
nucleated substructures. At YR-35, they are found in clusters of the
Types 5, 6, 7, and 9. Type 9 platforms are the smallest structures of
the sample: they are less than or equal to 70 cm in height and their
basal areas range between 5.0–19.5 m². The spatial association of
the Type 9 structures within groups of platforms is variable and does
not clearly suggest a functional interpretation. For example, they are
spatially isolated from the core platform group at YR-18 (fig. 12) and
tightly clustered with Types 6 and 7 at outlying groups at YR-35
(fig. 6). Their frequency within the small structure types is 49%,
which demonstrates they are a common type of structure.

The Types 5, 6, 7, and 9, and possibly 4 and 8, have areal ranges
which suggest that they may have functioned as prehistoric residential platforms. Floor areas of modern Maya houses have the basal

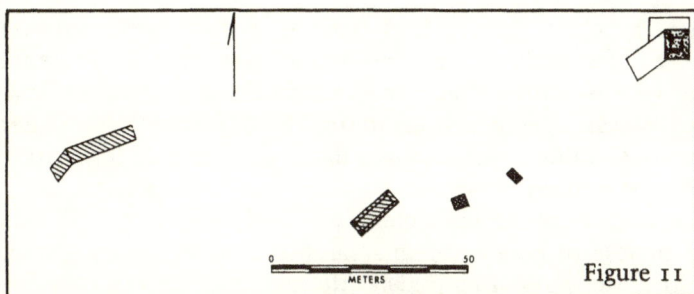

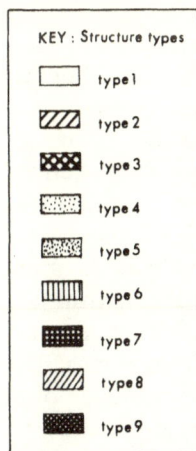

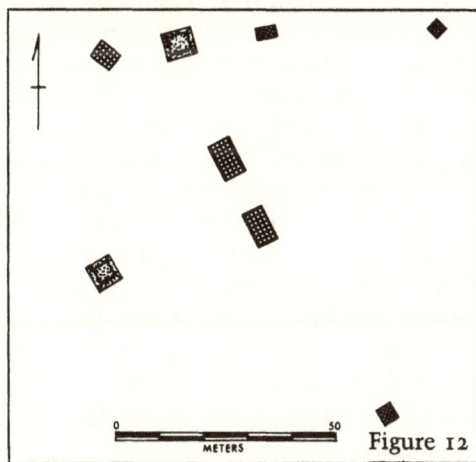

Figure 11. Site YR-57, Type 1 site.

Figure 12. Site YR-18, Type 2 site.

areas of the Types 7 and 9 combined: ethnographic house sizes range between 6.6 m²(Wisdom 1940: 147) and 46.45 m² (Wauchope 1934). The greater basal area of structures in Types 5 and 6 falls within an acceptable size range for probable residences at the central Peten Maya site of Tikal. Surface areas of 30 structures excavated by Haviland ranged between 27–96 m² (Rice and Puleston 1981: 137–138). The Types 4 and 8 exceed 100 m² and fall outside the range of recorded residence sizes; however, their association with other low platforms suggests that they were, at least, a functional part of a residential group. The greater height of the Type 4 mounds differentiates these platforms from others and suggests they may be of a special character.

Site Typology

The site typology defined four types; it is based primarily on the presence of increasingly large mounds at sites. Initially, I intended to isolate groups with cluster analysis, but found that the low frequency of variables per site prohibited meaningful assessment of similarities. Table 2 summarizes data pertaining to four site types extant in the transect sample.

Type 1 sites are the least complex of all; they have 1–3 mounds 90 cm or less in height. In this sample, mound Types 6, 7, and 9 constitute the sorts of mounds at these sites; they can occur as isolates or in combinations. The size of the sites ranges between the area of a single mound and 2,241 m².

Type 2 sites are differentiated from the Type 1 sites by the presence of the large-size structure Types 4 and 5 which have heights between 1 and 2.3 m. Sites characteristically have one to eight platforms; three mounds or more can have a formal rectilinear plaza arrangement (fig. 9a) or an informal organization (fig. 9b) or no central ambient space (fig. 12). Site areas range from 252 m² for nucleated settlements to 8,100 m² for dispersed groupings. Settlement data from north of Transect 1 in Section 1 (see fig. 3) provide an augmentation of our knowledge of the potential variability within the Type 2 category. At YR-47, there are three clustered Type 5 structures; at YR-29, 21 platforms are organized around two plazas. The outstanding characteristic of the Type 2 sites is the presence of at least one structure in a group that is usually distinguished by its height and location. At YR-29, a Type 5 mound stands alone on the south side of the plaza.

Site Types 1 and 2 make up 83% of the sites of the transect sample. They are, therefore, a predominant form of community

Table 2. Summary of the Data Pertaining to the Four Site Types Defined by the Survey

		Mound Type									Total Number of Mounds	Area of Site (m²)	Total Number Mounds per Community	Total Area of the Community (m²)
	Sites	1	2	3	4	5	6	7	8	9				
Type 1	YR-50						1				1			
	YR-51						1				1			
	YR-52									1	1			
	YR-53									1	1			
	YR-56							1		1	2	336		
	YR-58						1			2	3	2,241		
Type 2	YR-16					2		2			4	2,275		
	YR-17				1						1			
	YR-18					2		3		3	8	7,200		
	YR-19					1	1	1		1	4	782		
	YR-20				1		1	3		2	7	2,300		
	YR-32					1		1		1	3	375		
	YR-48					1					1			
	YR-49					1	1				2	252		
	YR-57					1			2	2	5	8,100		
Type 3	YR-22	1		2		2					5	6,000		
Type 4	YR-24	1	6	2	7	3	2	1		1	23	40,000	60	450,000
	YR-35		1	5	1	13	2	26	3	37	88	81,000	116	300,000

within the preserved remains on the east side of the Sula valley. The Type 2 sites are more frequent in the northern zone of settlement; they are prevalent in Transect 1 and Section 1. Type 1 sites, of which there are none in the northern area, are common in Transect 3.

Type 3 sites are quadrangle groups which incorporate the large structures of the Type 1 and 2 categories; platform heights can range from 2.5 to 3.5 m. Structures are oriented around a rectilinear plaza which tends to be approximately 50 m by 50 m; the entire site area of the single example of this type, YR-22, is 6,000 m^2. Type 3 settlements are structure-focused; at YR-22 (fig. 8), a Type 1 structure, 440 m long and 3.2 m high, dominates the group. There are also two Type 5 platforms at YR-22, which could be domestic structures. Two other sites, YR-46 and YR-21 located in Section 1, have nearly identical organizations. There are small structures of Types 5 and 9 at the former site, and Types 4, 5, 7, and 8 at the latter. The presence of structures of Types 5–9 suggests that domestic functions may have been carried out on the edges of the grand plaza at these quadrangle groups.

Type 4 sites are the most complex: they incorporate more structures, a greater frequency of large platforms, and more area than any other category. Their basic structural organization is a single plaza, as at El Balsamo (YR-35), or a multi-plaza core, as at Arenas Blancas (YR-24), and their circumambient Type 1 and 2 sites.

Site YR-24 is a large concentration of 21 cobble and earth-filled mounds covering an area ca. 200 m on a side, or 40,000 m^2 (fig. 7). A predominant aspect of the site is that most of them are parallel: 18 of the 22 mapped mounds are oriented 21 degrees east of true north. At the southern end of the site, four Type 2 structures and one Type 4 encircle a well-defined plaza 40 m by 100 m. Three irregular plazas, approximately 20 m by 60 m, are defined by the arrangements of structures of Types 2-4.

Other sites may have been part of the prehistoric community of Arenas Blancas. Workmen informed us that approximately 30 low mounds in five or six clusters were leveled in the cane field south of, and adjacent to, YR-24. Sites YR-25, YR-26, and YR-27 represent the remains of some of these mounds (see fig. 3). The community of Arenas Blancas probably spanned the quebrada of the same name as contiguous mounds exist on the north side of the river. Site YR-23 may be a northerly extension of the concentration of large mounds of YR-24; its two mounds, of Types 2 and 5, have been included in the mound tally for YR-24. The estimated total number of platforms at Arenas Blancas is 60. The maximum extent of the prehistoric Arenas Blancas community as represented by the location of YR-24,

YR-23, YR-25, YR-26, and YR-27, is 700 m (east-west) and 650 m (north-south) or 455,000 m².

El Balsamo is a prehistoric community of over 100 platforms (fig. 6). The core of YR-35 is a spatially distinct cluster of 66 structures. A large plaza in the middle of this cluster measures ca. 70 m by 35 m and is bounded by seven of the largest mounds, Types 2 and 3. South of the plaza group lies a dense clustering of mounds of Types 4 through 9 mounds. One cluster was situated on a raised platform which was constructed so as to take advantage of a natural 5 m contour. To the south, a large, irregularly shaped borrow pit measures 35 m by 45 m on its longest dimensions, and is approximately 1.5 m deep; it probably provided soil for much of the constructions. North of the large, centralized plaza, 17 mounds are found in a fairly regular spatial distribution. Three other concentrations of small mounds with the same formal qualities as Type 1 and 2 sites are located to the west of this core area: two groupings similar to Type 1 sites are situated to the east; and a cluster like a Type 2 site is located 170 m southwest of the central plaza. The extent of the community's mapped area is 81,000 m². Additionally, three small mounds were discovered approximately 200 m north of the main plaza and one large mound was located 190 m northeast of the same feature.

The true extent of El Balsamo is probably not fully characterized by the above description of YR-35, but probably also encompassed the sites numbered YR-34 through 40 (see fig. 3). These latter numbers represent small circumambient Type 1 or 2 settlements, almost all of them disturbed by plowing. Their clustered distribution around El Balsamo and the presence of open space devoid of sites beyond these cultural loci suggest that they form a single prehistoric community. If this were the case, the community form of El Balsamo was that of a large central plaza with conspicuously tall mounds surrounded by mound clusters which are 1) nucleated around the main plaza, and 2) dispersed to the north, south, and west. The settlements, peripheral to the main core of the site, are 10 m to 700 m distant from the central plaza; the frequency of mounds per group ranges from two to 13 structures. The spatial extent of this single, large hypothesized community is 400 m by 750 m, that is, 300,000 m²; the community has a total of 116 documented mounds.

Site Types 1 through 4 represent three different categories of settlements: nuclear family residences, extended family residences, hamlets, and villages, respectively. Parsons (1971: 22) following Sanders (1965) estimates that village populations range from 100 to 1,500 persons. The Type 4 sites were probably small prehistoric villages. Assuming all possible domestic mounds at each site, those of Types 4–9, were occupied contemporaneously by five persons each, Arenas Blancas may have had a population of about 250 people and El Balsamo approximately 550. Site Types 1–3, with more than a few mounds, probably represent small hamlets or extended family residences of 25 or fewer people. Nuclear family residences are evidenced by loci of one or two mounds of site Types 1 and 2.

Conclusions

Comparison to Maya Prehistoric Settlement Forms and Hierarchies

Two published Maya lowland site hierarchies and typologies facilitate comparisons between Sula and Maya site types. Hammond (1975) has distinguished nine levels of site organization in northern Belize and Willey and Levanthal (1979) have proposed a four-part stratification for sites in Zone 2, east of the Main Group at Copan. The Sula valley sites correlate to only the lowest levels of the Maya hierarchies.

Sula valley Types 1 through 3 roughly correspond to Levels 1, 2, 3, and 4 from Belize and Types 1 and 3 from Copan. Table 3 summarizes these correspondences.

Level 6 in northern Belize is a minor ceremonial center with multiple plazas and a 10 m pyramid, while at Copan, Type 4 sites are multi-plazaed, with platforms up to 10 m in height. There are no correspondences in the Sula valley corpus to the levels 6 through 9 of the Belize hierarchy which include sites with ballcourts, stone monuments, huge compounds, multiple pyramids, and so forth.

Parallels also exist between the settlement components or organizations of the Type 1 and 2 sites and documented forms of pre-

Table 3. Correspondences among Site Types Defined for Northern Belize and the Copan and Sula Valleys

Belize Levels	Sula Site Type	Copan Site Type	Sula Site Type
1	1, 2	1	1, 2
2	1, 2		
3	2	3	3
4? 5?	3		

historic Maya communities as delineated in other studies. The most obvious similarities exist at the Type 1 and 2 levels. The single platform has been recognized as an elementary unit of settlement within the Maya area (Ashmore 1981b, Bullard 1960, Rice and Puleston 1981) and has a parallel in the presence of the isolated platform of the Type 1 and 2 site categories. Various forms of platform clustering are typical of Maya site plans (Ashmore 1981b: 47–55). All the Sula Type 1 and 2 sites with more than two platforms have correlates in the Maya forms: YR-16, YR-57, and YR-58 are informal groups; YR-19, YR-20, and YR-32 are patio groups; and YR-18 is an informal cluster. A further parallel exists in the presence of a single, dominant structure in the Type 2 site category. Bullard (1960) recorded this pattern in plaza groups from the Peten, noting that one mound was usually higher than the others in the same cluster.

For the Sula valley Type 3 sites, affinities to Maya settlement forms break down, and no analogs to typical Maya forms exist. The closest parallel might be with the small, single plaza, minor ceremonial center (Bullard 1960: Figure 3b), but the Southeast Periphery examples lack the pyramidal structure diagnostic of this type. The formal cluster level 4, a type of site in northern Belize, is another analog type (Hammond 1975); commonalities with the Sula sites are the presence of 6 to 12 structures differentiated in size and function arranged around a well articulated plaza, mound heights in the range of 5 to 7 m and an absence of circumambient, low mound clusters. Comparisons with Maya minor ceremonial centers in peripheral areas near the southeastern frontier which did not develop dense populations or elaborate site hierarchies may yield closer affinities; Voorhies (1972) notes that minor centers around the Lago de Izabal, Guatemala, were not as large and employed less sophisticated construction techniques, e.g., river cobbles in place of cut stone, than the Peten examples.

The Sula Type 4 sites have no close analog within the Maya sample, although the general pattern of a Type 4 site, a single or multi-plaza core with low mounds clustered around the center or dispersed in the site periphery, is a common type of Maya organization. The parallels break down, however, in the elaboration of the core: the greatest platform heights in the Sula sample reach only 4.5 m, whereas, in the Maya area structures of 8–10 m in height are common.

If we assume that structure size is the material cultural representation of power variability within a society, then we must infer from present data that differences in status were not as pronounced in the Sula valley as in the central Maya zone. What emerges from the data presented here is that as site size increased in the Sula valley, there was not, as in the Maya area, a concomitant growth in structure size. The intrasite structural variability at Arenas Blancas and El Balsamo argue for less complex status differentiation, less powerful elites, and a different style of leadership than that of the Maya lowland area. Moreover, the strongest correspondence in settlement organization between the Sula and Maya types exists at the lowest levels of the site types and hierarchies. This suggests that the social and economic factors contributing to these site forms are similar in the two areas, i.e., that the organization of family or extended family residences was the same in the Maya core area and on the periphery.

Macro-Settlement Organization

Arenas Blancas and associated sites occupy the highest level of a site hierarchy. These sites probably performed different political, social, and economic functions within the alluvial fan subregional settlement system from those carried out at small platform clusters, and may have been interrelated in a valley-wide settlement network. Investigations in 1981 of settlements along the mountain slopes on the east side outside of the transect sample suggest that Type 4 sites are spaced at 5 km intervals along the valley edge. Sites YR-24 and YR-35 are separated by about 10 km, but the site of La Guacamaya, with approximately 200 platforms, two plazas of 4 to 5 m high mounds surrounded by seven low structure clusters, is situated halfway between YR-24 and YR-35. Approximately 5 km north of Arenas Blancas lies Rio Pelo, a site of 50 mounds, one reaching 7 m in height, and two large plazas. These four dominant settlements are located near or on quebradas and are between 0.5 km and 2 km from the base of the mountains. The regular spacing of similar large settlements is not found south of YR-35; 5 km south of this site are only Type 1 and 2 settlements in Transect 3 near Piletas. The absence of a larger center can possibly be explained by the presence of the prehistoric site of Santa Rita, located on the east bank of the Ulua River, situated only 2 km south of Piletas. Perhaps a major center in prehistoric times, its presence may have eliminated the need for a distribution center only 2 km away.

The regular spacing of YR-24, La Guacamaya, and YR-35 along the edge of the valley suggests that their domains may have been of comparable physical size. This is a possibility in an area which is ecologically undifferentiated and of equivalent agricultural potential. The exploitation of a single mineral resource or unique agricultural crop was probably not a significant factor in the selection of a site location. In addition Hudson's diachronic model (1969) of rural farm settlement location theorizes that if population densities are high, competition for land will regulate the spacing between major centers; if population densities are low, farmers new to an area will monopolize zones which do not infringe on the lands of already present groups. It may be that Arenas Blancas and El Balsamo were Late Classic colonizations of the east side and that their locations were conditioned by populations at Rio Pelo, La Guacamaya, and Santa Rita, all sites with occupations during the Ulua Bichrome phase (200 B.C.–A.D. 500).

In summary, the Late Classic settlement system of the east side alluvial fans is characterized by regularly spaced prehistoric villages at, perhaps, environmentally and socially optimal locations. The organization of the cores at these nucleated sites is similar to lowland Classic Maya community organization, but in actuality these sites are a regional, unique settlement form unlike any known from the Maya area.

Late Classic Settlements in the Comayagua Valley

Introduction

The Comayagua valley in central highland Honduras has been the subject of archaeological investigations since the first half of the nineteenth century, when the renowned pioneer E. G. Squier worked there (1853). Most of the research since then has concentrated on ceramic studies, with settlement and community pattern observations at a minimum. Recent work in settlement archaeology has, however, shown the enormous potential of such data for the study of past lifeways.

The present study does not pretend to be comprehensive. Rather, it is the product of a quick and biased reconnaissance of some of the more prominent sites in the valley. Its goals are to provide a reference point for, and act as a stimulus to, a more comprehensive settlement study of the area, and to give the many ongoing archaeological projects in Honduras a baseline for comparison of their finds to the Comayagua valley.

The Region

The Comayagua valley (fig. 1) is a high-lying interior plain located in the center of Honduras. At its greatest extent the valley is 16 km from east to west and 36 km from north to south. Its total surface area is approximately 518 km^2. The southern section of the valley has a higher mean elevation above sea level than the northern: the

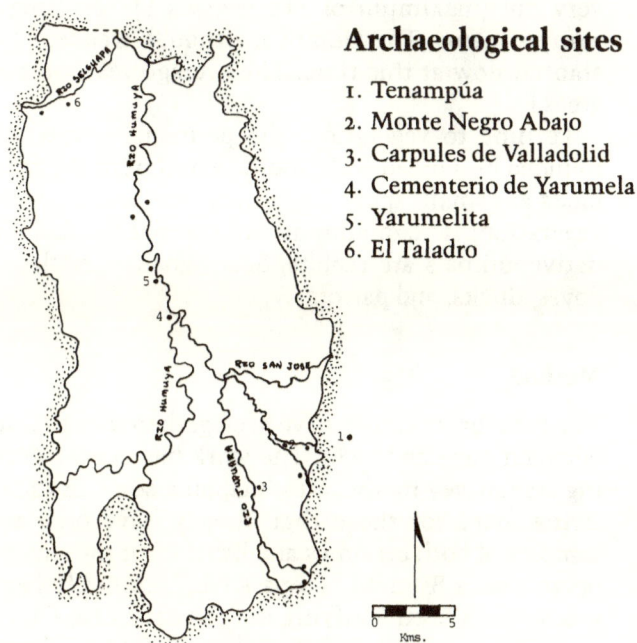

Archaeological sites

1. Tenampúa
2. Monte Negro Abajo
3. Carpules de Valladolid
4. Cementerio de Yarumela
5. Yarumelita
6. El Taladro

Figure 1. Map of the Comayagua valley, showing the location of sites referred to in the text.

southernmost modern town, Lamani, is at 740 m, while the northernmost, Comayagua, is at 579 m.

The valley is the catchment basin for the Humuya River, which originates in its southern section, flows north, and exits in the northwest. Along this route, the Humuya picks up tens of smaller streams which drain the high mountains delimiting the valley. The exit channel of the river is also the only natural exit and entry route to the area. Not far north of the valley the river changes its name to "Comayagua," flows into the Ulua drainage system in the Sula valley, thereby emptying, ultimately, into the Caribbean. Doris Stone has informed me that in her lifetime the Humuya was navigable by canoe to a point not far from the Comayagua valley. At present this is not possible outside of the stretch of the river in the Sula valley, and there only during the rainy season.

The climate of the research area is divided into two distinct seasons, rainy (*invierno*) and dry (*verano*). The rainy season begins in May and lasts till November with rainfall averaging 40 inches per year. The dry season, which makes up the other half of the year, is very hot (maximum of 111 degrees F), resulting in the drying of many streams. The Humuya, although weakened, maintains a substantial flow at this time. The average yearly temperature is 77 degrees F.

Turning to vegetation, the permanent water channels are surrounded by a broad-leaf canopy; adjacent to these zones in the flatter lands are small, spiny bushes and low trees (generally a xerophytic vegetation). The mountains are covered by pine forests. Among the native animals are rabbits, deer, iguanas, rattlesnakes, armadillos, doves, ducks, and parrots.

Method

The data for this study have been gathered in an intermittent fashion between 1974 and 1980. The work has primarily consisted of locating and surveying the sites, mapping some of the smaller ones, verifying maps for those that already have one, and taking surface samples of both ceramics and lithics. For the surveying and mapping operations a Brunton compass has commonly been used. A further interest has been verifying the putative Late Classic dates of many sites. This was accomplished through finding abundant quantities of Ulua Polychromes (the Babilonia Polychrome of Baudez and Becquelin, 1973), a Late Classic marker type.

The Sites

This study is primarily concerned with six sites: Tenampua, Monte Negro Abajo, Carpules de Valladolid, Cementerio de Yarumela, Yarumelita, and El Taladro (fig. 1). Many other sites were visited but were not integrated into this study because either the data on them were insufficient or the locales pertained to periods other than the Late Classic.

Tenampua

The mountain-top site of Tenampua is the most renowned of all the sites in the Comayagua valley. Popenoe (1935), Squier (1853), Yde (1938), Stone (1957), and others have studied and published on it; and collectors, amateurs, and "looters" have also paid the zone a good deal of less positive attention. Indeed, during the 1950s and 1960s it was a popular "sport" for affluent people and the diplomatic core of Tegucigalpa to go on "digging expeditions" to Tenampua. The result

Figure 2. Map of Tenampua (modified from Stone 1957: Fig. 3).

is, of course, that the mounds here have been more than decimated with only a tiny fraction of the archaeological data recorded in any fashion.

The site is located on a plateau which rises 240 m over the southeast section of the valley. It is a natural fortress with access being limited to two points at which tall stone walls were erected in ancient times. The surface area of the table-land is approximately 1 km². The mounds were found to cluster along the edges of the plateau, providing spectacular views.

According to the map made by Lothrop's expedition in 1917 (fig. 2), there once were over 300 mounds at the site. Analysis of the distribution of these mounds on the map, as well as of their remains in the field, made it clear that most of them were linearly arranged. The primary axis which the lines followed was north-south although some aligned east-west. Parallel lines of mounds, which amount to the formation of streets, also occurred but were infrequent, the result being a more dispersed distribution of individual lines.

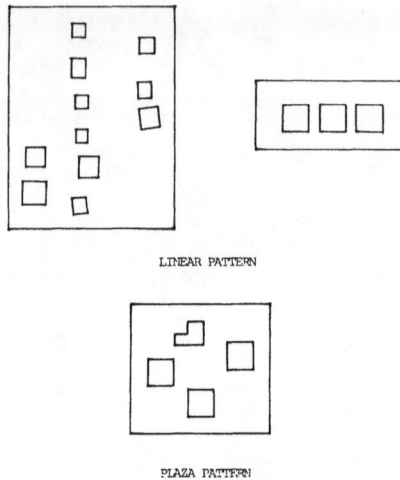

LINEAR PATTERN

PLAZA PATTERN

Figure 3. Mound patterns (examples from Tenampua).

A second pattern found, albeit rarely, was mounds at right angles to each other, forming plazas (fig. 3). A third pattern, actually something of a non-pattern, was that in which the mounds were placed in a haphazard fashion. This last pattern was frequently explained by topographic features (e.g., alignment along ridges or gullies).

All mounds were rectangular with "their sides conforming to the cardinal points" (Squier 1853: 4). The larger mounds, which were the only ones relatively well reported upon in excavation publications, were evidently terraced substructures for temples, and had staircases on their west sides. Construction apparently consisted of earthen cores with rough stone facings; the superstructures were supposed to have been of perishable materials (*Ibid.*). In size, these larger mounds were said to be "from sixty to one hundred and twenty feet in length, of proportionate width, and of different heights," whereas the smaller mounds (possibly housemounds) were "from twenty to thirty feet square, and from four to eight feet in height" (*Ibid.*: 4-5).

Stone (1957: 51) reported the use of "lime cement" (which I presume to be stucco) as flooring in the principal platform at Tenampua. This mound was also enclosed by a relatively large and elaborate rectangular wall which had its only entry on the west side. Stucco is not frequently found in the Comayagua area. The only other place where it has been recorded is Yarumela, in a Preclassic context (Canby 1949: 86). The main mound at the site of El Taladro was also said to have had an enclosure by a knowledgeable local informant, but I was not able to confirm this.

Another distinct architectural feature of Tenampua was its ballcourt. This is probably the only relatively well-preserved structure in Tenampua today. It was an open-ended court; many have been led to think otherwise by a linear arrangement of stones at the southern end of the court, but these are only the remains of a retaining wall of a large terrace that was created to put the ballcourt on flat terrain. Terraces of this sort were frequent at Tenampua.

Ulua Polychromes abounded at Tenampua. There are large private collections in Tegucigalpa that amply testify to this, and it is further verified by my own surface collections. Manos and metates, including some very elaborate ones (Popenoe 1935: fig. 4) were also plentiful at the site. These have been interpreted as indicative of ties with lower Central America (Popenoe 1935: 572; Stone 1957: 55).

Monte Negro Abajo

Monte Negro Abajo is a small valley bottom site in the immediate vicinity of Tenampua. Its 57 mounds stretch along 650 m of a rise between the Quebrada de Santa Rosa and Quebrada de Gualcoquita, which at this point in their courses run parallel to each other at a distance of about 250 m. This site had never been reported and was mapped and surface collected for the purpose of this report.

The mounds exhibited the same basic patterns as at Tenampua but in different proportions. Linear arrangements were present but were no more common than roughly strewn plaza arrangements or discordant groups of mounds. Most of the platforms were rectangular with their sides pointing in the cardinal directions. Those that were not were of irregular shapes.

Most of the mounds (55 of them) rose no more than 50 cm from the ground. At their edges one could frequently see lines of river cobbles which I interpreted as house foundations. On the basis of these lines the house sizes were estimated as from 3 to 7 m on a side. Clay daub with wattle impressions was found throughout the site, implying that these were the elements for the construction of the upper house walls. Houses with stone foundations and wattle-and-daub construction are frequent in the valley today serving as analogies for the Precolumbian situation.

The two larger mounds found at the site rise no more than two meters from the ground and average 15 m on a side. They seem to have been stone-faced earthen platforms. No stairways or terraces could be discerned on them.

In addition to the Ulua Polychromes scattered over the site, simple metate fragments and obsidian flakes were found.

Carpules de Valladolid

The site of Carpules de Valladolid stretches for over a kilometer on the high-lying eastern bank of the Rio Jupuara, a main affluent of the Humuya. This site lies 3 km to the southwest of the site previously described. There are over two hundred mounds at the site, of which about twenty are larger, probably ceremonial, structures. These cluster at the north end of the locus; the more numerous smaller platforms dot the landscape to the south, along the river.

This site has never been reported. It was surveyed and surface collected by the author. A map was begun but not completed.

The principal mound pattern at Carpules de Valladolid was the linear arrangement. Like Tenampua, north-south lines were favored over east-west, but the latter were also present. Parallel lines of platforms also occurred. Only one vague plaza group was identified at the site, among the larger structures. It is possible that with closer inspection and mapping operations more plaza groups will be found. Unpatterned mound groups were also found here.

All mounds checked were rectangular and cardinally oriented. The smaller mounds were very similar to those of Monte Negro Abajo: low (less than 50 cm), from 3–6 m on a side, and with lines of cobblestones on their edges. Similar construction techniques are inferred.

The larger mounds were found to run up to 40 by 15 m in basal dimensions and to rise to a height of 3.5 m. Construction seems to have been as noted from Monte Negro Abajo: cobble facing on an earthen core, and no terraces or stairways were discernable.

Finally, the expected Late Classic artifacts were found on the surface.

Cementerio de Yarumela

Next to the cemetery of the modern town of Yarumela in the center of the Comayagua valley lies the somber site of Cementerio de Yarumela. The site (fig. 4) sits on a high ridge at the base of which runs the Rio Humuya, and commands an impressive view of the valley to the east and south. It consists of an enormous plaza (over 130 m wide) bordered by nine large mounds, with a probable habitation area to the west.

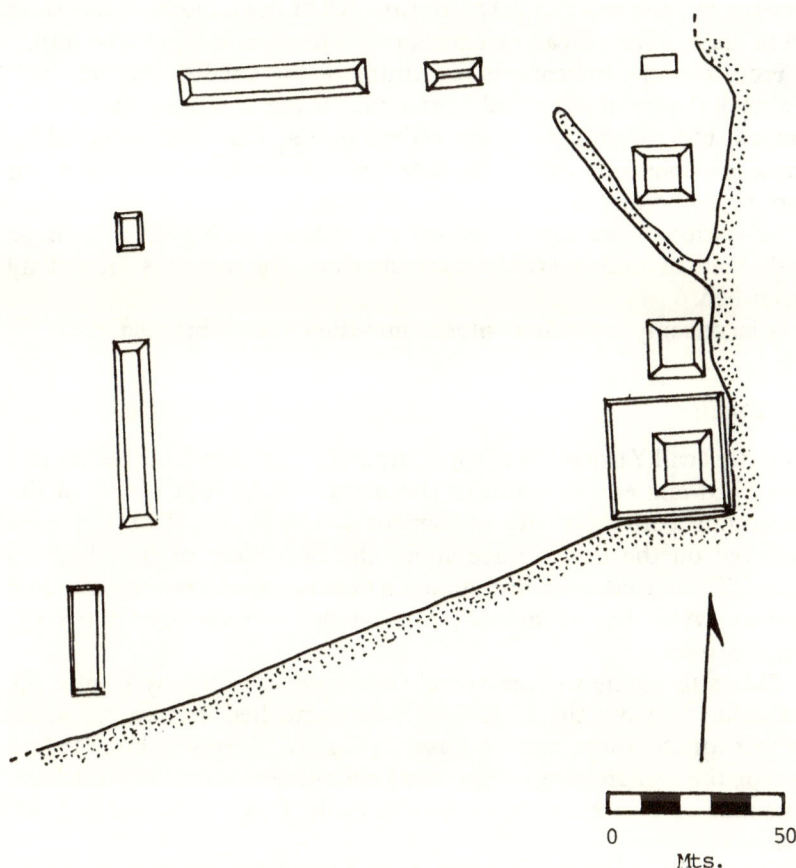

Figure 4. Map of Cementerio de Yarumela.

To my knowledge, this site has never been reported in a publication. I did a compass map of its plaza and took ceramic samples from its surface. The habitation area was too destroyed by agriculture to merit mapping.

The plaza was not a typical southern Mesoamerican or Maya plaza: it was open on its south side; there were too many mounds; and these were quite far dispersed. The platforms were also of a different complexion, particularly on the north and west sides of the site, where the principal structures were very long (over 50 m), narrow (10 m), and low (2.5 m) platforms. All of the larger mounds were rectangular. The plaza's orientation is 5 degrees west of true north.

From the few indications remaining of the smaller mounds (soil stains and very slight rises) I infer that these had been linearly arranged, but this must remain only a guess. The area occupied by these mounds was over a hectare but the actual number of them cannot be estimated.

Indications were that construction techniques for both the large and small mounds were the same as those for the sites previously described.

A large sample of Ulua Polychrome sherds was obtained.

Yarumelita

The site I call Yarumelita is approximately 2 km north of the site just described and 600 m south of the main mound (El Cerrito) of the enormous Formative site of Yarumela (Canby 1949). It was constructed on the first terrace above the floodplain of the Humuya River. There were over fifty mounds here in an area several hundred meters wide. Larger mounds were found interspersed with the smaller ones.

This site seems to correspond to the areas called by Canby the Roadside Site and the Rock Site. I distinguished it from Yarumela proper for the most part because, as Canby himself acknowledged (1949), the loci are temporally (and I believe geographically) distinct. The map of Yarumelita has yet to be made; I only surveyed and collected it.

The site was highly reminiscent of Monte Negro Abajo and Carpules de Valladolid: linear arrangements of mounds were prevalent, no plazas were observed, and the mounds were of the same categories in size, shape, orientation, and construction. Similar artifacts were also found on the surface.

El Taladro

El Taladro is located in the northwest section of the Comayagua plain, on the banks, or first terrace, of the Río Selguapa, another major affluent of the Humuya. The site consists of over one hundred mounds scattered along the river for about 1 km. The larger mounds tend to concentrate on the northern side of the site. A thorough survey of the locus was not possible as a good deal of it was in tall grass at the time of my visit. Enough of it was visible though, to make the observations needed. I have never seen information published on this site.

Ample evidence was found on the linear arrangements of mounds. No plaza groupings were observed. The data for this site on mound size, shape, orientation, construction, and surface artifacts were in accord with those from Yarumelita, Carpules, and Monte Negro Abajo.

Observations

With the exception of the first site discussed, Tenampua, the preferred location for Late Classic sites seems to have been on high ground along the major rivers and streams where good drainage, good agricultural land, and a year-round supply of potable water can be found. Whereas no one can convincingly argue that Tenampua had an abundance of any of these, and, much to the contrary, has often been cited for its lack of them, it offered two advantages not available to the other sites: 1) a superb defensive position, and 2) an exhilarating geographical setting (Squier 1853; Popenoe 1935; Stone 1957). Thus it seems likely that while agricultural considerations were the prime movers for the location of Late Classic sites on the valley floor, war and spiritual exaltation were those for Tenampua. All three of them, of course, we would expect to be major factors in the shaping of the cultural development of the region in Late Classic times.

Most of the sites seem to have been agricultural villages. These seem to have been composed of civic (probably ceremonial) structures and habitational structures which are the interpretations traditionally given to the larger and smaller mounds respectively (Baudez 1970: 66). In the relationship between the different kinds of mounds (i.e., large vs. small) no pattern was observed—more often than not, they intermingle freely. Nevertheless, in the interrelationship of the mounds in general (that is, regardless of size groupings) two main patterns were discernable.

The most prominent pattern seems to have been the linear arrangement of mounds in north-south lines. East-west arrangements were present but less frequent. At times, lines of platforms were placed parallel to each other, creating streets. Outside of the Comayagua valley, linear arrangements can be seen in Quelepa, eastern El Salvador (Andrews 1976: fig. 2) and in a few of the groups at Los Naranjos, Lake Yojoa (Baudez and Becquelin 1973: Figs. 40, 56). The

Sula valley, with which the Comayagua valley is closely affiliated (based on ceramic assemblages), is dominated by closely knit plaza groupings (e.g., Travesia, Curruste, Calabazas, etc.). Unfortunately, comparable data are not available for areas east of the valley with which it has been associated through stonework (as noted when discussing Tenampua). Further afield, one can find affiliation in linear community patterns in central Mexico.

It is possible that the linear pattern is an indigenous development. Some support for this can be seen in the linear arrangement of mounds in the Preclassic site of Yarumela (Canby 1949: sketch map of Yarumela). It also concurs with the ideas about indigenous sociocultural development in the region (central Honduras and eastern El Salvador) from the Late Preclassic on, as expressed by Andrews (1977) on the basis of his work at Quelepa.

Much to the contrary, the second pattern of mound arrangements discerned for the sites of the valley, that of plaza arrangements, seems to be intrusive, the reflection, in fact, of foreign (probably Maya) influence. Again, this would agree with the general view held by Andrews (1977: 129) who sees Quelepa as the recipient of diverse Mesoamerican influences in the Late Classic.

The secondary nature of this pattern is evidenced in its reduced frequency and in the fact that the plaza arrangements seen in the Comayagua valley are certainly not the clearest examples of the genre. This was already noted with respect to the best example of a plaza found in my survey, that of Cementerio de Yarumela. The contrast is particularly obvious when comparing site patterns with the nearby Sula valley and other regions farther afield, such as the Copan valley. Sites with "secondary" plaza arrangements like that of Cementerio de Yarumela have also been reported from other neighboring Maya periphery areas, for example the Department of Santa Barbara and the Rio Sulaco (Veliz and Hasemann 1978).

That the plaza arrangement is a Mesoamerican and, more specifically, a Maya pattern cannot be doubted (Bullard 1960; Willey and Bullard 1965; Willey, Leventhal, and Fash 1978). Thus, I consider the Maya world to be the source of the encroaching plaza pattern in the Comayagua valley. The fortified nature of Tenampua leads me to believe that the cultural relations that accompanied the contact seen in site patterns were not occurring under friendly conditions.

Observations on construction techniques based on surface features must be handled cautiously. I will therefore limit my discussion of these. The larger mounds at the sites visited seem to be the remains of earthen core platforms with river cobble facing. No evidence was found on the surface for superstructures; nor was evidence found for terracing, staircases, or ramps, like those reported for Tenampua, on any of the other sites.

The smaller mounds seem to be the remains of wattle-and-daub edifices with stone foundations. From my perspective, the mounds are too low and restricted in surface area to be considered platforms. I therefore believe that the houses were built directly on the ground and not, as is typical in Mesoamerica, on platforms.

All clearly defined structures had rectangular shapes with their sides pointing in the cardinal directions. This, of course, can be identified as a generalized Mesoamerican pattern.

Overall, I feel that observations of construction materials and techniques are too generalized to lead to valid temporal and geographical comparisons. Such are better left till after excavation when more substantial data will be available.

The specialized architectural features of Tenampua (the ballcourt, central enclosure, terracing of structures, and stucco) obviously also point to Mesoamerican influence in Late Classic times. Nevertheless, if the presence of the first two (ballcourt and enclosure) are predictions of the other two (terracing and stucco), and our sample of sites in the valley is in any fashion representative, we would not expect to find any of the four on the valley floor.

Conclusions

As stated in the introduction, this paper does not pretend to be the definitive work on the settlement and community patterns of the Comayagua valley. It is a preliminary scan of the area, with a main objective of stimulating ideas, hypotheses, and plans for future work. At the same time it tries to make available settlement data which up to now has been very limited.

The tentative conclusions reached in this work are as follows:

1) In the Late Classic the Comayagua valley was inhabited by people living in agricultural villages. 2) These villages were composed of civic and habitational structures with a distinctly non-Mesoamerican principal community pattern but one which also contained a secondary pattern and certain architectural features which were Mesoamerican. 3) Most of these Mesoamerican traits possibly were the result of Maya influence in the area. 4) This influence was warlike in nature. 5) The non-Mesoamerican settlement traits are shared mostly with regions to the south (mainly eastern El Salvador).

Most of these conclusions are not new in their general implications and can be found disseminated in the work of most of the scholars who worked in the area (e.g., Squier 1853; Stone 1957, 1972; Baudez 1966, 1970). What is new, however, is the data base used to arrive at these: community and settlement pattern archaeology.

PATRICIA A. URBAN **18**

Precolumbian Settlement in the Naco Valley, Northwestern Honduras

Introduction

The Naco valley lies in northwestern Honduras along the middle reaches of the Rio Chamelecon, roughly 20 km to the southwest of the modern city of San Pedro Sula. The valley is in the northeast corner of a rough square, the other apices of which are Quirigua (ca. 100 km to the west in Guatemala), Copan (approximately 120 km in straightline distance to the southwest), and Lake Yojoa (about 120 km to the south-southeast).

The valley has an area of approximately 90 km². It is essentially flat territory, lying for the most part between 100 and 200 m in elevation, and clearly outlined by the surrounding mountains. The Chamelecon cuts through the valley from south-southwest to north-northeast, exiting from the northeast "corner," and dividing the valley into a small east part and a much larger western segment. All watercourses in the valley drain, ultimately, into the Chamelecon. Of the many other streams and quebradas, only the Rios Manchaguala, in the far north, and Naco, running through the valley's center, carry good supplies of water year-round. Smaller streams dependable for at least season flow are the San Bartolo in the northwestern part of the valley, Manacal Creek in the north, the Agua Sucia to the far south, and Quebrada Grande, the major stream east of the Chamelecon. There are extensive networks of quebradas which are now either totally dry or which carry only trickles during the rainy season.

Little remains of the valley's natural vegetation due to disruption by agriculture, both commercial and private. Along Manacal Creek is a stand of tropical deciduous trees the likes of which may once have covered more of the area, according to the observations of

Strong and associates (Strong, Kidder, and Paul 1938). Today vast tracts of valley bottomlands are used for cattle pasture, and the cultivation of tobacco, sugarcane, and ornamental plants (for export) expands yearly. Additionally, there are areas of abandoned pasture and milpa which are covered with thorn scrub and cactus, as well as currently used milpas. In contrast, the hills retain a pine-oak forest cover, which is exploited for lumber, and a few coffee-growing fincas are located in the mountains, largely well outside the survey zone. The area's animal life is likewise disturbed, but informants report abundant local fauna in the past.

Although the valley is known from the accounts of early explorers (Cortes 1971; Chamberlain 1953), it had attracted relatively little archaeological interest. The joint Smithsonian-Harvard project of 1936 (Strong, Kidder, and Paul 1938) spent several weeks in the area, locating five sites, including the ethnohistorically-known center of Naco, and test-pitting Naco and two other sites. In 1974 J. S. Henderson (Cornell University) began investigations in the valley which were continued in 1975 and 1977 (Henderson *et al.* 1979). The survey program begun in 1975 was continued by Urban in 1977, 1978, and 1979, with the 1979 season including excavation (Urban 1978, 1979, n.d.).

The survey has attempted as close to a 100% coverage of the valley as limitations of preservation, vegetation, and financial resources would permit. The survey zone included all of the valley flats, the ridges within the valley proper, and portions of the less-steep hill flanks. Excluded from the survey area were the Naco zone, covered by A. Wonderley (this volume), and the La Sierra zone, investigated by J. S. Henderson. Within the survey's purview 130 sites were located. A site was considered to be any evidence of human occupation and/or use, taking in resource zones, sherd scatters, and more pronounced remains such as mound groupings. In practice, virtually all of the sites located in the valley had the remains of standing architecture visible on the surface as mounds (when not altered by plowing), or as heavy concentrations of river cobbles and artifactual debris, particularly sherds, when disturbed. The preserved structures themselves range in size from 0.1 m to 6.0 m in height, and are found in configurations ranging from isolated mounds to groupings of around 40 structures.

During excavations carried out in 1979, 19 sites were probed. The research design was fairly traditional in nature: because of the paucity of information relating to the area and its environs, an emphasis was placed on chronology; concurrent with this, material concerning site planning, architecture, and the functional differentiation of both structures within a site and sites of differing configurations was sought. The sites investigated ranged from sherd scatters with no attendant structures to several sites on the larger end of the continua of both site extent and structure size. Because of the need for chronological data, greater emphasis was placed on the larger sites, based on the hypothesis that these had grown through time by slow accretion and remodeling of structures and, therefore, represented long periods of continuous occupation. This presumption was in large part borne out by the excavations.

The Chronological Sequence

The sequence which has been established for the Naco valley is predicated on changes in the overall ceramic assemblage, which, while conservative, does show more variation with time than any other type of artifact, architecture, or site planning. The chronological series presented here contains six temporal divisions, not including the Late Postclassic, which largely fell outside my purview (Wonderley, 1980, 1981, this volume). In developing the sequence, information from both stratigraphically related deposits and seriation was used. Cross-ties to other areas of the southeast periphery can be seen in various modes and types (for example, in the Late Preclassic wares) as well as definite trade items, all of which are crucial to the approximate dating of the various complexes. Nonetheless, the internal changes have been by far the most important class of data for constructing the relative sequence. Table 1 lists the six time spans identified by my work in the Naco valley, and gives correspondences in the pervasive Mesoamerican schema of Pre-through Postclassic eras. It must be emphasized that the time spans presented here are not absolute; rather, in the absence of dates from such techniques as C^{14} analysis, the ranges for each epoch can only be regarded as tentative.

Period 1: Middle Preclassic

This time span is poorly known, with material coming only from limited excavation contexts at one site, #123 (Santo Domingo), on the far northern margin of the valley. Only two types of ceramics pertain to this period: Chaguites Burnished: Chaguites variety, and Peñonas Brown: Peñonas variety. The former is a well-burnished type with colors ranging from grayish-tan to black. The principal form is the tecomate, with some vertical- and flaring-walled bowls present. Many of the tecomates are decorated with grooving or incision be-

Table 1. Definition of Time Spans within the Naco Valley and Their Broader Mesoamerican Analogs

Period 1	800–400 B.C.	Middle Preclassic
Period 2	400–0 B.C.	Late Preclassic
Period 3		
Facet 3-A	A.D. 0–150	Late/Terminal Preclassic
Facet 3-B	A.D. 150–300	Protoclassic
Period 4	A.D. 300–600	Early Classic
Period 5		
Facet 5-A	A.D. 600–775	Late Classic
Facet 5-B	A.D. 775–950	Late Classic
Period 6		
Facet 6-A	A.D. 950–1100	Terminal Classic/Early Postclassic
Facet 6-B	A.D. 1100–1250	Early Postclassic

low the rim. Chaguites vessels appear very similar in form, color, and surface finish to El Congo ceramics from Chalchuapa (Sharer 1978c; and personal communication, 1979–1980). The second type, Peñonas, is dark orange to brown in color, usually with well-smoothed surfaces, and often showing shallow striations. A red wash also was inconsistently used, appearing on both striated and non-striated vessels. Forms are predominantly jars, the most common being one with a low vertical neck and a direct rim; some jars also have low, flared necks with direct rims.

Period 2: Late Preclassic

The two ceramic types of the previous era are virtually absent in this phase. In their place we find the earliest versions of the three basic wares which are present in all subsequent time spans: a series of unslipped vessels, typically jars; pottery, usually jars, with red-on-natural decoration; and a group of, usually, bowls with an orange-to-red slip and, in three varieties, painted decoration. The unslipped type, Fronton Unslipped, has three varieties—Fronton, Well-smoothed, and Red-decorated. It is predominantly of two forms, a jar with a flared neck and exteriorly thickened rim, usually having roughly incised cross-hatched or diamond-shaped designs on the neck, and tecomates which seem modally related to those of the previous period in both rim shape and decorative grooving. The tecomates often have the remains of a red wash in the grooves surrounding the opening. A virtually identical type, also called Fronton Unslipped (but with varietal distinctions) has been identified in the

Gualjoquito area to the south (Urban, field notes, 1983–84). Fronton jars also resemble the illustration of Candungo Incise at Los Naranjos (Baudez and Becquelin 1973: Figs. 88–89).

The red-on-natural tradition, which is much stronger in later periods, seems to begin here with some examples of vertical-necked jars with everted rims, and a few bowls; none of the types in this red-decorated group is common. The red-orange type, Sirena Orange-slipped, appears here and in later incarnations as a slant-walled to slightly incurved bowl, with occasional vertical-walled bowls and small jars; direct rims are the norm. It is also a relatively uncommon type in this time span.

The most striking aspect of the Period 2 assemblage is the presence of high percentages of Usulutan-decorated vessels which are similar to Chalchuapa's Izalco Usulutan (Sharer 1978c; Demarest and Sharer 1982, this volume) and the Usulutan-decorated ceramics of Los Naranjos (Baudez and Becquelin 1973). These sherds represent the highest concentrations of resist-decorated wares for any era.

In general, this epoch is not well understood, having been found in limited excavation contexts only at one site, again #123. Surface lots elsewhere have produced a few Usulutan-decorated sherds, but these are almost exclusively analogs of the later Chilanga Red-painted Usulutan. Moreover, continuities with the preceding era are weak, suggesting that a gap may exist in the Naco valley sequence.

Period 3: Terminal Preclassic

This time span is more widely seen, although excavated materials are still limited to site #123. The major type is Fronton Unslipped, with the red-on-natural types as a group coming in a distant second in frequency. The Sirena Orange-slipped vessels show the beginnings of varietal distinctions: in addition to the plain orange items, a few black-painted or red-painted specimens were encountered (Sirena Bichrome) and some black-and-red-on-orange polychromes (Sirena Polychrome). Among the types appearing in very small numbers are Izalco-like Usulutan-decorated sherds.

Period 4: Early Classic

This temporal division, like all subsequent ones, is dominated by the triad of unslipped and red-on-natural domestic jars, and the orange-slipped bowls with three varieties. The unslipped items fall into two types: Fronton Unslipped from the preceding eras, which appears in ever-decreasing quantities; and the early form of Jicaro Unslipped:

Jicaro variety. Jicaro, at this time, is a relatively fine-pasted, thin-walled type, found, first, in jars with flaring necks 3–4 cm in height to 8–12 cm, usually with direct rims, and second, in neckless, everted-rim jars. A very few bowls with out-slanted, incurved, or flared walls are also found. The red-painted type, Magdalena Red-on-natural: Magdalena variety, was manufactured with pastes of two distinct colors, a tan to buff paste, and a darker one of brownish orange. These vessels are almost exclusively jars with vertical necks and everted rims, although bowls appear rarely. The designs on the jars are generally geometric—cross-hatching, triangles, oblique stripes, dots, and so forth—and occur on the rims, necks, and, occasionally, on the shoulders (Henderson *et al.* 1979: Fig. 15D). These red-on-natural designs appear much like the Urupa Rouge Sur Beige vessel illustrated in the Naranjos report (Baudez and Becquelin 1973: Fig. 94G). In addition they may be related to the Chinda Rouge of Los Naranjos (Baudez and Becquelin 1973). Magdalena also shares some characteristics with red-on-natural vessels from Central Santa Barbara such as the La Isla type (Urban, field notes, 1983–1984). Such red-decorated types are also seen at Copan, e.g., Prospero (personal observations). Finally, analogous materials have been seen in the Sula plain, for example, littering the heavily-looted site of Travesia.

The orange-slipped items, now called Chamelecon Orange-slipped, are clearly differentiated into three varieties: Polychrome, Bichrome (almost entirely red-on-orange), and Chamelecon, which is the plain, unpainted form. The designs on the painted varieties (bowls and rare jars) are generally distinctive bird- and crab-like creatures. These are placed in open orange areas delineated by black and red bands (see Henderson *et al.* 1979: Fig. 7a–c; Fig. 15a). Usulutan-decorated sherds with red rims and red-painted designs (Chilanga Usulutan) are also found, although in very small quantities, usually less than 1% of any site's assemblage; they appear to be imported, seemingly from the Sula plain. Some imported polychromes are also present, again in very small numbers (1% or less). These seem to fall within the Ulua-Yojoa category and are most like examples from central Honduras (Urban *Ibid.*), but due to their small numbers and generally poor condition it is difficult to be more specific about their origins.

Period 5: Late Classic

This time span is divided into two facets, 5-A and 5-B. The distinction has been made on the basis of imported materials as well as internal change. During this period the Jicaro-Magdalena-Chamelecon triumvirate of types reigns supreme.

Facet 5-A. In this first facet Jicaro Unslipped begins to have a coarser paste and slightly thicker walls and, while well-smoothed on the exteriors, loses the almost burnished surface of the preceding period. The necks of the flaring-necked jars also increase slightly in height. Magdalena Red-on-natural continues to utilize both tan and orange pastes. In its designs crab and bird figures sometimes replace part of the geometric decoration. The presence of small quantities of non-local polychromes continues.

Facet 5-B. The second facet of Period 5 sees little change in the three major local types. Jicaro Unslipped continues to decline in surface finishing and the high flared necks attain their greatest size, sometimes reaching 15–17 cm in height. Their vertically-placed strap handles are notable for a decoration of short, parallel, vertical incised lines, and some handles are decorated with round punctations. Magdalena Red-on-natural jars often have a 2 to 4 mm raised horizontal band at mid-neck, and some jar bodies have indented medallions which are decorated with geometric designs inside the circumference of the medallion. Additionally, there are rare instances (fewer than a dozen) of wavy line incision replacing all, or part, of the painted neck design. These incised designs are similar to Masica Incised and related types found in various parts of the Southeast Periphery (Baudez and Becquelin 1973; Willey *et al.* 1980; Schortman 1984; Urban *Ibid.*) and have been separated as a distinct type, Masica Incised: La Sierra variety, within the Magdalena group. Chamelecon Orange-slipped's three varieties remain unchanged but a fourth variety, Fine-line Polychrome, is added. This is very similar to materials in the Sula valley's Chasnigua group, and it has been suggested that the Fine-line variety is the Naco valley's equivalent of Ulua-Yojoa polychrome (Henderson, personal communication, 1984).

For this facet, the small quantities of non-local wares are of extreme interest. There is a cream-to-buff unslipped but usually well-burnished type, Cerro Azul Buff, which characteristically is found in a hemispherical bowl with a thin band of red on the lip, and often having two small appliqued lugs on the rim exteriors. The affiliations of this distinctive type are unknown. More clearly understood are several types of fine-pasted ceramics which are also seen in other nearby regions. One group of these consists of Tipon Orange bowls apparently from the lower Motagua valley in Guatemala (Schortman 1984; Sharer, personal communications, 1979–1981). In addition to this unslipped group there are a few sherds of unmistakable Capulin White, which is typologically related to Tipon and is also found at Quirigua and in the lower Motagua area (*Ibid.;* Sharer *Ibid.*). There are, too, red-slipped fine paste bowls which are essentially identical to sherds found at Quirigua, where they are non-local; they may be San Augustine vessels from the eastern Maya area (Sharer *Ibid.*). The occurrence of non-local polychromes continues, with sherds again resembling central Honduran Ulua-Yojoa wares (Urban *op. cit.*). It should be noted that although these presumed imports loom large in the Naco sequence where they are essential for cross-dating, they are present in minute quantities (well under 1%) and are of very limited distribution in the valley; most examples come from La Sierra, with smaller elite residential sites having a few specimens.

Period 6

As with the preceding era, Period 6 is divided into facets, 6-A and 6-B. The division is largely based on internal criteria, although the very small quantities of imported materials are significant in the first facet. Compared to Periods 4 and 5, Period 6 is less well-defined, although it is vastly better understood than the first two valley time spans. It exhibits some precursors of the Late Postclassic assemblage as defined by Wonderley (1981), but the connection between my Period 6-B and his early facet of the Late Postclassic remains obscure. Wonderley (this volume) defines his Late Postclassic early facet as A.D. 1200 to 1250; this overlaps with my estimated Period 6-B end date. The dates for both Wonderley's and my facets are "guesstimates," and the overlap is merely indicative of the problems involved in grasping the Early to Late Postclassic transition.

Finally, it is interesting to note that the processes seen in the Naco valley are also being found elsewhere in Honduras as more work is accomplished on this elusive time span. For example, the simplification and coarsening of the Naco ceramic assemblage are mirrored in the ceramics of Central Santa Barbara (Urban, field notes, 1984), as are the trends in site planning and construction discussed below.

Facet 6-A. The three major Naco valley types continue into this facet, but are generally coarser in paste and less well finished than before. The proportions of all decline, and painted varieties of Chamelecon are rare. The principal change in the assemblage is the introduction of micaceous ceramics of the Naco Group (Wonderley 1981, this volume, personal communication 1979). These are generally simple undecorated and unslipped domestic jars in forms much like

Jicaro Unslipped flaring-necked jars and neckless jars with everted rims. The principal type found is Fulano Unslipped. The fine-paste, imported groups discussed above, especially the red-slipped ones, continue in diminishing quantities. Imported polychromes are also found, several of which are similar to Tenampua Polychrome from central Honduras (R. Viel, personal communication, 1979).

Facet 6-B. This facet sees an increase in the Naco Group ceramics at the expense of Jicaro and other types. Magdalena is much less well-made and -decorated than previously, and the pastes are definitely coarser. In Chamelecon, the Bichrome and Polychrome varieties are virtually extinct, as are the non-local fine paste ceramics discussed above. Finally, there is very little polychrome pottery found. While the complex is apparently transitional to Wonderley's Late Postclassic, none of his characteristic polychromes are seen in facet 6-B.

Summary

In summation, then, we see a strong local ceramic tradition, beginning with Period 2 (Late Preclassic) and continuing through Period 6, the Early Postclassic. Similarities between Naco ceramics and those of both Chalchuapa and Los Naranjos are evident during several early temporal periods, although imported resist-decorated wares are never common, and no local imitations are made. Likenesses to Central Santa Barbara and the Sula valley can be seen during the Classic, and the processes of change in Early Postclassic Naco valley ceramics are similar to those seen in Santa Barbara (Urban, field notes, 1983–1984). Imported wares are present in the Classic, but always in small quantities and with limited distributions—largely elite residential sites. This implies that while the valley maintained some external connections, possibly through trade, it was not extensively tied to even adjacent regions such as the Sula plain. This conjecture is supported by the relative paucity of Naco ceramics found elsewhere in the Periphery: a handful of Magdalena and Chamelecon sherds have come from Gualjoquito (Urban, field notes, 1983–84), and Chamelecon was found at Playitas in the lower Motagua valley (Schortman 1984)

Settlement Patterns

Turning now to the settlement history of the valley, let us examine the numbers and locations of sites for each time period. The dating of sites is based primarily on ceramics, using both excavation and surface samples. Not all sites had surface collections extensive enough to permit dating, but in addition to the 19 excavated sites, 34 had collections sufficient to permit at least tentative assignment to a time span. Also used to allocate sites to Periods 5 and 6 are data from site plans, since sites constructed in Period 6 differ from Period 5 sites in structure size and elaboration and overall site configuration. All told, 80 of the valley's 130 sites can be assigned to a time span. The differing bases of temporal assessment are reflected in the symbols used on the maps: sites marked by a large cross and large numerals had their principal occupations during the depicted time spans; secondary or lesser occupations are shown by smaller numerals and a dot, while some evidence of occupation and/or use appears as a small numeral and a dot. For Pers. 5 and 6 some sites could not be assigned to sub-phases; main occupations assigned to a whole phase are shown by a medium-sized number and a cross, and some evidence of use by an open circle and small numbers. Finally, if a site is assigned to a phase on the basis of site plan only, it has a cross within a circle and small numbers. For all appropriate time spans, data from Naco and La Sierra are displayed on the maps. Maps illustrating settlement distributions for Periods 4 through 6-B are included.

Settlement in the first three periods seems to have been very limited. Period 1 and 2 remains are found in only a few excavations at site #123. In addition, two sites have produced a few sherds of Period 1 wares, but only from surface collections. Period 3 is also principally from #123: the terminal use of most of the structures tested is during this time span, and the site, because of the large size of its structures—the largest in the valley regardless of age—was probably the most important locale in the valley during this era. In addition to #123, evidence of Period 3 is found at three other sites all of which are small in both extent and structure size.

During Period 4, the Early Classic, the focus of settlement activity seems to have been in the central part of the valley (fig. 1). Assignable to this era are eight sites with principal or major occupations, while six other sites have evidence of occupation. Site #116, a locale found virtually in the middle of the valley and having 28 platforms, appears to have been the valley's major center, although La Sierra, paramount in several later time spans, was most certainly occupied. It is not possible at present completely to assess the extent of occupation at La Sierra. but it may have rivaled #116 in importance. The core of #116, however, has structures which are larger and more

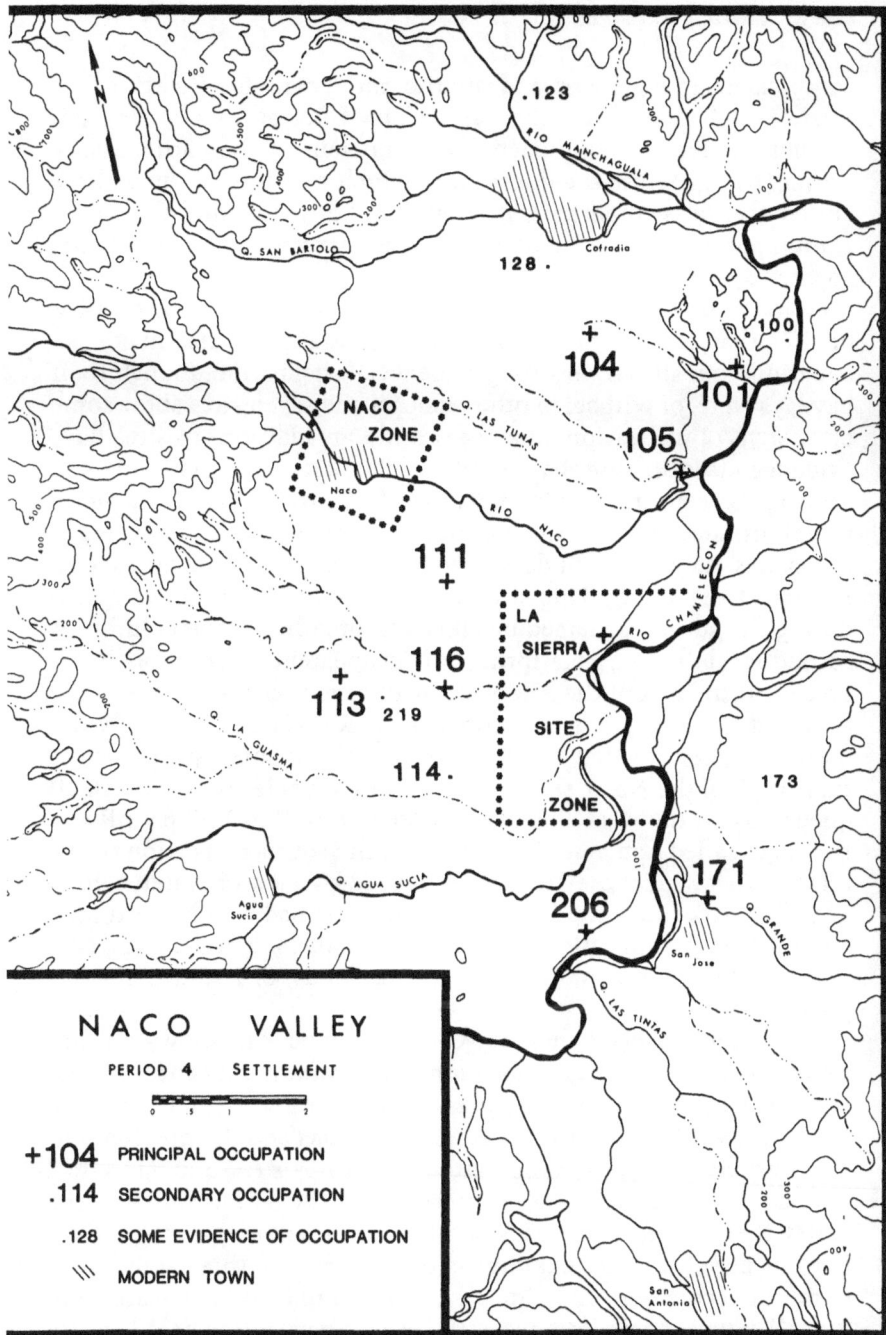

Figure 1. Naco Valley Settlement Distribution, Period 4.

complex in arrangement and architecture than the cluster at La Sierra which unequivocally was occupied during this epoch; and neither cluster even approaches the grandeur of the earlier major center (#123). While the question of which site housed the valley's Period 4 elite is important, it should be borne in mind that most contemporary sites are small in extent and structure size; they were, apparently, simple residential clusters.

Period 5-A, the early facet of the Late Classic, has a larger number of sites than any previous period (fig. 2): 30 sites evince major occupation; four sites have strong evidence of occupation, though their heydays were, or will be, in other epochs; and seven sites show some clear signs of utilization on a lesser scale. In addition, 16 sites have evidence of occupation based on site plan data. The main focus of settlement seems to shift from #116 to La Sierra. Second to La Sierra in extent, and possibly in importance, is #168 with 41 preserved structures and an area of destroyed mounds. It is on the far eastern margin of the valley. This site also has the only monument found during the survey, a shaped but unsculptured limestone column. A second locale with 41 platforms but no apparent destruction, #109 on the north bank of the Rio Naco, may have been a secondary elite center at this time. The area north of the Rio Naco is relatively unused, compared to that south of the river. It is interesting to note that south of the Naco, settlement is being intruded onto very small quebradas on the west side of the valley, as well as Jutiapa hill and the ridge called Loma de Jicaro, both in the southern portion of the region. Today all these zones are plagued by lack of water, which suggests either that the facet 5-A Naqueños had a more fortunate environment, or that they exploited marginal residential zones, possibly to clear better-watered agricultural lands, or because of overpopulation.

The second facet of the Late Classic, Period 5-B, shows no profound change in settlement location or the paramount center, which remains La Sierra (fig. 3). There is slightly more settlement north of the Naco, while utilization of small quebradas and the hillslopes in the southern part of the valley intensifies. Sites #109 and #168 may have continued as secondary centers, and in the far northwest of the valley there is a tertiary focus of elite settlement at site #120. During this period 27 sites exhibit major occupations, three show signs of minor occupation, and nine others appear to have been utilized to a small extent. Again, 16 sites with Period 5 occupation based on site plan have been included.

In the succeeding temporal unit, Period 6-A, the terminal Classic/

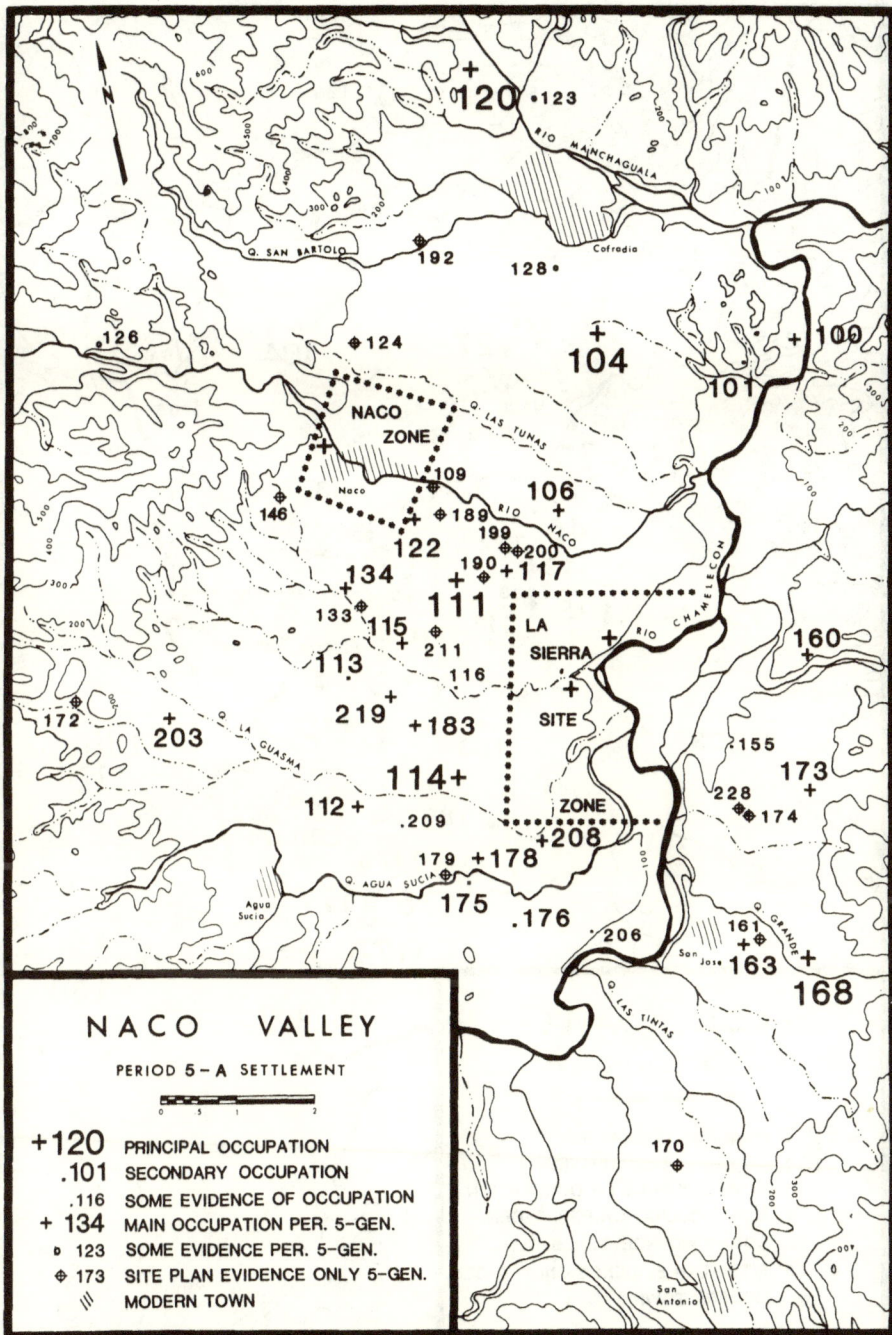

Figure 2. Naco Valley Settlement Distribution, Period 5-A.

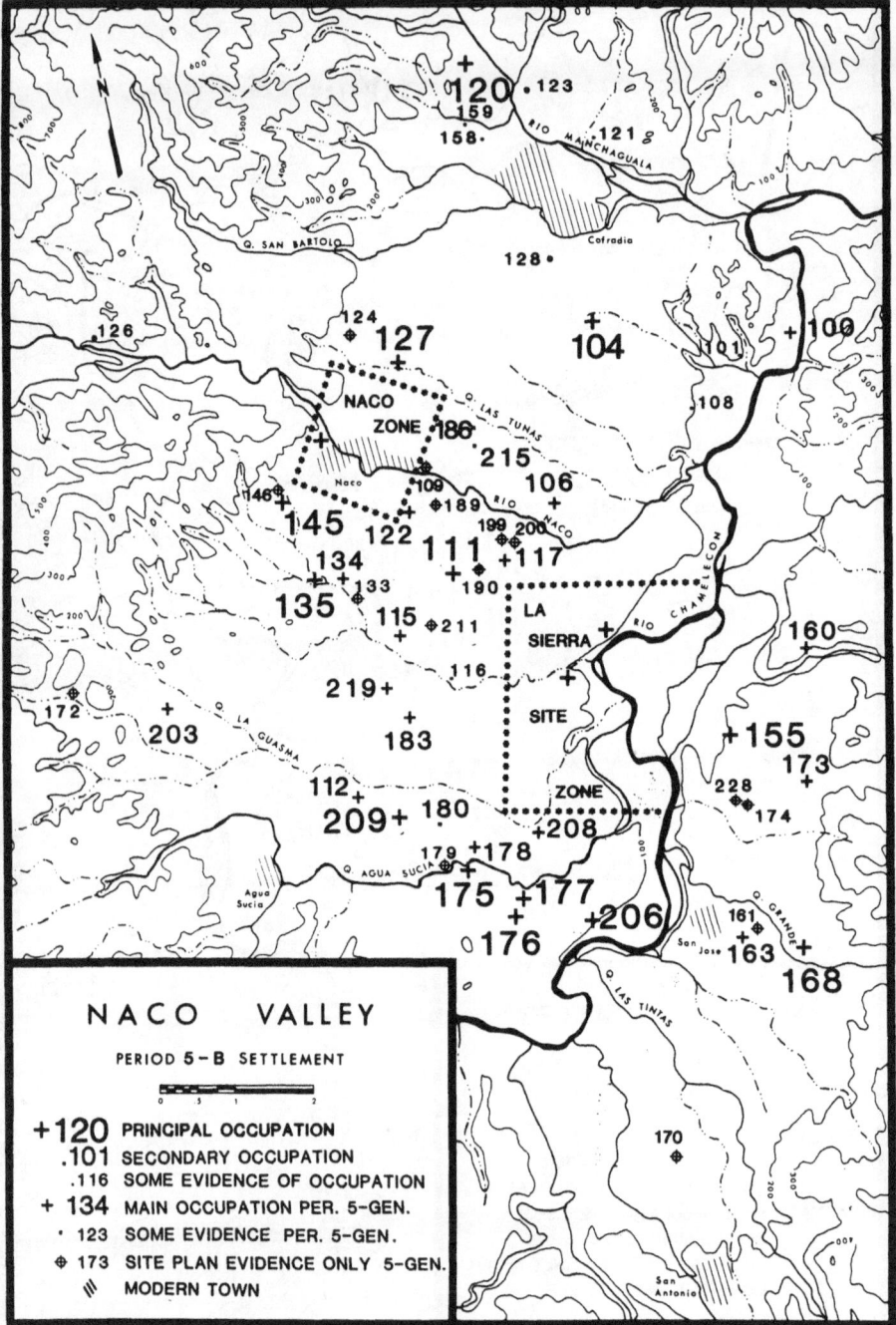

Figure 3. Naco Valley Settlement Distribution, Period 5-B.

first facet of the Early Postclassic, there is some diminution of settlement: there are 10 sites with major occupations, one with minor occupation, and seven with some evidence of use. An additional six sites are displayed whose attributions to Period 6 are based on site planning (fig. 4). This apparent diminution of the valley population may be in part an artifact of the research conducted to date: several excavated sites with typical Late Classic site plans proved to have been used through facet 6-A, suggesting that further excavation in similar sites will increase the Period 6 sample. La Sierra probably remains the valley's most important site during this facet, and the trend to settlement location north of the Naco continues. Continuity with earlier Classic period settlement is apparent: several sites which had minor usage during the preceding period are now experiencing their florescence, for example, #120, the center of settlement for the northwest part of the valley.

The trends noted in the early facet of the Early Postclassic continue in Period 6-B (fig. 5). The most striking change is the relative lack of sites south of the Rio Naco. There is also an apparent shift of major centers, from the centrally-located La Sierra to #110, eccentrically placed on the far west margin of the valley. Naco is, of course, increasing in importance during this period as pointed out by Wonderley (1981, this volume). All together, eight sites have main occupations, three have some evidence of occupation, and six sites are assigned on the basis of site plan. The diminution of population in this era seems clear from the data, but it should be noted that sites pertaining to Period 6 in general, and facet 6-B in particular, are more difficult to find than Period 4 and Period 5 sites: structures are much smaller, and site plans are more dispersed. For these reasons, as well as those stated above, Period 6, particularly its late facet, may be under-represented in the sample.

Finally, it should be noted that two sites located and excavated by the survey project are datable to the early facet of the Late Postclassic. One is a small midden without associated construction, and the other is an apparently reused (or continuously used) structure cluster which was constructed in earlier times, possibly as early as the Late Classic. The major Late Postclassic center was, of course, Naco proper (Wonderley *Ibid.*). That only two sites of this era were located is puzzling, given the large populations reported by Spanish conquerors: Montejo stated that 10,000 people lived in Naco itself, and Las Casas said that the valley was "thickly" populated (both cited in Strong, Kidder, and Paul, 1938).

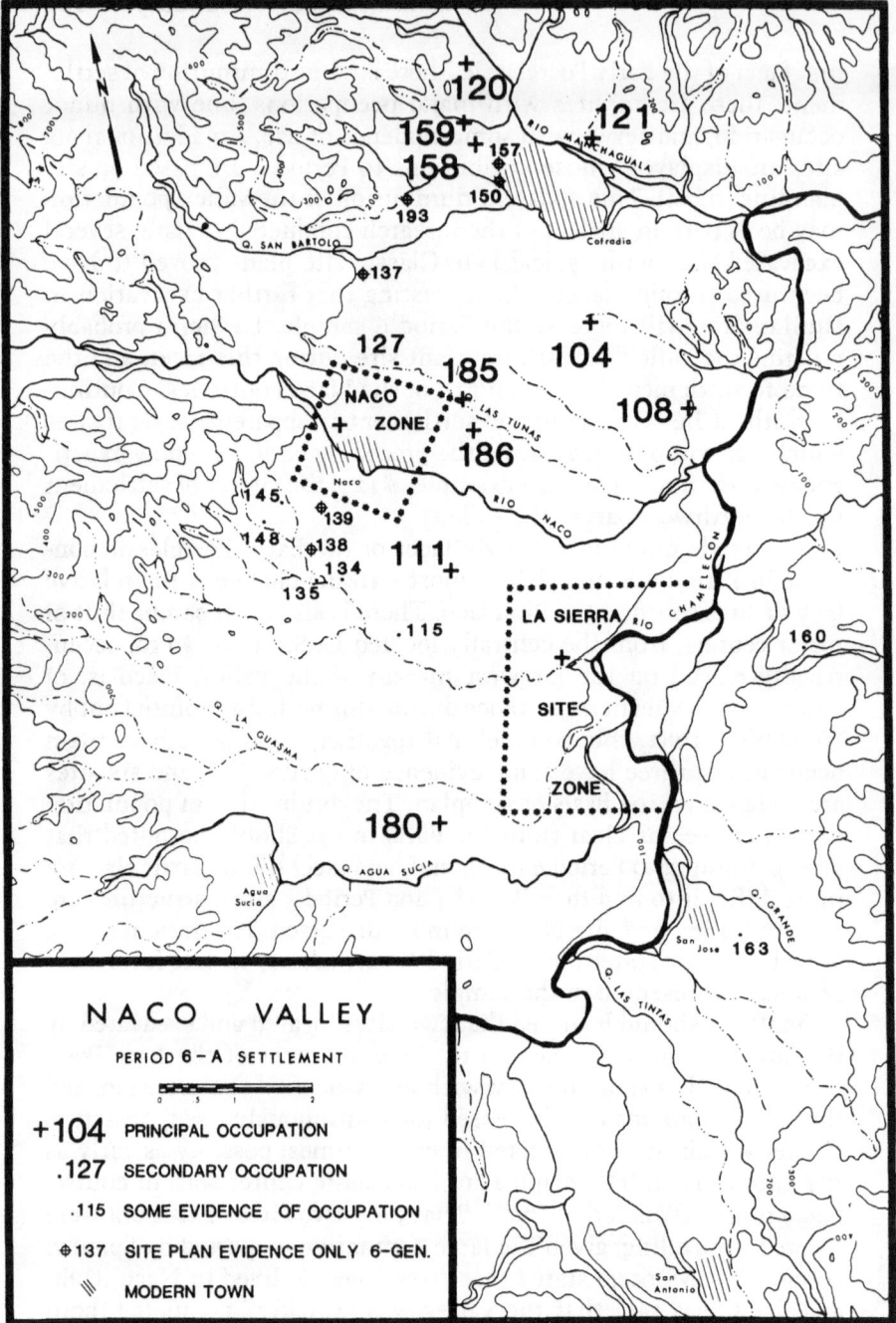

Figure 4. Naco Valley Settlement Distribution, Period 6-A.

Architecture and Site Planning

Even considering these brief summaries of ceramics and settlement location, a picture of the Naco valley as a stable, conservative area emerges. This is reinforced by a consideration of site planning, as seen in figs. 6 through 10, and architecture. Site #123 (fig. 6) is the principal site in the valley during Period 3, during which time the larger structures appear to have been constructed and utilized. The structures are not arranged orthogonally in a plaza arrangement; rather, the placement of structures is often determined by the presence of slight natural changes in elevation ranging from 20 cm to 1.1 m. The line of structures on the east margin of the site most clearly illustrates this placement schema.

The structures at #123 were constructed of rounded river cobbles, earth, and occasional flat rock slabs, usually of schist; superstructures, for the most part, were perishable. One well-preserved platform, Str. 20, shows a series of low cobble terraces which gave the west side the appearance of a stairway running the entire length of the structure. At the summit were low cobble walls outlining a cruciform room paved with flat stone slabs. The structure's fill consisted of cobbles and clay, and there was at least one fill retaining wall in the structure's interior, constructed of cobbles. Probes into other platforms at #123 also disclosed cobble and earth construction; nowhere at the site was any cut block masonry found. Remains of adobe and/or bajareque in various excavations suggest the nature of most superstructures, and some cobble foundations were encountered. A final architectural point of interest is the enhancement or paving of some of the natural contours to serve as connectors between structures, for example, on the east side of the site; in the absence of contours, raised walkways or saddles were sometimes constructed.

The second site illustrated, the Period 4 center #116 (fig. 7), shows the irregular arrangement already seen at #123. The site is defined on the south by a steep drop to a quebrada floor; the ground rises to the north, and small changes in elevation were used to determine the location of structures, in particular the line on the northwest. Again, there is no plaza-type rectilinear arrangement, and the site gives the impression of being constricted and crowded. Excavation revealed platform facings of cobbles and unmodified chunks of rock with earth and cobble fill. Traces of adobe/bajareque, again, indicate that the low platforms probably supported perishable superstructures. Enhanced contours used as structural connectors, seen at #123, are found here as well.

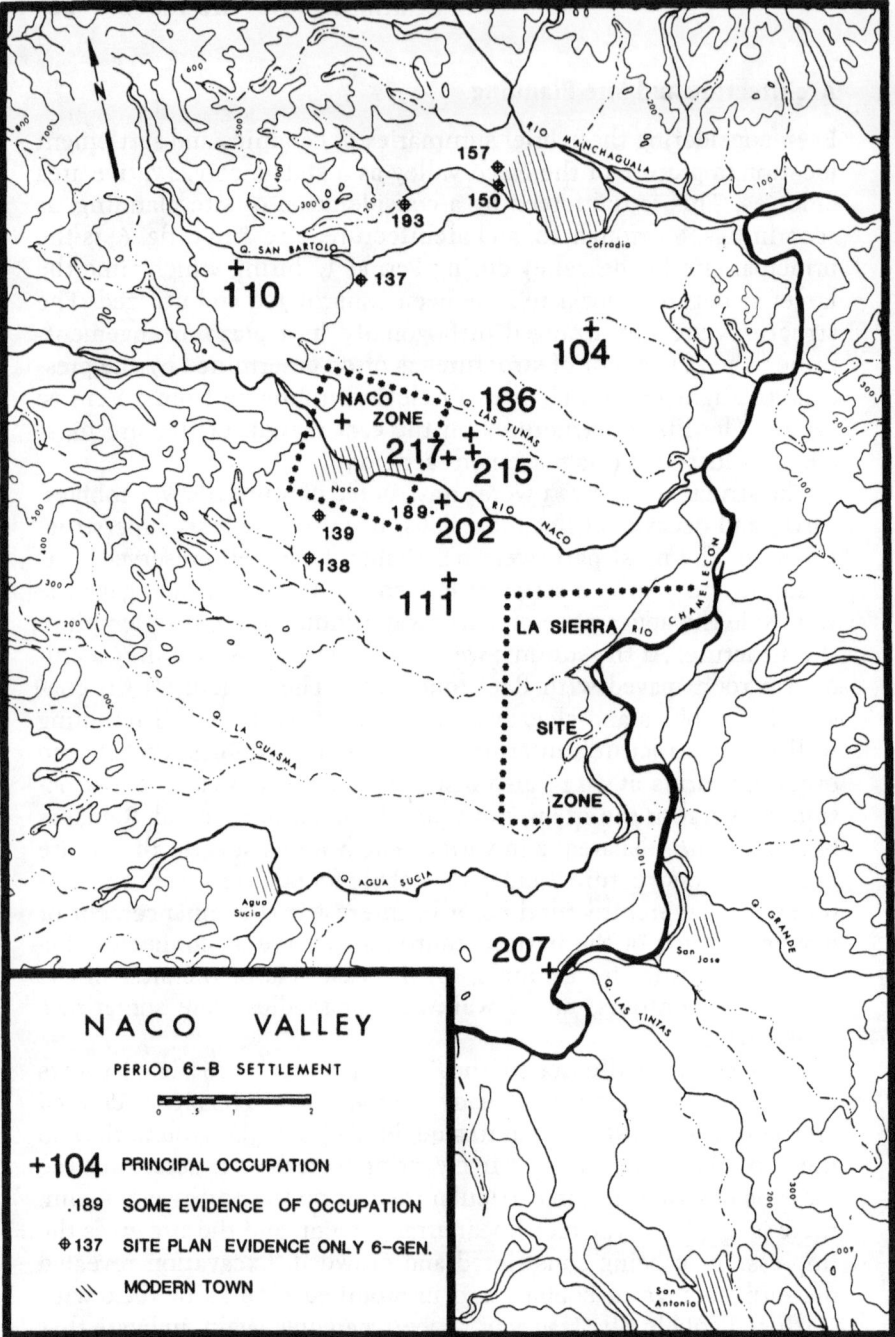

Figure 5. Naco Valley Settlement Distribution, Period 6-B.

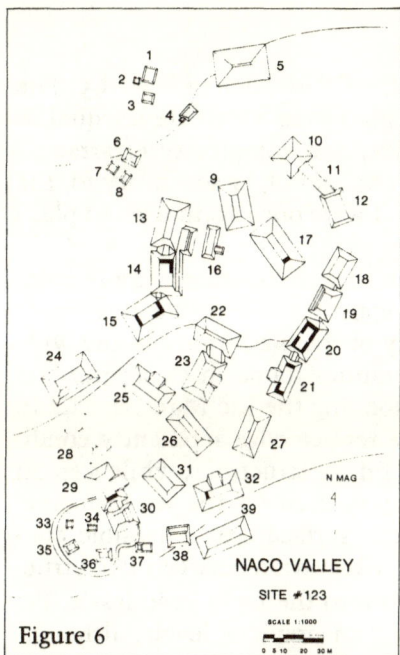

NACO VALLEY

SITE #123

SCALE 1:1000

0 5 10 20 30 M

Figure 6

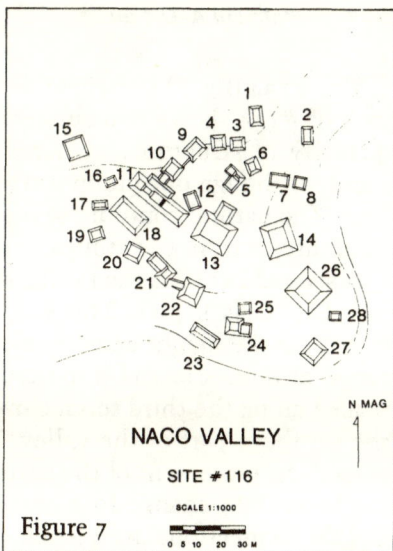

NACO VALLEY

SITE #116

SCALE 1:1000

0 5 10 20 30 M

Figure 7

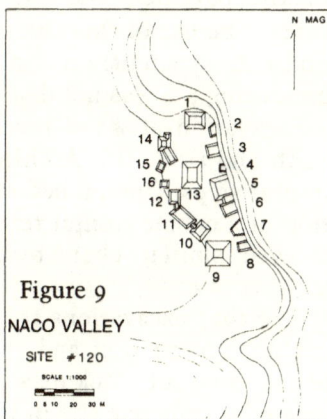

Figure 9

NACO VALLEY

SITE #120

SCALE 1:1000

0 5 10 20 30 M

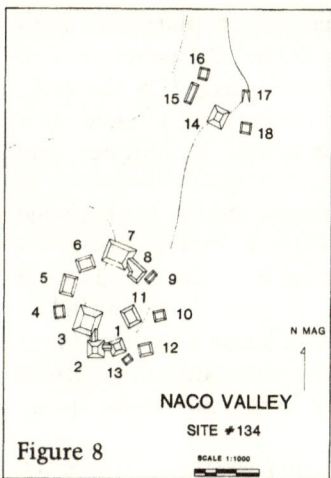

NACO VALLEY

SITE #134

SCALE 1:1000

Figure 8

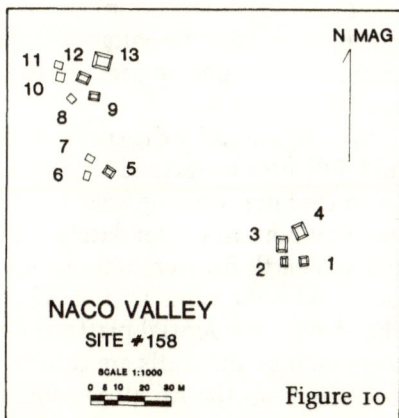

NACO VALLEY

SITE #158

SCALE 1:1000

0 5 10 20 30 M

Figure 10

Figure 6. Site #123, Santo Domingo.

Figure 7. Site #116, La Jamaica.

Figure 8. Site #134, Embacadora.

Figure 9. Site #120, Guayavial.

Figure 10. Site #158, Sin Arboles.

Site #134 (fig. 8) is assignable to the Classic era, or Period 5. The map of #134 shows two clusters of platforms which are unequal in quantity of structures, structure size, and complexity of arrangement, as though one group were an offshoot of, or secondary to, the first. The natural contours of the land were once again used to place structures within the groups.

A second Late Classic locale, #120 (fig. 9) illustrates a more compact Late Classic plan. This site, an apparent elite residential center (based on the height and complexity of the platforms and the wide range of domestic and imported ceramics found in excavation), is placed along the third terrace over looking the Rio Manchaguala in the northern part of the valley. The terrace edge apparently conditioned the placement of the eastern line of structures, while a small (30 to 40 cm) change in elevation was used for the western line. Saddle connections are visible on the surface, and a possible connecting pavement was uncovered in excavation between two structures. The use of this site continued into the Early Postclassic, Period 6-A, apparently undiminished from previous levels, although use during 6-B was not discerned.

Excavation at #120 revealed cobble facings on platforms with earth and stone fill. Architectural details included pavements and frontal steps. One probed structure had been enlarged by the addition of a cobble frontal terrace. Other excavated Late Classic sites showed similar characteristics of construction techniques and architecture.

The 1977 excavations at La Sierra (Henderson *et al.* 1979) revealed cobble construction and the use of extensive terracing; but at La Sierra some cut block masonry was also employed. Cut blocks were located at only one site in the survey zone, in a small wall buried by later cobble construction (site #209). The La Sierra site map (*Ibid.*: Fig. 6) shows that irregular placement of structures, utilizing natural changes in ground surface, is also a feature of this major site, as are saddle connectors.

Investigations by the survey project at Early Postclassic (facets 6-A and 6-B) sites unearthed structures with construction little different from that in preceding eras. For example, at #110, a large and apparently important center datable to Period 6-B, cobble facings and cobble and earth fill were ubiquitous. At smaller sites from both facets of Period 6 the same is true. The greatest change in construction is that small, residential platforms become lower with time, and platform facings and walls are thinner, employing fewer cobbles in their construction; the fill also seems to have more earth and fewer cobbles at many of the smaller sites. Inspection of the site maps for these later sites reveals change in site planning as well. For example, site #158 (fig. 10) shows a more dispersed plan than previously found, and the diminished sizes of platforms can also be clearly seen. Architecture is less elaborate as well: even excavated structures fail to show terracing, pavements, and other features seen earlier. These trends are documented at other excavated Early Postclassic sites.

The Late Postclassic, as delineated by Wonderley (1981, this volume) evinces profound changes in architecture, although site planning is difficult to assess. The lack of stone in Naco structures is notable, as is a use of plaster. Naco, of course, is the paramount center for the valley of this time; if smaller locales followed its architectural canons, that, combined with the previous trends towards smaller platforms, may help account for the lack of Late Postclassic material encountered by the survey—it may simply be a largely "invisible" time span.

Conclusions

The Naco valley represents an easily definable, coherent region within the Southeast Mesoamerican Periphery. Beginning in the Late Preclassic, the valley exhibits a striking conservatism in ceramics, architecture, and site planning. Population seems to have grown steadily through the Early Postclassic, experiencing a marked decline only in the second facet of the period: there was no striking "collapse" or disjunction in the valley's development until the middle of the Postclassic, as documented by Wonderley (*Ibid.*). External connections can be seen in several forms: the importation of obsidian; the presence of non-local ceramics albeit in small amounts; and the apparent ballcourts at La Sierra, site #110 and Naco.

The valley did not, however, share many common Southeast Periphery traits: imported Usulutan-decorated ceramics are uncommon, and no local imitations have been found; Masica Incised is encountered only at La Sierra, in minuscule quantities; Copador Polychrome is extremely rare; and even large centers such as La Sierra are not orthogonally arranged (#110, the Period 6-B center, is the sole exception). On the whole, the Naco valley is an area in which strong local traditions predominate throughout most of its history, despite its location along a major river which could have connected Copan to the Sula plain, and its proximity to other subregions, both Maya and non-Maya in character, of the Southeast Periphery.

The Role of Commercial Agriculture in Early Postclassic Developments in Central El Salvador: The Rise and Fall of Cihuatan

Introduction

The Early Postclassic period (ca. A.D. 900–1100), remains poorly understood throughout Mesoamerica. This is especially the case on the Southeastern Periphery of this large culture area in the modern states of Honduras and El Salvador. The available evidence indicates that, in general, the Early Postclassic was a period of rapid and extensive culture change in the form of population movements, increased intergroup conflicts, political and social unrest, changes in the organization and orientation of existing cultures, and an expansion of interregional commercial enterprises. Numerous discussions have pointed to the crucial role played by economics in effecting these wide-ranging changes. Of particular significance are the increased participation in long-distance trade by a broader spectrum of the population, which broke the elite monopoly over this activity, and changes in the location of trade routes. These have been causally linked to the series of social and political events which mark the close of the preceding Classic period, initiating the Postclassic era: the "fall" of Teotihuacan as a major power and then, somewhat later, the collapse of Classic Maya civilization (Sabloff *et al.* 1974; Sabloff and Rathje 1975b; Webb 1973, *inter alia*). These alterations in the nature of interregional commerce continued to be at the root of the sociopolitical changes which characterized Early Postclassic societies; and in the final era of the Precolumbian epoch, the Late Postclassic (ca. A.D. 1300–1500), new societies were founded on the revenues of vigorous long-distance commercial systems. Trade was also one of the few unifying factors in the turbulent period of the Early Postclassic, linking newly-developing societies in much of Mesoamerica. While the above reconstruction of the importance of trade is a reasonable one, and is certainly well-attested for the Late Postclassic when historic documents become available, we are still faced with a lack of hard data documenting the crucial period of transition from Classic to Late Postclassic societies. Nowhere is this more true than in the southern periphery of Mesoamerica.

It was, in part, to fill this intellectual vacuum that an intensive archaeological program was initiated at the large Early Postclassic center of Cihuatan, located on the middle Lempa drainage in central El Salvador. The purpose of this paper is to briefly summarize the results of work, relate it to what little is known of the Postclassic culture history of this portion of El Salvador, and offer an hypothesis based on commercial principles that is designed to account for the location, growth, and eventual abandonment of this major site. As in any situation where work is carried out in the absence of a sizable body of comparative material, the interpretations offered here are tentative and not proven. They are questions designed to encourage and to help direct research in this important area and time period.

Prehistoric Background

The prehistory of the area which now forms the modern state of El Salvador is tolerably well-documented for the Preclassic (ca. 1000 B.C.–A.D. 200) and Classic (ca. A.D. 200–900) periods as these are the eras which have traditionally attracted the greatest amount of archaeological interest (e.g., Sharer, ed., 1978; Andrews 1976; Longyear 1944). During these periods the local cultures were involved in interactions first with the Olmecs, and then the Maya and the cultures of Veracruz (Andrews 1976; Boggs 1943, 1945b, 1950b; Earnest 1976; Fowler 1976; Sharer, ed., 1978). While the extent and intensity of this interaction have not been fully documented, it was sufficiently close in the Classic period that the major Salvadoran centers underwent a collapse which parallels, and is apparently linked to, that of the Maya. Major centers such as those of the Chalchuapa zone, Quelepa, San Andres, and the Lempa valley, were abandoned.

There also seem to have been significant realignments of population and, if one may judge from the historic record, considerable political fractionation.

On the historic level, the division of El Salvador into small political entities of mixed Mexican and local culture is clearly documented. Although the Classic centers were now abandoned, El Salvador supported a prosperous and dense population organized as a series of small chiefdoms. On the basis of both the historical documents and the small amount of archaeological investigation which has been carried out in El Salvador, it appears that these chiefdoms were integrated into extensive Mesoamerican trading systems. Such areas as Sonsonate[1], Izalco, and Usulutan were large producers of cacao, an important item in Postclassic economics. Cotton and indigo apparently were also grown on a scale much larger than that necessary for local consumption as was, perhaps, maize. The documentary sources are not as complete as one might wish, however, and there are large areas of El Salvador which are not mentioned at all or mentioned only in passing. These areas, though, must have supported an equally large population, a population which was doubtless not completely divorced from neighboring groups either politically or economically.

History, of course, only deals with the situation at the time of the arrival of the Europeans and with the effects that their presence had on local cultures. It is evident that the Late Postclassic situation in El Salvador must have had its roots in earlier events. The disruption of life at the end of the Classic period can be documented archaeologically, yet the realignment of peoples is a subject which has hardly been touched upon. The development of commercial agriculture in Mexico and Yucatan along with commercial production of manufactured goods and the movement of these products through new routes and via new carriers are some of the major economic developments of this period to the north and west. The situation in El Salvador in the sixteenth century suggests strongly that similar events must have taken place in this area as well.

Cihuatan

Cihuatan is located in central El Salvador some 37 km to the northeast of the modern city of San Salvador. The main ceremonial centers lie less than 1 km to the east of the Carretera Troncal del Norte, the main road from San Salvador to the frontier with Honduras at Citala. The physical setting is a small, flat valley drained by the Acelhuate and Chalchigue Rivers. These rivers join and flow into the

Lempa about 15 km to the northeast near the Puente Colima. The elevation is low, averaging 250–300 m above sea level, and the climate is correspondingly hot and humid with strongly alternating wet and dry seasons. The modern vegetation consists of cultivated fields of sugar cane, maize, yuca, and coffee, with scrub and open pasture on less fertile lands. As recently as the 1950s the area was still covered with seasonal deciduous forest. The main portion of the site is located on a low volcanic ridge formed of ashy deposits and decaying andesites with a thin, rocky soil cover. This ridge is bounded by two perennial streams, the Acelhuate and the smaller Rio Izcanal. In addition, the ridge holds at least two perennial springs and six to eight which flow only in the wet season. Although the main part of the site seems to have been located on this ridge, there is evidence of contemporary population on the valley floor as well and there is a series of small ceremonial centers located in the valley; one of these, on the Hacienda San Francisco, directly to the east of the main site, is contemporary with Cihuatan. Material in local collections indicates that the majority of other sites are also Early Postclassic in date.

In 1975 an archaeological project investigating the settlement surrounding Cihuatan was begun. This project involved mapping as much of the habitation area around the ceremonial centers as is possible (given contemporary land use) and controlled excavations in domestic structures. The project was planned in conjunction with the excavation and reconstruction project centered in the Western Ceremonial Center sponsored by the Administracion del Patrimonio Cultural, Departamento de Arqueologia. To date, some 65 ha of the residential area have been mapped, perhaps one-third of the total area, and 10 structures have been excavated, largely by horizontal clearance of whole structures and surrounding areas. As it now appears that Cihuatan is a single component site dating to the Terminal Classic/Early Postclassic, these (admittedly incomplete) investigations provide an interesting source of hypotheses regarding cultural changes in the period.

The core of the site consists of two adjoining major ceremonial precincts, the eastern and western centers, and their surrounding suburbs, which together form a town covering the ridge and extending for an unknown distance into the surrounding valley. Maps of the close-packed area around the ceremonial centers and preliminary survey along the ridge to the south indicate a dense population. House clusters are found arranged around patios or organized in groups along terraces. Not all are closely contiguous, but the average distance from one group of structures to the next is less than 10 m.

Within the area mapped are some 900 structures including houses, terrace walls, civic or ceremonial buildings, and storage structures. Owing to the vegetation covering the site this is only an approximate figure. Excavations along one terrace indicate that a great many structures which were covered with eroded soil (as well as high grass and brush) had been missed. (On the first map this terrace appeared as only a terrace. Excavations showed four structures and patios on it, none of them visible before excavation.) Clearly, then, Cihuatan had a resident population of some size, much larger, in fact, than that which would have been required as a support population for the ceremonial centers.

The artifacts of Cihuatan form a very homogeneous assemblage and indicate that it was occupied for only a short time despite its size. Ceramics include, in addition to local plain red and tan wares and the common red-on-buff or red and white wares that typify Early Postclassic assemblages all over Mesoamerica, considerable quantities of Tohil Plumbate, some Mixteca-Puebla Polychromes, fine paste wares (not further identified as to group), and wares related to the lower Central American polychromes. Locally produced wares themselves give evidence of close contacts with outside areas, especially Guatemala and Veracruz. These include coarse paste modeled and applique wares formed into life- or near-life-sized images of Mexican deities (Tlaloc, Mictlantecuhtli, Xipe Totec), biconical incensarios, ladle incensarios, Mazapan-style figurines, wheeled figurines, and ceramics related to the Veracruz types FONDO SELLADO and BANO METALICO (Bruhns 1980b). Stone artifacts include very abundant obsidian, chert, quartzite, greenstone, chalk, jadeite, and serpentine. All of these, except perhaps the obsidian, are from non-local sources.[2] An effigy metate of a Costa Rican-Nicaraguan type found in a house associated with the Western Ceremonial Center indicates that larger manufactured stone artifacts may have been brought into the site.

Although the domestic architecture is of a type closely related to indigenous forms (which are themselves related to Mesoamerican types), the public architecture of the Western Ceremonial Center is clearly inspired by contemporary Mexican styles. Buildings include two I-shaped ballcourts with associated structures, small stepped platforms with central staircases, and a large stepped pyramid. The stepped construction exhibits Postclassic proportions in the talud-tablero elements and in the stair balustrades. The closest analogs of this architectural style, both stylistically and temporally, are to be found in central Veracruz.

Cihuatan was apparently destroyed by invaders in the early eleventh century A.D. although volcanic and seismic activities may have played their part. As far as can be reconstructed from the scanty historical records for this part of El Salvador, the site itself and much of the surrounding area were abandoned and in forest by the time of the arrival of Pedro de Alvarado in 1524. At this time the main centers of population were to the south at Viejo Cuscatlan, perhaps located on the slopes of the Volcan de Guazapa,[3] Guazapa, and Apopa, all located at the west entrance to the lower Acelhuate/Chalchigue valley, El Paisnal on the western mountains bordering the valley, and Suchitoto in the Lempa proper. The letters of Alvarado indicate that there was a considerable population in the area but mention few sites by name (Alvarado 1924). A census for 1542, the *Tasacion* of 1548, and later documents mention no towns in the vicinity of Cihuatan, and the first historical record of the site is not until 1879 when the German-American traveller S. Habel passed nearby on his way from Chalatenango to Guazapa (Feldman, personal communication; Anonymous 1548–1551; Habel 1879). The conquest of El Salvador was not accomplished easily and there was great loss of life from outright aggression, from epidemics, and from slaving. The Acelhuate-Chalchigue valley was largely depopulated, either in the early colonial period or before, the first resettlement coming shortly before 1807 with the establishment of the Hacienda Colima at the point where the Rio Limones (the united Acelhuate and Chalchigue) joins the Lempa (Gutierrez y Ulloa 1962). Aguilares, the market town of the region, was not incorporated until 1932 when the increasing population of El Salvador began to heavily recolonize the valley (Larde y Larin 1957). Sometime before that, in the late 1920s, Cihuatan was investigated by Samuel Lothrop and then by Antonio Sol and the increasing clearance of the forest for fields and pastures began to reveal the immense size of this forgotten town (Boggs 1971; Lothrop 1926a; Sol 1929).

As was noted earlier, it is currently very difficult to relate the events at Cihuatan to contemporary developments elsewhere in central El Salvador. The recent archaeological investigations precipitated by the construction of the Fifth of November Dam across the Lempa and carried out in the Lempa Valley adjacent to the Acelhuate-Chalchigue valley have revealed the presence of only one Postclassic site, Santa Maria, contemporary with Cihuatan. A series of Preclassic and Classic period villages and ceremonial centers was also discovered in this area on the valley floor and flanking hills (Crane 1976, 1978; Earnest 1976; Fowler 1976). Santa Maria is a small ceremonial (and perhaps residential) center, nowhere near as impressive as the by-then-abandoned Late Classic centers. Investigations at Santa Maria, carried out by William Fowler under the auspices of the Patrimonio Cultural, show a complete artifactual identity between this site and Cihuatan. Moreover, the same pattern of destruction by burning, including the smashing of large incensarios on the stairs of the ceremonial platforms, was observed at Santa Maria. The one radiocarbon determination from this site indicates that this destruction was probably contemporary with that of Cihuatan. Fowler has suggested that Santa Maria was a dependent of Cihuatan, although the nature of its connection with that site cannot be known as yet (Fowler and Solis A. 1977).

To date, then, the scant available information suggests that the events of the Late Classic in Mesoamerica were paralleled in El Salvador with abandonment of sites and major movements of population. The part of the Lempa valley in which Santa Maria is located was apparently strongly affected with a large number of ceremonial centers abandoned, and with evidence of only a small Early Postclassic occupation. It would seem that the population center shifted to the adjacent Acelhuate-Chalchigue valley where a large site of a somewhat different type, a town with a large resident population, was founded. This valley had not been an important population center previously. Such limited evidence of Classic occupation in the Cihuatan area as exists indicates small centers mainly located on the flanking hill slopes.[4] The site where Cihuatan was built was not occupied previous to the founding of the Early Postclassic center. Finally, after a relatively short period of use, 100–150 years maximum, Cihuatan itself was destroyed and abandoned. This part of the valley may well have been depopulated at this time, and a series of new centers arose to the southwest. The foundation dates for these centers are not known, but, as noted above, Guazapa, Apopa, and the now-lost Viejo Cuscatlan were all flourishing when Pedro de Alvarado entered the area.

Interpretation

Events of this scale suggest a major shift in cultural development in the area. One might postulate that new peoples were involved or a need for defense. There is some reason to think that the overlords of Cihuatan were of foreign origin, perhaps ultimately from Veracruz or part of the wave of Toltec migration which was happening in Guatemala at about the same time (Borhegyi 1965a, Carmack 1968). Cihuatan is defensible as it is located on the one piece of high ground in the middle of the valley and is protected by steep slopes and rivers on three sides. The Western Ceremonial Center is walled, however, the contemporary Eastern Ceremonial Center which adjoins it is not. The wall around the Western Ceremonial Center is as much a levelling terrace as a barricade, although in places it survives to more than 2 m in height. It may have been palisaded, but it more likely served to screen, and regulate access to, the ceremonial precincts. In any event, Cihuatan is neither more nor less defensible than some of the Classic Lempa sites.

To develop a reasonable hypothesis for the founding and brief prosperity of this site it is necessary to look to environmental and social factors. These can be augmented by the meager colonial sources to provide a firmer basis for theories of population movement and Early Postclassic events in El Salvador in relation to those of Mesoamerica.

Two factors involved in the Maya collapse proved to be of great importance to later cultural developments in El Salvador. These were, first, the appearance of Mexican peoples and a heavy influence of Mexican cultural ideas in the Maya and Mayoid areas, and second, the development of new long-distance trade routes carrying objects which were not destined for a small elite, but which eventually found their way down to a considerable number of people of lower social status. Among the items which were important trade goods were obsidian, ceramics of various sorts (especially fine paste wares and plumbate), cotton, and cacao.

When we look at the location of Cihuatan we can postulate, on this basis, some reasons for both the founding of the town and for its unusual form.

To begin, the site is located along a major access route from Honduras to the Pacific, as well as on routes to first, the ancient market center of Esquipulas in Guatemala and second, to lower Central America via the Lempa River. The modern Carretera Troncal del Norte follows the colonial Camino Real from San Salvador to Comayagua. This Spanish road seems to have, in its turn, closely followed the Precolumbian route. Thus Cihuatan is in an admirable position to have controlled traffic to and from a number of cultural and environmental areas, served as a distribution center for the rich region of its own and adjacent valleys, and overseen the very fertile lands of the Acelhuate-Chalchigue valley and the adjoining mountain slopes. That these are important considerations is shown by the location of the Late Postclassic sites of Guazapa and Apopa (and perhaps Viejo Cuscatlan), the one controlling access to the Lempa and to Honduras, the other on the road to the Zapotitan basin and the area of San Andres.

Location alone, however, is insufficient to explain the founding and importance of Cihuatan. Specifically, the question is what was newly important enough in this valley to found a site there instead of at either Guazapa or, perhaps, Colima, areas which would have had the same benefits in terms of control of traffic and trade? Here we can only find partial answers, based upon modern conditions and what historical information exists. Cihuatan itself is located on a ridge with thin leached soils which are very marginal for agriculture. Yet the elevated position of the site may have been attractive for other reasons including comfort in this hot, humid environment and easy access to ample year-round water sources and local building materials.

More importantly, however, the valley floor surrounding Cihuatan is flat to rolling land with deep, well-drained soils of recent volcanic origin. These soils are, in part, underlain by lenses of clay which hold in moisture at depths of 2–5 m. Today, with some irrigation, these soils are used for the commercial cultivation of coffee on the valley floor, yuca, and other crops. Sugar cane cultivation is of relatively recent origin. Previously, the main commercial crop was cotton, with coffee and fruit crops cultivated on the slopes and on part of the valley floor.

The current weather regime is one of rain beginning in late May and continuing with increasing force through September. The rains then gradually cease and little or no rain falls from January to March. This climatic pattern is no different from that of the adjacent Lempa, but differences in topography and amount of water carried mean that the Acelhuate and Chalchigue seldom flood. The climate is uniformly mild, even though there are gross differences in the amount of water available in the different seasons, and temperatures range from the mid-60s F to an extreme of the low 90s F. These soil, temperature, and moisture conditions are ideal for growing cotton, maize, yuca, indigo, and cacao. Of these cotton and cacao are known to have been important commercial crops in the rest of Postclassic Mesoamerica. Indigo, which was an extremely important crop in the colonial period, seems largely to have been introduced by the Spanish in the seventeenth century (Guevara 1976). It may well have been a crop of some importance previously, however. Maize was (and is) a staple crop probably grown more for local consumption than for trade. In a situation in which most movement of goods is on human backs, bulky low value items do not tend to be important in long distance trade. Cotton and cacao are another matter. Both are, when processed, relatively low in weight and bulk compared to value.

Further cacao was the only commercially-important crop grown in Precolumbian Mesoamerica which demanded constant year-round attention. Cacao is prone to disease and to insect infestation. The only way that these can be dealt with in a situation of plantation (that is to say, fields where the cacao trees are contiguous, not separated from each other by individuals of many other species) growing without insecticides is by constant inspection of the plants and hand removal of insects and diseased plants and leaves. Cacao also demands a considerable labor input in sprouting the seeds (done in nurseries), transplanting the seedlings, and general care. Harvesting the beans and even preliminary preparation of them for transport or use also demand a high labor input. In areas in which cacao must be irrigated, and El Salvador is one of these, the construction and maintenance of irrigation systems adds another major and continual labor input. The necessity for large permanent labor forces to grow cacao on any but a home-use basis is attested to both from modern cacao plantations and from historical documents from El Salvador itself. In Sonsonate and Izalco the major cause of the decline of the cacao industry was the failure of the labor force through epidemics and mismanagement. It became impossible to keep up existing cacao plantations or to rehabilitate those which had fallen behind in maintenance, and cacao was largely replaced in the seventeenth century by crops which needed less labor (MacLeod 1973).

In sum, cacao needs deep fertile soils, moisture, and a high average temperature to flourish. Environmentally the Acelhuate-Chalchigue valley meets these requirements and is, in fact, better land for such an enterprise than the adjacent Lempa with its large areas of seasonally flooded land: cacao will not stand flooding. The area around Cihuatan is suitable for cacao growing and, indeed, some was grown in the area until quite recently (Gregorio Quijano, personal communication). It is evident from the sheer size of Cihuatan that a large labor force would have been available and indeed one can argue that the size and nature of Cihuatan is directly related to the need for a large concentrated labor force to grow cacao.

Direct evidence of cacao production is hard to come by. Cacao is pollinated by insects and leaves few, if any, traces in the palynological record. The usual evidence for cacao production and use in tropical areas involves a combination of environmental information, historical data, and artistic representations coupled, where possible, with evidence from preserved macro-specimens.[5] Only the first of these is, so far, available for Cihuatan. There is also the evidence of a large town being built where none had existed before, and such a change in settlement could be interpreted as an adaptation to the need for a permanent labor force of some size for some locally important activity. Cacao growing is one of the few activities which requires this sort of labor input.

We also now have evidence of Precolumbian irrigation in this area. Irrigation is necessary to grow cacao except, first, in situations where the roots can be kept damp by natural means the year round. (Hammond [1978] has discussed one such situation in the core Maya area), or second, a situation in which the trees are planted in very deep soil and can send down extremely long tap roots (Urquhart 1961). The soils of the valley floor are deep enough in places for the latter situation to occur and the existence of clay lenses which maintain moisture may have been helpful in keeping trees alive during the dry season. Irrigation, though, would have been necessary in much of the valley and for any intensive and reliable production of this crop. During 1977 and 1978, in a survey of the north and east sides of the Cihuatan ridge, a series of check dams was discovered. The modern inhabitants do not practice gravity flow irrigation or erosion control and are largely ignorant of the methods involved. Moreover, in 1978 two constructions which seem to have been reservoirs were located on the northwest side of the ridge. These are large circular depressions, partly walled on the downslope side and with a few small structures on the rims. They are fed by seasonal springs and, although no longer operative, could have provided a certain surplus of water during the months of no rain. Unfortunately, the valley floor has been repeatedly deep-plowed for sugar cane planting and any further evidences of Precolumbian irrigation will have to be sought on the hill slopes bordering the valley. In the absence of any survey of these areas we cannot say if water control was extensive or not: that it was understood is attested to by the evidence from Cihuatan.

An indirect source of evidence for cacao cultivation is the cultivation of yuca (*Manihot escuelenta* var.). Today, and in the past, this was an important food crop. A preliminary analysis of soil samples from two house floors at Cihuatan shows what may be yuca bark phytolith in the samples (Arlene Miller, personal communication). No maize phytolith was found in the samples. It is probable that maize, then as now, was stored in cribs outside the house. Yuca is usually dumped on the kitchen floor preparatory to being processed.

A common use of yuca is as an intercrop with cacao. Fields are cleared, leaving some trees, and then yuca and cacao are planted. The yuca can be eaten, perhaps by the plantation workers, or used for other purposes, and the cacao, when bearing, sold. This kind of intercropping has been largely abandoned in modern plantations because of problems in plant spacing. Laborers today are usually fed through the company store, but this could not have been a viable proposition in Precolumbian America.

Another use for yuca is the manufacture of starch, a purpose for which it is still grown in central El Salvador (Christina Crane, personal communication). Although the non-food uses of yuca have been little considered, starch is a necessary product in cotton cloth production as well as being used in costumes. The use of starch by the Maya is attested to by numerous representations of persons wearing what appear to be starched netting or gauze headdresses (e.g., Piedras Negras Stela 40). A more essential use of starch is in weaving cotton. When making cotton textiles, especially those which involve any manipulation of the warps (as in gauzes, brocades, etc.) the warps must be starched to keep them from fuzzing up (Ann Rowe, personal communication). Owing to climatic conditions, few Precolumbian Mesoamerican textiles have been preserved. These limited specimens, however, together with evidence from ancient art, historic accounts, and ethnographic textile manufacture all testify to elaborate textiles having a long history in this part of the world. Starch manufacture today in El Salvador is largely on a part-time family basis. People who own *yucales* manufacture starch for trade in the market. This business has gotten smaller in recent times, owing to competition in city markets from industrially-produced commercial starches, but is still important in more rural economies.

There is some indication that cotton was an important crop in central El Salvador in Late Postclassic and early Colonial times. In the sixteenth century, tribute in cotton was being paid by the surviving towns in the Departments of Cuscatlan and San Salvador. Census materials, however, also indicate that maize cultivation, fishing, and honey and wax manufacture were almost as important (L. Feldman, personal communication). (In these documents, which are mid-sixteenth century in date, only one *cacatal* is mentioned. It belonged, or the rights to buy and process the cacao belonged, to an *encomendero* from Apopa.)

This area of El Salvador suffered very heavily from the epidemics, massacres, slaving, and forced movements of peoples to the coast in the early Colonial period and one would expect that any labor intensive crop, such as cacao, would have been soon abandoned. In more recent times the recolonization of the Acelhuate-Chalchigue valley went hand in hand with the expansion of cotton growing. Cotton was replaced as the major cash crop of the region by sugar cane only some twenty years ago.

On the archaeological level we have little direct information for cotton cultivation in the environs of Cihuatan. Heat, humidity, and acid soils have led to a lack of organic preservation at Cihuatan. Trial flotation of archaeological soils yielded almost no material and none that was unequivocably ancient. Excavation of domestic structures has shown that spindle whorls are found in household refuse but in such small numbers that probably only domestic manufacture was taking place. In the excavations of the NW-1/NW-3 group in 1978, a group which was burned and very hastily abandoned, only eleven spindle whorls were found. Most of these were encountered in such a context as to suggest that they formed the contents of a single spinning or sewing kit. Other structures contained on average three to five spindle whorls.

All of the structures excavated outside the ceremonial precincts have been close to the Western Ceremonial Center and all but three are manifestly residential in function. A single workshop, located on the West Terrace (the supposed central market place), was apparently given over to the manufacture of obsidian tools and, perhaps, to woodworking. This is currently our only evidence for the non-domestic manufacture of any product. The possibility exists that there were workshops specializing in cotton spinning and weaving but that they are in some other sector of the site. It may also have been that raw cotton was produced for trade rather than thread or *mantas*. Certainly in the sixteenth century, tribute was paid in cotton, not cloth (L. Feldman, personal communication). However, cotton cultivation would not explain the very distinct change from a dispersed population to a highly nucleated one. Cotton production, like that of maize and indigo, calls for a large labor force on a seasonal basis. Cacao cultivation needs a large labor force year-round and the concentration of the population in a single large town (with perhaps outlying villages) would be extremely useful in terms of organizing and overseeing the care of extensive cacao plantations.

Summary

In sum, on the basis of environment, settlement pattern, and observable trading relationships, one can look at Cihuatan's founding and unusual form as being a response, in part, to the development of large-scale production of cacao for the enlarged markets opening up in Mesoamerica. Unfortunately, physical evidence for cacao cultivation is still lacking. The impetus for this change may well have come from an immigrant elite, perhaps from Veracruz. The closest ties of Cihuatan, in artifacts and architecture, are with central Veracruz, not with the adjoining Maya area. Cacao production was thoroughly established in Veracruz and there is every indication that the Veracruz cultures were heavily involved in the development of the new trading patterns of the Terminal Classic and Postclassic. If one looks at Cihuatan from the standpoint of Veracruz traders, it is in what was, at the time, a prime position. The later important production areas of Honduras were, most probably, in some disarray owing to the collapse of the Classic centers. This doubtless affected agricultural production as well as construction and maintenance of civic architecture. The reconstructed Chorti migrations of the ninth century may also have contributed to general unrest, and the lack of centralized controls would have provided little impetus to farmers to produce more than that needed to meet their own immediate needs (Thompson 1970). Peoples coming in overland and establishing themselves as an elite in El Salvador, in much the same way as the Toltecs came into Guatemala, may well have looked at the Acelhuate-Chalchigue with its deep fertile soils and its sparse population as an ideal area for a new center and the introduction of a cash crop. The location of Cihuatan means that it could control access to the major north-south and east-west routes to Mesoamerica. It is also close to the Rio Lempa, the traditional border between Mesoamerica and lower Central America. Evidence of trade with Guatemala and Veracruz is found at Cihuatan as well as some evidence of trade with Central America. Simple control of access routes would not explain the amount of imported goods found in Cihuatan residences and ceremonial contexts and it seems self-evident that the Cihuatecos were producing desired materials as well as profiting from the movement of goods across their territory. Of the goods that could have been produced, cacao fits the given evidence of settlement type and local environment the best.

A combined cacao production-trade model also provides insights into the brief prosperity and rapid abandonment of Cihuatan. Cihuatan, though close to major trade routes and in a generally good position, is not at a key control point for any of these routes. Also, the amount of prime land is definitely limited. The major Salvadoran centers of cacao production in the Late Postclassic were to the west in Izalco and Sonsonate, both much nearer the coast and directly on those routes along the coast and heading east to San Miguel and Usulutan. By this time there had been economic recovery in Honduras and cotton, tobacco, and cacao were once again being produced in the lands to the northeast of Cihuatan. The political situation had also changed. The Pipil had made their thrust into central El Salvador and had established towns on the routes to the coast, the

Lempa, and to the Zapotitan basin. Any taxation of goods that these centers would have imposed would have raised the price of Cihuatan products, prices which already would have been high owing to the distances to main markets. Warfare and other political problems could also have contributed to an economic collapse. Interruption in tending plantations and reduction in the labor force (through war, payment of tribute, etc.) may well have led to a series of events which made the abandonment of the plantations more feasible than their rehabilitation. Deforestation and leaching of soils may also have played a part. By the Middle Postclassic period (ca. A.D. 1100– 1300) Cihuatan was gone. The Western Ceremonial Center and its surrounding residential area had been burned and not reoccupied. There may have been people living in the site area, but there were evidently not many and the major concentrations of population were, once again, on the flanking hills.

Cihuatan's founding and brief florescence can, therefore, be interpreted as being tied directly to major political and economic events in southern Mesoamerica. Changing trade routes, political unrest in former production areas, and the appearance of a foreign elite with ties to southern Mexico seem to have led to the establishment of a new center whose economy was based on commercial production of a much desired commodity, cacao. This center was admirably located for both this production and for the movement of the product to Mesoamerican markets.

However, the recovery of the Honduran production areas in the Middle Postclassic and the establishment of Naco as a major trade center (Wonderley, this volume), the Chorti migrations into the eastern highlands across the routes to the Gulf of Honduras and to Esquipulas, and the movement of Pipil groups across the access routes to the coast, combined with the florescence of the cacao production areas of Sonsonate and Izalco, cut the economic base from under Cihuatan. In this situation the burning of the main site by persons unknown can be seen as simply the *coup de grace* to a moribund center.

Given the lack of comparative data from Early and Middle Postclassic centers on the southern periphery of Mesoamerica and the small amount of evidence from Cihuatan itself, the previous statements can only be a highly tentative hypothesis. This hypothesis fits the available evidence and explains the enigmatic events of the founding and abandonment of Cihuatan as well as its evident close involvement with southern Mesoamerica. Further work in El Salvador and Honduras will doubtless modify this hypothesis or even force its abandonment. At present, however, commercial agriculture involving cacao, or possibly cotton, and control of trade routes provides a useful explanatory model for a major population shift and related events in the Early Postclassic in this southernmost area of Mesoamerica.

Acknowledgments

The fieldwork upon which this paper is based was supported by Earthwatch/The Center for Field Research, Inc., National Science Foundation through the Frederic Burk Foundation for Education, San Francisco State University, the Department of Anthropology and the Treganza Museum of Anthropology, San Francisco State University, and numerous private donors. I would like to thank all of these institutions and people for their aid, especially the Earthwork volunteers who worked with us. Stanley Boggs, Richard Crane, and William Fowler of the Administracion del Patrimonio Cultural, Departamento de Arqueologia, have been unstinting in their practical help and in discussing problems of Cihuatan and El Salvador in general. Only the author is responsible, however, for the opinions herein expressed.

Notes

1. Santisima Trinidad de Sonsonate was founded in 1551–1553 in an attempt to control the activities of European and mestizo merchants exploiting the cacao growers (who were all Indians). The large Precolumbian site of Cara Sucio, which reportedly has a Postclassic component, is not far from Sonsonate and there were numerous smaller centers in the immediate area.

2. It has been steadily rumored that there is an obsidian source on the Volcan de Guazapa. Wolfgang Haberland (personal communication) has reported a large obsidian workshop on the finca El Mico, but no further survey or exploration has been carried out in this area. The Cihuatan obsidians, for lack of funds, have not yet been sourced.

3. There is some doubt as to the location of the main Pipil center of Viejo Cuscatlan. Some have placed it near Santa Tecla (which is, however, also called Nuevo Cuscatlan), others more towards Tonocatapeque. Stanley Boggs has suggested that it may well have been in the Guazapa region. San Salvador itself was founded in an area previously unoccupied by a large town (in the so-called "Valle de las Hamacas") but which was ringed by smaller Indian centers.

4. No archaeological survey has been carried out on the slopes of the Volcan de Guazapa in the Acelhuate-Chalchigue valley. Extant

evidence of other centers comes from reports of local informants, sightings (and some visits) of mound groups or on aerial photographs, and the like.

5. Cacao pods may have been found in materials floated from the midden at El Perical (Richard Crane, personal communication), and were found along with cotton seeds in soils from domestic contexts floated by Charles Miksicek in the 1979 Cihuatan season.

Naco, Honduras—Some Aspects of a Late Precolumbian Community on the Eastern Maya Frontier

Introduction

It seems curious that the period associated with written descriptions provided by Spanish conquerors should be the least known archaeologically along the Mesoamerican-Central American border. The Ahal phase defined by about 1500 sherds at Chalchuapa, El Salvador (Sharer 1978c: 61–66), the Malalaca phase known from a largely destroyed site near the Gulf of Fonseca (Baudez 1966), an unnamed component at Lake Yojoa, Honduras (Baudez and Becquelin 1973: 66), and apparently late assemblages at Agalteca and El Rincon del Jicaque, Honduras (Stone 1957: 67–69; Stromsvik and Longyear 1946) form a list virtually exhaustive of the inventory of Late Postclassic material culture known from the Southeast Periphery of Mesoamerica. The archaeological vacuum is attributable, in part, to a practical consideration: Late Postclassic sites have proved to be difficult to locate even in areas known to have been densely populated in the early sixteenth century.

Naco, in northwestern Honduras, provides an ideal preface to archaeological studies concerned with the three elusive centuries prior to Spanish domination since its precise location and ethnohistoric identification are beyond conjecture (Strong, Kidder, and Paul 1938: 27–34). The site has been under investigation since 1975 by a Cornell University team directed by John S. Henderson. Initial

research has focused on basic archaeological systematics but we
have also begun to perceive a few of the institutional and organizational patterns operative within the ancient community. This paper
presents some of the results to date in the form of a broadly synchronic portrait of Naco during one portion of the Late Postclassic
phase.

I will summarize certain aspects of the site as they appear to have
been between A.D. 1250 and 1450. This time span is the middle facet
of the Naco Late Postclassic and happens to be best represented in
current samples. These dates are estimates based, in large measure,
upon ceramic similarities between Naco and more distant sites. For
example, basal flanges, characteristic of the Naco middle facet, are
also reported from the late facet of the Isla complex in the Peten
(ca. A.D. 1200–1450) and the early portion of the Tulum complex
along the east coast of the Yucatan Peninsula (ca. A.D. 1200–1300
[Rice 1979: 39; Sanders 1960: 186, 207]). Small tripod cups associated with the Naco middle facet are duplicated in Tases phase collec-

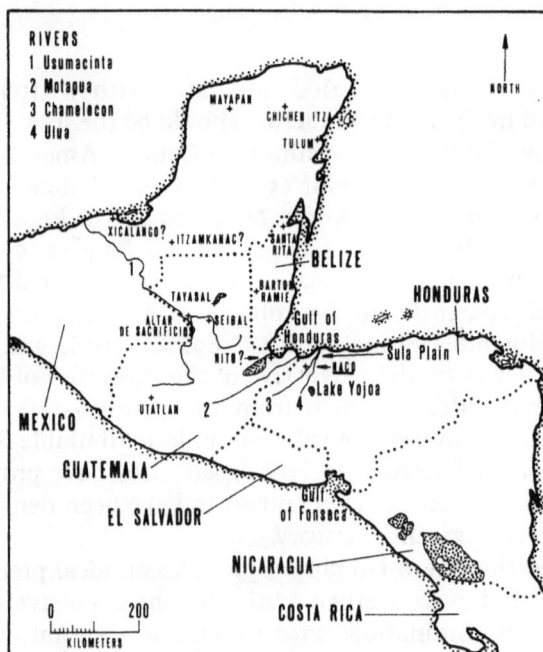

Figure 1. Naco and the Southeastern Periphery of Mesoamerica.

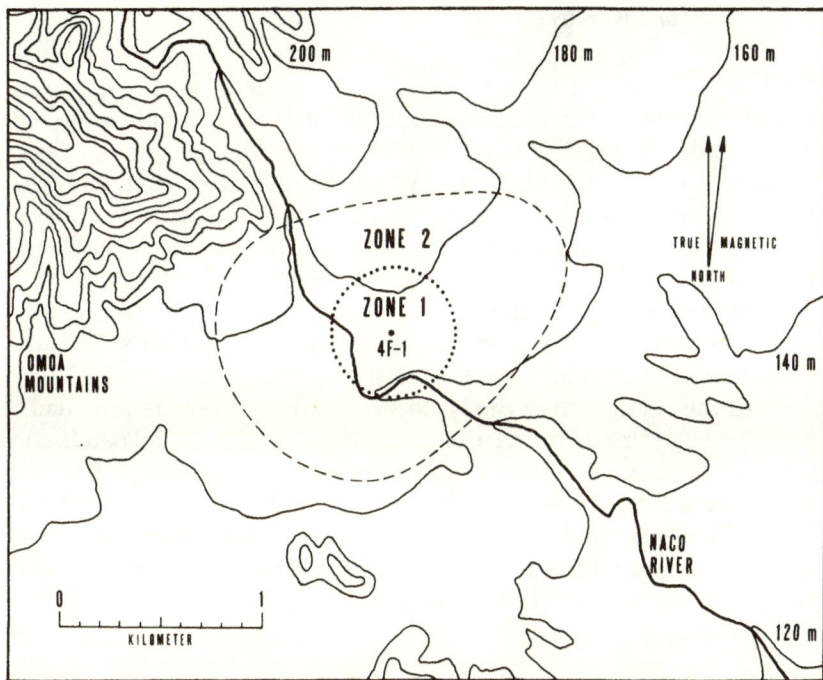

Figure 2. Topographic setting of the Naco site. The egg-shaped configuration indicates the approximate extent of middle facet occupation. Also shown are the zones used in distributional studies and defined by distance from Structure 4F-1. Magnetic declination is 6 degrees 44 minutes east of north.

tions at Mayapan (ca. A.D. 1300–1450 [Smith 1971: 215]). Altogether, the Late Postclassic phase at Naco (composed of three facets) is roughly bracketed between A.D. 1200 and 1536.

The Naco valley is a small mountain pocket of low altitude along the Chamelecon River some 40 km south of the Caribbean shore (fig. 1). Its topographic setting is intermediate between the high, rugged landscape of the mountainous interior to the south and the low, fairly level coastal plain to the north. Rainfall is heavy between May and November and the mean annual temperature probably would be a frost-free 20–25 degrees C. It is likely that the valley floor was originally enveloped in tropical forest vegetation. Slopes of surrounding hills are still covered by a pine-oak zone.

Ancient Naco is situated in the approximate center of the western valley edge, 7 km due west of the Chamelecon (fig. 2). The site is set against the base of the Omoa Mountains at 160 to 190 m above sea level and is bisected by the Naco River—a small, swift, perennial stream. The soil in this region is alluvial in origin and characterized by "remarkably high" fertility (Olson 1975: 69).

Patricia Urban, who has studied Precolumbian settlement patterns in the Naco valley, emphasizes the region's "striking conservatism in ceramics, architecture, and site planning" (1980: 16). Inhabited by at least Late Preclassic times, the valley supported a steadily expanding population up to about A.D. 1100. Urban perceives "no striking 'collapse' or disjunction in the valley's development until the middle of the Postclassic" (*Ibid.*).

From the standpoint of the Naco site itself, the demographic nadir may have occurred during the early facet of the Late Postclassic (ca. A.D. 1200–1250) since remains associated with this period are relatively scarce. It seems likely that sites such as those around Lake Yojoa, Honduras and Barton Ramie, Belize, also experienced dramatic population diminishment at about the same time (Baudez and Becquelin 1973: 407; Bullard 1973: 227–230; Rice 1979: 8; Willey 1973: 101).

The Early Facet of the Late Postclassic

The early facet at Naco witnesses the appearance of the red-on-white painted type Nolasco Bichrome, although surfaces are too eroded to permit recognition of design elements. Ladle censers with hollow, tubular handles and bowls with appliqued spikes displace the plate or lid censer form characteristic of the Early Postclassic phase. The new painted type and the new censer forms are diagnostic of the entire Late Postclassic phase at Naco. A *molcajete* tripod bowl form with appliqued raised relief also occurs at this time as does, evidently, the practice of fabric impressing.

These innovations should not obscure the fact that ceramics of the Late Postclassic's early facet manifest extremely close ties to those of the previous phase. Two minor types, Cofradia Unslipped and Salto Red, are clearly direct descendants of pottery types common in the Naco valley throughout the Late Classic and Early Postclassic phases. And, in a larger sense, major utilitarian types (Fulano Unslipped, Algo Red) and vessel forms (bowls with outcurving, slanting, and hemispherical walls; wide-mouthed jars with low flaring necks and occasional vertical strap handles; comals) of the Naco Late Postclassic undoubtedly were present sometime during the Early Postclassic as well. These traits strongly suggest a local continuity of population.

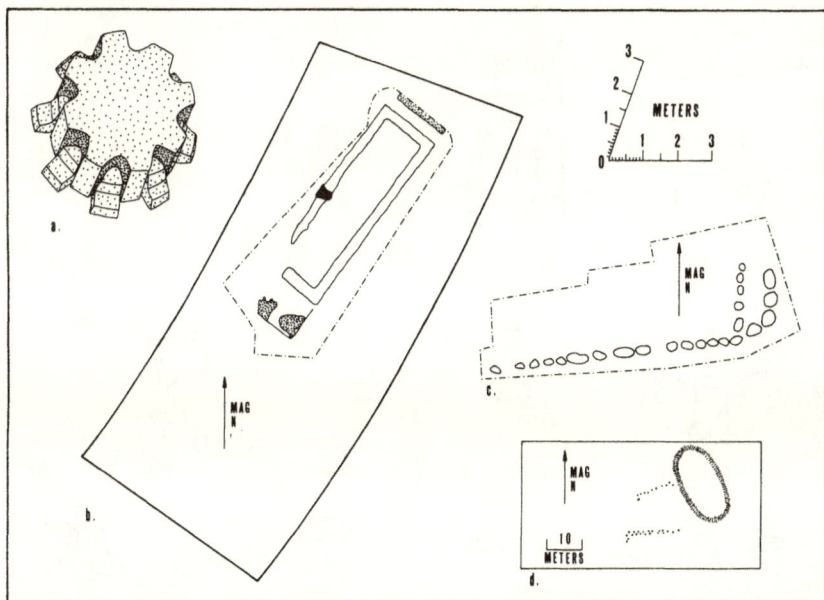

Figure 3. Middle facet architecture in Zone 1. a) Suggested reconstruction of Structure 4F-1 (isometric projection), a white plaster column with an earth fill. b) Plan of rectangular structure excavated on Structure 4F-8, a low, crescentic mound of earth. The southwest corner has been destroyed by a huaquero pit but the rest of the mud-and-gravel wall survived to a height of 10–15 cm. A packed clay surface (darkened) defined the entrance and a rectangular surface of red plaster (stippled) flanked each end of the building. c) Plan of partially excavated Structure 6F-4, a ground-level building with boulder foundations. d) The Smithsonian-Harvard Expedition noted and sketched similar boulder lines in 1936 (after Strong, Kidder, and Paul 1938: Figure 3).

The transmutation of Naco during the middle facet is viewed against the backdrop of this early facet characterized by an apparently dwindling local population.

The Middle Facet of the Late Postclassic

The middle facet is ceramically defined by the addition of new types, forms, and modes to the early facet inventory. Burnished pottery (Tal Burnished, Algo Red: Glossy variety) appears and it is probable that Salto Red is no longer present. New vessel forms include jars with high vertical necks, bowls with incurving walls, tripod

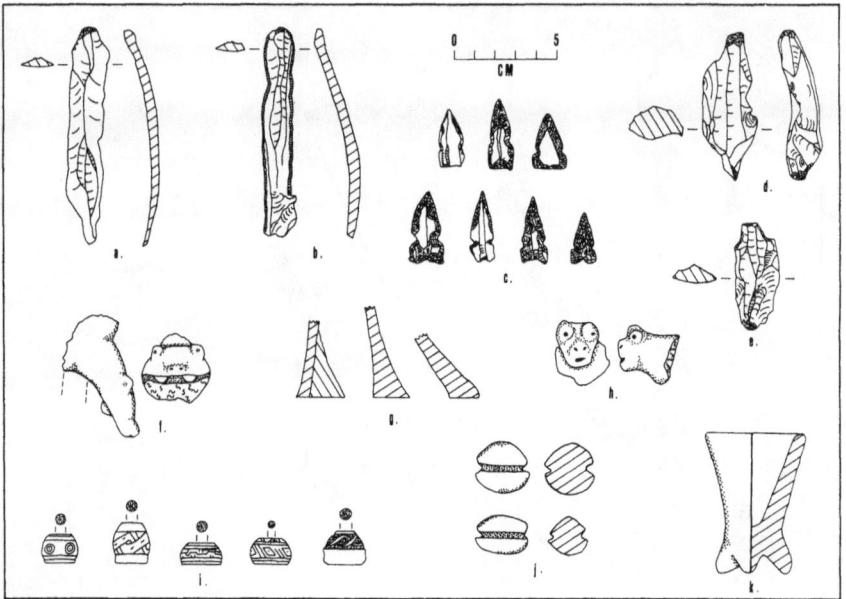

Figure 4. Nolasco Bichrome: Red-on-White Painted Pottery of the middle facet. a) Ladle censer showing pinched distal end of the tubular handle. b) Hemispherical bowl. c–i) Fragments of tripod bowls. c, d) Type I hollow legs. The second example is a section view of a bowl with a reed-stamped basal flange. e) Type II hollow leg with stamp-impressed basal interior plane. f, g) Rims. h–i) Body sherds.

cups (fig. 5k), potstands, drums (?) (fig. 5g), and perforated vessels. Finger-impressed fillet bands, horizontal strap handles, effigy lugs (fig. 5h), reed stamping, and bowl flanges (fig. 4d) all occur for the first time. Whether the three ubiquitous design elements of Nolasco Bichrome: Nolasco variety—the "serpent jaw" (e.g., fig. 4g: left view), guilloche (e.g., fig. 4a), and feather (e.g., fig. 4b: left side)—are middle facet innovations is unknown. The type does boast other unmistakably new features such as the owl-like Type II effigy leg (fig. 4e), its more common Type I pseudo-effigy counterpart (fig. 4c,d), and the production of raised relief grater surfaces by means of stamp impressing rather than applique (fig. 4e: top view).

There are several new artifact types in other categories such as small, obsidian projectile points with side notches and concave or straight bases (fig. 5c), ceramic spindle whorls (fig. 5i), and, less certainly, flat ceramic stamps, obsidian tools made from shattered polyhedral cores (fig. 5d, e), and tripod metates.

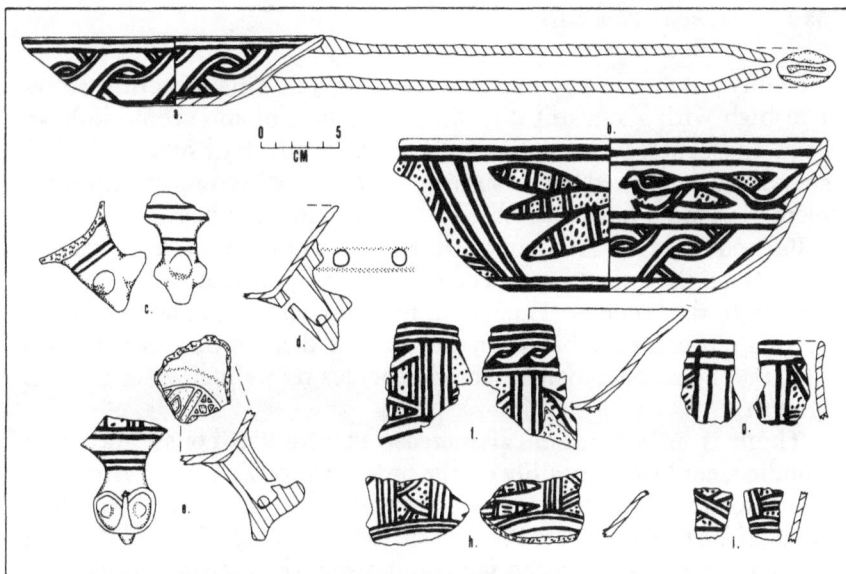

Figure 5. Miscellaneous artifacts of the middle facet. Examples a–e are obsidian, f–k ceramic material. a, b) Blades. The second example is unifacially retouched. c) Side-notched projectile points with straight (upper row) and concave (lower row) bases. d, e) Polyhedral core fragment tools. f) Solid effigy leg, unslipped—a serpent lacking its mandible. g) possible drum fragments—one is unslipped, two are red. h) Effigy lug, unslipped—monkey. i) Incised spindle whorls, unslipped. j) Net weights, unslipped. k) Tripod cup, unslipped.

Residential mounds, frequently placed on natural eminences, continue to be constructed during the middle facet as they had been in the past. But, as in other classes of material culture, the older practices are supplemented by several new architectural techniques. Rectangular structures built at ground level are characteristic of this facet. One excavated residence of this sort, 6F-4, consisted of boulder foundations on at least two sides with an apparent open front indicated by an absence of foundation features (fig. 3c). A mass of clay, suggesting the collapse pattern of mud-covered, vertical pole wall construction (Wauchope 1938: 70, 86–88), covered the interior surface. This architectural style probably was common in middle facet Naco (fig. 3d).

A second architectural innovation is the widespread use of plaster. Plaster appears most frequently in the form of white or red-stained patio and floor surfaces (fig. 3b). It is also employed as a sort of white exoskeleton around earth cores of odd configuration. The most completely known example of the latter use is the earliest stage of 4F-1, probably datable to the middle facet (fig. 3a). This structure stood 1 m high with a summit diameter of about 4 m and seems to have been the centerpiece of the main plaza. Only half of its original shape was uncovered but, assuming a generalized symmetry, its complete plan must have resembled a wheel with eight cogs.

Beyond a simple listing of traits, there are new elements in middle facet Naco that must have been of profound political and economic import to that society. The site at this time encompasses an area of 160 ha, an estimate based on the surface distribution of ceramics (fig. 2). The archaeological record provides no indication of gradual growth.

There is an astronomical increase in obsidian consumption in middle facet Naco, possibly on the order of 2500%. Early Postclassic operations at Naco yielded 0.4 g of obsidian per m³ of excavated soil, while the early facet Late Postclassic figure is 0.8 g. The middle facet value is 20.3 g. As a very rough comparison, the highest corresponding figures from the Classic period are Copan (27.5 g) and Tikal (15.3 g). Other Postclassic measurements are Mayapan (3.7 g) and Tulum (1.4 g) (Sidrys 1976a: 453). The increment suggests the development of an interregional procurement system effective by any prehistoric Mesoamerican standard.

This period is also notable for a significant shift in dietary preference. Freshwater shells, almost completely absent from the earlier archaeological record of the Naco valley, are found throughout the middle facet site in immense quantities. One midden excavation produced over 14 kg of the freshwater snail *Pachychilus* per m³ of excavated soil. Net weights in the form of small, grooved spheroids of clay are one more new artifact type common in middle facet Naco (fig. 5j). The shells, in conjunction with the weights, suggest the establishment of a new subsistence regime at least partially oriented towards the river.

Interpretation

The middle facet is characterized by innovation in every class of material culture. There also occurs, in all probability, a profound modification of structural and infrastructural relations within the community.

The middle facet phenomenon may be considered a remarkable local florescence occasioned by factors unknown and unpresaged in the archaeological record. This interpretation would emphasize continuity between the early and middle facets as manifest in the presence of most ceramic types, many major vessel forms, and possibly the construction of house platforms on ground rises. Much of this continuity would extend into the Early Postclassic phase also.

An alternate interpretation would invoke a site unit intrusion with a subsequent fusion of foreign and local elements. I favor this explanation because it seems in better accord with the archaeologically abrupt and pervasive transformations apparent at this time. It is not without theoretical difficulty for it necessitates a "pure" intrusive material culture inventory, one that I have not isolated in excavations to date. It also requires a particular cultural dynamic in which the societies in question amalgamate to produce an archaeologically perceptible hybrid entity. That assumption is a plausible one since cultural reformulations involving migration and ethnic admixture seem to have been rather common during the Postclassic. The Peten Postclassic tradition, for example, is interpreted in precisely these terms.

The true picture was possibly that Classic Peten people survived in some places and that other Maya groups moved in from several areas to exploit the vacuum created by the Classic breakup. I would guess that at least some came from Quintana Roo and Campeche, perhaps as refugees from the Putun Maya invasions of which Thompson speaks. The cultural amalgamation of these groups is expressed archaeologically mainly by Augustine and Paxacaman pottery (Bullard 1973: 241; cf. Sharer and Chase 1976: 289).

If a site unit intrusion at the beginning of the middle facet is considered a strong possibility, why would the event occur at this time and place? About A.D. 1250, a number of population displacements occurred in the Maya area as part of the general reshuffling of power and commercial relationships that followed the collapse of Toltec Chichen Itza. The Peten "is thought to have received migrating groups of Itza peoples" (Rice 1979: 5) at this time. Fox believes other Mexicanized Maya groups such as the Quiche and Cakchiquel simultaneously moved into the highlands from the Gulf Coast area (1978: 1–2, 274–275).

In such "epigonal" Toltec circumstances, Naco would have been a prize to any migrating group able to exploit its commercial potential. The Naco valley is conveniently situated to dominate the cacao-rich Sula plain to the north. More importantly, it is part of a natural trans-isthmian corridor between the Caribbean and the Pacific, and would benefit from any connection between culturally distinct zones to the north (Maya) and south (lower Central America). In a discussion of metal trade between Maya territory and lower Central America, Bray observes that the

> Costa Rican links were probably by way of the Pacific side of the Isthmus, through what Baudez has called the Zone of Meso-american Influence, which embraces Guanacaste, western Nicaragua, western Honduras and all of El Salvador. Some of the traffic must have followed the Pacific coast, but from the map provided by Baudez the strategic significance of the Naco region of northwest Honduras stands out at a glance. Not only was it "a land rich in gold mines" and the centre of a major cacao-growing area—it also stood at a commercial crossroads, a port of entry for the Yucatan trade, and the one region where the Zone of Meso-american Influence touches the Caribbean shore to link with the canoe routes along the coast of Honduras (1977: 392).

A region suspected as the source of intrusive elements at Naco is the riverine base of the Yucatan Peninsula. To judge by Spanish accounts, this archaeologically unknown area seems to have been characterized by many of the traits appearing without antecedent in middle facet Naco.

There is some reason to suppose that the molluscan utilization pattern evident at Naco may have been widespread across the base of the Yucatan in late prehistoric times. Feldman, for example, describes a species of *Pachychilus* as "the river snail whose broken remnants are encountered among the structures of Seibal" (in Willey 1978: 166). No frequencies are given but it would appear that *Pachychilus* was common at that Usumacinta site primarily occupied during the Terminal Classic Bayal phase, a time of Mexicanized Maya domination. Lee reports phenomenal quantities of *Pachychilus* at a colonial Maya site on the upper Grijalva (1979). "[O]ver 48,000 common freshwater snail shells," he notes, were "the most significant single food species" (Lee and Markman 1977: 62) of the area. A sixteenth century Spaniard campaigning against the Chol Maya around the southeastern base of the Yucatan Peninsula wrote ". . .it seemed that they had eaten the mountains of snail shells that they had gathered together to eat" (quoted in Hellmuth 1977: 424).

The most common ceramic net weight form throughout the prehistoric sequence of southern Mesoamerica is a notched potsherd (Sanders 1960: 261; Willey 1978: 44). In contrast, the distribution of grooved, clay spheroids found in middle facet Naco seems limited and sporadic. They are reported in Campeche probably in Late Classic contexts, the Tehuantepec region during Late Classic-Early Post-classic times, Chiapas in the Late Postclassic, and Veracruz in un-dated provenience (Berlin 1956: 144, fig. 6aa; Drucker 1943: Pl. 65n–p; Navarrete 1966: 79; Wallrath 1967: 136). Here again, there is reason to suspect the presence of these objects around the rivers of the lower Yucatan Peninsula. The geographical occurrence nearest to Naco is a single specimen with uncertain dating from Altar de Sacrificios (Willey 1972: 86, fig. 70). An early Spanish reference de-scribes the use of similar artifacts among the Chol Maya: "And in two of said houses two large nets were found. . .with their floats, and for weights clay (balls) well sewn on" (quoted in Hellmuth 1977: 426).

Ground level buildings, such as the 6F-4 residence mentioned above, are an important aspect of the Naco middle facet innovations. Most of these structures appear to have been rectangular with an open side and three walls probably composed of mudcovered vertical poles. Somewhat north of the area I believe crucial to the hypothe-sized intrusion, ground level houses are reported in contexts likely postdating the appearance of this form at Naco (Chase 1979: 99; Har-rison 1979: 202, 204). Chols of the Conquest period favored similar architecture and, while the practice is of unknown antiquity, their residences would yield remains corresponding to the archaeological examples at Naco: "And all the houses have their fronts open, and the sides and rear built up of stakes covered with clay" (quoted in Hellmuth 1977: 425).

Another ground level structure, 4F-14, stood in or near the central plaza area of middle facet Naco. This building is unlikely to have been strictly residential as nearly half of its ceramics belong to the painted type Nolasco Bichrome, whereas contemporary midden ac-cumulations contain 13% to 21% of that type. Structure 4F-14 had an unusually high percentage of utilitarian jar rims relative to bowls (38% as opposed to midden values of 20% to 25%). Most painted sherds derived from ladle censers (fig. 4a) and an enormous bowl with a plaster-coated center and perforated spikes is also from this building. The 4F-14 excavation yielded evidence of musical instru-ments such as a bone rasp and the ceramic form thought to be a drum (fig. 5g). This archaeological inventory is congruent with a description of a centrally located community building in the Chol town of Dolores or Sac Balam (Hellmuth 1977: 425). That building was a "combined temple and men's hut" (Thompson 1938: 603) serv-ing as a repository for pottery incense burners and "full of vessels for the (ceremonial) drinking" (*Ibid.*: 595).

Thompson strongly advocated the view that the Chol lacked

"idols" at the close of the sixteenth century (1938: 585, 593; 1970: 187). He considered the distinction of ethnological significance since it set the Chols apart from other Maya groups to the north character- ized by an effigy censer cultus after about A.D. 1200 (Andrews 1943: 43; Bullard 1970: 304; Harrison 1979: 203; Rice 1979: 79; Sanders 1960: 245; Smith 1971: 255–256). If Thompson's interpretation is correct, the absence of effigy censers in 4F-14 and, indeed, through- out the Naco site, would strengthen the similarity between Chol culture and archaeological remains at Naco.

One other aspect of the comparison of 4F-14 with the Chol men's hut is of interest. Snail shells, easily the most common domestic refuse in middle facet Naco, were not present in 4F-14. If the build- ing served as a men's house, could an absence of mollusc accumula- tions signal a segregation of activity along sexual lines? There is no evidence to suggest this was or was not so among the Chol. Among the present-day Lacandones of the same area, however, *Pachychilus* is regarded as a supplementary food source "chiefly for women and children" (Nations 1979: 569). This speculation should be testable in the archaeological record.

Snail shell consumption, clay ball weights, residential and cere- monial architecture—these are the strongest points of similarity be- tween ethnohistorically known Maya culture along the lowland base of the Yucatan and new traits in middle facet Naco. An examination of other characteristics does not materially strengthen the resem- blance. This is not to say that the archaeology of Naco and the Span- ish accounts of riverine Maya are in disagreement. The problem is that written descriptions are frequently so vague as to preclude any meaningful comparison. White plaster, for example, was known to the Chols and one chief's house possessed a verandah (Thompson 1938: 599). Whether such observations can be equated with the new plaster architecture of Naco generally, and the patios excavated within 4F-8 specifically (fig. 3b), is unclear. Similarly, the Spanish noted "bowls, *cantaros*, frying dishes," as well as "flat bowls" and "well made *comales*" (quoted in Hellmuth 1977: 425, 426) among the Chols. These phrases could apply easily enough to the ceramics of Naco but they are not very helpful.

The curious cogwheel-shaped structure, 4F-1, is another impor- tant element among the middle facet innovations with equivocal ties to Maya culture at the base of the Yucatan (fig. 3a). The plaster- coated column may be a variant of circular altar constructions found in much of the Late Postclassic Maya area (Fox 1978: fig. 1, 31; Chase 1981: 30). Structure 4F-1 particularly resembles some of the lowland examples as these were typically low, round platforms built in open plaza areas (Harrison 1979: 191) and not spatially associated with ballcourts. Thompson, for example, mentions the occurrence, in early colonial times, of "a crudely made altar of stone and mud, about an arm's breadth in diameter" (1938: 594) standing in the plaza of a Chol settlement.

Lowland altars were not necessarily strictly circular as illustrated by a masonry column at Mayapan forming, in plan, a rounded cruciform (Pollock *et al.* 1962: 128, fig. 1). Deviance from the round form may have been motivated by the desire to present an iconographically meaningful image as in the case of the Tayasal column representing "Yaxcheelcab, the ceiba tree of the world" (Thompson 1977: 27).

The plan of the Naco column may have been similarly conceived. Perhaps 4F-1 was meant to be a cosmographic representation, its eight cogs corresponding to the cardinal and intercardinal divisions of the universe as presented, for example, in the calendar of the Madrid Codex (pp. 75–76). Alternatively, the 4F-1 design could have duplicated the plan of the Caracol tower at Chichen Itza. By the Late Postclassic, the Caracol may have acquired a symbolic significance transcending an original astronomical function, a situation which apparently occurred during the Early Classic with the nonfunctional imitations of the Group E observatory at Uaxactun (Aveni 1980: 277–281; Ruppert 1940).

A third possibility is that the Naco column was an architectural elaboration of the glyph Chicchan—a day name in Yucatec Maya (Kelley 1976: 65–67, 108–109; Thompson 1962: 310). The specific form of the glyph most nearly identical to 4F-1 occurred exclusively, so far as I know, as body markings on serpents depicted in several late Maya pictorials approximately contemporary with the Naco middle facet. In the Codex Madrid (p. 30; see fig. 6a), the cogged Chicchan markings are visible on a serpent associated with Ix Chebel Yax and one of the Chacs in the act of pouring "rain water earthward" (Thompson 1970: Pl. 9). One of the figures in the Santa Rita murals stands in front of a temple engulfed in the jaws of a serpent similarly decorated (fig. 6b).

The coeval appearance of this design in the Yucatan Peninsula and at Naco seems unlikely to be fortuitous although I cannot develop the analysis beyond a level of formal resemblance. If the comparison is valid, however, the Chicchan symbol probably would be appropriate to the Chol area. The word itself, as Kelley notes, is "apparently borrowed from some Cholan dialect" (1976: 109). To the Chorti, the only Cholan group to receive major ethnographic attention, Chicchans are easily "the most important of the native deities" (Wisdom

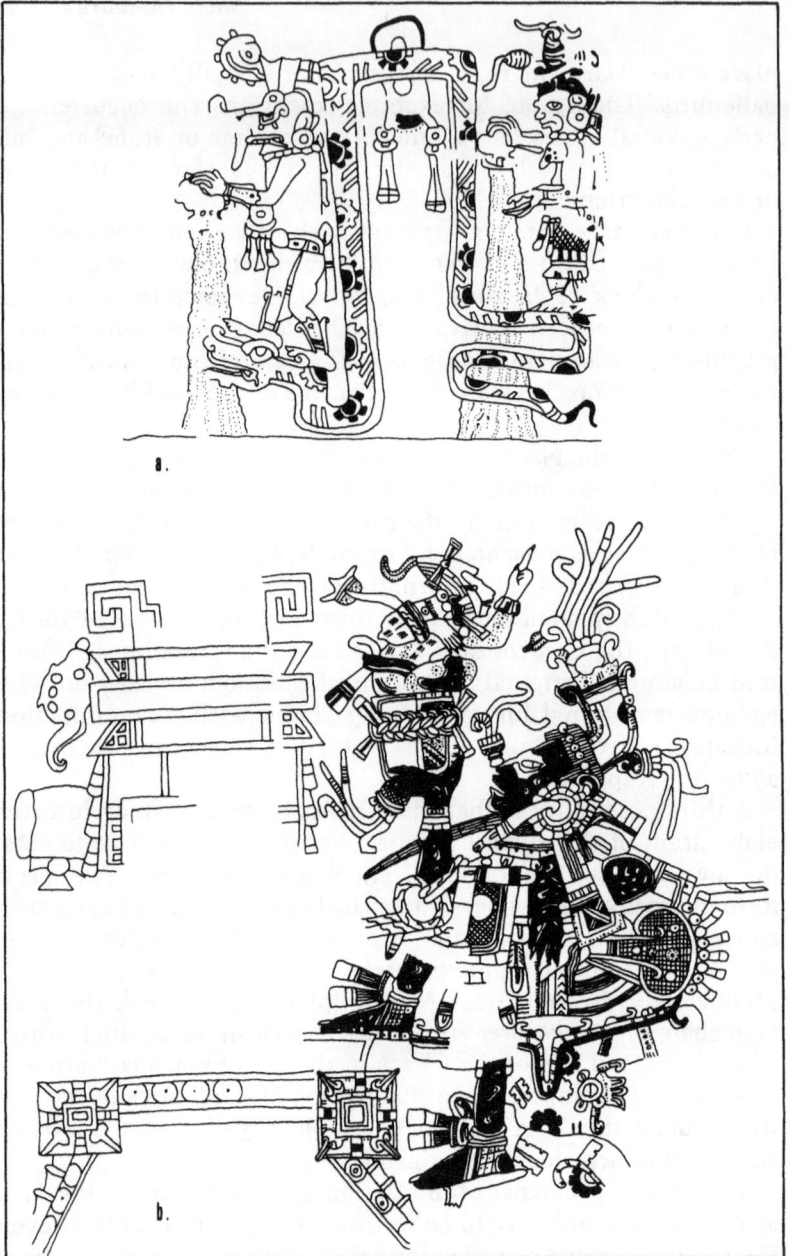

Figure 6. "Chicchan Markings" in Postclassic Maya art. a) Codex Madrid, the upper panel of page 30. b) Figure 3 on the west half of the north wall in Mound 1, Santa Rita, Belize (after Villacorta and Villacorta 1930; Gann 1900: Plate 30).

1940: 392). They are ophidian beings "responsible for both the beneficial and the harmful conditions of the earth and sky" (*Ibid.*: 395).

The middle facet, in sum, is marked both by continuity in major
types and vessel forms and a tremendous amount of quantitative and
qualitative change in every class of material culture. I think it likely
the archaeological record resulted from the fusion of migrant and
autochthonous groups, a common enough occurrence at this time
and in this region. The intrusive element must have originated in a
riverine environment and the base of the Yucatan Peninsula provides
a likely setting. That area, archaeologically unknown during the
Postclassic, was home to various Maya groups characterized by a life-
style similar, in important respects, to the congeries of traits appearing without antecedent in middle facet Naco. Many of the riverine
Maya groups were Chol speakers and there is a reasonable possibility
that it was they who introduced freshwater mollusc utilization, ceramic net weights, unelevated residential and ceremonial buildings,
and possibly all of the middle facet innovations to Naco. This suggested affiliation can hardly be considered revolutionary in view of
the fact that Naco was situated very near to known Chol territory
and is sometimes associated with that language (Feldman 1975;
Thompson 1970: 84–102, 130).

Whether Naco achieved status as a major commercial center during the middle facet is unclear. Storage facilities may have existed at
this time although evidence for this function, negative at best, is
somewhat stronger in the late facet. Most goods that presumably
flowed through Naco would have been perishable and archaeologically undetectable (Parsons and Price 1971: 175; Thompson 1970:
124–158). Others, such as metal and trade pottery, are not currently
known from reliable middle facet contexts. Several fragments of ves-
icular ground stone, a green obsidian blade, and a chert flake from
this period imply at least indirect contact with the volcanic highlands, central Mexico, and, possibly, the east coast of Yucatan. Certainly the quantity of obsidian strongly suggests the existence of an
efficient procurement network linking Naco, in some fashion, to the
southeastern Guatemala highlands. Although it is clear that almost
all obsidian arrived at Naco in the form of decorticated macro cores,
specific mechanisms of importation remain unknown as does the
issue of whether obsidian was subsequently exported from Naco to
other areas. The commercial activity may have been directed by a
central zone elite at Naco but, if so, a subsequent dispersion (redis-
tribution?) of the material throughout the site prevents recognition
of any such association.

The middle facet is the period best represented in the Naco sample and it becomes possible at this time to infer certain aspects of the social structure from intra-site distributional patterns. These spatial analyses are based on a division of the site into two zones. Zone 1 is the area within a 300 m radius of 4F-1 containing what is believed to be the ceremonial precinct as well as a number of residences. Zone 2 is all of the site beyond Zone 1, an area lacking any indication of exclusively civic-ceremonial activity (fig. 2).

In many respects, the distribution of material culture seems uniform over the entire site. In ceramic terms, both zones produce roughly comparable amounts of utilitarian types such as Algo Red: Algo and Glossy varieties, Tal Burnished, and Cofradia Unslipped. Both zones have the same utilitarian bowl forms in equivalent proportions and in both, utilitarian bowl rims are about twice as common as jar rims. Zones 1 and 2 have the same frequencies of strap handles and fabric impressions.

Many chipped stone characteristics are also evenly distributed. Each zone has the same amount of blade retouch and specific retouch techniques are present in both areas in similar proportions.

Furthermore, the homogeneous distribution of chipped stone provides an insight into the character of obsidian tool production in middle facet Naco. Flakes, cores, and cortex are present equally in Zones 1 and 2, a circumstance implying the absence of localized workshops for blade production. Mistake rates and technologically determined blade attributes are about the same throughout the site indicating a rather uniform level of manufacturing competence. These data suggest that blade production in the middle facet community probably was a non-localized and unspecialized activity performed, in all likelihood, at the household level.

There is also little indication that ceramic production was specialized or standardized. Appendages are hand-modeled, quality of line application on painted design is diverse, and rim diameters of almost every vessel form vary widely. A possible exception to the latter statement is the Nolasco Bichrome: Nolasco variety ladle censer with out-curved bowl wall. Almost every example of this vessel form bears the guilloche element on exterior and interior surfaces, lacks a bowl-to-handle air vent, and possesses a pinched handle termination (fig. 4a). Rim diameter variation is only 4 to 6 cm, compared with the next lowest range of 10 cm.

There is no evidence for differential access to the important substances obsidian and freshwater mollusks. Data gathered from residential midden deposits indicate, in a general fashion, that people living on the outskirts of middle facet Naco could consume (and necessarily obtain) fully as much obsidian as those living in the central area. It is also clear that substantial quantities of shellfish were universally available and, to judge by relative proportions of the genera consumed in the two zones, molluscan dietary preferences appear to have been identical.

Thus, the archaeological picture emerging from middle facet Naco seems to be that of a generally homogeneous, unspecialized, and, in several respects, egalitarian community. This is not to say that evidence for differential standing within the community is nonexistent. It does appear that certain architectural and dietary prerequisites are associated with the central area of the site. Plaster was employed in some domestic architecture of Zone 1 only (fig. 3b). There is also an intriguing indication that Zone 1 residents consumed more types of meat (mostly white-tailed deer and dog) in substantially greater quantities (perhaps ten times as much) than their Zone 2 contemporaries. Higher Zone 1 frequencies of projectile points and perpendicular scratch abrasion on blade tools (butchering activity?) may be correlated with the greater amount of bone in the central area.

There are other zonal differences suggestive of preference rather than privilege. The practice of grinding instead of striating core platform surfaces is far more popular in Zone 1. Zone 1 has relatively more Nolasco Bichrome and less Fulano Unslipped pottery than Zone 2. The Nolasco Bichrome hemispherical bowls with their elaborate design treatments (fig. 4b) are more common in Zone 1 as are vertical-necked jars and comals of the utilitarian types. In contrast, pseudo-effigy (Type I) legs of Nolasco Bichrome are overwhelmingly associated with Zone 2 (fig. 4c, d) and most of the reed-stamped decoration and bowl flanges are from that area also.

While some of these contrasts conceivably could be attributed to functional differences or status-related privileges, they more easily could be the material correlates of kin-based and/or cultic diversity within the middle facet site. In this regard, it seems to me that many of the distinctive traits of Zone 1 possess a more Mexicanized flavor than those of Zone 2. It would appear that high frequencies of ground platform abrasion and side-notched projectile points (particularly those with concave bases) are very generally associated with Mexican or Mexicanized cultures in Postclassic southern Mesoamerica. The comal vessel form could reflect a Mexican or Mexicanized preference for tortillas largely absent from the Maya lowlands. There is a more explicit ophidian emphasis, possibly indicative of a Mexicanized stance, in the iconography of Zone 1 as seen in the painted feathered serpent in figure 4b and the fanged effigy support in figure

5f. Characteristic traits of Zone 2 such as the Type I pseudo-effigy legs (and, possibly, their Type II effigy counterparts) presumably imply an alternate iconographic emphasis, perhaps that of a peasant-oriented cultus.

This interpretation cannot be pressed on existing evidence but is worthy of further consideration. Thompson observed that every expansionist polity in the southern region of the Maya lowlands about the time of the Spanish Conquest was dominated by a Mexicanized Putun elite (1970: 73–79). Tayasal and Chetumal, in his view, consisted of a Chan (Yucatec-speaking) peasantry ruled by Putun invaders (1977: 36). A Putun elite dominated what Feldman terms the "Tamactun Chontal" at Itzamkanac (1975: 8; Scholes and Roys 1948). The Torquegua Chol around Nito "can be placed alongside other protohistoric Chols as a people dominated by a Mexicanized mercantile elite who lived on water borne lines of communication" (Feldman 1975: 8). One can only speculate what form this association would take in the archaeological record (cf. Rice 1979: 12) but it could well show up as the kind of variation noted in the material culture of Naco.

To summarize, Naco's external relationships during the middle facet are poorly understood but minimally included an effective arrangement to procure obsidian from the southeastern highlands of Guatemala. In view of Naco's later commercial reputation and its enormous site area at this time, the generally uniform, unspecialized, and even egalitarian character of the artifact distributions is rather surprising. It is probable, however, that those who lived near the central plaza were accorded some architectural and dietary privileges. This centrally located group also manifested certain preferences in chipped stone and pottery, possibly indicative of a more Mexicanized orientation.

Conclusions

Ethnohistoric information relevant to Naco is associated with the late facet (ca. A.D. 1450–1536), a time span largely beyond the scope of this presentation. Spanish accounts indicate that Naco had a population of about 10,000 and was almost certainly the principal commercial center of the Ulua region (Henderson 1979). Archaeologically, the community size remained about the same as during the middle facet and there was little change in the material culture of Zone 2. Within Zone 1, however, two new and distinctive painted pottery types appeared. The affinities and significance of one type are unknown. Very speculatively, this may have been the pottery of foreign commercial agents residing at Naco. Affinities of the second type lie with a series of ceramics related to the Mixteca-Puebla horizon and distributed along the Pacific slopes of Central America. This type probably was the pottery of an intrusive Mexican or Mexicanized elite responsible for extensive remodeling of Naco's central precinct.

The recent work at Naco has produced a wealth of new data, many of which suggest that evidence of cultural boundaries—very possibly the material correlates of ethnic groupings—is manifest in the archaeological record. If interpretations presented in this paper are even partially correct, interaction among groups of more-or-less distinct cultural affiliation played a fundamental role in the functioning of the community. Future research will be more specifically concerned with the character of intrusive groups as well as the nature of subsequent interaction between foreign and autochthonous peoples. We particularly wish to examine the manner in which variegated cultural relationships may have influenced economic, political, and ritual patterns within the community. At Naco, such questions are bound up closely with the concept of Mexicanization—a diffusion process increasingly perceived in southern Mesoamerica but only vaguely defined.

Archaeological study of the effects of ethnicity is clearly fraught with uncertainty but it may be that working along the Late Postclassic eastern Maya frontier is tantamount to accepting this issue as a primary research focus. During the Terminal Classic and Postclassic periods of southern Mesoamerica, cultural change is frequently due less to multi-causal chains of local development than to the sudden appearance of foreign peoples. Movements of smaller groups consisting of itinerant elites or warrior-traders may have been even more common. The presence of culturally distinct barrios of specialized craftsmen or merchant enclaves implies that much of society's economic business may have been institutionalized along ethnic lines. But these are perhaps nothing more than the garden variety forms of interaction; all may be present at Naco and all are well-attested in the archaeology and ethnohistory of heartland Mesoamerica. The peripheral zone presents the additional challenge of coping with a fluid and complicated transition from Maya to Central American cultural traditions. As we learn more about the Southeast Periphery of Mesoamerica in late prehistoric times, I suspect relations of ethnicity will prove to be inextricably associated with the flow of goods and ideas throughout much of the region.

Acknowledgments

I gratefully acknowledge the cooperation of Vito Veliz R. (Instituto Hondureno de Antropologia e Historia) as well as much assistance provided by John S. Henderson, Pauline Caputi, Patricia Urban, and Edward Schortman in all aspects of the Naco work.

21

Southeast Mesoamerican Periphery
Summary Comments

The Southeast Mesoamerican Periphery means a zone which has been part of Mesoamerica but peripheral to its higher civilizations. It is a frontier zone whose limits, nature, and role have frequently changed through time. It is only thanks to researches undertaken these last years that one can get a glimpse at its complex history.

Our documentation on the Early Preclassic is too scanty for any generalization. More data are available on the Middle Preclassic which indicate that between 800 and 400 B.C. southeastern Mesoamerica as a whole was peripheral to the Olmecs. We do not know to what extent, and we do not yet understand through which mechanisms, the Guatemalan, Honduran, and Salvadoran cultures were participating in this civilization. What we do know is that remains from Kaminaljuyu, Chalchuapa, Playa de los Muertos, Los Naranjos, and Copan demonstrate Olmec "influence," and a rather high level of craftsmanship and aesthetic excellence in already complex societies (at least at Los Naranjos and Chalchuapa). I do not understand Kennedy's point of defending the Playa de los Muertos reputation of being unjustly accused of belatedness and marginality. If the Ulua valley is marginal for most of its known history, it is not so before the Late Preclassic period. In fact, many authors such as Popenoe, Vaillant, Strong, and Porter have been aware of the precocity and quality of the Playa de los Muertos ceramics and artifacts.

From 400 B.C. on, the major elements which combined to give birth to the Classic Maya civilization of the lowlands begin to appear. Civilization is slowly emerging with a higher level of social organization, a major art style illustrated in many media, and an elaborate writing system. At the same time, and perhaps even earlier, the Southeastern Highlands experience an analogous period of gestation and take off. Demarest and Sharer convincingly demonstrate the cultural homogeneity of this large zone which extends from Bilbao to a few miles west of the Zapotitan basin. It has nothing to envy in the Maya lowlands, does not belong to its periphery, and appears, rather, as a challenger. The territory comprising eastern Guatemala, western and central Honduras, and most of El Salvador, is quite different in nature as much as in homogeneity. As far as urbanism, architecture, sculpture, and writing are concerned, these regions are obviously less developed than the Maya lowlands and highlands. Although this area as a whole shares a common taste or interest in certain classes of artifacts (i.e., Usulutan decorated ceramics), the diversity of ceramics from one site to the other points to strong regionalist tendencies. Because of that, I would object to the creation of a Uapala sphere: very few types, if any, would be shared by all this territory's sites.

Towards the end of the 3rd century A.D., the lowland Maya civilization is officially born with the generalized use of vaults, carved stelae, hieroglyphic writing, and polychrome pottery. Early in the fifth century, the new civilization expands southward and Maya centers are created at Quirigua and Copan. Curiously enough, no further expansion will occur later. Meanwhile, the Southeastern Highlands break down as a culture area. If Kaminaljuyu reaches its climax under Teotihuacan's control, the other regions or centers to the east are either abandoned or depopulated; the population loss and cultural regression may be due, at least in part, to volcanic activity. Nevertheless, one can observe a comparable stagnation or regression in Early Classic times in non-Maya Honduras, with no accompanying evidences of disastrous eruptions. The ceramics show a strong continuity with the preceding period with very few inventions and a lack of interest in adopting foreign innovations. Because of this continuity it is often hard to date a Periphery site through its ceramics; when Sheets claims that there are no Early Classic sites in the Zapotitan basin, his claim may be based on their lack of recognition as such. In any event, the hypothesis of a migration, following volcanic disaster, of Protoclassic Salvadorans to Belize has to be abandoned, as it cannot be sustained any more by supposed similarities between orange ceramic types from both regions (Demarest and Sharer, this volume).

The climax of Maya lowland civilization is reached during the Late Classic period. In the highlands, there is no more unity than in the Early Classic, but now it is Kaminaljuyu which regresses while

Chalchuapa (Tazumal) makes a fresh start. Farther east, the Zapotitan basin is reoccupied—assuming it has been abandoned—by Maya Chorti people, according to Sheets. His hypothesis rests on the reconstruction by Thompson (1970) of a Chorti territory which has, I think, no reality as it is made up of data from different periods: archaeology of Classic times as well as ethnohistoric documents from the sixteenth and eighteenth centuries (including Galindo's "Chorti Empire"). In fact, all "evidence" of Chorti-speaking peoples in El Salvador dates from the eighteenth century. If Sheets uses the word Chorti for designating the language, it cannot be proven that the people speaking Chorti in eighteenth century El Salvador were already there in the Classic period. If Sheets means the Chorti Classic culture, i.e., a variant of Maya lowland civilization as it blossomed at Copan and beyond (Sensenti and Asuncion Mita?), does he have any evidence of it in the Zapotitan basin? Where are the vaulted buildings, the carved stelae, the hieroglyphic stairways, the ballcourts?

The new information available from the Sula and Comayagua valleys is still very partial and preliminary and any interpretation has to be very cautious. The sample presented by Robinson is not as representative as she claims: if the transects represent 14% of her universe (the southeastern part of the Sula Valley), her maps show that the area really surveyed is much less. But for a few exceptions, the sites are concentrated on the easternmost edges of her transects. She assumes as a "working hypothesis" that all of her 18 sites are Late Classic, on the basis of tests in two sites. There is a strong probability that at least some sites have major Late Preclassic or Early Classic components; in these cases, even if they were occupied in the Late Classic as well, the inhabitants had to take into account the earlier constructions and the site plan would not reflect "pure" Late Classic settlement norms, but, rather, an adaptation, or even a tolerance, to an earlier pattern. Besides, most of the inferences that Robinson draws from her data are disputable insofar as she has no picture of the whole settlement network in the valley. The very limited areas she presents can very well be marginal to others with larger sites, higher mounds, and so forth.

According to the short and preliminary descriptions by Agurcia of Late Classic settlements in the Comayagua valley, (dates were checked through surface ceramics), these look much like the Sula sites. When compared to the Maya lowland settlement pattern(s), the Honduras settlements appear to be more dependent on topographic constraints. The disposition of the structures is partly determined by the contours. This means that the Periphery peoples were not ready to undertake large earth-moving work, unlike the Maya.

Quelepa, in eastern El Salvador, is a notable exception. In the Periphery, the structure arrangements are less rigid and less systematic; they even sometimes look haphazard. Most often the linear pattern is the result of topography. The plaza arrangement is not a Maya nor even a Mesoamerican exclusive trait; as Thompson noted (1970: 85) it is found from the United States to Panama.

In architecture, the use of cut stone is rare and is replaced by cobble masonry. When structures are built that way they do not well survive the ravages of time, and it is often hard to ascertain whether they were terraced or not. I would guess, through comparison with examples I know at Los Naranjos and Curruste, that most of the structures higher than 2 m were terraced and had a ramp or stairway for access. The public buildings are relatively modest in size, execution, and decoration. Because of the poor quality of cobble architecture, the destruction rate is important and the mounds represent the remains of much higher structures. Even so, their estimated cost in manpower is relatively lower than what was required for most of the Maya civic or public works. Use of plaster is uncommon. I think that Robinson's Types III and IV (large hamlets and small villages) do exist among the Maya even if the major buildings are lower in the Sula valley than in the Maya area. A lesser mound height does not imply that "differences in status were not as pronounced in the Sula valley as in the central Maya zone." A site like Travesia (Stone 1941) would constitute a Type V, an analog to the Maya minor ceremonial center. The major difference between the Sula valley and any lowland Maya region is the absence of a major center comparable to Copan or Quirigua, and this difference is an expression of the chiefdom-state opposition. At the village level, no significant differences between periphery and center are noticeable; it is only a matter of degree: sites are smaller, buildings are lower, more simply and crudely built. But the Maya patterns (stepped pyramids, stairways, ballcourts, etc.) are a permanent source of inspiration. The Sula and Comayagua valleys, along with the Lake Yojoa region, not only had many traits in common (in settlement pattern but also in ceramics and artifacts) but shared a common history. Although they never experienced the social and cultural complexity of the Classic Maya civilization, they developed in its shadow, reaching their demographic and cultural zenith and nadir when the Maya had theirs. In other terms, they rose and fell with the Maya.

Within this symphony, the Naco valley sounds a discordant note, as it offers a very fascinating case of "inner marginalism" within an already marginal area. The settlement pattern as well as the ceramics are remarkably conservative; one does not observe major cultural changes at the beginning as at the end of the Late Classic period. The Naco valley does not share its neighbors' interest toward the Usulutan pottery in Late Preclassic and Early Classic times, nor in the Babilonia (Ulua-Yojoa) Polychrome of the Late Classic, nor in the Las Vegas of the following period. The Maya collapse does not seem to have affected it as the valley population does not shrink before A.D. 1100, i.e., at least two centuries later. I do not have any hypothesis to offer for explaining this strange case of cultural isolation. I cannot help but observe how paradoxical it is that perhaps the most peripheral region of the Periphery is located not far, but at the same distance, from the major centers of Copan and Quirigua and "is part of a natural trans-isthmian corridor between the Caribbean and the Pacific" (Wonderley, this volume). This shows that distance from the center and marginality are not directly correlated and that there are no natural trade routes or corridors. These become "natural" only when they are used as such.

The Postclassic period is very poorly known in the Periphery and the investigations at Naco only deserve comment here. The major changes experienced by Naco around A.D. 1250 certainly require major attention as far as their origin may throw light on southern Mesoamerican history after the fall of Toltec Chichen. Unfortunately, too little is known of this period to allow fruitful comparisons. Personally, I am not wholly convinced by Wonderley's attempts to interpret these new data, which do not seem to confirm the site intrusion hypothesis: intrasite oppositions between a supposed "Mexican" elite and an indigenous peasantry are far from being evidenced. The stimulus diffusion process would be another likely possibility. As for the origin(s) of the new traits, it (they) cannot be pinpointed in the present state of our knowledge.

The papers here reviewed and commented upon are witnesses of the amount of archaeological work undertaken in the Periphery these last years. Most of these studies are in their early beginnings but we may rather soon expect to get a much clearer picture of the cultural history of the Southeast Periphery.

ROBERT J. SHARER   **22**

Summary of Southeastern Periphery Papers

Introduction

The papers included in this section are illustrative of the recent advances made in the archaeology of the Southeastern Periphery. Several of these studies (especially those by Agurcia, Robinson, and Urban) are based in settlement archaeology and thereby generate hypotheses concerning ancient socio-political organization founded on the premise that settlement patterning reflects these systems. Often the settlement data is used in conjunction with artifactual and architectural evidence, with the predominant data, not surprisingly, being provided by ceramics. Most of the remaining papers, less directly based in settlement archaeology, rely more exclusively on material culture (Bruhns, Demarest and Sharer, Kennedy, and Wonderley) to develop hypotheses usually quite consistent with the settlement studies. Sheets' contribution stands somewhat apart in that it begins with a theoretical position—the impact of volcanism on human population—to provide a framework for describing the consequences of volcanism within a specific region (Zapotitan Basin, El Salvador).

Implicit in comparing these approaches, as in any collection of papers representing separate research, is a series of methodological and theoretical differences. In a few cases, these are made explicit, as with the procedures and ends of ceramic analysis discussed by two papers (Kennedy, Demarest and Sharer).

This variability in methodological and theoretical approaches may, to a greater or lesser degree, inhibit comparison and synthesis. In this summary, to encourage the goal of understanding the prehistoric developments in the Southeastern Periphery, I will downplay these differences and emphasize the complementary and reinforcing ideas advanced by each author.

Summary of Papers

The contribution by Agurcia, while clearly a preliminary study, is a significant initial step towards defining a settlement typology in the Comayagua valley. It can only be hoped that the tantalizing conclusions drawn from this survey can be followed by further investigation. Agurcia describes the known settlement patterns of sites in the Comayagua valley, including four previously undocumented centers, approximately dated by ceramic surface collections. Two of these newly reported sites are sizeable: Carpules de Valladolid (over 200 mounds) and El Taladro (over 100 mounds). Within the valley he defines two major classes of remains, large civic-type platforms and small residential-type platforms, together with two recognizable patterns: linear arrangements and plaza groupings. The former is seen as reflecting an indigenous pattern (reinforced by noting that similar arrangements predominate at Yarumela and at sites in eastern El Salvador), and the latter is identified with lowland Maya prototypes. Agurcia then notes how this settlement dichotomy parallels previously proposed contrasts between indigenous and Maya affiliations in the artifactual (largely ceramic) remains of the Comayagua valley. After describing these data, Agurcia correctly cautions about premature conclusions, pending further research. He does venture his preliminary opinion that conflict played a role in the apparent intrusion of Maya patterns into the Comayagua valley—as evidenced by the famed fortified site of Tenampua—but this seems to be only one of many possibilities to be investigated in the future.

Robinson reports the results of a methodologically complex settlement survey in the Sula valley, but her results are compatible with more traditional surveys such as those reported by Agurcia and Urban. The Sula valley study utilized a 14% stratified random transect sample to locate the mapped sites. The 1 km wide transects extended east-west across the valley, cross-cutting the major biotic zones paralleling the river course. Within each transect, survey coverage varied according to local conditions, with techniques ranging from walking major roads and use of local informants in densely cultivated areas, to total coverage in the alluvial fans along the eastern edge of the valley when visibility and preservation were optimal.

The analysis reported here is based solely on data from these areas of maximum coverage (18 of the best-preserved sites).

Size and form were emphasized to construct, by means of cluster analysis, a typology of mounds and sites. Nine mound classes are defined: Types 1–3 represent large, special function platforms associated with the largest plazas. Types 4 and 5 are intermediate—the first form plazas with Types 1–3 while the second are associated with the smaller mound Types 6–9. Types 6–9 correspond in size and shape to what are usually labeled housemounds. Four site classes are defined and interpreted as representing (from smallest to largest) nuclear family residences, extended family residences, hamlets, and villages. The two types of residential groupings are equivalent to lowland Maya settlement types (informal groups, patio groups, and informal clusters, cf. Ashmore, 1981b), but the hamlet and village patterns are without close analogs in the Maya lowlands and represent, presumably, an indigenous tradition.

Urban describes her settlement survey of the Naco Valley (less the sites of Naco and La Sierra) aimed at establishing a chronological sequence based primarily on ceramics, a definition of settlement patterns, and a description of architectural form and function. A near 100% coverage of the valley resulted in the location of 130 sites and test excavations were subsequently concluded at 19 of these. Excavated materials dating to the Preclassic and to the Protoclassic (Periods 1 through 3) are limited to one site (#123), although there are three smaller sites containing Period 3 ceramics. During the Early Classic (Period 4) settlement disperses to at least 14 sites, but none is as large as the previously dominant site #123. Settlement expands during the Late Classic (at least 30 sites occupied during Period 5-A and 27 occupied during Period 5-B, with an additional 16 sites inhabited during Period 5, facet unspecifiable on present evidence), and the valley appears dominated by the center of La Sierra. There is continuity in settlement during the Early Postclassic, although some decrease in occupation may be indicated (18 sites occupied in Period 6-A and 11 in Period 6-B; six sites are assigned to Period 6 in general, with no facet indicable). Site planning is similar in all periods, with non-orthogonal arrangements and use of "saddle" platform connections, as are construction methods using earth and cobble fills with bajareque and cobble walls. Cut stone is rare, found only at La Sierra and one other site.

A local and conservative tradition in ceramics, architecture, and site planning is delineated by Urban, from the beginning of the Classic era through the Early Postclassic. No reflection of the lowland Maya Classic "collapse" is detectable here, and external trade contacts seem to be a constant, although minor, constituent. The most dramatic shift in the Naco valley occurs in the Late Postclassic.

Wonderley's study of the site of Naco continues the reconstruction provided by Urban for the entire valley. At Naco, there appears to be considerable continuity in the local ceramic traditions through the early facet of the Late Postclassic period. At this point in time the appearance of a series of new ceramic types and modes added to the indigenous inventory defines the middle facet of the Late Postclassic. Similar additions in the rest of the artifactual, culinary, and architectural record also mark this period. The most dramatic evidence of this change is a sudden increase in the volume of obsidian importation and use at Naco. Wonderley considers a sudden in situ population growth as an explanation for these shifts, but concludes, rightfully I believe, that the available record reflects a significant intrusion of new population elements at Naco. He then presents some convincing evidence linking this intrusive population with the riverine southern Maya lowlands. From this he infers the identity of the outsiders as Mexicanized Chontal Maya from this region, consistent with ethnohistoric accounts. Intrasite patterning also reflects a subtle, but seemingly significant, contrast between a central area with more prevalent "Mexicanized" traits—seen as the probable zone occupied by foreign elites—and the surrounding area, probably occupied by the indigenous population.

Bruhns reviews the available evidence concerning the use and abandonment of the important Early Postclassic center of Cihuatan, long known for its explicit Mexican-style artifacts and architecture. Her paper is concerned more with interpretation than with details of evidence, so that the reconstructions seem very speculative, although intriguing.

The founding of Cihuatan, possibly by elite colonists from Veracruz, according to Bruhns, is seen as part of a major reorientation of settlement in El Salvador following a widespread disruption at the close of the Classic, apparently linked to the "collapse" in the Maya lowlands. Yet the evidence for this southeastern disruption remains elusive and, in some cases, indicates quite the contrary—a continuity of occupation from Late Classic to Early Postclassic as at Chalchuapa (Sharer, ed., 1978).

The primary function of Cihuatan is postulated as a trading and commercial agricultural center, specializing in the production of cotton and cacao. The best evidence for this seems to be a suitable local environment for growing these crops, and the remains of check-dams in the vicinity of Cihuatan presumably once functioning as part of an irrigation system (although these features remain undated). Also, of course, both cotton and cacao were important products of this region at the time of the Conquest. But, as Bruhns points out, there is even less archaeological information concerning the Late Postclassic or the period linking the abandonment of Cihuatan with the historically recorded centers of the Spanish period. Nonetheless, economic factors are also seen as responsible for the abandonment of Cihuatan, ca. 100–150 years after its founding, although warfare is also advanced as playing a role. Clearly, much work remains to be done to test the propositions outlined in Bruhns' paper.

The paper by Demarest and Sharer is based on comparative ceramic data provided by several research projects. With allowances for the obscuring of pottery similarities by use of different classificatory methods, two new separate ceramic spheres are proposed for the Late Preclassic Southeastern Maya Highlands. Termed the Providencia and Miraflores ceramic spheres, they are defined by an unusually large number of homologous types and modes. Their tentative spatial and temporal limits are hypothesized based on available data, as are their known intra-sphere variations. It is also suggested that these Late Preclassic spheres derive from an earlier, Middle Preclassic sphere, but definition of this entity must await an expanded data base. The cultural significance of the Late Preclassic spheres is explored by noting their correspondence to the distributions of a series of homologous material remains, including pottery figurines and other ceramic artifacts, incensarios, sculptured monuments, lithic assemblages, and, to the extent known, architecture and settlement patterning. In sum, this distribution suggests a unified cultural area, reflecting rather intense and continuous interaction among (perhaps) a single linguistic and ethnic group. I might add that in many ways these Late Preclassic highland ceramic spheres appear to reflect a socio-political situation analogous to that reflected in the Chicanel ceramic sphere of the Maya lowlands. The paper concludes by suggesting means to refine and test these assumptions.

Based on her research at Playa de los Muertos, Kennedy defined three Preclassic ceramic complexes demonstrating both local continuity and increasing connections with external regions through time. The earliest of these, Zanjos (ca. 650–450 B.C.), in its external ties, is equated with the Isthmian "Pre-Mayan tradition" defined by Lowe (1978). The Sula Complex (ca. 450–300 B.C.) reflects ceramic modes apparently originating in the Southeastern Highlands recombined within the local Playa de los Muertos tradition. Finally, the Toyos Complex (ca. 300–100 B.C.) features broadening external ties, including those to the Southeastern highlands, the Maya lowlands, and Lake Yojoa (Los Naranjos), as well as more distant areas. These outside connections are seen as reflecting involvement by Playa de Los Muertos in an expanding long-distance trade network.

Kennedy's interpretation contrasts with Strong, Kidder, and Paul's (1938) pioneering research at the site. She explains how the original ceramic classification was only preliminary and emphasized specialty wares, thus overlooking the more common and diagnostic Preclassic modes. As a result, Playa de los Muertos was inaccurately seen as peripheral, or even retarded, in its ceramic development due to its seemingly unusual pottery and its apparent lack of the more typical elements found in neighboring ceramic inventories.

The recent research by Kennedy has corrected these distortions and firmly established Playa de los Muertos in its proper perspective, well integrated in the Mesoamerican Preclassic ceramic tradition. Furthermore, she argues with justification that terms such as peripheral or frontier are inappropriate for this area, at least during the Preclassic. Instead, Kennedy suggests a more neutral term, such as ethnotone (analogous to ecotone) to describe areas of apparent ancient ethnic transition.

Sheets presents a resume of the research design that guided the Proyecto Protoclassico in its investigation of the Zapotitan basin in El Salvador. The central theme of this research was the study of the impact of volcanism in a prehistoric setting. Evidence for four volcanic eruptions was revealed in the archaeological record. The most profound of these was the Ilopango event dated to the Late Preclassic-Classic period transition. Sheets presents three alternative hypotheses to describe the consequences of the Ilopango eruption and ash fall in the Zapotitan basin together with the test implications for each: 1) incomplete emigration with survivors continuing to subsist in less devastated areas such as hilly flanks of the basin; 2) complete emigration followed by eventual and gradual recolonization by peripheral Maya groups from the north (Motagua-Ulua region); 3) complete emigration followed by eventual and rapid recolonization by lowland Maya groups. Tested against the archaeological data, Sheets reports that hypothesis 1 receives the least support, hypothesis 2 is partially supported, and hypothesis 3 receives the strongest support.

This evidence suggests the unusually profound disruptive effects of the Ilopango eruption, for most volcanic eruptions, including the other three documented in the Zapotitan sequence, produce only local and short-term consequences. In fact, in reviewing the world-wide incidence of ancient eruptions, Sheets points out only two other volcanic events with comparable consequences (Thera in the Aegean and Mt. Saint Elias on the Alaska-Canada border).

Conclusions

To conclude this all too brief summary, I would like to focus on two related issues raised by the foregoing papers: the question of prehistoric ethnicity, and general cultural historical trends as presently known in the Southeast Mesoamerican Periphery.

Several strategies are pursued in attempting to identify prehistoric ethnic groups in these papers, as in distinguishing between lowland Maya and local settlement patterns, reinforced with data from other artifactual and architectural sources. Schortman (this volume) provides a detailed examination of the archaeological basis for the identification of Maya and non-Maya affiliation, together with the underlying assumptions and pitfalls in this endeavor, and these need not be repeated here. Suffice it to say that in cases devoid of historical evidence, ancient ethnic identification should be approached with caution, despite the fact that I once ventured such a hypothetical identification for one region of the Southeastern periphery (Sharer 1974). This is not to say that ethnic identification should not remain a goal in prehistoric archaeological research. Several of the papers in this volume have made important contributions to this topic. But at present we appear limited by the archaeological evidence to a rather simple (and thereby unrealistic) distinction between the lowland Maya and non-lowland Maya (or indigenous populations in the southeastern area). Obviously we should expect a more complex situation, recognizing at a minimum a continuum between these divisions, rather than a dichotomy, and eventually, perhaps, taking into account the diversity of ethnic groups in both time and space at both ends of this continuum.

The papers reviewed here also provide new insights into the culture history of the Southeast Periphery. It is becoming increasingly obvious that in a series of more favored regions of the southeast, long processes of cultural development during the Preclassic culminated in the emergence of complexly organized societies, interconnected by extensive regional and long distance exchange networks. Subtle variations seen in the archaeological evidence (settlement patterning, architectural form, ceramics, and other material remains) are, I believe, best described by Kennedy's concept of ethnotones. And following the suggestion made by Demarest and Sharer, these ethnotones may be subsumed within at least two widespread cultural traditions, one situated in the highlands of the Pacific Coast from central Guatemala to western El Salvador, and the other (still not well defined) seemingly extending from Honduras into eastern El Salvador. But above all, these emerging complex societies of the Late Preclassic are not well described by the term peripheral, as Kennedy makes clear. Instead, each should be viewed as a dynamic center of socio-political developments, such as those in the Ulua valley, the Copan valley, the valley of Guatemala, the Ahuachapan basin (Chalchuapa), and the Zapotitan basin.

The Late Preclassic-Classic transition appears to be marked by drastic changes throughout these areas brought about directly in some regions, or indirectly in others, by the devastating eruption of Ilopango and the population disruptions and decline that followed. Thereafter, a series of outside groups seem to impinge upon many areas effected by the Ilopango disaster. The Early Classic period is marked by lowland Maya colonization of the Motagua and Copan valleys and beyond, eventually reaching as far south as the Zapotitan basin in El Salvador. Also in the Early Classic, central Mexican colonists became established on the Pacific coast and at Kaminaljuyu to begin a period of active interaction with the lowland Maya at Tikal and elsewhere. It would appear that here the term peripheral becomes valid in application to the southeast, since in the Classic period this region did become economically, politically, and developmentally marginal to the centers of power in the Maya lowlands and central Mexico.

The Classic and Postclassic eras in this area can be typified as times of interaction and assimilation, as indigenous populations accommodated to the ebb and flow of outside influences and peoples. One illustration of these processes would be the apparent Mexican presence at Cihuatan and elsewhere in El Salvador. The last episode seems to have been the Mexicanized Maya colonization at Naco, although future research will doubtless reveal additional details of events during this period.

We still do not possess an adequate data base to flesh-out the details of culture history, and the reconstruction of the developmental trends in this area remain elusive. But the contributions offered here are indicative of the progress being made, and should provide an essential step towards a better understanding of the prehistory of the southeastern area.

Bibliography

Adams, R.

1971

The Ceramics of Altar de Sacrificios. Papers of the Peabody Museum, vol. 63, no. 1. Harvard University, Cambridge, Mass.

1981

Settlement Patterns of the Central Yucatan and Southern Campeche Regions in *Maya Lowland Settlement Patterns.* W. Ashmore, ed., pp. 211 – 258. Albuquerque: University of New Mexico Press, School of American Research Advanced Seminar.

Adams, R., and R. Jones

1981

Spatial Patterns and Regional Growth Among Classic Maya Cities. *American Antiquity* 46: 301–322.

Agrest, D., and M. Gandelsonas

1977

Semiotics and the Limits of Architecture in *A Perfusion of Signs.* T. Sebeok, ed., pp. 90–120. Bloomington: Indiana University Press.

Agurcia Fasquelle, R.

1976a

A Research Design for Archaeological Investigation in the Comayagua Valley. Ms., Department of Anthropology, Tulane University, New Orleans, La.

1976b

Los petroglifos de Valladolid, Comayagua in *Las Fronteras de Mesoamerica,* XIV Mesa Redonda de la Sociedad Mexicana de Antropologia vol. 1, pp. 229–236. Mexico.

1980

Late Classic Settlements in the Comayagua Valley. Paper presented at the 45th Annual Meeting of the Society for American Archaeology, Philadelphia, Pa.

Alvarado, P. de

1924

An Account of the Conquest of Guatemala in 1524. S. Mackie, ed. and trans. Documents and Narratives Concerning the Discovery and Conquest of Latin America, no. 3. New York: Cortes Society.

Anderson, B.
1978
Excavations at Laguna Cuzcachapa and Laguna Seca in *The Prehistory of Chalchuapa, El Salvador*. R. Sharer, ed., vol. 1, pp. 43–60. Philadelphia: University of Pennsylvania Press.

Anderson, D.
1978
Monuments in *The Prehistory of Chalchuapa, El Salvador*. R. Sharer, ed., vol. 1, pp. 155–180. Philadelphia: University of Pennsylvania Press.

Andrews, E. W., IV
1943
The Archaeology of Southwestern Campeche. Carnegie Institution of Washington Contributions to American Anthropology and History 8: 1–101. Washington, D. C.

Andrews, E. W., V
1972
Correspondencias fonogicas entre el Lenca y una lengua Mayance. *Estudios de Cultura Maya* 8: 341–387.
1976
The Archaeology of Quelepa, El Salvador. Middle American Research Institute, publication 42. Tulane University, New Orleans, La.
1977
The Southeast Periphery of Mesoamerica: A View from Eastern El Salvador in *Social Process in Maya Prehistory*. N. Hammond, ed., pp. 113–134. New York: Academic Press.

Andrews, G.
1975
Maya Cities: Placemaking and Urbanization. Norman: University of Oklahoma Press.

Anonymous
1548–1551   Tasaciones de los Naturales de las Provincias de Guathemala y Nicaragua y Yucatan e Pueblos de la Villa de Comaiagua se Sacaron por Mandado de los Senores Presidente y Oidores del Audiencia y Chancilleria Real de los Confines 1548–1551. Ms., Archivo General de las Indias, Audiencia de Guatemala. leg. 128, 410 folios. Seville.

Arnold, J., and A. Ford
1980
A Statistical Examination of Settlement Patterns at Tikal, Guatemala. *American Antiquity* 45: 713–726.

Ashmore, W.
1980a
The Classic Maya Settlement at Quirigua. *Expedition* 23: 20–27.
1980b
Discovering Early Classic Quirigua. *Expedition* 23: 35–44.
1980c
The Classic Maya Settlement at Quirigua. Paper presented at the 45th

Annual Meeting of the Society for American Archaeology, Philadelphia, Pa.

1981a

Precolumbian Occupation at Quirigua, Guatemala: Settlement Patterns in a Classic Maya Center. PhD Dissertation, Department of Anthropology, University of Pennsylvania, Philadelphia, Pa.

1981b

Some Issues of Method and Theory in Lowland Maya Settlement Archaeology in *Lowland Maya Settlement Patterns*. W. Ashmore, ed., pp. 37–69. Albuquerque: University of New Mexico Press, School of American Research Advanced Seminar.

1984

Quirigua Archaeology and History Revisited, *Journal of Field Archaeology* 11: 365–380.

in press

Research at Quirigua, Guatemala: The Site Periphery Program in *The Periphery of the Southeastern Maya Realm*. G. Pahl, ed., Los Angeles: UCLA Latin American Center.

Ashmore, W. (ed.)

1981

Lowland Maya Settlement Patterns. Albuquerque: University of New Mexico Press, School of American Research Advanced Seminar.

Ashmore, W., and R. Sharer

1975

A Revitalization Movement at Late Classic Tikal. Paper presented at the Area Seminars in Ongoing Research, Westchester State College, Westchester, Pa.

1978

Excavations at Quirigua, Guatemala: The Ascent of an Elite Maya Center. *Archaeology* 31: 10–19.

Ashmore, W., E. Schortman, and R. Sharer

1983

The Quirigua Project: 1979 season. *Quirigua Reports*. E. Schortman and P. Urban, eds., vol. II, pp. 55–78. Museum Monographs, University of Pennsylvania, Philadelphia, Pa.

Aveni, A.

1980

Skywatchers of Ancient Mexico. Austin: University of Texas Press.

Ball, J.

1983

Teotihuacan, the Maya, and Ceramic Interchange: A Contextual Perspective. in *Highland-Lowland Interaction in Mesoamerica: Interdisciplinary Approaches*. A. Miller, ed., pp. 125–145. Washington, D. C.: Dumbarton Oaks.

Barth, F.

1969

Introduction. in *Ethnic Groups and Boundaries: The Social Organization of Culture Difference*. F. Barth, ed., pp. 9–38. Boston: Little, Brown, and Co.

Barth, F. (ed.)

1969

Ethnic Groups and Boundaries: The Social Organization of Culture Difference. Boston: Little, Brown, and Co.

Baudez, C.

1966

Niveaux ceramiques au Honduras: une reconsideration de l'evolution culturelle. *Journal de la Societe des Americanistes* 55: 299–341.

1970

The Ancient Civilization of Central America. London: Barrie and Jenkins.

1976

Arqueologia de la frontera sur de Mesoamerica. in *Las Fronteras de Mesoamerica*, XIV Mesa Redonda de la Sociedad Mexicana de Antropologia, vol.1, pp. 133–146. Mexico.

Baudez, C., and P. Becquelin

1973

Archeologie de Los Naranjos, Honduras. Mission Archeologique et Ethnologique Francaise au Mexique. vol. II, Etudes Americaines. Mexico.

Beaudry, M.

1977

Classification and Analysis of Painted Ceramics from La Canteada, Copan, Honduras (D-4). Master's Thesis, Archaeology, University of California, Los Angeles, Ca.

1978

Preliminary Analysis of Ceramics from the 1978 Protoclassic Project, Zapotitan Basin, El Salvador. in *Research of the Protoclassic Project in the Zapotitan Basin, El Salvador*. P. Sheets, ed., pp. 73–82. Department of Anthropology, University of Colorado, Boulder, Co.

Bebrich, C., Jr.

1969

Kaminaljuyu During the Terminal Formative Period. Paper presented at the 68th Annual Meeting of the American Anthropological Association, New Orleans, La.

Becker, M.

1971

The Identification of a Second Plaza Plan at Tikal, Guatemala, and its Implications for Ancient Maya Social Complexity. PhD Dissertation, Department of Anthropology, University of Pennsylvania, Philadelphia, Pa.

1972

Plaza Plans at Quirigua, Guatemala. *Katunob* VIII: 47–62.

Benyo, J.

1979

The Pottery Censers of Quirigua, Izabal, Guatemala. Master's Thesis, Department of Anthropology, State University of New York, Albany, NY.

Bergmann, J.
1969
The Distribution of Cacao Cultivation in Pre-Columbian America. *Annals of the Association of American Geographers* 59: 85–96.
Berlin, H.
1952
Novedades Arqueologicas. *Antropologia e Historia de Guatemala*, Publicacion no. 2: 41–46.
1956
Late Pottery Horizons of Tabasco, Mexico. Carnegie Institution of Washington Contributions to American Anthropology and History 12: 95–153. Washington, D. C.
1977
Signos y significados en las inscripciones Mayas. Guatemala.
Binford, L.
1962
Archaeology as Anthropology. *American Antiquity* 28: 217–225.
Bishop, R.
1980
Aspects of Compositional Modeling. in *Models and Methods in Regional Exchange.* R. Fry, ed., pp. 47–66. Society for American Archaeology, SAA Papers no. 1.
Bishop, R., and R. Rands
1982
Maya Fine Paste Ceramics: A Compositional Perspective. in *Analyses of Fine Paste Ceramics, Excavations at Seibal.* J. Sabloff, ed., pp. 35–67. Memoirs of the Peabody Museum, vol. 15, no. 2. Harvard University, Cambridge, Mass.
Bishop, R., A. Demarest, and R. Sharer
n.d.a.
Chemical Analysis and the Interpretation of Late Preclassic Intersite Ceramic Patterns in the Southeast Highlands of Mesoamerica. Brookhaven National Laboratory Report BNL 30699. Upton, NY.
n.d.b.
An Interregional Pattern of the Late Preclassic in Southeastern Mesoamerica: Compositional Analyses and Interpretation of the Highland Ceramic Spheres. Ms., Smithsonian Institution, Washington, D. C.
Bishop, R., G. Harbottle, and E. Sayre
1982
Chemical and Mathematical Procedures Employed in the Mayan Fine Paste Ceramics Project. in *Analyses of Fine Paste Ceramics, Excavations at Seibal.* J. Sabloff, ed., pp. 272–282. Memoirs of the Peabody Museum, vol. 15, no. 2. Harvard University, Cambridge, Mass.
Bishop, R., R. Rands, and G. Harbottle
1982
A Ceramic Compositional Interpretation on Incense-Burner Trade in the

Palenque Area. in *Nuclear and Chemical Dating Methods*. L. Currie, ed., pp. 411–419. Washington, D. C.: American Chemical Society.

Bishop, R., R. Rands and G. Holley

1982

Ceramic Compositional Analysis in Archaeological Perspective. in *Advances in Archaeological Method and Theory*. M. Schiffer, ed., vol. 5, pp. 275–330. New York: Academic Press.

Bishop, R., M. Beaudry, R. Leventhal, and R. Sharer

in press

Compositional Analysis of Classic Period Painted Ceramics in the Southeast Maya Area. *Yaxkin*.

Black, K.

1979

Preliminary Report on the Survey of the Zapotitan Basin area. in *Research of the Protoclassic Project in the Zapotitan Basin, El Salvador: A Preliminary Report of the 1978 Season*. P. Sheets, ed., Department of Anthropology, University of Colorado, Boulder, Co.

Blackith, R. and R. Reyment

1971

Multivariate Morphometrics. New York: Academic Press.

Boas, F.

1948

Race, Language, and Culture. New York: Macmillan.

Boggs, S.

1943

Observaciones respecto a la importancia de "Tazumal" en la prehistoria Salvadoreña. *Tzunpane* 3: 127–133.

1944

Excavations in Central and Western El Salvador. in *Archaeological Investigations in El Salvador*. J. Longyear, III, ed., appendix C. Memoirs of the Peabody Museum, vol. IX, no. 2. Harvard University, Cambridge, Mass.

1945a

Archaeological Materials from the Club International. Carnegie Institute of Washington, Notes on Middle American Archaeology and Ethnology, vol. 2, no. 60. Washington, D. C.

1945a

Informe sobre la tercera temporada de excavaciones en las ruinas de "Tazumal." *Tzunpane* 5: 33–45.

1950a

Archaeological Investigations in El Salvador. in *For the Dean: Essays in Anthropology in Honor of Byron S. Cummings*. E. Reed and D. King, eds., pp. 259–276. Hohokam Museums Association and the Southwest Monuments Association, Santa Fe, New Mexico.

1950b

Olmec Pictographs in the Las Victorias Group, Chalchuapa Zone, El Sal-

vador. Carnegie Institution of Washington, Notes on Middle American Archaeology and Ethnology, no. 99. Washington, D. C.

1972

Figurillas con ruedas de Cihuatan y el oriente de El Salvador. *Ministerio de Educacion, Coleccion de Antropologia,* no. 2. San Salvador, El Salvador.

Borhegyi, S.

1951a

A Study of Three-Pronged Incense Burners from Guatemala and Adjacent Areas. Carnegie Institution of Washington, Notes on Middle American Archaeology and Ethnology, no. 101. Washington, D. C.

1951b

Further Notes on Three-Pronged Incense Burners and Rim-Head Vessels in Guatemala. Carnegie Institution of Washington, Notes on Middle American Archaeology and Ethnology, no. 105. Washington, D. C.

1965a

Archaeological Synthesis of the Guatemalan Highlands. in *Handbook of Middle American Indians.* R. Wauchope and G. Willey, eds., vol. 2, pp. 3–58. Austin: University of Texas Press.

1965b

Settlement Patterns of the Guatemalan Highlands. in *Handbook of Middle American Indians.* R. Wauchope and G. Willey, eds., vol. 2, pp. 59–75. Austin: University of Texas Press.

Bray, W.

1977

Maya Metalwork and its External Connections. in *Social Process in Maya Prehistory.* N. Hammond, ed., pp. 365–403. New York: Academic Press.

Bricker, V.

1983

Directional Glyphs in Maya Inscriptions and Codices. *American Antiquity* 48: 347–353.

Brooks, D., A. Bieber, Jr., G. Harbottle, and E. Sayre

1974

Biblical Studies through Activation Analysis of Ancient Pottery. in *Archaeological Chemistry.* C. Beck, ed., pp. 48–80. Advances in Chemistry Series 138. Washington, D. C.: American Chemical Society.

Brose, D.

1979

A Speculative Model for the Role of Exchange in the Prehistory of the Eastern Woodlands. in *Hopewell Archaeology: The Chillicothe Conference.* D. Brose and N. Greber, eds., pp. 3–8. Kent, Ohio: Kent State University Press.

Brown, K.

1977

The Valley of Guatemala: A Highland Port of Trade. in *Teotihuacan and*

Kaminaljuyu: A Study in Prehistoric Culture Contact. W. Sanders and J. Michels, eds., pp. 205–395. University Park: The Pennsylvania State University Press.

Bruhns, K.

1980a

Cihuatan: An Early Postclassic Town of El Salvador. The 1977–1978 Excavations. University of Missouri Monographs in Anthropology, no. 5. Columbia, Mo.

1980b

Plumbate Origins Revisited. *American Antiquity* 45: 845–848.

Bullard, W., Jr.

1960

Maya Settlement Pattern in Northeast Peten, Guatemala. *American Antiquity* 25: 355–372.

1970

Topoxte: A Postclassic Maya Site in Peten, Guatemala. in *Monographs and Papers in Maya Archaeology.* W. Bullard, Jr., ed., Papers of the Peabody Museum, no. 61, pp. 245–307. Harvard University, Cambridge, Mass.

1973

Postclassic Culture in Central Peten and Adjacent British Honduras. in *The Classic Maya Collapse.* T. Culbert, ed., pp. 221–242. Albuquerque: University of New Mexico Press, School of American Research Advanced Seminar.

Burton, I., R. Kates, and G. White

1978

The Environment as Hazard. New York: Oxford University Press.

Caldwell, J.

1970

Interaction Spheres in Prehistory. in *Hopewellian Studies.* J. Caldwell and R. Hall, eds., pp. 133–143. Illinois State Museum Scientific Papers no. 12. (originally published in 1964).

Campbell, L.

1976

The Linguistic Prehistory of the Southern Mesoamerican Periphery. in *Las Fronteras de Mesoamerica,* XIV Mesa Redonda de la Sociedad Mexicana de Antropologia, vol. 1, pp. 157–183. Mexico.

Canby, J.

1949

Excavations at Yarumela, Spanish Honduras. PhD Dissertation, Department of Anthropology, Harvard University, Cambridge, Mass.

1951

Possible Chronological Implications of the Long Ceramic Sequence Recovered at Yarumela, Spanish Honduras. in *The Civilizations of Ancient America.* S. Tax, ed., pp. 79–85. Chicago: University of Chicago Press (selected papers from the 29th International Congress of Americanists).

Carmack, R.
1968
Toltec Influence on the Post-Classic Culture History of Highland Guatemala. Middle American Research Institute, publication 26. Tulane University, New Orleans.

Chamberlain, R.
1953
The Conquest and Colonization of Honduras: 1502–1550. Carnegie Institution of Washington, publication no. 598. Washington, D. C.

Chase, A.
1979
Regional Development in the Tayasal-Paxcaman Zone, El Peten, Guatemala: A Preliminary Statement. *Ceramica de Cultura Maya* 11: 86–119.

Chase, D.
1981
The Maya Postclassic at Santa Rita Corozal. *Archaeology* 34: 25–33.

Chase, D., and A. Chase
1982
Yucatec Influence in Terminal Classic Northern Belize. *American Antiquity* 47: 596–614.

Cheek, C.
1977a
Excavations at the Palangana and the Acropolis, Kaminaljuyu. in *Teotihuacan and Kaminaljuyu: A Study in Prehistoric Culture Contact.* W. Sanders and J. Michels, eds., pp. 1–224. University Park: The Pennsylvania State University Press.

1977b
Teotihuacan Influence at Kaminaljuyu. in *Teotihuacan and Kaminaljuyu: A Study in Prehistoric Culture Contact.* W. Sanders and J. Michels, eds., pp. 441–452. University Park: The Pennsylvania State University Press.

1983
Las excavaciones en la Plaza Principal: Resumen y conclusiones. in *Introduccion a la Arqueologia de Copan,* vol. 2. SECTUR, Tegucigalpa, Honduras.

Childe, V.
1947
Archaeology as a Social Science. in *Third Annual Report of the Institute of Archaeology,* pp. 49–60. London: University of London.

Coe, M.
1961
La Victoria: An Early Site on the Pacific Coast of Guatemala. Papers of the Peabody Museum, vol. 53. Harvard University, Cambridge, Mass.

Coe, W.
1965
Caches and Offertory Practices of the Maya Lowlands. in *Handbook of*

Middle American Indians. R. Wauchope and G. Willey, eds., pp. 441–461. Austin: University of Texas Press.
1970
Tikal, a Handbook of the Ancient Maya Ruins. 3rd ed. Philadelphia: The University Museum, University of Pennsylvania.
Coggins, C.
1967
Palaces and the Planning of Ceremonial Centers in the Southern Maya Lowlands. Ms., Tozzer Library, Peabody Museum, Harvard University, Cambridge, Mass.
1975
Painting and Drawing Styles at Tikal: An Historical and Iconographic Reconstruction. PhD Dissertation, Department of Fine Arts, Harvard University, Cambridge, Mass.
1980
The Shape of Time: Some Political Implications of a Four-Part Figure. *American Antiquity* 45: 727–739.
Cohadas, M.
1976
The Iconography of the Panels of the Sun, Cross, and Foliated Cross at Palenque: Part III. in *The Art, Iconography and Dynastic History of Palenque, Part III.* M. Robertson, ed., pp. 155–176. Pebble Beach, Ca.: Robert Louis Stevenson School.
Cohen, R.
1978
Ethnicity: Problem and Focus in Anthropology. in *Annual Review of Anthropology.* B. Seigel, A. Beals, and S. Tyler, eds., vol. 7, pp. 379–403. Palo Alto: Annual Reviews Inc.
Collins, T.
1975
Behavioral Change and Ethnic Maintenance Among the Northern Ute: Some Political Considerations. in *The New Ethnicity: Perspectives from Ethnology.* J. Bennett, ed., pp. 59–74. New York: West Publishing Co.
Cortes, H.
1908
Hernando Cortes: His Five Letters of Relation to the Emperor Charles V. F. MacNutt, trans. 2 vols. New York and London.
1971
Hernan Cortes' Letters from Mexico. A. Pagden, ed. and trans. New York: Grossman.
Crane, R.
1976
Informe preliminar de las excavaciones arqueologicas de rescate efectuadas en 1974 en la Hacienda "Colima," Departamento de Cuscatlan (proyecto no. 2, Programa "Cerron Grande"). *Anales del Museo Nacional "David J. Guzman,"* nos. 42–48: 13–28.

1978
Notes on a Pre-Columbian Grave from North-Central El Salvador. *Codex Wauchope, Human Mosaic* 12: 145–150.
Culbert, T.
1973
The Maya Downfall at Tikal. in *The Classic Maya Collapse*. T. Culbert, ed., pp. 63–92. Albuquerque: University of New Mexico Press, School of American Research Advanced Seminar.
Dahlin, B.
1976
An Anthropologist Looks at the Pyramids: A Late Classic Revitalization Movement at Tikal, Guatemala. PhD Dissertation, Department of Anthropology, Temple University, Philadelphia, Pa.
1978
Figurines. in *The Prehistory of Chalchuapa, El Salvador.* R. Sharer, ed., vol. 2, pp. 134–178. Philadelphia: University of Pennsylvania Press.
1979
Cropping Cash in the Protoclassic: A Cultural Impact Statement. in *Maya Archaeology and Ethnohistory.* N. Hammond and G. Willey, eds., pp. 21–37. Austin: University of Texas Press.
Daugherty, H.
1969
Man-Induced Ecological Change in El Salvador. PhD Dissertation, Department of Geography, University of California, Los Angeles, Ca.
Demarest, A.
1981
The Development of Complex Society in the Highlands of Southeastern Mesoamerica. PhD Dissertation, Department of Anthropology, Harvard University, Cambridge, Mass.
in press
Santa Leticia Project, First Preliminary Report. *Anales del Museo Nacional "David J. Guzman"* 1977–78.
Demarest, A., and R. Sharer
1982
The Origins and Evolution of the Usulutan Ceramic Style. *American Antiquity* 47: 810–822.
Demarest, A., R. Switsur, and R. Berger.
1982
The Dating and Cultural Associations of the Pot-Bellied Sculptural Style. *American Antiquity* 47: 557–571.
Despres, L.
1975
Ethnicity and Ethnic Group Relations in Guyana. in *The New Ethnicity: Perspectives from Ethnology.* J. Bennet, ed., pp. 127–147. New York: West Publishing Co.

Doxiadis, C.
1970
Ekistics, the Science of Human Settlements. *Science* 170: 393–404.

Drucker, P.
1943
Ceramic Sequences of Tres Zapotes, Veracruz, Mexico. Smithsonian Institution Bulletin 140. Washington, D. C.

du Toit, B.
1975
Introduction: Migration and Population Mobility. in *Migration and Urbanization.* B. du Toit and H. Safa, eds., pp. 1–15. The Hague: Mouton.

Earnest, H., Jr.
1976
Proyecto de rescate "Cerron Grande." Excavaciones-interpretaciones "Hacienda Santa Barbara." *Coleccion de Antropologia e Historia*, no. 7. Administracion del Patrimonio Cultural, San Salvador, El Salvador.

Erasmus, C.
1965
Monument Building: Some Field Experiments. *Southwestern Journal of Anthropology* 21: 277–301.

Fash, W.
1980
Informe final, reconocimiento del valle. Ms., Proyecto Arqueologico Copan, Copan, Honduras.
1982
A Middle Formative Cemetary at Copan, Honduras. Paper presented at the 81st Annual Meeting of the American Anthropological Association, Washington, D. C.
1983a
Deducing Social Organization from Classic Maya Settlement Patterns: A Case Study from the Copan Valley. in *Civilization in the Ancient Americas: Essays in Honor of Gordon R. Willey.* R. Leventhal and A. Kolata, eds., pp. 261–288. Albuquerque: University of New Mexico Press and Peabody Museum of Archaeology and Ethnology, Harvard University.

Fash, W., and S. Lane
1983
El Juego de Pelota B. in *Introduccion a la Arqueologia de Copan*, vol. 3. SECTUR, Tegucigalpa, Honduras.

Fash, W., and K. Long
1983
La mapa arqueologica del Valle de Copan. in *Introduccion a la Arqueologia de Copan*, vol. 3. SECTUR, Tegucigalpa, Honduras.

Feldman, L.
1975
Riverine Maya—the Torquegua and other Chols of the Lower Motagua Valley. University of Missouri, Columbia Museum, Brief 15. Columbia, Mo.

Fishman, J.
1977
Language and Ethnicity. in *Language, Ethnicity and Intergroup Relations.* H. Giles, ed., pp. 15–57. New York: Academic Press.

Flannery, K.
1968
The Olmec and the Valley of Oaxaca: A Model for Inter-Regional Interaction in Formative Times. in *Dumbarton Oaks Conference on the Olmecs.* E. Benson, ed., pp. 79–110. Washington, D. C.: Dumbarton Oaks.

Flannery, K. (ed.)
1976
The Early Mesoamerican Village. New York: Academic Press.

Fowler, W., Jr.
1976
Programa de rescate arqueologica "Cerron Grande," sub-proyecto Hacienda Las Flores. *Anales del Museo Nacional "David J. Guzman"* 49: 13–50.

Fowler, W., Jr. and E. Solis A.
1977
El mapa de Santa Maria: Un sitio post-clasico de la region "Cerron Grande." *Anales del Museo Nacional "David J. Guzman"* 50: 13–20.

Fox, J.
1978
Quiche Conquest. Albuquerque: University of New Mexico Press.
1981
The Late Postclassic Eastern Frontier of Mesoamerica: Cultural Innovation Along the Periphery. *Current Anthropology* 22: 321–346.

Freidel, D.
1976
Late Postclassic Settlement Patterns on Cozumel Island, Quintana Roo, Mexico. PhD Dissertation, Department of Anthropology, Harvard University, Cambridge, Mass.
1979
Cultural Areas and Interaction Spheres: Contrasting Approaches to the Emergence of Civilization in the Maya Lowlands. *American Antiquity* 44: 36–54.
1981a
Continuity and Disjunction: Late Postclassic Settlement Patterns in Northern Yucatan. in *Lowland Maya Settlement Patterns.* W. Ashmore, ed., pp. 311–332. Albuquerque: University of New Mexico Press, School of American Research Advanced Seminar.
1981b
Civilization as a State of Mind: The Cultural Evolution of the Lowland Maya. in *The Transition to Statehood in the New World.* G. Jones and R. Kautz, eds., pp. 188–227. Cambridge: Cambridge University Press.

n.d.
World Image and World View: The Structural Foundations of Lowland
Maya Civilization. Paper prepared for a volume on interdisciplinary ap-
proaches to Maya archaeology, R. Sharer and A. Miller, eds.
Fritz, J.
1978
Paleopsychology Today: Ideational Systems and Human Adaptations in
Prehistory. in *Social Archaeology: Beyond Subsistence and Dating.*
C. Redman, M. Berman, E. Curtin, W. Langhorne, Jr., N. Versaggi, and
J. Wanser, eds., pp. 37–59. New York: Academic Press.
Gann, T.
1900
Mounds in Northern Honduras. Bureau of American Ethnology Annual
Report 19: 655–692. Washington, D. C.
Gifford, J.
1976
*Prehistoric Pottery Analysis and the Ceramics of Barton Ramie in the
Belize Valley.* Memoirs of the Peabody Museum, vol. 18. Harvard Uni-
versity, Cambridge, Mass.
Glass, J.
1966
Archaeological Survey of Western Honduras. in *Handbook of Middle
American Indians.* G. Eckholm and G. Willey, eds., vol. 4, pp. 157–
179. Austin: University of Texas Press.
Glassie, H.
1975
*Folk Housing in Middle Virginia: A Structural Analysis of Historic Ar-
tifacts.* Knoxville: University of Tennessee Press.
Gonzalez, D. de, and R. Wetherington
1978
Incensarios and other Forms at Kaminaljuyu. in *The Ceramics of Kaminaljuyu.* R. Wetherington, ed., pp. 279–298. University Park: Pennsylvania State University Press.
Gordon, G.
1898a
*Caverns of Copan, Honduras. Report on Explorations of the Museum,
1896-1897.* Memoirs of the Peabody Museum, vol. 1, no. 5. Harvard
University, Cambridge, Mass.
1898b
Researches in the Uloa Valley, Honduras. Memoirs of the Peabody Museum, vol. 1, no. 4. Harvard University, Cambridge, Mass.
1902
The Hieroglyphic Stairway, Ruins of Copan. Memoirs of the Peabody Museum, vol. 1, no. 6. Harvard University, Cambridge, Mass.

Graham, J.

1976

Maya, Olmecs, and Izapans at Abaj Takalik. Paper presented at the 42nd International Congress of Americanists, Paris.

1978

Abaj Takalik 1976: Exploratory Investigations. Contributions of the University of California Archaeological Research Facility, vol. 36: 85–110. Berkeley, Ca.

Green, D., and G. Lowe

1967

Altamira and Padre Piedra, Early Preclassic Sites in Chiapas, Mexico. Papers of the New World Archaeological Foundation, 20. Provo, Utah.

Grim, R. and W. Bradley

1948

Rehydration and Dehydration of the Clay Minerals. *American Mineralogist* 33: 50–59.

Guevara, C. de

1976

Etnografia del anil, su artesania actual del Departamento de Chalatenango. *Coleccion de Antropologia*, no. 4. Administracion del Patrimonio Cultural, San Salvador, El Salvador.

Guillemin, G.

1968

Development and Function of the Tikal Ceremonial Center. *Ethnos* 33: 1–35.

Guitierrez y Ulloa, A.

1962

Estado General de la Provincia de San Salvador, Reyno de Guatemala, Ano de 1807. 2nd ed. Coleccion Historica, Ministerio de Educacion, Direccion General de Publicaciones, San Salvador, El Salvador.

Haaland, G.

1969

Economic Determinants in Ethnic Processes. in *Ethnic Groups and Boundaries: The Social Organization of Culture Difference.* F. Barth, ed., pp. 58–73. Boston: Little, Brown, and Co.

Haaland, R.

1977

Archaeological Classification and Ethnic Groups: A Case Study from Sudanese Nubia. *Norwegian Archaeological Review* 10: 1–31.

Haas, J.

1977

Introduction and Overview. in *Reconstruction Following Disaster.* J. Haas, R. Kates, and M. Bowden, eds. Cambridge: MIT Press.

Haas, J., R. Kates, and M. Bowden (eds.)

1977

Reconstruction Following Disaster. Cambridge: MIT Press.

Habel, S.
1879
The Sculpture of Santa Lucia Consumalwhuapa (sic) in Guatemala with an Account of Travels in Central America and on the Western Coast of South America. Smithsonian Contributions to Knowledge, vol. 269. Washington, D. C.
Hall, E.
1973
The Silent Language. Garden City: Doubleday, Inc.
Hammond, N.
1972
Obsidian Trade Routes in the Mayan Area. *Science* 178: 1092–1093.
1975
Maya Settlement Hierarchy in Northern Belize. in *Studies in Ancient Mesoamerica.* J. Graham, ed., pp. 40–55. University of California Archaeological Research Facility, vol. 27. Berkeley, Ca.
1977
The Earliest Maya. *Scientific American* 236: 116–133.
1978
The Myth of the Milpa: Agricultural Expansion in the Maya Lowlands. in *Prehispanic Maya Agriculture.* P. Harrison and B. Turner, II, eds., pp. 23–34. Albuquerque: University of New Mexico Press.
1981
Settlement Patterns in Northern Belize. in *Lowland Maya Settlement Patterns.* W. Ashmore, ed., pp. 157–186. Albuquerque: University of New Mexico Press, School of American Research Advanced Seminar.
Hardoy, J.
1973
Pre-Columbian Cities. New York: Walker and Co.
Harris, M.
1968
The Rise of Anthropological Theory. New York: Thomas Y. Crowell Co.
Harrison, P.
1979
The Lobil Postclassic Phase in the Southern Interior of the Yucatan Peninsula. in *Maya Archaeology and Ethnohistory.* N. Hammond and G. Willey, eds., pp. 189–207. Austin: University of Texas Press.
Hasemann, G., V. Veliz R., and L. Van Gerpen
1978
Informe preliminar, Curruste: Fase 1. Ms., Instituto Hondureno de Antropologia e Historia, Tegucigalpa, Honduras.
Hatch, M.
1975
A Study of Hieroglyphic Texts at the Classic Maya Site of Quirigua, Guatemala. PhD Dissertation, Department of Anthropology, University of California, Berkeley, Ca.

Healey, P.
1974
The Cuyamel Caves: Preclassic Sites in Northeast Honduras. *American Antiquity* 39; 435–447.
Hellmuth, N.
1977
Cholti-Lacandon (Chiapas) and Peten-Ytza Agriculture, Settlement Pattern, and Population. in *Social Process in Maya Prehistory*. N. Hammond, ed., pp. 421–448. New York: Academic Press.
Henderson, J.
1979
The Valle de Naco: Ethnohistory and Archaeology in Northwestern Honduras. *Ethnohistory* 24: 363–377.
Henderson, J., I. Sterns, A. Wonderley and P. Urban
1979
Archaeological Investigations in the Valle de Naco, Northwestern Honduras: A Preliminary Report. *Journal of Field Archaeology* 6: 169–192.
Hewett, E.
1916
Latest Work of the School of American Archaeology at Quirigua. in *Holmes Anniversary Volume Anthropological Essays*, pp. 57–162. Washington, D. C.
Hirth, K., P. Urban, G. Hasemann, and V. Veliz R.
1980
Regional Settlement Patterns in the Cajon Region, Department of Comayagua, Honduras. Paper presented at the 79th Annual Meeting of the American Anthropological Association, Washington, D. C.
1981
Patrones regionales de asentamiento en la region de El Cajon, Departementos de Comayagua y Yoro, Honduras. *Yaxkin* 4: 33–55.
Hodder, I.
1977
The Distribution of Material Culture Items in the Baringo District, Western Kenya. *Man* 12: 239–269.
1978a
Simple Correlations Between Material Culture and Society: A Review. in *The Spatial Organization of Culture*. I. Hodder, ed., pp. 3–24. Pittsburgh: University of Pittsburgh Press.
1978b
The Spatial Structures of Material "Cultures": A Review of Some of the Evidence. in *The Spatial Organization of Culture*. I. Hodder, ed., pp. 93–111. Pittsburgh: University of Pittsburgh Press.
1979
Economic and Social Stress and Material Culture Patterning. *American Antiquity* 44: 446–454.

Hodder, I. (ed.)
1978
The Spatial Organization of Culture. Pittsburgh: University of Pittsburgh
    Press.
Holmes, G.
1914
Areas of American Culture Characterization Tentatively Identified as an
    Aid in the Study of Antiquities. *American Anthropologist* 16: 413–416.
Hudson, J.
1969
A Location Theory for Rural Settlement. *Annals of the Association of
    American Geographers* 59: 365–381.
Johnson, J.
1975
Micropatterns in the Settlement of the Intermediate Plains, Chiapas,
    Mexico. Paper presented at the 40th Annual Meeting of the Society for
    American Archaeology, Dallas, Texas.
Jones, C.
1969
*The Twin-Pyramid Group Pattern: A Classic Maya Architectural As-
    semblage at Tikal, Guatemala.* PhD Dissertation, Department of An-
    thropology, University of Pennsylvania, Philadelphia, Pa.
1977a
Research at Quirigua: the Site-Core Program. Paper presented at the 42nd
    Annual Meeting of the Society for American Archaeology, New Or-
    leans, La.
1977b
Inauguration Dates of Three Late Classic Rulers of Tikal, Guatemala.
    American Antiquity 42: 28–60.
1983
Quirigua Monument 26. in *Quirigua Reports.* E. Schortman and P. Urban,
    eds., vol. 2, pp. 118–128. Museum Monographs, University of Pennsyl-
    vania, Philadelphia, Pa.
Jones, C., and R. Sharer
1980
Archaeological Investigations in the Site-Core of Quirigua. *Expedition* 23:
    11–19.
Jones, C., W. Ashmore, and R. Sharer
1983
The Quirigua Project: 1977 Season. in *Quirigua Reports.* E. Schortman
    and P. Urban, eds., vol. 2, pp. 1–38. Museum Monographs, University
    of Pennsylvania, Philadelphia, Pa.
Josserand, J.
1975
Archaeological and Linguistic Correlations for Maya Prehistory. *Proceed-
    ings of the 41st International Congress of Americanists,* vol. 1, pp. 501–
    510. Mexico City, Mexico.

Joyce, R.
1981
El sistema de asentamientos en Cerro Palenque. Paper presented at the Primer Seminario de Arqueologia Hondurena. Tegucigalpa, Honduras.

Kates, R., and D. Pijawka
1977
Models of the Reconstruction Process: Reconstruction as Disaster Recovery. in *Reconstruction Following Disaster*. J. Haas, R. Kates, and M. Bowden, eds. Cambridge: MIT Press.

Kaufman, T.
1976
Archaeological and Linguistic Correlations in Mayaland and Associated Areas of Mesoamerica. *World Archaeology* 8: 101–118.

Kelley, D.
1962
Glyphic Evidence for a Dynastic Sequence at Quirigua, Guatemala. *American Antiquity* 27: 323–335.

1976
Deciphering the Maya Script. Austin: University of Texas Press.

Kennedy, N.
1972
El informe preliminar de algunos sitios arqueologicos en el Valle de Sula de Honduras, America Central. Ms., Tegucigalpa, Honduras.

1978
Acerca de la frontera en Playa de los Muertos, Honduras. *Yaxkin* 2: 203–215.

1981
The Formative Period Ceramic Sequence from Playa de los Muertos, Honduras. PhD Dissertation, Department of Anthropology, University of Illinois, Urbana-Champagne, Ill.

Kidder, A., J. Jennings, and E. Shook
1946
Excavations at Kaminaljuyu, Guatemala. Carnegie Institution of Washington, Publication no. 561. Washington, D. C.

Knutsson, K.
1969
Dichotomization and Integration: Aspects of Inter-Ethnic Relations in Southern Ethiopia. in *Ethnic Groups and Boundaries: The Social Organization of Culture Difference*. J. Barth, ed., pp. 86–100. Boston: Little, Brown and Co.

Kramer, C.
1977
Pots and Peoples. in *Mountains and Lowlands*. L. Levine and T. Young, eds., pp. 91–112. Biblioteca Mesopotamia, vol. 7. Malibu, Ca.

Kramer, G., and S. Lowe
1940
Archaeological Sites in the Maya Area. Middle American Research Insti-

tute, Tulane University (revision of F. Blom and O. Ricketson, Jr., *Ruins in the Maya Area*, 1924).

Kroeber, A.

1939

Cultural and Natural Areas of Native North America. University of California Publications in American Archaeology and Ethnology, vol. 38. Berkeley, Ca.

Kurjack, E.

1974

Prehistoric Lowland Maya Community and Social Organization: A Case Study at Dzibilchaltun, Yucatan, Mexico. Middle American Research Institute, Publication 38. Tulane University, New Orleans, La.

1978

Final Report, Operation IV, 1978. Ms., Proyecto Arqueologico Copan, Copan, Honduras.

Kurjack, E., and S. Garza T.

1981

Precolumbian Community Form and Distribution in the Northern Maya Area. in *Lowland Maya Settlement Patterns.* W. Ashmore, ed., pp. 287–309. Albuquerque: University of New Mexico Press, School of American Research Advanced Seminar.

Lange, F.

1976

The Northern Central American Buffer: A Current Perspective. *Latin American Research Review* 11: 177–183.

1979

Theoretical and Descriptive Aspects of Frontier Studies. *Latin American Research Review* 14: 221–227.

Larde y Larin, J.

1957

El Salvador: Historia de sus Pueblos, Villas, y Ciudades. Colleccion Historica, vol. 3. Ministerio de Cultura, San Salvador, El Salvador.

Lathrap, D.

1962

Yarinacocha: Stratigraphic Excavations in the Peruvian Montaña. PhD Dissertation, Department of Anthropology, Harvard University, Cambridge, Mass.

1974

Ancient Ecuador: Culture, Clay and Creativity. Chicago: Field Museum of Natural History.

Lattimore, O.

1962

Studies in Frontier History: Collected Papers 1928–1958. London: Oxford University Press.

Lee, T., Jr.

1979

The Sixteenth Century Coxoh Maya Village on the Camino Real. in *Maya*

Archaeology and Ethnohistory. N. Hammond and G. Willey, eds., pp. 208–222. Austin: University of Texas Press.

Lee, T., Jr., and S. Markman

1977

The Coxoh Colonial Project and Coneta, Chiapas, Mexico: A Provincial Maya Village under the Spanish Conquest. *Historical Archaeology* 11: 56–66.

Leone, M.

1977

The New Mormon Temple in Washington, D. C. in *Historical Archaeology and the Importance of Material Things*. L. Ferguson, ed., pp. 43–61. Washington, D. C.: Society for Historical Archaeology.

Leventhal, R.

1979

Settlement Patterns at Copan, Honduras. PhD Dissertation, Department of Anthropology, Harvard University, Cambridge, Mass.

Longyear, J., III

1944

Archaeological Investigations in El Salvador. Memoirs of the Peabody Museum, vol. 9, no. 2. Harvard University, Cambridge, Mass.

1947

Cultures and Peoples of the Southeastern Maya Frontier. Theoretical Approaches to Problems, 3. Carnegie Institution, Washington, D. C.

1952

Copan Ceramics: A Study of Southeastern Maya Pottery. Carnegie Institution of Washington, Publication no. 597. Washington, D. C.

Lothrop, S.

1921

The Stone Statues of Nicaragua. *American Anthropologist* 23: 311–319.

1926a

Lista de los sitios arqueologicos en El Salvador. *Revista de Etnologia, Arqueologia, y Linguistica*, Tomo 1: 19–23.

1926b

Stone Sculptures from the Finca Arevalo Ruins, Guatemala. Museum of the American Indian, Heye Foundation, Indian Notes, vol. 4, pp. 12–13. New York.

1939

The Southeastern Frontier of the Maya. *American Anthropologist* 41: 42–54.

Lowe, G.

1978

Eastern Mesoamerica. in *Chronologies in New World Archaeology*. R. Taylor and C. Meighan, eds., pp. 331–393. New York: Academic Press.

Lunardi, F.
1948
Honduras Maya: Etnologia y Arqueologia de Honduras. Tegucigalpa: Imprenta Calderon.
MacLeod, M.
1973
Spanish Central America: A Socio-Economic History, 1520-1720. Berkeley: University of California Press.
Marcus, J.
1976
Emblem and State in the Classic Maya Lowlands. Washington, D. C.: Dumbarton Oaks.
Marquina, I.
1964
Arquitectura Prehispanica. Memorias del INAH, Segunda Edicion. Mexico: Instituto Nacional de Antropologia e Historia.
Michels, G.
1975
El Chayal Guatemala: A Chronological and Behavioral Assessment. *American Antiquity* 40: 103–106.
1976
Some Sociological Observations on Obsidian Production at Kaminaljuyu, Guatemala. in *Maya Lithic Studies.* T. Hester and N. Hammond, eds., pp. 109–118. Special Report no. 4, Center for Archaeological Research, University of Texas, San Antonio, Texas.
1979a
Settlement Pattern Excavations at Kaminaljuyu, Guatemala. University Park: The Pennsylvania State University Press.
1979b
The Kaminaljuyu Chiefdom. University Park: The Pennsylvania State University Press.
Miles, S.
1957
The Sixteenth-Century Pokom-Maya: A Documentary Analysis of Social Structure and Archaeological Setting. *Transactions of the American Philosophical Society* 47: 731–781.
1965
Sculpture of the Guatemala-Chiapas Highlands and Pacific Slopes, and Associated Hieroglyphs. in *Handbook of Middle American Indians.* R. Wauchope and G. Willey, eds., pp. 237–276. Austin: University of Texas Press.
Mileti, D., T. Drabek, and G. Haas
1975
Human Systems in Extreme Environments: A Sociological Perspective. Monograph 21, Program on Technology, Environment, and Man. Institute of Behavioral Science, University of Colorado, Boulder.

Miller, A.
1980
Art Historical Implications of Quirigua Sculpture. Paper presented at the 45th Annual Meeting of the Society for American Archaeology, Philadelphia.

Molloy, J., and W. Rathje
1974
Sexploitation Among the Late Classic Maya. in *Mesoamerican Archaeology: New Approaches*. N. Hammond, ed., pp. 431–444. Austin: University of Texas Press.

Morley, S.
1920
The Inscriptions at Copan. Carnegie Institution of Washington, Publication no. 219. Washington, D. C.

1935
Guide Book to the Ruins of Quirigua. Carnegie Institution of Washington, Supplemental Publication no. 16. Washington, D. C.

1937–8
The Inscriptions of Peten. Carnegie Institution of Washington, Publication no. 437. Washington, D. C.

Morley, S., G. Brainerd, and R. Sharer
1983
The Ancient Maya. 4th ed. Stanford: Stanford University Press.

Nations, J.
1979
Snail Shells and Maize Preparation: A Lacandon Maya Analogy. *American Antiquity* 44: 568–571.

Navarrete, C.
1966
The Chiapenec History and Culture. New World Archaeological Foundation, Paper 21. Provo, Utah.

Nie, N., C. Hull, J. Jenkins, K. Steinbrenner, and D. Bent
1975
Statistical Package for the Social Sciences. New York: McGraw-Hill.

Nievens, M.
n.d.
Neutron Activation Analyses and the Santa Leticia Obsidian. Ms., Vanderbilt University, Nashville, Tn.

Norman, V.
1981
Comment on: Caves, Gods, and Myths: World-View and Planning in Teotihuacan, by D. Heyden. in *Mesoamerican Sites and World-Views*. E. Benson, ed., p. 37. Washington, D. C.: Dumbarton Oaks.

Nowak, T.
1973
Mercantilism and Colonization: A Study of Prehistoric Regional Commu-

nity Patterning and Cultural Change in the Lower Motagua Valley, Guatemala. Ms., Peabody Museum, Harvard University, Cambridge, Mass.

1975
Prehistoric Settlement and Interaction Networks in the Lower Motagua Valley, Guatemala: A Regional Analysis. Ms., Peabody Museum, Harvard University, Cambridge, Mass.

Olson, G.

1975
Study of Soils in Valle de Naco and La Canteada, Honduras. Department of Agronomy, Cornell University, Mimeo 75-19. Ithaca, NY.

1971
Prehistoric Settlement Patterns in the Texcoco Region, Mexico. Memoir no. 3. Museum of Anthropology, University of Michigan, Ann Arbor, Mich.

Parson, J.

1974
The Development of a Prehistoric Complex Society: a Regional Perspective for the Valley of Mexico. *Journal of Field Archaeology 1: 81–108.*

Parsons, L.

1967
Bilbao, Guatemala. Vols. 1 and 2. Publications in Anthropology, nos. 11–12. Milwaukee Public Museum, Milwaukee, Wi.

1969
Summary Report on the First Season of Excavations at Monte Alto, Escuintla, Guatemala, 1968–1969. Ms., Harvard University, Cambridge, Mass.

1976
Excavations of Monte Alto, Escuintla, Guatemala. *National Geographic Society Research Reports, 1968 Projects:* 325–332. Washington, D. C.

1981
Post-Olmec Stone Sculpture: The Olmec-Izapan Transition on the Southern Pacific Coast and Highlands. in *The Olmec and their Neighbors: Essays in Memory of Matthew W. Stirling.* E. Benson, ed., pp. 257–288. Washington, D. C.: Dumbarton Oaks.

Parsons, L., and P. Jenson

1965
Boulder Sculpture of the Pacific Coast of Guatemala. *Archaeology* 18: 132–144.

Parsons, L., and B. Price

1971
Mesoamerican Trade and Its Role in the Emergence of Civilization. in *Observations on the Emergence of Civilization in Mesoamerica.* R. Heizer and J. Graham, eds., pp. 169–195. University of California Archaeology Research Facility, Department of Anthropology, Contribution 11. Berkeley, Ca.

Pasztory, E.
1974
The Iconography of the Teotihuacan Tlaloc. in *Studies in Precolumbian Art and Archaeology*, no. 15. Washington, D. C.: Dumbarton Oaks.

Pendergast, D.
1981
Lamanai, Belize: Summary of Excavation Results 1974–1980. *Journal of Field Archaeology* 8: 29–53.

Peterson, F.
1963
Some Ceramics from Mirador, Chiapas, Mexico. Papers of the New World Archaeological Foundation, no. 15. Provo, Utah.

Peterson, W.
1968
Migration: Social Aspects. *International Encyclopedia of the Social Sciences* 10: 286–292.

Phillips, P., J. Ford, and J. Griffin
1951
Archaeological Survey in the Lower Mississippi Alluvial Valley, 1940–1947. Papers of the Peabody Museum, no. 25. Harvard University, Cambridge, Mass.

Plafker, G.
1976
Tectonic Aspects of the Guatemala Earthquake of 4 February, 1976. *Science* 193: 1201–1208.

Pollock, H.
1965
Architecture of the Maya Lowlands. in *Handbook of Middle American Indians*. R. Wauchope and G. Willey, eds., vol. 2, pp. 378–440. Austin: University of Texas Press.

Pollock, H., R. Roys, T. Proskouriakoff, and A. Smith
1962
Mayapan, Yucatan, Mexico. Carnegie Institution of Washington, Publication no. 619. Washington, D. C.

Popenoe, D.
1934
Some Excavations at Playa de los Muertos. *Maya Research* 1: 61–81.
1935
The Ruins of Tenampua, Honduras. *Annual Report, Smithsonian Institution*: 559–572. Washington, D. C.

Porter, M.
1953
Tlatilco and the Preclassic Cultures of the New World. Viking Fund Publications in Anthropology, 19. New York: Wenner-Gren.

Price, B.
1979
Turning States' Evidence: Problems in the Theory of State Formation. in

New Directions in Political Economy: An Approach from Anthropology. M. Leons and F. Rothstein, eds., pp. 269–306. Westwood: Greenwood Press.

Proskouriakoff, T.

1950

A Study of Classic Maya Culture. Carnegie Institution of Washington, Publication no. 593. Washington, D. C.

1963a

Historical Data in the Inscriptions of Yaxchilan..Part I. *Estudios de Cultura Maya* 3: 149–167.

1963b

An Album of Maya Architecture. Norman: University of Oklahoma Press.

1973

The Hand-Grasping-Fish and Associated Glyphs on Classic Maya Monuments. in *Mesoamerican Writing Systems.* E. Benson, ed., pp. 165–178. Washington, D. C.: Dumbarton Oaks.

Rands, R., and R. Bishop

1980

Resource Procurement Zones and Patterns of Ceramic Exchange in the Palenque Region, Mexico. in *Models and Methods in Regional Exchange.* R. Fry, ed., pp. 19–46. Society for American Archaeology, SAA Papers 1.

Rao, C.

1964

The Use and Interpretation of Principal Components Analysis in Applied Research. *Snakhya* 26: 329–358.

Rapoport, A.

1982

The Meaning of the Built Environment: A Nonverbal Communication Approach. Beverly Hills: Sage Publications.

Rathje, W.

1972

Praise the Gods and Pass the Metates: A Hypothesis of the Development of Lowland Rainforest Civilizations in Mesoamerica. in *Contemporary Archaeology: A Guide to Theory and Contributions.* M. Leone, ed., pp. 365–392. Carbondale: Southern Illinois University Press.

1973

Classic Maya Development and Denouement: A Research Design. in *The Classic Maya Collapse.* T. Culbert, ed., pp. 405–454. Albuquerque: University of New Mexico Press, School for American Research Advanced Seminar.

1975

Last Tango in Mayapan: A Tentative Trajectory of Production-Distribution Systems. in *Ancient Civilization and Trade.* J. Sabloff and C. Lamberg-Karlovsky, eds., pp. 409–448. Albuquerque: University of New Mexico Press, School of American Research Advanced Seminar.

Reina, R., and R. Hill, II
1978
The Traditional Pottery of Guatemala. Austin: University of Texas Press.
Rice, P.
1977
Whiteware Pottery Production in the Valley of Guatemala: Specialization and Resource Utilization. *Journal of Field Archaeology* 4: 221–233.
1978
Ceramic Continuity and Change in the Valley of Guatemala: 'A Technological Analysis. in *The Ceramics of Kaminaljuyu*. R. Wetherington, ed., pp. 401–510. University Park: The Pennsylvania State University Press.
1979
Ceramic and Nonceramic Artifacts of Lakes Yaxha-Sacnab, El Peten, Guatemala. Part I. The Ceramics. Section B, Postclassic Pottery from Topoxte. *Ceramica de Cultura Maya* 11: 1–85.
Rice, D., and D. Puleston
1981
Ancient Maya Settlement Patterns in the Peten, Guatemala. in *Lowland Maya Settlement Patterns*. W. Ashmore, ed., pp. 121–156. Albuquerque: University of New Mexico Press, School of American Research Advanced Seminar.
Richardson, F.
1940
Non-Maya Monumental Sculpture of Central America. in *The Maya and Their Neighbors*. C. Hay, R. Linton, S. Lothrop, H. Shapiro, and G. Vaillant, eds., pp. 395–416. New York: Dover.
Riese, B.
1979a
Hel-Heiroglyphen. Paper presented at the Albany Conference on Phonetecism in Maya Writing, State University of New York, Albany, NY.
1979b
Copan: Reutilizacion disfuncional de monumentos jeroglificos. Ms., Proyecto Arqueologico Copan, Copan, Honduras.
1980a
Late Classic Relationships Between Copan and Quirigua: Some Epigraphic Evidence. Paper presented at the 45th Annual Meeting of the Society for American Archaeology, Philadelphia, Pa.
1980b
Katun Alters-Angaben in Klassischen Maya-Inschriften. *Baessler Archiv* 28: 155–180.
1982
Hel-Hieroglyphen. Materialien der Maya Inschriften Dokumentation no. 8. Berlin.

Rohlf, F.
1967
Correlated Characters in Numerical Taxonomy. *Systematic Zoology* 16:
109–126.

Rouse, L.
1939
Prehistory in Haiti: A Study in Method. Yale University Publications in
Anthropology, 21. New Haven, Conn.

Ruppert, K.
1940
A Special Assemblage of Maya Structures. in *The Maya and Their Neighbors.* C. Hay, R. Linton, S. Lothrop, H. Shapiro and G. Vaillant, eds.,
pp. 222–231. New York: Appleton-Century.

Ruz, L.
1965
Tombs and Funerary Practices in the Maya Lowlands. in *Handbook of
Middle American Indians.* R. Wauchope and G. Willey, eds., vol. 2,
pp. 441–461. Austin: University of Texas Press.

Sabloff, J.
1975
Excavations at Seibal, Department of Peten, Guatemala: Ceramics.
Memoirs of the Peabody Museum, vol. 13, no. 2. Harvard University,
Cambridge, Mass.

Sabloff, J., and R. Rathje
1975a
The Rise of a Maya Merchant Class. *Scientific American* 233: 72–82.
1975b
*A Study of Changing Pre-Columbian Commercial Systems: The 1972–
1973 Seasons at Cozumel, Mexico.* Peabody Museum Monographs, no.
3. Harvard University, Cambridge, Mass.

Sabloff, J., R. Rathje, D. Freidel, J. Connor, and P. Sabloff
1974
Trade and Power in Postclassic Yucatan: Initial Observations. in *Mesoamerican Archaeology: New Approaches.* N. Hammond, ed., pp. 397–
416. Austin: University of Texas Press.

Safa, H. and B. du Toit (eds.)
1975
Migration and Development. The Hague: Mouton.

Sanders, W.
1960
Prehistoric Ceramics and Settlement Patterns in Quintana Roo, Mexico.
Carnegie Institution of Washington Contributions to American Anthropology and History 12: 155–264. Washington, D. C.
1965
The Cultural Ecology of the Teotihuacan Valley. Pennsylvania State University, Department of Sociology-Anthropology. University Park, Pa.

1970
The Teotihuacan Valley Project Final Report. Occasional Papers in Anthropology, no. 3, Department of Anthropology, Pennsylvania State University. University Park, Pa.

1972
Population, Agricultural History, and Societal Evolution in Mesoamerica. in *Population Growth: Anthropological Implications.* B. Spooner, ed., pp. 101–153. Cambridge: MIT Press.

1974
Chiefdom to State: Political Evolution at Kaminaljuyu, Guatemala. in *Reconstructing Complex Societies: An Archaeological Colloquium.* C. Moore, ed., pp. 97–116. Supplement to the Bulletin of the American Schools of Oriental Research, no. 20.

1977
Ethnographic Analogy and the Teotihuacan Horizon Style. in *Teotihuacan and Kaminaljuyu: A Study in Prehistoric Culture Contact.* W. Sanders and J. Michels, eds., pp. 397–410. University Park: The Pennsylvania State University Press.

1981
Classic Maya Settlement Patterns and Ethnographic Analogy. in *Lowland Maya Settlement Patterns.* W. Ashmore, ed., pp. 351–369. Albuquerque: University of New Mexico Press, School of American Research Advanced Seminar.

Sanders, W., and J. Michels (eds.)
1977
Teotihuacan and Kaminaljuyu: A Study in Prehistoric Culture Contact. University Park: The Pennsylvania State University Press.

Santley, R.
1980
Obsidian Trade and Teotihuacan Influence in Mesoamerica. Paper presented at the Dumbarton Oaks Symposium on Inter-Disciplinary Approaches to the Study of Mesoamerican Highland-Lowland Interaction. Washington, D. C.

Sapper, K.
1895
Altindianische ansiedlungen in Guatemala und Chiapas. Veroffentligingen aus den Koniglichen Museum zur Volkerkund. Bd. IV, heft 1.

1897
Das Nordliche Mittel-America nebst Cinem Ausflug nach dom Hochland von Anahuac. Berlin.

Satterthwaite, L.
1979
Quirigua Altar L (Monument 12). in *Quirigua Reports.* W. Ashmore, ed., vol. 1, pp. 39–43. Museum Monographs, University of Pennsylvania, Philadelphia, Pa.

Sayre, E.
1973
Brookhaven Procedures for Statistical Analysis of Multivariate Archae-ometric Data. Brookhaven National Laboratory Report, BNL-21693. Upton, NY.
Sayre, E., A. Murrenhoff, and C. Weick
1958
The Non-Destructive Analysis of Ancient Potsherds through Neutron Ac-tivation. Brookhaven National Laboratory Report, no. 508. Upton, NY.
Schele, L.
1981
Sacred Site and World-View at Palenque. in *Mesoamerican Sites and World-Views.* E. Benson, ed., pp. 87–117. Washington, D. C.: Dumbar-ton Oaks.
Scholes, F., and R. Roys
1948
The Maya Chontal Indians of Acalan-Tixchel. Carnegie Institution of Washington, Publication no. 560. Washington, D. C.
Schortman, E.
1980a
Archaeological Investigations in the Lower Motagua Valley, Guatemala. Paper presented at the 45th Annual Meeting of the Society for American Archaeology, Philadelphia, Pa.
1980b
Archaeological Investigations in the Lower Motagua Valley. *Expedition* 23: 28–34.
1984
Archaeological Investigations in the Lower Motagua Valley, Department of Izabal, Guatemala. PhD Dissertation, Department of Anthropology, University of Pennsylvania, Philadelphia, Pa.
Schortman, E. and P. Urban (eds.)
1983
Quirigua Reports, vol. 2. Museum Monographs, University Museum, University of Pennsylvania, Philadelphia, Pa.
Sedat, D. and R. Sharer
1972
Archaeological Investigations in the Northern Maya Highlands: New Data on the Maya Preclassic. Contributions of the University of Cali-fornia Archaeological Research Facility, vol. 16: 23–35. Berkeley, Ca.
Sharer, R.
1974
The Prehistory of the Southeast Maya Periphery. *Current Anthropology* 15: 165–187.
1975
The Southeast Periphery of the Maya Area: A Pre-historic Perspective. Paper presented at the 74th Annual Meeting of the American Anthropo-logical Association, San Francisco, Ca.

1978a
Archaeology and History at Quirigua, Guatemala. *Journal of Field Archaeology* 5: 51–70.

1978b
Excavations in the El Trapiche Group. in *The Prehistory of Chalchuapa, El Salvador*. R. Sharer, ed., vol. 1, pp. 61–87. Philadelphia: University of Pennsylvania Press.

1978c
Pottery and Conclusions. in *The Prehistory of Chalchuapa, El Salvador*. R. Sharer, ed., vol. 2. Philadelphia: University of Pennsylvania Press.

1979
Classic Maya Elite Occupation in the Lower Motagua Valley, Guatemala: A Preliminary Formulation. Paper presented at the Ethnohistory Workshop, University of Pennsylvania, Philadelphia, Pa.

1984
Lower Central America as Seen from Mesoamerica. in *The Archaeology of Lower Central America*. F. Lange and D. Stone, eds., pp. 63–64. Albuquerque: University of New Mexico Press, School of American Research Advanced Seminar.

Sharer, R. (ed.)
1978
The Prehistory of Chalchuapa, El Salvador. 3 vols. Philadelphia: University of Pennsylvania Press.

Sharer, R., and A. Chase
1976
New Town Ceramic Complex. in *Ceramics of Barton Ramie* by J. Gifford. pp. 288–314. Memoirs of the Peabody Museum, vol. 18. Harvard University, Cambridge, Mass.

Sharer, R. and J. Gifford
1970
Preclassic Ceramics from Chalchuapa, El Salvador and their Relationships with the Maya Lowlands. *American Antiquity* 35: 441–462.

Sharer, R., C. Jones, W. Ashmore, and E. Schortman
1979
The Quirigua Project: 1976 Season. in *Quirigua Reports*. W. Ashmore, ed., vol. 1, pp. 45–64. Museum Monographs, University of Pennsylvania, Philadelphia, Pa.

Shaw, T.
1977
Notas sobre los datos historicos en las inscripciones de Quirigua y Palenque. *Estudios de Cultura Maya* 10: 139–148.

Sheets, P.
1971
An Ancient Natural Disaster. *Expedition* 14: 24–31.

1972
A Model of Mesoamerican Obsidian Technology Based on Preclassic Workshop Debris in El Salvador. *Ceramica de Cultura Maya* 8: 17–33.

1975
Behavioral Analysis and the Structure of a Prehistoric Industry. *Current Anthropology* 16: 369–391.
1976
The Ilopango Volcanic Eruption and the Maya Protoclassic. University Museum Studies no. 9. Carbondale: Southern Illinois University Press.
1978
The Artifacts. in *The Prehistory of Chalchuapa, El Salvador.* R. Sharer, ed., vol. 2, pp. 2–107. Philadelphia: University of Pennsylvania Press.
1979a
Environmental and Cultural Effects of the Ilopango Eruption in Central America. in *Volcanic Activity and Human Ecology.* P. Sheets and D. Grayson, eds., pp. 525–564. New York: Academic Press.
1979b
Posibles repercusiones en el occidente de Honduras a causa de la erupcion de Ilopango en el siglo tercero d.c. *Yaxkin* 3: 47–68.
1983
Guatemalan Obsidian: A Preliminary Study of Sources and Quirigua Artifacts. in *Quirigua Reports.* E. Schortman and P. Urban, eds., vol. 2, pp. 87–101. Museum Monographs, University of Pennsylvania, Philadelphia, Pa.
Sheets, P. (ed.)
in press
Volcanic Eruptions in Prehistoric Central America: The Zapotitan Valley of El Salvador. Austin: University of Texas Press.
Sheets, P. and D. Grayson (eds.)
1979
Volcanic Activity and Human Ecology. New York: Academic Press.
Sheets, P., W. Loker, H. Spetzler, R. Ware, and G. Olhoeft
in press
Geophysical Exploration for Ancient Maya Housing at Ceren, El Salvador. *National Geographic Society Research Reports.* Washington, D. C.
Shennan, S.
1978
Archaeological "Cultures": An Empirical Investigation. in *The Spatial Organization of Culture.* I. Hodder, ed., pp. 113–139. Pittsburgh: University of Pittsburgh Press.
Sheptak, R.
1981
Reconocimiento del Valle de Sula con fotos aereas. Paper presented at the Primer Seminario de Arqueologia Hondureña. Tegucigalpa, Honduras.
Shibutani, T., and K. Kwan
1965
Ethnic Stratification: A Comparative Approach. New York: The MacMillan Co.

Shook, E., and A. Kidder
1952
Mound E-III-3, Kaminaljuyu, Guatemala. Carnegie Institution of Washington, Publication no. 596. Washington, D. C.
Sidrys, R.
1976a
Classic Maya Obsidian Trade. *American Antiquity* 41: 449–464.
1976b
Mesoamerica: An Archaeological Analysis of a Low-Energy Civilization. PhD Dissertation, Department of Anthropology, University of California, Los Angeles, Ca.
1978
Archaeological Measurement of the Matter-Energy Flow in Mesoamerican Civilization. in *Papers on the Economy and Architecture of the Ancient Maya.* R. Sidrys, ed., pp. 1–39. Monograph VII, Institute of Archaeology, University of California, Los Angeles, Ca.
Sidrys, R., J. Andresen, and D. Marcucci
1976
Obsidian Sources in the Maya Area. *Journal of New World Archaeology* 1: 1–13.
Smith, A.
1950
Uaxactun, Guatemala, Excavations of 1931–1937. Carnegie Institution of Washington, Publication no. 588. Washington, D. C.
Smith, R.
1971
The Pottery of Mayapan. Papers of the Peabody Museum, no. 66. Harvard University, Cambridge, Mass.
Sneath, P., and R. Sokal
1973
Numerical Taxonomy. San Francisco: W. H. Freeman.
Sol, A.
1929
Exploraciones arqueologicas realizadas por el Departamento de Historia del Ministerio de Instruccion Publica. La antigua ciudad de Cihuatan. *Revista del Departamento de Historia* Ano 1: 57–59. San Salvador, El Salvador.
Spaulding, A.
1960
The Dimensions of Archaeology. in *Essays in the Science of Culture in Honor of Leslie A. White.* G. Dole and R. Carneiro, eds., pp. 437–456. New York: Thomas Y. Crowell.
Spinden, H.
1913
A Study of Maya Art, Its Subject Matter and Historical Development. Memoirs of the Peabody Museum, vol. 6. Harvard University, Cambridge, Mass.

Squier, E.
1853
Ruins of Tenampua, Honduras, Central America. *Proceedings of the Historical Society of New York*. New York.
Steinmayer, R.
1932
A Reconnaissance of Certain Mounds and Relics in Spanish Honduras. Middle American Research Institute, Publication 4. Tulane University, New Orleans, La.
Stone, D.
1941
Archaeology of the North Coast of Honduras. Memoirs of the Peabody Museum, vol. 9, no. 1. Harvard University, Cambridge, Mass.
1957
The Archaeology of Central and Southern Honduras. Papers of the Peabody Museum, vol. 49, no. 3. Harvard University, Cambridge, Mass.
1972
Pre-Columbian Man Finds Central America: The Archaeological Bridge. Cambridge, Mass.: Peabody Museum Press.
Streuver, S., and G. Houart
1972
An Analysis of the Hopewell Interaction Sphere. in *Social Exchange and Interaction*. E. Wilmsen, ed., pp. 47–79. Anthropological Papers no. 46. Museum of Anthropology, University of Michigan, Ann Arbor, Mich.
Stromsvik, G.
1941
Substela Caches and Stela Foundations at Copan and Quirigua. Carnegie Institution of Washington, Publication 528. Washington, D. C.
1952
The Ball Courts at Copan with Notes on Courts at La Union, Quirigua, San Pedro Pinula and Asuncion Mita. Carnegie Institution of Washington, Contributions to American Anthropology and History, no. 55. Washington, D. C.
Stromsvik, G., and J. Longyear, III
1946
A Reconnaissance of El Rincon del Jicaque, Honduras. Carnegie Institution of Washington. Notes on Middle American Archaeology and Ethnology 3: 44–53. Washington, D. C.
Strong, W., A. Kidder, II, and, A. Paul, Jr.
1938
Preliminary Report on the Smithsonian-Harvard University Archaeological Expedition to Northwestern Honduras, 1936. Smithsonian Miscellaneous Collections, vol. 97, no. 1. Washington, D. C.
Swadesh, M.
1967
Lexicostatistics and Classification. in *Handbook of Middle American In-*

dians. R. Wauchope and N. McQuown, eds., vol. 5, pp. 79–115. Austin: University of Texas Press.

1939

Excavations at San Jose, British Honduras. Carnegie Institution of Washington, Publication no. 506. Washington, D. C.

1962

A Catalog of Maya Hieroglyphs. Norman: University of Oklahoma Press.

1966

The Rise and Fall of Maya Civilization. Norman: University of Oklahoma Press.

1970

Maya History and Religion. Norman: University of Oklahoma Press.

1977

A Proposal for Constituting a Maya Subgroup, Cultural and Linguistic, in the Peten and Adjacent Areas. in *Anthropology and History in Yucatan.* G. Jones, ed., pp. 3–42. Austin: University of Texas Press.

Tourtellot, G., J. Sabloff, and R. Sharick

1978

A Reconnaissance of Cancuen. in *Excavations at Seibal.* Memoirs of the Peabody Museum, vol. 14. Harvard University, Cambridge, Mass.

Turner, B., II

1979

Interim Report of the Ecological Section of the Proyecto Arqueologico Copan. Ms., Proyecto Arqueologico Copan, Copan, Honduras.

Turner, B., II, W. Johnson, G. Mahood, G. Wiseman, B. Turner, and J. Poole

1983

Habitat y agricultura en la region de Copan. in *Introduccion a la Arqueologia de Copan,* vol. 1. SECTUR, Tegucigalpa, Honduras.

Turner, E., N. Turner, and R. Adams

1981

Volumetric Assessment, Rank Ordering, and Maya Civic Centers. in *Settlement Patterns in the Maya Lowlands.* W. Ashmore, ed., pp. 71–88. Albuquerque: University of New Mexico Press, School of American Research Advanced Seminar.

Urban, P.

1978

A Brief Summary of the Naco Valley Survey Project, 1978 Season. Ms., Department of Anthropology, University of Pennsylvania, Philadelphia, Pa.

1979

The 1979 Season of the Naco Survey Project. Ms., Department of Anthropology, University of Pennsylvania, Philadelphia, Pa.

1980

Precolumbian Settlement in the Naco Valley, Honduras. Paper presented at the 45th Annual Meeting of the Society for American Archaeology, Philadelphia, Pa.

Urquhart, D.
1961
Cocoa. London: Longmans, Green and Co. Ltd.
Vaillant, G.
1934
The Archaeological Setting of the Playa de los Muertos Culture. *Maya Research* 1: 87–100.
Veliz R. V., and G. Hasemann
1978
Prospeccion arqueologica de la presa El Cajon: Localizacion preliminar de sitios, conclusiones tentativas, recomendaciones iniciales. Ms., Instituto Hondureno de Antropologia e Historia, Tegucigalpa, Honduras.
Villacorta, J., and C. Villacorta
1930
Codices Maya. Guatemala: Tipografia Nacional.
Vio Escoto, J.
1964
Weather and Climate of Mexico and Central America. in *Handbook of Middle American Indians*. R. Wauchope and R. West, eds., vol. 1, pp. 187–215. Austin: University of Texas Press.
Voorhies, B.
1972
Settlement Patterns in Two Regions of the Southern Maya Lowlands. *American Antiquity* 37: 115–126.
Wallrath, M.
1967
Excavations in the Tehuantepec Region, Mexico. *Transactions of the American Philosophical Society*, vol. 57, no. 2. Philadelphia, Pa.
Warren, B.
1961
The Archaeological Sequence at Chiapa de Corzo. in *Los Maya del Sur y Sus Relaciones con los Nahuas Meridionales*. Sociedad Mexicana de Antropologia, Mexico.
Warrick, R.
1975
Volcano Hazard in the United States: A Research Assessment. Institute of Behavioral Sciences, University of Colorado, Boulder, Co.
Wauchope, R.
1934
House Mounds of Uaxactun, Guatemala. Carnegie Institution of Washington, Publication no. 436, Contribution F. Washington, D. C.
1938
Modern Maya Houses: A Study of Their Archaeological Significance. Carnegie Institution of Washington, Publication no. 502. Washington, D. C.
Webb, M.
1973
The Peten Maya Decline Viewed in the Perspective of State Formation. in

The Classic Maya Collapse. T. Culbert, ed., pp.367–404. Albuquerque: University of New Mexico Press, School of American Research Advanced Seminar.

Webster, D.
1980
Spatial Bounding and Settlement History at Three Walled Northern Maya Centers. *American Antiquity* 45: 834–844.

Wells, P.
1980
Culture Contact and Culture Change: Early Iron Age Central Europe and the Mediterranean World. Cambridge: Cambridge University Press.

West, R.
1964
Surface Configuration and Associated Geology of Middle America. in *Handbook of Middle American Indians.* R. Wauchope and R. West, eds., pp. 33–83. Austin: University of Texas Press.

West, R., and J. Augelli
1976
Middle America, Its Lands and Peoples. 2nd ed. Englewood Cliffs: Prentice-Hall, Inc.

Wetherington, R.
1978
The Ceramics of Kaminaljuyu. University Park: The Pennsylvania State University Press.

White, G. (ed.)
1974
Natural Hazards: Local, National, Global. New York: Oxford University Press.

White, G., and J. Haas.
1975
Assessment of Research on Natural Hazards. Cambridge: MIT Press.

Willey, G.
1953
A Pattern of Diffusion-Acculturation. *Southwestern Journal of Anthropology* 9: 369–384.
1969
The Mesoamericanization of the Honduran-Salvadoran Periphery: A Symposium Commentary. *Proceedings of the 38th International Congress of Americanists* 1: 533–542.
1972
The Artifacts of Altar de Sacrificios. Papers of the Peabody Museum, vol. 64, no. 1. Harvard University, Cambridge, Mass.
1973
Certain Aspects of the Late Classic to Postclassic Periods in the Belize Valley. in *The Classic Maya Collapse.* T. Culbert, ed., pp. 93–106. Albuquerque: University of New Mexico Press, School for American Research Advanced Seminar.

1974

The Classic Maya Hiatus: A Rehearsal for the Collapse? in *Mesoamerican Archaeology: New Approaches*. N. Hammond, ed., pp. 417–430. Austin: University of Texas Press.

1977

The Rise of Classic Maya Civilization: A Pasion River Perspective. in *The Origins of Maya Civilization*. R. Adams, ed., pp. 133–158. Albuquerque: University of New Mexico Press, School of American Research Advanced Seminar.

1978

Excavations at Seibal: Artifacts. Memoirs of the Peabody Museum, vol. 14, no. 1. Harvard University, Cambridge, Mass.

1981

Maya Lowland Settlement Patterns: A Summary Review. in *Lowland Maya Settlement Patterns*. W. Ashmore, ed., pp. 385–415. Albuquerque: University of New Mexico Press. A School of American Research Advanced Seminar.

Willey, G., and W. Bullard, Jr.

1965

Prehistoric Settlement Patterns in the Maya Lowlands. in *Handbook of Middle American Indians*. R. Wauchope and G. Willey, eds., vol. 2, pp. 360–377. Austin: University of Texas Press.

Willey, G., and R. Leventhal

1979

Prehistoric Settlement at Copan. in *Maya Archaeology and Ethnohistory*. N. Hammond, ed., pp. 75–102. Austin: University of Texas Press.

Willey, G., T. Culbert, and R. Adams

1967

Maya Lowland Ceramics: A Report from the 1965 Guatemala City Conference. *American Antiquity* 32: 289–315.

Willey, G., R. Leventhal, and W. Fash, Jr.

1978

Maya Settlement in the Copan Valley. *Archaeology* 31: 32–43.

Willey, G., C. Dipeso, W. Ritchie, I. Rouse, J. Rowe, and D. Lathrop

1956

An Archaeological Classification of Culture Contact Situations. in *Seminars in Archaeology: 1955*. R. Wauchope, ed., pp. 3–30. Salt Lake City: Society for American Archaeology.

Willey, G., R. Sharer, R. Viel, A. Demarest, R. Leventhal, and E. Schortman

1980

A Study of Ceramic Interaction in the Southeastern Maya Periphery. Paper presented at the 45th Annual Meeting of the Society for American Archaeology, Philadelphia, Pa.

Williams, H., and H. Meyer-Abich

1955

Vulcanism in the Southern Part of El Salvador. *University of California Publications of the Department of Geological Science* 32: 1–64.

Wisdom, C.
1940
The Chorti Indians of Guatemala. Chicago: University of Chicago Press.
Wishart, D.
1978
Clustan. User Manual. Program Library Unit, Edinburgh University, Edinburgh.
Wissler, C.
1917
The American Indian: An Introduction to the Anthropology of the New World. New York: D. C. McMurtrie.
Wonderley, A.
1980
Postclassic Naco, Honduras. Paper presented at the 45th Annual Meeting of the Society for American Archaeology, Philadelphia, Pa.
1981
Late Postclassic Excavations at Naco, Honduras. Latin American Studies Program Dissertation Series 86. Cornell University, Ithaca, NY.
Workman, W.
1979
The Significance of Volcanism in the Prehistory of Subarctic Northwest North America. in *Volcanic Activity and Human Ecology.* P. Sheets and D. Grayson, eds., pp. 339–371. New York: Academic Press.
Yde, J.
1938
An Archaeological Reconnaissance of Northwestern Honduras. Middle American Research Institute, Publication 9. Tulane University, New Orleans, La.
Zier, A.
1976
Classic Period Reoccupation of El Salvador. Ms. Department of Anthropology, University of Colorado, Boulder.
1980
A Classic Period Maya Agricultural Field in Western El Salvador. *Journal of Field Archaeology* 7: 65–74.

Index

Jicalapa Usulutan, 211, 212
Jinuapa, 199
Mizata Buff, 204, 209
Naco, 282, 283
Olocuitla, 203, 211, 212
Pajonal Cream, 204
Pinos, 199, 203, 212, 219
Puxtla, 211, 212
Santa Tecla, 203
Soyapango White-on-Orange, 204
Tepecoyo Usulutan, 204
Ceramic horizon style, 207
Ceramic sphere, 204–207
  Chicanel, 211, 342
  Mamon, 211
  Miraflores, 208–213, 218, 219, 342
  Providencia, 208, 210–213, 218, 219, 342
  Tepeu, 211
  Tzakol, 211
  Uapala, 212, 219, 334
  Xe, 183
Ceramic types
  Abelino red, 183
  Achiotes unslipped, 183
  Algo red, 316–317, 328
  Aguacate orange: Atecozol variety, 201
  Arambala polychrome, 142, 144
  Arenal coarse-incised, 209
  Arenal fine-incised, 210
  Candungo incise, 279
  Capulin white, 282
  Casaca striated, 106, 111
  Caterpillar polychrome, 111
  Cementerio incised, 106, 111
  Cerro Azul buff, 281
  Chaguitas burnished, 277–278
  Chamelecon orange-slipped, 280–283
  Chamelecon polychrome, 280–283
  Chilanga Usulutan, 144, 153, 161–164, 279, 280
  Chinda rouge, 280
  Cofradia unslipped, 316, 328

Copador polychrome, 56, 84, 85, 105, 106, 109, 111–113, 143–147, 151–153, 162, 175, 295
Fronton unslipped, 278–279
Fulano unslipped, 283, 316, 329
Gualpopa polychrome, 144, 153–154, 158, 161, 163–166
Izalco Usulutan, 211, 212, 279
Jicaro unslipped, 279–280, 281, 283
Jorgia coarse-incised, 203
La Isla red-on-natural, 280
Lorenzo red, 106, 111
Magdalena red-on-natural, 280, 281, 283
Masica incised, 106, 111, 281
Mixteca-Puebla polychrome, 300, 331
Nolasco bichrome, 316, 318, 323, 328, 329
Olocuitla orange, 219
Olocuitla Usulutan, 212
Penonas brown, 277–278
Prospero rojo, 280
Providencia purple-painted, 209
Salto red, 316, 317
San Augustine red, 282, 321
Santa Tecla red, 219
Sirena orange-slipped, 279
Tal burnished, 317, 328
Tenampua polychrome, 283
Tipon orange, 281, 282
Tohil plumbate, 300, 303
Ulua polychrome, 105, 106, 111, 112, 264, 267, 268, 270, 280–282, 336
Urupa rouge-sur-beige, 280
Verbena black-brown coarse-incised, 203
Verbena black-brown fine-incised, 210
Verbena fine red, 219
Verbena ivory, 209
Verbena ivory: Usulutan variety, 209–210
Verbena red-orange, 219

www.ingramcontent.com/pod-product-compliance
Lightning Source LLC
Chambersburg PA
CBHW030634270326
41929CB00007B/80